## About The Author

Photo taken August '96

When John Thomas began his pursuit of agelessness, his *calendar age* was only 27 while his *real* age, that is, his **bio-electric age** was 39. Today (2002) John is 58 years by the calendar; yet his bio-electric age has declined to just 19 years "young!" Thomas is living proof that aging reversal can be a reality for anyone who wishes to experience it.

John was heavily influenced by the exemplary lives of Paul C. Bragg and Jack LaLanne.

Thomas spent 31 years researching every aspect of aging, challenging accepted dogmas, and daring to "rock" the boat of both conventional and alternative medicine.

John discovered that "medical science" asks the *wrong* questions and generates useless answers—while "alternative" medicine labors under gross misconceptions and half truths that fail to produce long term results.

Thomas was encouraged to write *Young Again!* because he does **NOT** age! Time stands still for John because he uncovered the **mystery** behind the aging process, applied it and reversed his **bio-electric** age to only 19 years "young!"

For a book like *Young Again!* to be *meaningful,* the author would need to have "personally lived" the subject matter AND be *living* proof that aging reversal and body rejuvenation are within every person's reach. The author would need a broad background in the sciences, philosophy, politics, history, and nutrition. He would also need to think "low tech" and incorporate a style of writing that would educate and ensure *communication* with the reader.

John wrote *Young Again!* as a practical, useful guide book of information spelling out **exactly** what must be done to **recapture** lost youth, **reverse** disease and extend one's life into the hundreds of years while "looking" and "feeling" young!

This book was NOT written for "experts" who claim to have answers, but who cannot demonstrate evidence of it in their lives or in that of their patients.

*Young Again!* is a living *testimony*—a mosaic of nature's secrets pieced together for the very first time. It encourages everyone to talk the talk AND walk the walk! Enjoy!

## Thoughts From Patricia Bragg

What a masterpiece! *Young Again!* is the best of the best! It will help millions of people.

We are a nation of half dead people! Cancer, heart trouble, high blood pressure, osteoporosis, etc. The health of our people is slipping fast. The question is why?

Good health is something that cannot be purchased from a doctor or in a bottle of pills. Good health is the product of a healthy lifestyle. America needs to know more about how to achieve health and vitality. Staying youthful, no matter what your age, is central to the health message and to the message of this book.

My father, Dr. Paul C. Bragg N.D., Ph.D. was a teenager dying of tuberculosis when he *chose* a life of health. Dad was ninety-seven years "young" when he died of a surfboard accident. During his life, he helped thousands of people find the path to agelessness. One of those people was Jack LaLanne.

Jack was a sickly boy. His health was so poor he was forced to drop out of school. Dad's message changed his life. Today, Jack LaLanne is a legend. He is living proof that the health message really works.

Dad said the world was lacking strong, courageous men and women who were not afraid to buck the trend of commercialism in the food industry and in the healing arts—people who could stand tall.

Here we have a strong crusader who *believes* in the health message and who *lives* what he preaches. John Thomas' wonderful book is his gift of love to the world.

Now, dear reader, it is your turn to experience a life of boundless energy and health. The keys are in your hand. Read and follow this book and it will change your life. *Young Again!* is the most thorough and concise message ever written on the subject of healthy living.

No excuses. You know right from wrong. Remember, what you eat and drink you become. It's either sickness or it's health. It's time to choose. Now! Today!

*Young Again!* is truly a personal guide to ageless living. I am honored to be a part of it.

Authored and published under the jurisdiction of
Title 4 U.S.C. 1 Flag of Peace of the united States of America
(see front cover)

Printed in the united States of America

# How To REVERSE The Aging Process

John Thomas

Plexus Press
Mead, Washington, united States of America

Authored and published under the jurisdiction of the
Title 4 U.S.C. 1 Flag of Peace of the united States of America
(see front cover)
Printed in the united States of America

# *young* AGAIN!

## *How To Reverse The Aging Process*

**By John Thomas**

**Plexus Press**
P.O. Box 1240 Mead, WA 99021
Phone (509) 465-4154 Fax: (509) 466-8103
**(800) 659-1882**



**Cataloging-In-Publication Data**
Thomas, John
Young Again! How to Reverse The Aging Process / by John Thomas. (1st edition April, 1994)
p. cm. • References: p. • Includes index and glossary.
ISBN 1-884757-79-0 (5th edition, October, 2002)
1. Aging. 2. Rejuvenation. 3. Longevity. 4. Health. I. Title
RA776.75.T56 2002
613.04—dc20 94-65131

Printings: 20 19 18 17 16 15 14 13 12 11 10 9 8 7

## LEGAL NOTICE

**RESPONSIBILITY DISCLAIMER UNDER U.C.C. 3-501.** UNDER TITLE 42 U.S.C. 1986 FOR KNOWLEDGE OF THE LAW, VENUE AND JURISDICTION OF ALL ACTIONS/CASES RELATING TO THIS BOOK ARE UNDER COMMON LAW JURISDICTION OF THE TITLE 4 U.S.C. 1 AMERICAN FLAG OF PEACE OF THE united STATES OF AMERICA, REFERENCED UNDER PRESIDENTIAL EXECUTIVE ORDER 10834, AND UNDER ARTICLE (6) SECTION (3), OATH OF FIDUCIARY OFFICERS OF THE COURT, AND UNDER ARTICLE (IV) (4) SECTION (3), NO "state" (JUDGE) SHALL CREATE A STATE (AREA OF THE BAR), AND united STATES CODE ANNOTATED 11: NO "FOREIGN STATE" (LAW OF THE FLAG) SHALL HAVE JURISDICTION OVER A SOVEREIGN CITIZEN IN PARTY, AND ARTICLE (1) SECTION (9),AMENDMENT 13: NO TITLES OF NOBILITY (ESQUIRES) UNDER ANY FOREIGN FLAG JURISDICTION AND IN BREACH OF THE TREATY OF TITLE 28 U.S.C. 1605 "FOREIGN SOVEREIGN IMMUNITY ACT OF October 21, 1976 AND IN BREACH OF THE CONSTITUTION OF THE united STATES OF AMERICA, WILL BE ALLOWED IN THE JURISDICTION OF THE CASE. BREACH OF CONTRACT BY ANY PARTY WILL CAUSE SANCTIONS UNDER FEDERAL RULES OF CIVIL PROCEDURE RULE 16(f), WHEN THE CONSTITUTION OF THE untied STATES OF AMERICA IS SURRENDERED FOR A FOREIGN STATE/POWER, AND BREACH OF CONTRACT OF OATH OR AFFIRMATION FOR THE united STATES OF AMERICA, THEN CHARGES FOR PERJURY OF OATH (TITLE 18 U.S.C. 1621), CONSTRUCTIVE TREASON, AND FALSE SWEARING WILL BE BROUGHT AGAINST THE OFFICERS OF THE COURT. THE CONSTITUTION OF THE united STATES OF AMERICA IS MADE A PART OF THE BOOK *YOUNG AGAIN!* BY REFERENCE AND IN A "REAL TIME" "PRESENT TENSE" STATE OF BEING.

Aging reversal requires the investment of time, energy, and money by the reader/Citizen desiring the experience knowing that aging reversal is "personal and unique" to the indivdual. The **"intent of mind"** of the author and publisher in making *Young Again!* available in the public domain is limited to the dissemination of health related information for causing THINKING among Citizens and QUESTIONING of medical modalities and advice. Neither the publisher nor author offer "medical" advice and the book *Young Again!* is not to be used for medical diagnosis. The author and publisher believe the information provided is complete and accurate, but mistakes both typographical and in content may be dicovered after printing; and therefore, the reader should use *Young Again!* as a general guide only and not as the ultimate source of information. Neither author nor publisher have liability or responsibility for any reader/Citizen respecting loss or damage caused or alleged for reliance on information in *Young Again!* **THE READER IS RESPONSIBLE FOR SEEKING "PROFESSIONAL" MEDICAL CARE BY THE READER'S OWN CHOICE.**

## DEDICATED TO...

**Robert McLeod**—You will meet Bob in Chapter One. He became my mentor, a living example, and a good friend.

**Dr. Paul C. Bragg N.D., Ph.D.**—Paul Bragg was the point man of the health movement in the United States. Millions of people owe their lives to him. He served his fellow man well, and his Creator to the fullest. Paul Bragg saved my life!

**Charles Walters**—Charlie is the editor of *Acres USA*. He taught me to winnow the wheat from the chaff. He helped me establish the link between "live" food and "live soil." His editorial pen is the harbinger of TRUTH in matters of agriculture and national economics. He is another Thomas Paine!

**Diane DeFelice M.S., R.D.**—Diane was my upper level college nutrition instructor. She is unselfish in her effort to help students make the connection between diet, lifestyle and good health. She helped me realize that *Young Again!* simply had to be written.

**Patricia Bragg N.D., Ph.D.**—Patricia *challenged* me to write this book. She also challenged me to pick up the baton her father handed to her and to Jack LaLanne. Patricia is the daughter of the great Wizard—"Paul Bragg." Patricia is a mighty force in the health movement worldwide. She is a voice crying in the wilderness!

**Jack LaLanne**—Beginning in the 1950's, Jack LaLanne became "Mr. Fitness." He is a living example of the benefits that accrue from a healthy lifestyle and regular exercise. Jack has been the point man in the fitness industry for over forty years! He deserves our applause and thanks. Many people have been blessed by his work.

**Leonard Ridzon**—Of all the people I've known in 58 years, this farmer makes me think more than any other. Leonard is a simple man, but he isn't simple. He sees the Creator's handiwork and asks questions to whoever will listen. His questions can hold a pack of doctors at bay; they seldom risk an answer. And when Leonard talks, you had best be listening. He says as much *between* the lines as he does in words. Thank you, Leonard, for teaching me to observe, think and challenge!

## TABLE OF CONTENTS

# Acknowledgements

The author would like to take this opportunity to acknowledge and thank the following people who were involved, directly and indirectly, in bringing this book to fruition and to the attention of the public.

Robert Stephan D.D.S., Dr. John Briggs D.C., Dennis Higgins M.D., Linus Pauling M.D., Edward Arana D.D.S., Hal Huggins D.D.S., Joseph Kramer M.D., Ignaz Semmelweis M.D., Thomas Gerber M.D., Arnold Lorand M.D., Max Gerson M.D., Dr. Carey Reams, Drs. Paul C. and Patricia Bragg, Dr. Bernard Jensen, Guenther Enderlein M.D, and Robert F. Hofman M.D.

Also, Bob Mcleod, Jack LaLanne, Charles Walters, Christopher Bird, Roger Lent, Ellen Rosbach, Merlyn Anderberg, Diane DeFelice, Ray and Carolyn Teagarden, Dan Poynter, Tom Mahoney, Pat and Kay Lee, Cathy Cameron, Keith Ries, and the family into which I was blessed to have been born.

Special thanks to Gretchen Gardner, William C. Lawson and Elizabeth Beryl for their assistance in editing and clarification.

**Cover design by:** Dunn + Assoicates
P.O. Box 870
Hayward WI 54843
(715) 634-4857

Credit hereby given for Progressive *Spinal Deformation In Osteoporosis* medical illustration shown on page 100, per:

## Introduction by Robert B. Stephan D.D.S.

Man's ways are the antithesis of Nature's ways. They have little resemblance to the natural healing process. Nature provides the basis of life and the potential to help man correct his tendency towards disease, but drug based medicine has chosen to increase health care productivity rather than identify the constraints which inhibit good health.

Allopathic medicine seems to be infatuated with technology, powerful drugs, and the suppression of symptoms. It prefers to *cut, poison,* and *burn,* when less would do. Medicine's world is physical and chemical.

We are moving away from this physical and chemical based system of disease care and into the realm of energy and spirit. This is not a new movement, but a rediscovery of ancient wisdom. It is a mix of "proven" wisdom combined with technology.

As we move away from a *disease* care system and into a *health* care system, we will need a compass and a road map to navigate by if we hope to find our way through the maze of exploding knowledge and rediscovered tradition that is fast approaching us.

*Young Again!* serves the dual purpose of a navigation tool and a survival manual. It is easy to read and it is a very complete gathering of information. It will guide you to a healthy, vibrant life; *and* it will take you where Western Allopathic doctors fear to tread.

It is a divine privilege to be involved in the march to a preferred future, and it is a great pleasure to have John Thomas' wonderful book to use as a fount of information in my position as a Holistic Biological Dentist. Discover in this book the joy and path of good health!

Dr. Robert B. Stephan, D.D.S., B.S., F.A.P.D.
Spokane, Washington
Holistic Dental Association, Board of Directors
International Academy of Oral Medicine and Toxicology
American Academy of Biological Dentistry
Occidental Institute, Research Faculty
Environmental Dental Association

## Introduction by Dr. John A. Briggs

Our body is an incredible work of art. Unfortunately, it does not come with an owner's manual—as does a car—that tells us *how* to care for our body.

Consider the master mechanic. He has knowledge of the workings of his car. He knows how to protect his investment. His world is a world of regular maintenance and mechanical details. He avoids the pitfalls of ownership through individual responsibility. He knows *how* to maintain his car's youthfulness and vigor.

The medical world is not like the world of the master mechanic. In my practice, I have seen people with the full range of health related problems—problems directly related to modern living—problems that could be avoided if people only had an owner's manual.

These people come to me willing to spend their fortunes. They have tasted the bitterness of disease and old age—they cry out for good health. They also DREAM of regaining the health of their youth.

I help them as best I can. I point the way, but my time is limited as is their money. What these people really need is an owner's manual for the care and maintenance of their body. I have wished for such a manual.

My wish was fulfilled when John Thomas wrote *Young Again!* It contains all the information my patients need to maintain their youth and vigor.

*Young Again!* arms the reader with practical, valuable information. This book is correctly aligned with the concepts of Naturopathic medicine. It will help the reader to stay young no matter what their age.

Thomas' research is exhaustive. He has a thorough working knowledge of the healing arts. Most importantly, he drives home his points with simple examples designed to help the reader understand.

Read this book and follow the information it contains. If you do, you too can achieve the radiant health I observed when John Thomas first introduced himself.

Dr. John A. Briggs
Naturopathic Physician
Clatskanie, Oregon

## Foreword by Charles Walters

"People can be **fed** to live peacefully or fight, to think or dream, to work or sleep, to be virile or pathologic, physically, mentally, and spiritually developed or retarded, and for any possible degree of advance or variation within the mechanical limits of the organism."

This was the late Albert Carter Savage speaking during the early years of WW II, and Winston Churchill took him seriously. After all, the health of England's fighting men was all that stood between the freedom of Englishmen and Hitler's thirst for world domination.

It was realized that food had to carry a fair complement of minerals in order to confer health, and the idea that vitamins could function without minerals was at least as strange as the concept that coal-tar drugs—capable of making a healthy person ill—could make a sick person well.

These few thoughts came to mind when John Thomas' manual *Young Again!* arrived on my editorial desk.

Individual health is too important to be left in the hands of physicians. How can a person make informed decisions to preserve health and conquer sickness as well? Most books deal with individual problems—single factor analysis, we call it—but leave unanswered the silent killer in our lives, namely *shelf life.* For it is shelf life in the grocery store that annihilates the quality of life for the consumer.

When most of today's senior citizens were still youngsters, strange words in type too small to read became an indispensable part of almost every label. First came the emulsifiers and stabilizers—carrageenan in cheese spreads, chocolate products, evaporated milk, ice cream and dairy products. All evidence of mutagenicity, carcinogenicity, and teratogenicity remained neatly tucked away in the scientific literature.

Dioctyl sodium sulfosuccinate became the wetting agent of choice, even though infants suffered gastrointestinal irritation and reduced growth rates as a consequence of its use. There were also dozens of flavorings and colors other than Red Nos. 2 & 4, all inimical to sustained human health. Aspartame (Nutrasweet™) is a sweetener with approximately one hundred sixty times the sweetness of sugar. The problem is that people with phenylketonuria can't handle it. It accumulates in the system and causes mental retardation and even death. Cereals, chewing gum, and gelatins are loaded with it.

As shelf life for foods improved, strange anomalies in the population multiplied. The public prints became filled with reports of bizarre crimes (youths dumping gasoline on old ladies and setting them on fire, for instance); and asylums for the insane became a growth industry, finally to emerge with credentialed practitioners and a new nomenclature—mental health!

Did shellac—a food grade version of furniture finish—used as a confectioner's glaze have anything to do with this? Or xylitol, a sugar substitute that is a diuretic and causes tumors and organ damage in test animals? Or propylene glycol alginate or oxystearin (a modified glyceride) or glycerol ester of wood resin, or guar gum? All annihilate lesser life and whittle away at human health a bit at a time!

John Thomas' message in his manual on health is clear and to the point. Witless science has worked its mischief, but we are not helpless. We have only to take command of our own health and make sensible judgements without reference to higher approved authority.

*Young Again!* has little to do with mirror image vanity and everything to do with the "mechanical limits of the organism," as Albert Carter Savage put it, meaning the human body.

*Young Again!* has to be read with a box of marker pens handy. It is a matchless narrative and an encyclopedia of health. It covers the secrets of the ancients and projects forward to encompass the range of the electromagnetic spectrum. The advice—page by page, chapter by chapter—may not entirely reverse aging, but it is certain to put the process on hold.

Charles Walters
Editor, Acres USA
Kansas City, Missouri

## Aim High!

The "object" of this book is to provide the reader with ANSWERS to health concerns and improve the quality of the reader's life. Hopefully, these are the reasons you are reading Young Again.

Your author's approach to health and longevity is total and BASIC! He does NOT believe in band aids or magic bullets. He wants readers to understand how loss of control of the body's **terrain** occurs and exactly what must be done to experience aging reversal.

It is not the author's *intent* to be absolute or overzealous. Few people will be able to comply 100% with all of the suggestions contained in these pages. The reader is encouraged to advance in personal knowledge at his/her own pace. Do not feel doomed because you are unable to follow all suggestions at once. Please realize, the material presented represents the BEST you can shoot for—the goal—the ideal!

The ideal world of health is a lifestyle that includes wholesome food, pure water, moderate exercise, adequate rest, low stress, a clean body and a strong mind. These things are worth striving for even though the *perfect* lifestyle is very difficult to "live" in a world where disease and human suffering are the norm.

Hopefully, this book will help the reader find a middle ground where enjoyment of good health can be realized and perpetually maintained, consistent with one's circumstances.

We live in an imperfect world, and we fall short of the ideal. Sometimes we are subject to events and circumstances beyond our control. Yet, each day, we DO have the opportunity to make "choices" that affect our lives and health—and the lives of those around us—for good and bad. We must strive to make the BEST choices we can each and every day of our lives.

The reader is reminded that health and disease are **cumulative** states of being, and the *alternative* to good health is a sorry existence indeed. Poor health cheats us of happiness—and of "life."

Aim high—and do the very best you can. Good health is worth **whatever it takes** to get it and keep it!

## Think About It!

*"In the health arena, there are only two classes of people. Those who are young and healthy and those who are old or sick. The former want to hold onto their youth and the latter desperately want to reclaim what they have lost."*

John Thomas

# 1

# Something Of Value

*"If you want to look and feel as I do when you are my age, you must begin!"*
Robert McLeod

It was a strange place for me to meet the person who would become my mentor. Stranger still were the circumstances—a restaurant meeting room in San Bernardino, California in 1971. The event: A district sales meeting for ARCO (Atlantic Richfield Company), formerly Richfield Oil Company.

Having graduated from college the previous September, I stood in awe of the grandeur of it all. The Company, the oil industry and all that.

We had instinctively corralled ourselves into groups based on our position on the corporate ladder. Barnyard pecking order they call it.

And as a few of us were talking, I overheard my immediate superior and his cronies laughing and poking fun in a rather contemptuous way at one of their peers—a man named, Bob McLeod.

McLeod was outside people of his own level—"status inconsistent" the sociologists call it. Instead, his peers mocked him. As I listened to their gossip, something caught my attention.

"You know," one of them said, "McLeod is a vegetarian. He doesn't eat meat. He's...real strange!" "Yah! He's into health, whatever that is," said another.

It was difficult to compare McLeod to this arrogant, egocentric bunch of executives. I could NOT account for the differences between the *group* and the stranger, McLeod.

McLeod looked young. His smile, his eyes, his laugh—nothing squared with someone of forty-nine years. His hair was vibrant! His waistline was trim and slim. I liked what I beheld!

The "other" executives, well, they all looked twenty years older than McLeod. Paunchy stomachs, grayed hair, bald heads, fat, cigarettes blazing—and booze. Many were ready for their gold watches. But by this time in history, gold watches had been replaced by the old glass hand, a slap on the back and the epitaph on the grave stone, ***"He was a good old boy!"***

## McLeod Knew

McLeod knew something they did not, for he was forty-nine years "young" and the others, who were in their late thirties and early forties, were, well,...older!

I took my first step into the world of ageless living as I navigated in McLeod's direction. Life would never again be the same for me. I was destined to be there on that day, at that moment, and Bob McLeod was destined to become my mentor. God works in strange ways!

I introduced myself to this forty-nine years *young* enigma, and as we talked it became crystal clear that he was a very special human being. Immediately, my mind was made-up! "When I reach forty-nine, I am going to *LOOK* and *FEEL* like Bob McLeod!" (I was 27 years of age, then.)

"It's a long story, and you are going to have to search it out for yourself, but I would consider it a privilege if I can assist you," he said.

Instant friends we were! Fellow travelers for sure! Our paths only crossed a few times in the months that followed. When they did, he would take me under his wing and talk with me and point the way.

"If you want to understand how I have managed to look and feel twenty years younger than I am, you will have to study. I recommend you begin by reading a book by Dr. Paul C. Bragg entitled *The Miracle of Fasting.*

"You will not find all the answers there, but this book is a good place to start," he said.

Six months after meeting Bob, I left the company and lost ALL contact with him until August of 1993. He still looks *young and vibrant!* If you saw him on the street today you would guess him to be in his late forties. Not too bad for someone age 69 years YOUNG!

Thirty-one years have passed and now it is my turn. As I approach fifty-nine years of age, I am here to tell you that you **CAN** stop the clock and you **CAN** reverse the aging process—that is, if you will follow my lead and stay the course.

### Fear

People are reluctant to venture out, to break new ground, to sail uncharted waters—particularly when it involves being *different*. Perhaps it is social pressure. Perhaps people think they are giving up *something of value*. Regardless, fear and ignorance are the primary stumbling blocks that keep people from following the path of good health. Instead, people hang onto destructive habits—habits that become the glue by which they seal their coffin.

Most of my peers at that fortuitous meeting are well on their way into old age. All of them were past their anabolic PEAK at that time. Today, most of them suffer from degenerative conditions, and many of them are dead. **All** of them are old beyond their years—each the product of poor choices. There is no room for blame. We are responsible for our CHOICES!

People do not think "they" are going to get old. They know they have to die, but it is the other guy who gets old, never them. One day they wake up and look in the mirror, and their mind says, "Heh! Better enjoy it while you can! Time is short!" As friends grow old and die, the image in the mirror is confirmed—disease and old age have arrived.

It's important to understand the difference between disease and a condition. A disease is a condition that has "officially" been given a name. Diseases and conditions BOTH alter our lifestyle and prevent us from enjoying life as we normally would if we were in a healthy state of being.

We do not CATCH diseases. We DEVELOP conditions. Disease should be hyphenated. It should be spelled **"dis-ease,"** and I will do so for the remainder of this book to drive home the point. We die of conditions, not dis-eases!

How we define our health problems greatly influences our **attitude** about aging and our ability or inability to take control of our lives and redirect those forces that cause the bio-electric body to grow OLD.

### It's Your Decision

Would YOU like to become *Young Again*? All that is required is that you complete this book and apply its lessons in your life. If you want to experience the **miracle** of reversing the aging process, you MUST *visualize* the end result in your mind's eye. The miracle is available to ***anyone*** who wants it, but it is **NOT** free. You will become acquainted with the price as each chapter unfolds.

Once you understand HOW you become old, you will understand HOW to become *Young Again!*

**PREVIEW:** *In the next chapter, you will discover that you have four different ages. You will also determine your anabolic PEAK and learn about its significance in your life.*

***The choice of which road to take is up to the individual. He alone can decide whether he wants to reach a dead end or live a healthy lifestyle for a long, happy, active life.*** **–Paul C. Bragg**

**REALITY SELF CHECK**

When you look down the street, do you see a STOP sign instead of the horizon? Young people see only the horizon because their entire life is in FRONT of them.

Don't lose sleep over the doctor's diagnosis—for it is nothing but a confirmation of yesterday's poor choices. Instead, focus on today and tomorrow will be yours.

When you look in the mirror and the image looking back at you isn't the image you remember, you better believe the image looking back at you!

*"In this book (Young Again), the author goes a long way to provide hope that, in a world beset by health threatening pollution of all kinds, we are afforded some tools with which to build healthier, longer, and perhaps happier lives."*
Christopher Bird, *The Secret Life of Plants*

# *young Again!*

*"Youth is a wonderful thing. What a crime to waste it on children."*
George Bernard Shaw

**Old age follows days filled with new hopes and new dreams of good times to come.** Good times that go unfulfilled because our body fails to keep up with our mind.

An **old body** with a **young mind** is a phenomenon where conflict and misunderstanding abound. It is a condition where the body we once knew becomes *lost* in Time and unable to communicate with the mind. Flip side of the same coin: a young mind, an old body. Each expressing itself in a different language with no interpreter to translate.

Aging occurs through ignorance—and by **CHOICE!** People grow old because they do not know HOW to stay young. They are becoming old much faster than they once did. This is particularly true among the young—especially women between ages 25-45. The young now experience the ONSET of old age by year 24. Dis-eases that were once the domain of the old are now the domain of the young—and it's all a matter of **CHOICE!**

Despite the statistical claims of the *experts,* life expectancy is *not* greater today than it was yesterday. The statistics used to support this claim of greater life expectancy have been skewed by the number of children reaching adulthood. At one time, half the population of the United States died prior to reaching age twenty. Those deaths held life expectancy down. The *statistical* rise in life expectancy over the last fifty years has caused a gullible public to accept medicine's false claim of greater life expectancy. This is a serious mistake.

We are NOT better off today than we were yesterday. Degenerative **conditions** have replaced infectious **conditions**. Moreover, contagious conditions are on the rise and are returning with a vengeance. They are MORE than an old enemy returned. Their resurgence bodes ill for those who are unprepared and unwilling to conform to nature's plan.

A long, HEALTHY life is what we were meant to experience during our sojourn on Mother Earth. That is what this book is all about.

### Dividing Line

At my initiation into the study of aging in 1971, it was considered difficult to turn the body's biological clock backward if someone had *survived* thirty-five years of NORMAL living. If we made the same statement today, we would have to reduce age thirty-five down to age twenty-four. The dividing line between youth and the ONSET of old age is falling—fast!

When we are young, our health is at its peak and the body is able to repair itself quickly and easily. The word ***anabolism*** best describes this "state-of-being." Anabolism is the "absence" of slowdown or loss of function in body tissues and systems. It also implies healthy, ongoing repair and the return to good health and function. It is a *building up* process.

As we age, body functions slow and we become fragile. Injuries do not heal as quickly. *Catabolism* best describes this "state-of-being". Catabolism is the opposite of anabolism. These **conditions** are central to the Young Again Protocol™.

Catabolism releases energy. It is a kind of *self-digestion* where the body lives off the energy released from the digestion of its own tissues. This is bare-bones energy used to meet the body's *minimum* energy needs. Energy produced through catabolic activity is starvation energy. Catabolic activity can keep us alive, but it should NOT be equated with health and longevity. Catabolism has its roots in death.

When we are young, we are anabolic. When we are old, we are catabolic. Of course, there are degrees within these two categories. In this book, when we use the words *anabolism* and *catabolism* we are referring to the OVERALL condition or direction of the bio-electric body and its implications to the aging process.

The age twenty-four dividing line we spoke of earlier is our **anabolic PEAK.** It is that point in **TIME** when the young begin their slide into old age. Some people experience their anabolic peak earlier than age twenty-four. For others it comes a little later. The *point* is that its onset is arriving much too soon.

## Once Upon A Time

There was a time when it was uncommon to see the first signs of old age until the fortieth or forty-fifth year—unless one was subject to hardships beyond the norm. Obesity, gray hair, balding, slowing of sexual function, wrinkled skin, diminished vitality etc. are all classic *SIGNS* of old age.

Before we can erase the signs of old age, we must come to understand *why* they occur. We also need to understand *how* they express themselves. When we become AWARE of the passing of TIME, we also become aware of the invisible forces of aging—forces that cause the young to wake up old.

When we reach our ***anabolic peak,*** we are at the crossroads of Time. We are caught between the wonder of youth and the approach of old age.

*Aging initiates quietly and without notice.* It is a **self-ordained** process that speeds the passing of Time and hastens our date with death.

## Change The Script

**Life does NOT have to be this way!** We can change the script if we *choose*—no matter what our age! We can *reverse* our course if we are willing to learn and then act upon our new-found knowledge.

It is not the idea of growing old that people fear. Rather, it is the idea that old age will *cheat* them of the enjoyment of the things they once took for granted. For most, the thought of old age gives rise to visions of a dead-end street, loneliness, pain, suffering and finally death.

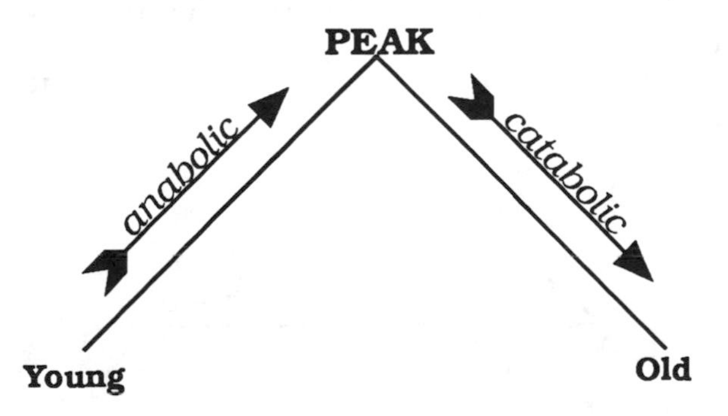


**Anabolic Peak**—That point in TIME when our youth is spent and the onset of old age has begun.

When I chose the title for this book, I wrestled between *Forever Young* and the present title, *Young Again!* The former title did not fit those people who are on the *anabolic* side of the pyramid. They will not read this book because they cannot grasp the meaning of the word *old*. Their world is *young*. They are never going to get old—or so they think.

Only those who realize that they have *passed* their anabolic peak understand the implications of the word ***OLD***. To them, the idea of becoming *Young Again!* is only a dream.

Hosea proclaims, "My people are destroyed for lack of knowledge." However, it is not knowledge that mankind lacks, but the wisdom to discern the difference between false knowledge and truth. ***Old age*** and ***old*** are not necessarily synonymous. They do not have to mean the same thing.

## The Doctor

When we are dying, we hear the pronouncements of medical science, "Nothing can be done!" "Accept that which cannot be changed!" and other expressions designed to worm their way into our consciousness. These expressions numb our wits and excise our will to live.

Oral pacifiers, these pronouncements! Empty words designed to help us accept and rationalize the phenomena we call life and death.

In the beginning—when poor health manifests itself—the medical folks talk of recovery. In time, recovery gives way to **high-tech jargon** and **HOPE**.

For the terminal patient, who has cast himself or herself before the altar of science, medical science quickly exhausts its mumbo-jumbo, turning instead to steely words that chisel our name on the tombstone.

The doctor announces death's call. The patient answers that call with forced preparation and/or frustration and the questions "Why?" "How?"

The ***mystery*** of health and happiness, life and death goes unanswered.

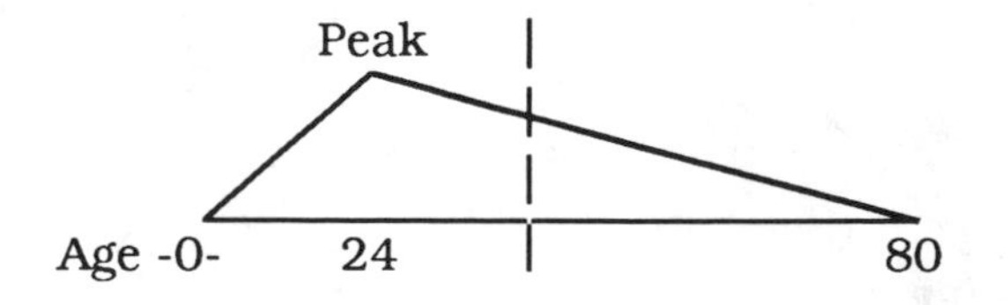


**Aging Pyramid**—note how far left of center the anabolic peak is located. In this case, it is shown at age 24.

## The Clergy

Religious training convinces us that we have an "appointed time" and to "accept what God has foreordained"—soothing words that placate our emotions and numb the reality of the moment. Few people dare to question religion's pronouncements. There is little quarter for rationality here.

Instead, we elevate to dogma that which we do not understand. We blindly follow our beliefs, never pausing to question "Why?" and "How?" as life slips away.

We give up. We grow old. We accept what we have been taught, and we die decades ahead of **TIME** because medical science said, *"Sorry!"* and our religious leaders offered us little consolation—except a, *"hereafter!"*

The balance of society attempts to buffer the "Why?" and "How?" with cynicism set to music in songs like Peggy Lee's *Is That All There Is!* Because we do NOT know where to find the answers, we keep dancing, pausing only to break out the booze.

Our inability to winnow truth from lies is *not* totally our fault. We have been schooled to accept the flood of distortions that emanate from our societal organs—government, newspapers, schools and universities. They are bullhorns—all of them—wired to the halls of Science, the present god of our civilization. Science has become a cult, a national religion, but science fails to answer *"Why?" and "How?"*

## Pilgrimage

Daily, we *voluntarily* make the pilgrimage to Science's cultic altar, paying homage to the idea that cause and effect can be explained using single factor analysis. We accept the *theory* that there is a **bug** responsible for every dis-ease, a **pill** to cure every ailment.

We are told we have a built-in alarm clock that signals our time to die, when longer days—good days—filled with health and happiness are within our reach if we will only act and accept our greatest gift of all—good health!

Medical science blames the bacteria and viruses for our dilemma and health problems, while Christianity blames Eve for bringing the curse of sickness and death upon Adam and his progeny. Both are dead wrong!

Instead of taking responsibility for ourselves, we blame other people and events we believe were beyond our control. We then prostrate ourselves before the *Altar of Science* and pay homage with the fruits of our labor. We buy medicines and pills that treat our symptoms, but leave the **causes** untouched, and more importantly, ***unidentified!***

***Palliation*** is a term that comes to mind. It says much about medical science in a few syllables. It means relief of SIGNS and SYMPTOMS without relief of underlying cause(s).

Drugs produce change in body function. They are prescribed to **prevent, diagnose or cure** dis-ease. *Palliation* is the **fourth** reason pharmacology texts use to **justify** drug administration. Palliation *tricks* the patient and leads the physician astray.

How different life would be if people had a correct knowledge about dis-ease and the aging process, and then acted upon that knowledge. Sadly, mankind lives in a medically induced stupor where the "Why?" and "How?" of life and death, health and dis-ease goes unanswered.

Make no mistake, 99% of the aging process is under our direct, personal control. We can possess and maintain a young body AND a young mind—if we wish. This book was written to answer the "Why?" and "How?" and to point the way to the **path** of ageless living.

### What Is Your Age?

How we define age can make a big difference in our *attitude* toward life. Our attitude dictates our daily actions. Our actions in turn draft our physiological future and our *bio-electric age.*

Age can be defined on the basis of chronological age, mental age, functional age and most importantly, *bio-electric* age. *Carefully* review each.

**Calendar age** is how old we are in years upon this earth. We celebrate our calendar age each year with a birthday party. Unfortunately, we celebrate in *past tense* and in the *negative* by defining age in years *old*, instead of years *young!*

**Mental age** is defined by the way we think. Mental age is our perspective on life. It is a kind of mental cohort effect. A mental cohort is a "mental" time capsule where the person's mind is *stuck* in a past time period—like in the the Great Depression when the person grew up. Many older people are living proof of a *mental* cohort effect. These are people who are mentally young, but *physically* old.

Most of us know someone like this; perhaps a loved one. Regardless of how young the person thinks, it is obvious that their body long ago passed its anabolic peak—losing cadence with their mind. ***Old* body, *young* mind**—not a very exciting prospect, is it?

**Functional age** is based on our ability to function. *Nursing* and bogus *holistic* medicine define functional health as our ability to experience normal, everyday desired activities.

These **bogus** medical definitions allow for one or more degenerative "conditions," while *wellness* is based on the way we perceive ourselves, **without respect** to mental or physical limitations that deprive us of a youthful lifestyle.

The above "plastic" definitions bother me because they lead us astray! They *dodge* the issues and causes of aging and dis-ease! They are **dead-end** definitions.

We can only experience *peak* health in the ABSENCE of dis-ease. This book teaches you HOW to achieve that goal every day of your life for as long as you desire to live.

Reversing your ***bio-electric*** **age**—your body's *actual age*—is what this book is about. Your *bio-electric* age can be measured and it is **malleable.** You will learn more in future chapters. Hopefully, this prospect will motivate you to finish reading this book. When you learn how to manipulate and control the forces that influence your bio-electric age,TIME'S effect on your life ceases to be a concern. When you *LOOK, THINK* and *FEEL* young—you are *Young Again!*

**PREVIEW:** *In the next chapter, you are going to determine your REAL age and identify those things that are causing you to become old before your time. The information you provide will become YOUR foundation for the balance of this book. Are you ready?*

**Brown Eyes Green**

We are taught that eye color, balding, diabetes, obesity and hormonal problems are "genetic" in origin. But it's not so. Children are ***born*** with blueish eyes ***before*** they change to brown or black. Men ***with*** hair become bald after they ***lose*** it. People ***become*** diabetics! Women **develop** female problems. Blondes become brunettes. People **become** fat. People **grow** deaf. The list goes on...

I once had dark brown eyes. **Now,** the're half green. Bald men **can** grow hair. Diabetics can **become** normal. Women can **resurrect** their "hormone cycle." Fat people can **become** thin. "Genetic" problems are solved by restoring the **TERRAIN.** Genetic problems are symtomatic and "past tense" in nature, **never** causitive. I "regrew" my hair and saw my health in all aspects **blossom** AFTER 50 years of age—and so can you, if you will follow my lead.

**Who's In Control**

Question medical authority. Get-up off your knees. It's YOUR body and YOUR life. Take control of YOUR future.

## NORMAL COLON AND SICK COLONS

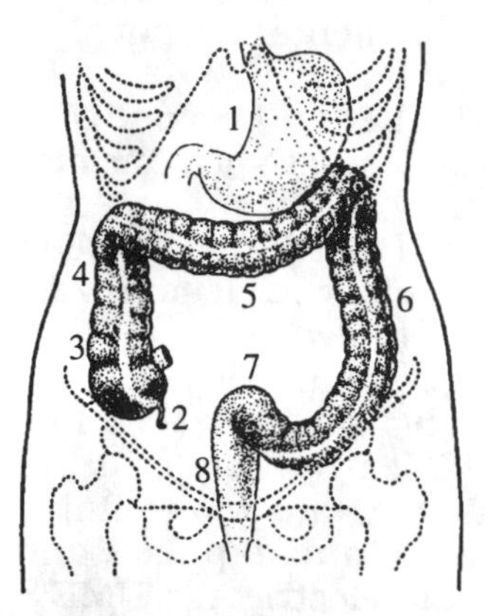


A. The Normal Colon

The normal colon in the proper position in relation to other structures: 1) stomach 2) appendix 3) cecum 4) ascending colon 5) transverse colon 6) descending colon 7) sigmoid flexure 8) rectum

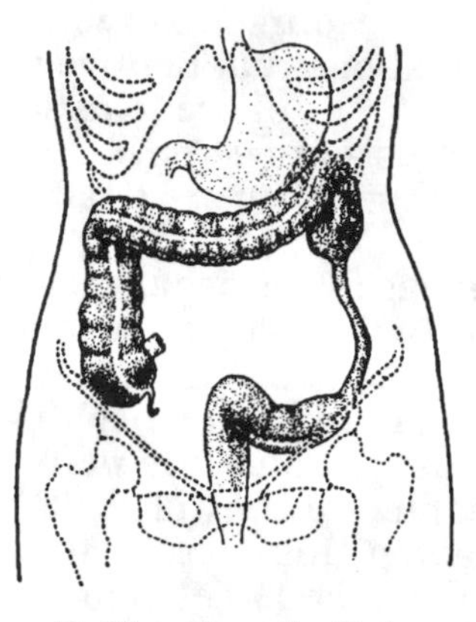

B. The Spastic Colon

The colon in spastic constipation.

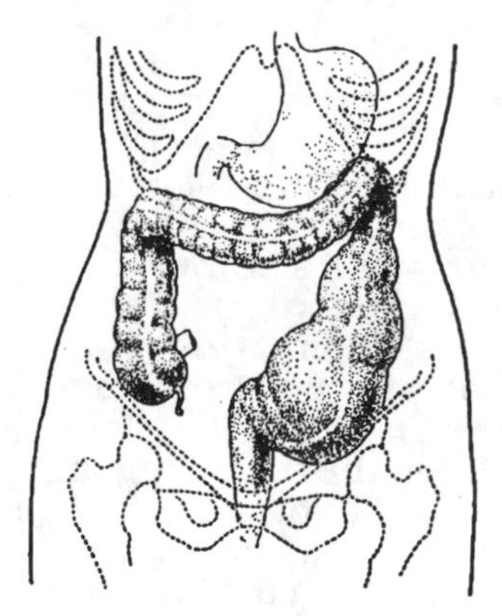

C. The Engorged Colon

The colon in engorged constipation.

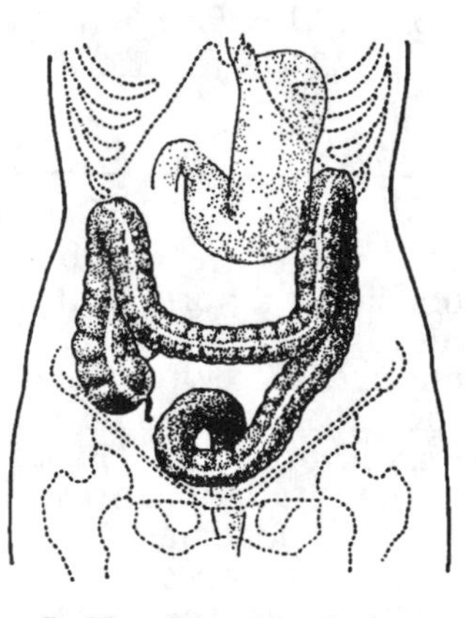

D. The Sagging Colon

Ptosis, or sagging, of the transverse colon, accompanied by displacement of the stomach.

**Programmed To Die**

We *program* ourselves to die by our actions, words and thoughts. And as we prepare, the *reaper* takes our friends and siblings—a signal that "our" time is approaching. We do our best to make sure we are not left behind.

# 3

# Any Old Road

*"If you don't know where you're going,*
*how will you know when you get there?*
*If you don't know how you got there,*
*any old road will NOT take you back."*
John Thomas

Aging is considered to be part of the normal life process. In actuality, it is the *abnormal* part of the process. Normal growth takes us from infancy to our anabolic peak. Abnormal aging takes us from our PEAK to our grave.

Aging follows a procession of TIME-related **events** we identify with descriptions like: gray hair, menopause, balding, diabetes, wrinkles, PMS, cold body, loss of energy, low sex drive, dental problems, obesity, etc. These "things" that occur in our lives **document** the passing of TIME. They are symptomatic—and they are also SIGNS of aging!

The aging process can be slowed, stopped and reversed. But doing so is ONLY possible when we have correct knowledge and understanding supported by action. Fundamental to seeing "results" is **personal responsibility.**

People speed the aging process and the passing of TIME when they **ignore** the SIGNS along the way. "Tuning-out" shortens their days on the Earth, and they age by default. Instead, let us choose to ***re-cycle*** TIME, **not** by reliving our experiences, but by ***exchanging*** TIME spent for TIME we can choose to live anew.

Aging and **TIME** are related, but they are not the same. Aging is the result of **TIME** poorly lived, whereas **TIME** is the *vehicle* of aging. For example, cancer is the product of TIME *poorly* lived. Cancer causes the passing of Time to accelerate. When this occurs, our body experiences a slump in its *bio-electric* balance and we become OLD! Think of dis-ease as **TIME** in motion. Dis-ease *warps* our concept of TIME! Aging is

**TIME's** trail—a confirmation of biological deterioration.

### *Rate* Yourself

Shortly, you will be asked to *personalize* each of the types of aging we discussed in Chapter Two. This simple project will give the concepts of *aging* and *Time* more tangible meaning.

Use an erasable pen or pencil. *Estimate* and place *your* age on each line. Leave the last line blank until *after* you have scored your *bio-electric* age at the END of this chapter.

| | | |
|---|---|---|
| Mental Age | 0____________________ | 80 yrs |
| Calendar Age | 0____________________ | 80 yrs |
| Functional Age | 0____________________ | 80 yrs |
| Age You Feel | 0____________________ | 80 yrs |
| ***Bio-electric Age*** | **0____________________** | **80 yrs ++** |

### Signs & Symptoms

**TIME** poorly lived produces SIGNS and SYMPTOMS of *bio-electric* aging and dis-ease. They represent *change* and diminished function in the **vital organs** and **glands**.

***Symptoms*** of dis-ease are *subjective* changes in body function that are NOT apparent to an outside observer—like nausea, anxiety, pain, dryness of mouth, anorexia and low sex drive. Symptoms often go unnoticed by the host. Symptoms, however, do indicate *subtle* alterations in body function and changes in the tissues, hormones, and fluids. Aging is a "nice" word for slow-down. Slow-down eventually leads to shut-down. Aging is falling apart one day at a time.

**Aging initially occurs in the *"invisible"* realm where the "electric" body resides. Eventually, aging is seen in the mirror and/or confirmed by the doctor's diagnosis.**

### TIME Made Visible

***Signs*** are different from symptoms. They are *external* events and are observable. Signs of aging and/or dis-ease can be observed and measured. Signs support a doctor's diagnosis of a morbid condition. Signs cause the host to become acutely aware of alteration of normal body function—like pain or inflammation. Hence, signs are a *confirmation* of aging and the passing of TIME. ***Signs** are Time made visible!* Signs are *bio-*

*electric* **TIME** capsules—frozen messages from the past.

Signs are *abnormal* events in the life process. They represent dis-ease and pathology. When we think of them as ***normal***, we diminish their impact on our consciousness and compound their effect. Aging and dis-ease become one.

Dis-ease is like the unwelcome guest who drops in, causing upset. Unlike the guest, dis-ease doesn't go away. Dis-ease steals away our life—as when we can no longer do the things we once did. Full manifestation of the aging process is delayed until we find ourselves in serious trouble. Only then does dis-ease remove its cloak and the passing of **TIME** accelerates before our very eyes.

**Damage to the vital organs is dis-ease's shadow. Slow down and loss of vital function should be our cue to change our lifestyle before it is too late.**

### Charting Your Bio-electric Age

The following list is your **key** to *your* bio-electric age. Additionally, it is the brush and canvas you will use to determine *how* and *why* your *bio-electric* age is what it is. This list is **your *personal* road map** to ageless living that points the way back in *bio-electric Time*—that is, if you absorb the simple lessons contained in the balance of this book. Each item on this list will be fleshed-out as the *Young Again!* story unfolds.

Each item reflects an assigned point value that is based on its long term **cumulative effect**. Most items are unisex and apply to both sexes while the male/female list applies to the respective sex only. *Contributing factors* that accelerate the aging process are also listed and carry heavy scores.

**NOTE:** This list is not a diagnosis of a particular dis-ease condition. Rather it is a list of markers. It gives you a close approximation of your ***bio-electric age***, providing you are honest with yourself.

Check the boxes that apply. Serious *past* health conditions **should** be counted if they have left their mark or are of recent vintage. If you are under care, or take medications for a condition, it should be counted. Complete this exercise NOW and **again** after you have completed the book when you better understand the significance of each item on this list. Each item will add direction and meaning to your quest for agelessness.

Please **do not** diminish or pass judgement on the items listed. The list is comprised of signs, symptoms and contributing factors that affect people's lives—for good and for bad.

Let me assure you that every item deserves your *attention*. Their **cumulative** effect can easily BLOCK your path and prevent you from becoming *Young Again!*

## Signs, Symptoms & Contributing Factors Of Bio-electric Aging

| | | | |
|---|---|---|---|
| Height: | Loss of physical height | | |
| | •1/4" shorter | 50 | ❑ |
| | •1/2" or more | 200 | ❑ |
| Facial: | •Crow's feet around eyes/upper lip lines | 30 | ❑ |
| | •Cheeks sunken, hollow | 35 | ❑ |
| | •Cheeks sagging/puffy | 65 | ❑ |
| | •Cheeks/nose have spider capillaries | 50 | ❑ |
| | •Face losing "tone" | 40 | ❑ |
| Skeletal: | Muscle deterioration/loss of muscle mass | 60 | ❑ |
| | •Flabby body; no muscle tone | 40 | ❑ |
| | •Leg cramps/charleyhorse | 18 | ❑ |
| | •Stature mildly hunched-back | 80 | ❑ |
| | •Stature severely hunched-back | 120 | ❑ |
| Belly: | •Paunchy/pot | 20 | ❑ |
| | •Grossly distended | 200 | ❑ |
| Eyebrows: thick, bushy | | 25 | ❑ |
| Nose & Ear hair (external) | | 25 | ❑ |
| Body Odor: | •Needs deodorant | 50 | ❑ |
| | •Overpowers deodorant | 80 | ❑ |
| Bad Breath: Chronic | | 30 | ❑ |
| Teeth: | •Decayed | 40 | ❑ |
| | •Cleaning required once a year | 25 | ❑ |
| | •Cleaning every 6 months | 40 | ❑ |
| | •Mercury amalgam fillings | 150 | ❑ |
| | •Root canal(s) present in mouth | 40 | ❑ |
| | •Gingivitis, bleeding gums | 70 | ❑ |
| Nails: | •Fungus/yeast growth under toe/finger nails | 80 | ❑ |
| | •Slow growth | 30 | ❑ |
| | •Thickening of toe nails | 40 | ❑ |
| Hearing: | Progregressively worse with age | 60 | ❑ |
| | •Tinnitis | 60 | ❑ |
| Skin: | •Dry, scaly (includes dandruff) | 20 | ❑ |
| | •Psoriasis/seborrhea/eczema | 50 | ❑ |
| | •Wrinkled/leathery | 40 | ❑ |
| | •Fat bumps on upper arms ; back | 10 | ❑ |
| | •Pimples/acne /skin blemishes | 30 | ❑ |
| | •Do not sweat easily | 20 | ❑ |
| | •Brown *liver* spots on hands/body | 40 | ❑ |
| | •Bruise easily; painful to touch | 60 | ❑ |
| | •Heavy oil secretion | 15 | ❑ |
| Hair, Mustache, & Beard: | | | |
| | •Predominantly gray/white | 50 | ❑ |
| | •Bald head | 50 | ❑ |
| | •Loss of body hair(legs, chest, groin) | 80 | ❑ |
| | •Slow hair growth | 30 | ❑ |
| | •Head hair (once wavy, now straight) | 40 | ❑ |
| | •Gray or white pubic, axillary, or leg hair | 40 | ❑ |
| Physical Activity: | | | |
| | •Inability to perform hard physical work | 30 | ❑ |
| | •Joint pain/inflammation after hard work | 20 | ❑ |
| | •1-3 days required to recover from hard work | 30 | ❑ |
| Weight: | | | |
| | •Easily gain pounds | 30 | ❑ |
| | •Unexplained large weight loss | 40 | ❑ |

| Category | Symptom | Points | |
|---|---|---|---|
| Mental: | •Depression | 50 | ❑ |
| | •Confusion/can't face day | 45 | ❑ |
| | •Need coffee to get/keep going | 30 | ❑ |
| Stools: | •Lack of medium dark brown color | 30 | ❑ |
| | •Formed/hard or dry | 50 | ❑ |
| | •Defecation requires effort | 20 | ❑ |
| | •Food transit time over 24 hours | 40 | ❑ |
| | •Overly foul gas/odor | 40 | ❑ |
| | •Bright red blood on stool | 15 | ❑ |
| | •Less than "complete" bowel evacuation | 20 | ❑ |
| Illness: | •Often feel sick, but no fever | 30 | ❑ |
| | •Colds more than once a year | 25 | ❑ |
| | •Succumb to flu most years | 30 | ❑ |
| Eyes: | •Require reading glasses | 20 | ❑ |
| | •Sensitive to sunlight | 40 | ❑ |
| | •Poor night vision (car lights bother) | 20 | ❑ |
| | •Brown spots in iris (colored portion) | 30 | ❑ |
| | •Racoon shadows under eyes | 90 | ❑ |
| | •Macular degeneration/glaucoma | 50 | ❑ |
| | •"Floaters" in eyes | 30 | ❑ |
| Joints: | •Joint pain (general) | 40 | ❑ |
| | •Osteo arthritis, bursitis | 100 | ❑ |
| | •Rheumatiod arthritis | 200 | ❑ |
| Minor Wounds: | | | |
| | •Scab drop-time requires over 1 week | 20 | ❑ |
| | •Subject to secondary infections | 50 | ❑ |
| | •Scars form easily | 40 | ❑ |
| Capillary Blood: | | | |
| | •Does not form a "pearl" when finger is pricked (i.e. blood flows instead) | 75 | ❑ |
| | •Color is dark red; not bright red | 60 | ❑ |
| | •Non-instant color return when nail beds are squeezed and released | 40 | ❑ |
| | •Blood full of "debris" (Rouleau effect) | 80 | ❑ |
| | •Use of blood thinners/aspirinrequired | 50 | ❑ |
| Respiratory (lungs): | | | |
| | •Heavy breather/can't catch breath | 90 | ❑ |
| | •Prone to pneumonia/bronchial trouble | 80 | ❑ |
| | •Angina-tightness of breath | 150 | ❑ |
| | •Asthma | 80 | ❑ |
| Gut & Bowel/gastro-intestinal: | | | |
| | •Constipation (less than 2 BM's/day) | 90 | ❑ |
| | •Irregular bowel habits | 60 | ❑ |
| | •Alternating diarrhea/constipation | 30 | ❑ |
| | •History of appendix problems | 50 | ❑ |
| | •Appendix removed | 60 | ❑ |
| | •Colitis /diverticulitis/Crohn's | 75 | ❑ |
| | •Removal of any part of small intestine | 90 | ❑ |
| | •Colostomy | 90 | ❑ |
| | •Untreated for intestinal/organ parasites | 90 | ❑ |
| | •Gas, indigestion, cramping after meals | 30 | ❑ |
| | •Acid reflux syndrome | 50 | ❑ |
| | •Abundant/ongoing foul gas | 40 | ❑ |
| | •Diagnosed with "leaky-gut syndrome | 90 | ❑ |
| | •Bloated abdomen after meals | 50 | ❑ |

Blood Circulatory System:

| Item | Points |
|---|---|
| •Heart Attack | 80 ❑ |
| •Anemia (low "iron") | 40 ❑ |
| •Diagnosed arterio/atherosclerosis | 100 ❑ |
| •Poor circulation | 50 ❑ |

Lymphatic System:

| Item | Points |
|---|---|
| •Lymph nodes swollen/painful groin, armpits, breasts | 50 ❑ |
| •Lymph nodes surgically removed | 50 ❑ |
| •Cancer of lymph system (lymphoma) | 200 ❑ |
| •Spleen surgically removed | 60 ❑ |
| •Tonsils have been removed | 70 ❑ |

Fat: Body & Dietary

| Item | Points |
|---|---|
| •10-20 lbs overweight | 20 ❑ |
| •30-75 lbs overweight | 90 ❑ |
| •75-200 lbs overweight | 200 ❑ |
| •Fatty tumors beneith skin covering body | 50 ❑ |
| •Dietary fat intake (butter/olive oil) less than 20% of diet | 50 ❑ |
| •Use of ANY type margarine | 50 ❑ |
| •Use of soy/canola oils or products | 70 ❑ |
| •Fat free diet | 100 ❑ |

Urinary:

| Item | Points |
|---|---|
| •High albumin in urine | 50 ❑ |
| •High urea level in urine | 40 ❑ |
| •A/G ratio below 1.6 | 90 ❑ |
| •Prone to kidney stones | 40 ❑ |
| •Generally **dark** urine color | 25 ❑ |
| •Foul urine odor | 30 ❑ |
| •Sweet urine odor | 50 ❑ |
| •Bladder infections (female) | 75 ❑ |
| •Urine volume small (less than 4 oz) | 35 ❑ |

General Metabolic:

| Item | Points |
|---|---|
| •Drink less than 1/2 gal water/day | 100 ❑ |
| •Drink water/liquids with meals | 80 ❑ |
| •Drink chlorinated/fluoridated $H_20$ | 60 ❑ |
| •Substitute soft drinks/juice for water | 95 ❑ |
| •Failure to drink 1 qt. of mineralized water with fresh lemon immediately upon rising | 50 ❑ |
| •Failure to drink 12-24 oz. of mineralized water per hour in heat, during hard work, when flying | 30 ❑ |
| •Use fluoridated toothpaste | 50 ❑ |
| •Use common deodorants | 30 ❑ |
| •Drinking water comes from city "tap" | 80 ❑ |
| •Regularly drink over-counter store "bottled" water | 30 ❑ |
| •Use any medications for headaches | 40 ❑ |
| •Regularly take Rx drugs | 80 ❑ |

Liver/Gallbladder:

| Item | Points |
|---|---|
| •Diagnosed/prone to gallbladder problems | 60 ❑ |
| •Surgical removal of gallbladder | 60 ❑ |
| •Diagnosed for hepatitis A, B, C, D, E, mononucleosis, Epstein-Barr, malaria, Chronic Fatigue, or "lime" disease | 95 ❑ |
| •Diagnosed with Herpes (genital) | 60 ❑ |
| •Suffer with "shingles" (past/present) | 80 ❑ |

| Category | Item | Points |
|---|---|---|
| Saliva: | •Dry mouth | 30 ❑ |
| | •Require liquids to swallow food | 30 ❑ |
| Body Temperature: | | |
| | •Below normal body temperature | 60 ❑ |
| | •Cold hands and feet | 60 ❑ |
| | •Sensitive to cold temperatures | 30 ❑ |
| | •Suffer in hot weather | 30 ❑ |
| Connective Tissue & General Energy | | |
| | •Diagnosed with lupus, MS, fibromyalgia, peripheral neuopathy, restless legs syn. | 200 ❑ |
| | •Suffer from gout (use medication for) | 80 ❑ |
| | •Stiff joints/loss of flexibility | 50 ❑ |
| | •Must eat often to have energy | 30 ❑ |
| | •Subject to mood swings/energy drops | 30 ❑ |
| | •Knee, shoulder or hip problems (cartilage) | 80 ❑ |
| | •Poor energy; energy "drops" | 40 ❑ |
| | •Sleepy/listless after lunch meal | 35 ❑ |
| Stress and Headaches: | | |
| | •Inability to function under stress | 30 ❑ |
| | •Regularly stressed-out | 40 ❑ |
| | •Chronic headaches | 70 ❑ |
| Cancer: | | |
| | •Diagnosis of any type of cancer | 200 ❑ |
| | •Received chemo/radiation therapy | 300 ❑ |
| | •Cysts or tumors of any kind | 50 ❑ |
| Tobacco: | •Smoke or chew | 95 ❑ |
| Tongue: | •Coated, pasty white-daytime | 40 ❑ |
| | •Coated upon rising in morning | 20 ❑ |
| | •Heavily grooved | 40 ❑ |
| Sleep: | •Sleep less than 7 hours per night | 20 ❑ |
| | •Sleep less than 6 hours per night | 80 ❑ |
| | •Sleep broken; usually interrupted | 20 ❑ |
| | •Sleep with windows closed | 30 ❑ |
| | •Sleep under electric blanket | 50 ❑ |
| | •Insomnia (can't sleep) | 70 ❑ |
| | •Hypersomnia (sleep all time) | 40 ❑ |
| | •Narcolepsy (involuntary daytime sleep lasting about 15 minutes) | 40 ❑ |
| Dietary: | | |
| | •Use "non food based" vitamins/minerals | 20 ❑ |
| | •Take calcium supplements | 30 ❑ |
| | •Lump in throat (difficulty swallowing) | 50 ❑ |
| | •Use insulin for diabetes | 80 ❑ |
| | •Vomit after meals (bulimia) | 95 ❑ |
| | •Eat when nervous | 30 ❑ |
| | •Increased appetite w/o weight gain | 30 ❑ |
| | •Acid foods upset stomach | 30 ❑ |
| | •Nervous stomach | 20 ❑ |
| | •Always hungry | 60 ❑ |
| | •Poor appetite | 25 ❑ |
| | •Milk causes indigestion/bloating | 50 ❑ |
| | •Spicy foods a problem | 20 ❑ |
| | •Greasy foods cause indigestion | 50 ❑ |
| | •Eat or snack more often than every 4 hrs | 55 ❑ |
| | •Devour food...fast eater | 30 ❑ |
| | •Salt food | 30 ❑ |
| | •Eat alfalfa sprouts | 20 ❑ |
| | •Food not "organic" or home grown | 80 ❑ |

| | |
|---|---|
| •Eat restaurant food often | 90 ❑ |
| •Eat junk, packaged or preserved foods | 100 ❑ |
| •Prepare food in a microwave oven | 200 ❑ |
| Computer & Cell phone: | |
| •Use computer more than 1 hour daily | 50 ❑ |
| •Computer closer than 30 inches | 50 ❑ |
| •Use cell phone daily | 100 ❑ |
| Fluorescent, Mercury, Sodium Vapor lights: | |
| •Use for work light | 30 ❑ |
| •Receive under 1 hour sunshine daily | 50 ❑ |
| Exposure to electrical interference devices: | |
| •Radar (police/military) | 40 ❑ |
| •Electronic Equipment | 30 ❑ |
| •Smoke Detector | 20 ❑ |
| Exercise: Lack of aerobic activity 3x week | 80 ❑ |
| Wake-Up: Slow; require hours to get going | 40 ❑ |
| Blood Pressure: | |
| •Resting pressure above 70/120 | 50 ❑ |
| •Working pressure above 90/140 | 90 ❑ |
| Emotions: | |
| •Keyed-up, can't relax | 30 ❑ |
| •Melancholy/unhappy | 40 ❑ |
| •"Snap" personality | 50 ❑ |
| Vegetable Juicing: | |
| •Failure to drink 1 glass of fresh beet, carrot and ginger juice daily | 50 ❑ |
| Eat according to rules for blood type/food combining | 30 ❑ |
| Colon Therapy: | |
| •Do not do colon therapy weekly | 100 ❑ |
| •Do not do colon therapy at all | 200 ❑ |

**Females Only**

| | |
|---|---|
| Menstruation & Menopause: | |
| •Over age 40; & no vitamin B-12 shots | 70 ❑ |
| •Over age 40; WITH vitamin B-12 shots | 50 ❑ |
| •Exposure to mammograms | 60 ❑ |
| •Premenstrual tension (PMS) | 50 ❑ |
| •Painful/difficult menses | 40 ❑ |
| •Depression before menstruation | 20 ❑ |
| •Painful intercourse | 60 ❑ |
| •Vaginal dryness; itching | 50 ❑ |
| •Ovaries/uterus removed | 80 ❑ |
| •Thinning hair | 40 ❑ |
| •Vegetarian/vegan | 70 ❑ |
| •Menses irregular/skip often | 40 ❑ |
| •Acne worse during menses | 30 ❑ |
| •Painful breasts | 60 ❑ |
| •Body painful to touch | 60 ❑ |
| •Ovarian cysts /uterine fibroid tumors | 95 ❑ |
| •Hot flashes | 95 ❑ |
| •Can detect active ovary each month | 40 ❑ |
| •Used birth control pills (ever) | 150 ❑ |
| •Used any form of estrogen replacement | 150 ❑ |
| •Thyroid condition/thyroid medication | 90 ❑ |
| •Yeast/bladder infections; vaginal itching | 80 ❑ |
| •Endometriosis | 200 ❑ |
| •Food binges/cravings before menses | 40 ❑ |

| | |
|---|---|
| •Brain fog, poor memory, confusion | 90 ❑ |
| •Lack of sexual interest | 90 ❑ |
| •Cellulite formation (hips or thighs) | 100 ❑ |
| •Vertigo (dizziness) | 70 ❑ |

**Male Only**

| | |
|---|---|
| •Impotence | 90 ❑ |
| •Prostate problems | 90 ❑ |
| •PSA count elevated | 60 ❑ |
| •Painful ejaculation | 60 ❑ |
| •Urination dribble, can't release | 90 ❑ |
| •Frequent night urination | 80 ❑ |
| •Pain inside leg or heels | 30 ❑ |
| •Leg spasms, cramps at night | 20 ❑ |
| •Vegetarian/vegan | 50 ❑ |
| •Over age 40; & no vitamin B-12 shots | 50 ❑ |
| •Lack of sexual interest | 100 ❑ |

Total Score............................................ ______

Divide (men divide by 226; women by 243)

Your *bio-electric* "reference score" is.......... ______

Add your points together and divide your score by 226 for men or 243 for women to obtain your *bio-electric* reference score. Example: If you are man and your score is 1790, divide by 226 to obtain a **reference score** of 7.92, and so on.

Next, use the conversion scale to convert your reference score to your *bio-electric* age of 70 years. This is your **"real"** age!

**Bio-electric Score Conversion Scale**

The number on the left is your reference score. The number on the right is your *bio-electric age.*

| | | | |
|---|---|---|---|
| .18 = 18 | .22 = 20 | .30 = 22 | .33 = 24 |
| .66 = 28 | 1.10= 30 | 2.42 = 35 | 2.86 = 40 |
| 3.30 = 45 | 3.96 = 50 | 4.40 = 55 | 5.28 = 60 |
| 6.60 = 65 | 7.92 = 70 | 8.81 = 75 | 11.0 = 80+ etc. |

Your bio-electric age *should* motivate you to evaluate your life. **DO NOT panic or feel hopeless if your bio-electric age is older than you think it should be. It is only a reference age.** Remember, it took your entire life to reach your present *bio-electric* age. Allow yourself a little time to undo the damage. ***Circle*** your age and ***transfer*** your score to the chart earlier in this chapter. You should re-calculate your *bio-electric age* every year to determine if you are aging or growing younger. Your *bio-electric age* is a VERY important **reference** number.

### Think About It!

If your *calendar age* is twenty-seven years and your bio-electric age is thirty-nine years—as mine was when I began the reversal process—you are **losing** the battle. Consider the impact each additional *bio-electric* year exerts upon you. The younger you are, the less effect a few extra years will have. BUT, if you are already thirty-five, forty, fifty, sixty or MORE *bio-electric* years OLD, a few extra years can mean a lot and they must not be ignored or written off.

The older you are, the faster **TIME** flies and the faster you become old! You "know" you are in trouble when the SIGNS appear. Most signs and symptoms appear between *bio-electric* ages 25-55. Things like: hormonal issues, obesity, diagnosed dis-eases, low energy, cellulite, menstrual problems, arthritis, falling and graying hair, heart attack and stroke, etc. Deal with these problems now on your terms, or deal with them on the doctor's terms later. It's a matter of **CHOICE**!

**Time is NOT on your side if your bio-electric age is equal to or greater than your calendar age.** There is NO time to waste! Don't look back! Make yourself finish this book and apply what you learn! The answers you SEEK are here.

My calendar age is 58, but my bio-electric age is holding at 19 years *young!* **TIME** is standing still for me—and it can stand still for you, too—if take responsibility for your life!

**No one's situation is hopeless!** The *bio-electric* body has AMAZING resiliency! Follow the lessons contained herein, and your body will heal itself. Let your body prove to you that you can become *Young Again!*

***ACTION STEPS TO AGELESS LIVING***

1. Evaluate your score & review items checked.
2. Complete the reading and study of this book.
3. Recalculate your score at least once a year.
4. Accept responsibility for your life.
5. Implement the truths contained herein.

Each thing you do to improve your health—no matter how small—will produce big benefits. Several small steps are more effective than one big step. The combined effect of many steps is simply astounding!

**PREVIEW:** *In our next chapter, you will meet a few great people of science, get a glimpse of the "behind-the-scenes" maneuvering within medical science, and you will be offered an explanation of mankind's present environmental dilemma.*

## Shedding "Your" Skin

Humans and snakes have something in common: they both shed their skin. Snakes shed their skin from the "outside" as often as necessary as they grow. Humans, on the other hand, shed their skin from the "inside" during the process of deacidification. The human process is done ONLY by choice.

Everyone acquainted with alternative healing has been taught that deacidification of the body often causes the body to "shed" a rubber like mucoid matter from the colon wall. Victor Irons, Bernard Jensen and Paul Bragg often referenced the phenomenon in their writings.

Your author has had many discussions with gastro-enterologists, surgeons, etc. about the "mystical" mucoid matter that is supposed to inhabit bowel and coat the colon wall. They tell me they have NEVER seen it. When they look inside someone's colon when doing a colonoscopy," they see only nice, pink tissue, but no mucoid lining. So as far as they are concerned, us "health" folks are, well, NUTS!

The answer to the riddle goes something like this. When people go on fasts, do major cleansing, perform colon therapy and drink fresh vegetable juice, their body begins dumping tissue waste into the blood and lymphatic system where it finds it's way to the liver, is filtered out of the blood and sent on its way down the "gut" until it reaches the colon where it accumulates. The colon is the last six feet of the intestine.

During a good cleanse, waste **COLLECTS** on the colon wall. Using colon hydrotherapy (colonic), the person will often shed the mucoid matter from the colon wall **much like the skin of a snake,** only we humans shed our skins from the inside.

The reason the medical folks never see it is because prior to doing their procedure, they give the patient some rather caustic stuff to drink in order to empty the colon. So who is correct? BOTH parties are correct, they are simply out of time and sequence with each other.

When humans shed their skin, the stuff that comprises the "skin" is best described as "cancer that hasn't happened yet!"

The process of **"deacidification"** is undoubtedly one of the most valuable and inexpensive processes available to us.

In Dr. Jensen's colon book, there are pictured forty colored slides of people's "skins." And while they aren't very pretty to look at, they are real as real can be. Your author has seen this "stuff" exit his body many times—and so will anyone who takes this simple message to heart.

So what's it going to be, dear reader? Take responsibility for your life and rid your body of the horrible burden it is laboring under? Or do you wish to continue to suffer, grow old and die young?

If you follow the Young Again Protocol™ you will be choosing to "deacidify" on your own terms now, instead of suffer-ing on the doctor's terms later.

It's more fun to be healthy and young every day of your life, than sick and old for the rest of your life. You decide.

## Yeast

What are just a few of the symptomatic health complaints associated with Candida Albicans (yeast)? Eye floaters, bad breath, depression, constipation, foul and excessive gas, low energy, bloated abdomen, aching joints, arthritis, moodiness, low blood sugar, acne, skin dryness, hearing problems, ear aches, colic in babies, hair loss, etc.

Yeast is associated with all dis-eases and health problems. It is NOT the cause of the problems, but it is a player. The **cause** is an acid "terrain." The solution for yeast related issues is what the Young Again Protocol is and the book *Young Again!* is all about.

## Vitamin B-12

Symptoms of vitamin B-12 related conditions are: Memory loss, sleeplessness, nervousness, irritability, spinal problems, constipation, poor motor function, heart palpitations, ringing in ears, chronic fatigue, the list goes into the hundreds of symptoms.

Central to the vitamin B-12 molecule is the cobalt atom, hence cyan-o-cobal-o-min. Even when B-12 is present in the diet, the mucoprotein "intrinsic factor" must be secreted from the stomach wall or B-12 is lost. Sublingual tablets don't work. And the only place in the small intestine that B-12 can be absorbed is in the ileum.

Vitamin B-12 injections are commonly given to women, and especially after age 40. But this is synthetic B-12, and it leaves a lot to be desired. The Young Again Protocol™ calls for the application of Cobo-12™ metabolite creme directly to the skin where it is absorbed easily. Women deplete their B-12 stores about 20 years ahead of men.

## Osteoporosis

The LAST thing women need is calcium. Contrary to popular belief, calcium intake is NOT the issue. Osteoporosis has "two" common denominators—and the reader will discover what they are as this book unfolds.

## All Played Out

Life is like a record player that plays in three speeds: 33, 45 and 78. At 33 life is great. At 45 you're not so sure. At 78, you're all played out. To avoid being a 78 at 45, all you have to do is "reduce" your bio-electric age to decimal **.33!**

## Foaming Urine

In the mid 1950's, Ajax cleanser was a popular household product. The advertisements sang a little song that went like this: *"Ajax, the foaming cleanser, baba baba ba ba, sends stains, right down the drain!"*

It is a very good sign if your urine produces massive amounts of foam. The more Medical Grade Ionized Water™ I drink, the more the urine foams. This water has an extremely high ORP potential. The more ATP the cells can produce, the healthier the tissues. As I have watched the aging process reverse itself, my urine has become more and more foamy! Just thought you might like to know.

## Diabetes

Adult Onset Diabetes (Type-II) is closely associated with leaky gut syndrome and Insulin Growth Factor 1 (IGF-1). Typically, this form of diabetes is contracted by people over 40 and overweight. Careful monitoring of dietary intake can manage insulin levels for some forks. Others take a glucose management pill like Glucophage™, others take insulin shots. Leaky gut syndrome is part of the diabetes story. So is a stressed liver, a sluggish bowel and an acid body.

The Young Again Protocol™ for diabetics calls for colon therapy, the Tissue and Liver Program and the use of R/C™, OX™ and Microbe-ize™. Fresh juice is used with care since the glycemic index is quite high. Lastly, green beans—steamed, raw, canned, etc.—all you can eat. I don't know why they work, but they do. Green beans is an old time remedy.

Diabetes is one of the "BIG 4" dis-eases, cancer, arthritis and heart attack/stroke are the other three. All four have one thing in common. They are TERRAIN conditions!

## Food & Light

After the body digests food energy, it passes those energy molecules by way of the blood through the capillary beds behind the eyes where "light" activates the energy. Hence, the Bible phrase, *"Let there be light!"* takes on new meaning.

## West Nile Fever

Like malaria, West Nile Fever is a virus transmitted by mosquitoes. Encephalitis can follow and kill. Problem is, the medical folks don't have any answers, but your author does and its called OX™. Any viral condition is a "terrain" issue.

### "The Experts"

When a system becomes overly *complex*, a cadre of *experts* soon appear with their agenda, codes, and private vocabulary. And in the people, this spawns resentment followed by skepticism as to the system's fairness.

Most of what we're taught and much of what we believe either isn't true or doesn't work. The experts understand this fact—so should you.

To learn the rules of the game and learn how to avoid "experts," read *If You Want To be Rich & Happy, Don't Go To School*, *Winning Through Intimidation*, and *Looking Out For Number One.* (See Source Page 384)

The latter two books teach the **opposite** of what their titles imply. All three books should be "mandatory" reading—complete with book reports—every month of every year from grades K-12.

Do yourself—and your children a favor—by reading these classics. **The only thing that counts is the way things are, NOT the way they ought to be.**

### Puberty & The "Middle Years" Window

Hormones DRIVE the changes that occur as children enter adulthood. When the hormones kick in, baby fat turns to lean muscle mass. Boys become as strong as mules; girls become shapely. Physical height is attained.

Most teens enjoy good health in spite of the abuse they deal themselves. But by age 25, degeneration of the vital organs is in progress, particularly in women. Birth control pills do their damage, as do food borne antibiotics, hormones and "zeno" estrogens that mimic hormones, but are not hormones. All of these things cause people to lose control of their lives.

Between ages 20-35, cellulite makes its appearance; thyroid related stress manifests; energy declines, menstrual changes appear; muscle tone is lost; leaky-gut syndrome increases; loss of cobalt accelerates; yeast infections increase; hair grays and thins—the list goes on.

Central to these things is the closing of the "puberty window." By age 40-45, the process is complete and the middle years are over. To reopen this window, follow the Young Again Protocol™. (See pages 72, 164, 212 and 384.)

**The Young Again Protocol™ turns the body into a "pass through" system that perpetually sheds its wastes.**

# 4

## *See* What You Look At

### Said Dorothy to the Wizard:

*"You're a very bad man!"*
*"Oh no!" responded the Wizard.*
*"I'm just a very bad Wizard!"*

**It's difficult to comprehend the human dilemma without some understanding of the forces within science and medicine that blur our vision and confuse our thought processes. Once understood, however, the reader will more fully grasp why he or she is discovering the path of agelessness in the pages of this book versus the media or medical system literature.**

The truly Great Wizards of science and medicine are a breed of their own. They are often light years ahead of their time. They are also a problem for those who want to control and manipulate society. There have been many of these great people in science and medicine. Many of them lived out their lives on the fringe—away from mainstream medicine and science. We hear little about them, but the impact of their vision is all around us—often with another's name on their discoveries. A few hardy souls chose to function *within* the system. Their insight usually created craters that could neither be denied nor erased by the powers that be.

I refer to these people as WIZARDS. Wizards understand medical science's loss of direction and the dilemma of TRUTH vs. theory.

Medical science's tragic loss of direction did NOT occur by accident; rather, it was foreordained. It is a tale of manipulation and *behind-the-scene* control.

Let us paint the historical landscape of a few great men and women of REAL medical science so we will better understand: the politics of medical science, and why we must accept responsibility for our own lives and **"UNPLUG"** from the medical system. Here's a brief history of a few medical Wizards.

**The Great Wizards**

**Dr. Carey Reams** was a Wizard. Reams had a sixth sense about nature and the energy forces of life at the subatomic level, and most of his life's work was in the agricultural arena. Reams *dared* to expose the connection between diet, lifestyle and dis-ease. He used simple, inexpensive testing procedures to determine the "state" of people health, procedures that only called for the pH of the urine and saliva plus the mapping of the blood capillaries in the whites of the eyes. He suffered professional ridicule and legal abuse for his efforts.

**Dr. Linus Pauling** was a Wizard! He gave us his monumental discoveries about vitamin C. He also suffered professional ridicule for the TRUTH he heralded. Dr. Pauling was the harbinger of the fantastic DNA molecule discovery in 1954. I spoke with Dr. Pauling three times before he died at age 94. Even at age 94, he was teaching at Stanford. We are indebted to Dr. Pauling. He was a wonderful scientist and a monument to TRUTH. Truth separates a good scientist from a poor one. Pauling won TWO nobel prizes in his life.

**Dr. Guenther Enderlein** was a Wizard. He proved that the blood is NOT a sterile medium. He heralded the **pleomorphic** nature of microbial life forms that are always present in the blood of healthy people. He further elucidated exactly why and how various life forms, from viruses and bacteria to yeast and fungi, predictably appear in the blood as people lose control of their body's "terrain." Enderlein was the first person to use body fluid pH to detect the presence of cancer. His final exam question to test his understanding of life before becoming a doctor in 1898 was: *"What is the difference between plant and animal?"* Enderlein responded, *"There is NO difference!"* He was correct and his discoveries proved it.

*P.S. When your author returned to school at age 45 to become "enlightened" in the ways of science, he also had a sound understanding of plant and soil physiology. As with Reams and Enderlein, that knowledge opened the door to far greater understanding than what was taught to me. Soils and plants provided the genesis of what is now called the* ***Young Again Protocol***™*, and the basis of this book.*

**Rene M. Caisse, R.N.** was a Wizard. Rene was Canada's "cancer nurse." She was a good student and a keen observer of nature's ways. Rene understood life at the subtle energy level and was hounded by health officials unmercifully.

**Dr. Max Gerson** was a Wizard. His discoveries are of tremendous importance to the aging process. He was an excellent example of "low-tech" medical brilliance. What made Gerson unique was that his therapies worked. He cared about people. He was an astute observer. He *cured* cancer with simple, inexpensive modalities; and therein was the *rub.* Gerson was hounded mercilessly by established medical authorities because he threatened their dogmatic position on the nature of cancer. He died in 1959 tired and overworked.

**Rachel Carson** was a Wizard. She was the lady scientist who took on the military industrial complex by herself. In 1959, she wrote the book, *Silent Spring.* Rachel was the beginning of the ***legitimate*** environmental movement. Her findings shattered Science's litany of lies and brought the evils of pesticides into focus. She was proclaimed a witch and was verbally burned at the stake before and after she died in 1964. Her epitaph reads: TRUTH!

**Theo Colborn** is a Wizard. She is the author of *Our Stolen Future,* and the woman who took on the entire medical and scientific world in the grand style of Rachel Carson, author of *Silent Spring.* Colborn's book defines the hormonal dilemma we face. The Young Again Protocol™ offers the solution to it.

**Dr. Ignaz Semmelweis** was a Wizard. He has particular significance to medical science and our story. He was a physician in Budapest during the middle 1800's. Semmelweis made the mistake of confronting a thoroughly entrenched male dominated profession that had only recently wrestled away control of the healing arts from female healers—midwifery, in this case. His contribution to medical science was a simple one, but it involved the use of uncommon good sense—a dangerous commodity in the face of arrogance. Semmelweis said, **"Doctors, wash your hands between patients!"**

There had been unrelenting outbreaks of childbirth fever (Puerperal Fever) among women and hundreds of deaths in area hospitals. The year was 1840. His detractors laughed good Dr. Semmelweis from the scene. They destroyed his reputation by character assassination—a ploy that leaves neither trail nor record of those in bloody robes.They also used professional ostracism—a time-tested tool of the trade. Today, they resort to revocation of a physician's license to practice—

putting a doctor out of his trade. Ostracism, licenses and belittling are *common* maneuvers used to this day to CONTROL physicians who dare to step out of line.

**Morton Walker** was a Wizard. Walker was a health researcher and reporter who wrote extensively and published many books. His primary contribution to the alternative health arena was his ability to piece-together seemingly unrelated pieces of medical landscape into a cohesive fabric of usable information. His life was a tribute to TRUTH.

**Bernard Jensen** is a Wizard. Jensen expanded the fields of colon therapy and iridology and is 93 years of age at this time (2002). Jensen has served his fellow man well.

**Victor Irons** was a Wizard. It was Irons who first brought colon therapy to the fore as a viable medical modality, and mankind owes him our utmost gratitude for such a wonderfully simple, yet effective gift.

**This codicil is offered to stimulate the reader's perspective.** *A doctor's status derives from the State. When the State grants its permission, the professional is created by way of a license. The doctor is a political being that exists at the whim of the State.*

*Licenses are supposed to protect the public. More often than not, they are a mockery that does little more than soothe. Behind the scenes, the professional boards and medical organizations badger and control the doctor who "sees truth" and dares to challenge scientific and medical dogma.*

*History provides us with a long list of good Wizards—Galileo and Copernicus for example,—who were driven out and destroyed.* ***Control*** *is the name of the game. Control is ALWAYS carefully maintained despite brush-fire political events that are provided for their theatrical effect. Keep these thoughts in mind as future chapters unfold.* ***In history, nothing happens by accident!***

The history books tell us *nothing* of the political maneuvering by Dr. Semmelweis' peers, nor of the women who died, nor of the money siphoned-away from people who prostrated themselves at medicine's altar. Today, in the year 2002, many arrogant doctors fail to wash their hands between patients. The more things change, the more they are the same.

### How It Happened

To understand how science and medicine lost their way and why mankind is at war with Mother Earth, let us go to the roots of Christianity, for it is there that we will find our clue.

And God said to Adam, *"Take dominion over the Earth and every living thing thereon."*

This one command, credited to Deity, has done more to pillage the Earth and its inhabitants—plant, animal and man—than any words ever put to task. The problèm isn't the command, but its *interpretation* and *implementation.*

*Misunderstood* and certainly *misapplied,* the biblical edict to *"take control of Nature and hold dominion over Her"* set the course and destiny of history from the time of Christ to Isaac Newton and the present day order.

By *blaming* the sin and fall in the garden on Eve—instead of acknowledging that BOTH male and female made their own choice—*man* dogmatized jurisdiction over woman and proclaimed WAR against Nature and the Earth. It was done in the *name* of GOD. Mankind's present dilemma is the result of blame instead of mutual respect for life.

**Adam & Eve**

*"Power and dominion OVER nature"* shaped science and its tributary, medicine, into the cult it is today. Man over God. Man over the Earth. Man over Woman—for it says, "Eve caused Adam to sin."

Interwoven in this tragic story was the shift from mankind's original primeval state as a *matriarchal* society to that of a *patriarchal* one. No longer would the blood line flow through the woman. Instead it would flow through the man. No more would Woman be exalted and recognized as the *giver* of life. Instead, she would be looked upon as the *ONE* who caused Adam (man) to sin in the garden.

*"And from this day forward, you will experience pain in childbirth as a REMINDER of your transgression."* And so, Woman became the villain. A commodity to be controlled, bought, sold and *"blamed"* for Adam's transgression—which was Adam's own **CHOICE**!

It was into this arena that Dr. Semmelweis wandered. Little did he realize that the powers behind the scene did not care about Puerperal Fever. It was profitable business. *"So what if some women die as long as WE control access to choice in medical care, access to God and, of course, control over the creation of a nation's money supply."*

**Control** is the name of the game. If we want control over our lives and destinies, we must recognize that in matters of health and finance, things are NOT what they seem (please read *Winning Through Intimidation,* and *Looking Out For #1*).

TRUTH in medicine causes problems; and the greater medical science's ***backlash*** to a Wizard's message, the greater the probability that TRUTH is on the loose.

In the business of medicine and science, TRUTH prospers OUTSIDE the mainstream—out on the fringe. The fringe is where we will be taking our lessons in reversing the aging process. On the fringe you can become *Young Again!*

**PREVIEW:** *Our next chapter is where you will become acquainted with the "energy forces" that CONTROL the aging process and you will learn HOW to identify them.*

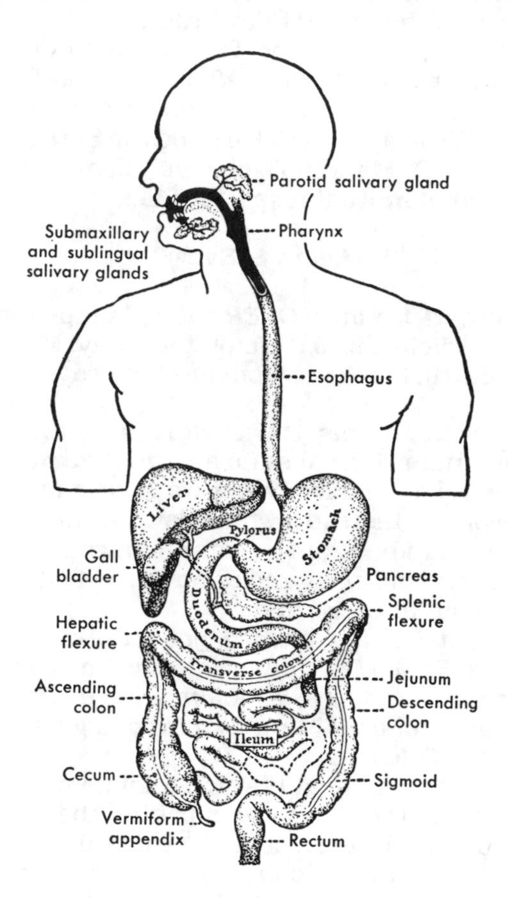


## Visceral Organs Of The Abdominal Cavity

**Dark Circles Under The Eyes**

Circles under the eyes are a SIGN of liver overload, kidney malfunction, under-hydration, lymphatic congestion, and systemic toxicity. A change in lifestyle and diet can eliminate this SIGN of premature aging.

# 5

# Energy & Matter

> *"Reason, of course, is weak when measured against its never-ending task. Weak, indeed, compared with the follies and passions of mankind, which, we must admit, almost entirely control our human destinies, in great things and small."*
>
> Albert Einstein

Little in life is seen in concrete terms of black and white. This is particularly true in the healing arts. For example, consider just a few of the differences in the following modalities (therapies) of healing presently in use.

**Allopathic medicine** (allopathy) attempts to heal using chemotherapy, which is *"chemically induced"* restoration of health. It also includes surgical intervention, emergency medicine and *palliation.* This is the predominant medical modality practiced in the West today. It uses chemical drugs to force ***submission*** and ***overpower*** body systems to induce change. Allopathy believes that "opposite cures opposite."

**Homeopathic medicine** (homeopathy) is the exact opposite of allopathic medicine. It is called the medicine of "similars." Homeopathy focuses on *unfriendly energy fields* in the body that vibrate at anti-life frequencies—frequencies that create stress in the vital organs and imbalances within the system. Homeopathy uses **vibrational** *remedies* instead of chemical drugs. Remedies are potent substances *tuned* to cancel renegade energy frequencies in the body—as represented by drugs, vaccines, toxins, etc. Remedies ***erase the footprint*** of offending frequencies, clear the body of their signature, and return the patient to health and homeostasis (*homeo*-resemblance; *stasis*-[restore to] standing).

**Chiropractic** considers dis-ease to be the result of the incorrect alignment of the spinal column and the nerve plexus issuing therefrom. Poor alignment negatively influences the vital organs served by the central and peripheral nervous systems. Chiropractic has much in common with other vibrational modalities. Chiropractors often wear several hats at once, and at best are "tolerated" by M.D.'s. The reason: a good chiropractor is trained to be results and patient oriented, AND they are generally open to alternative healing modalities.

**Network Spinal Analysis** (NSA) is a new form of chiropractic that integrates various "levels" of care in such a way as to *unfold* and *awaken* spinal energy flow. Healing occurs as a by-product of the freedom of the *body-mind* to utilize its natural, self-regulatory and self-expressive capabilities. In other words, healing is not the direct product of chiropractic, but of the "forces" of life itself *at the subtle energy level.*

The purpose of NSA is to determine the appropriate *timing* and *application* of mechanical forces to the tissues ***before*** chiropractic adjustment. NSA enables patients to release *non*-productive neurological patterns that block healing. NSA allows the *whole* person to express and experience their body's own self-intelligence and vital energy force.

It is the author's belief that NSA brings about healing by helping the patient to become *aware* of negative energy *memory* patterns *at* and *below* the cellular level, and to "erase" their memory from the tissues.

Network Spinal Analysis produces significant improvement in patient self-awareness and ability to make life changes. This promising new healing modality was developed by Donald Epstein, D.C., and is offered to the public by highly trained healers under the trade name *Network Chiropractic*™.

**Yoga & Pilates** are not exactly new to the health scene, but they are an absolutely wonderful and **proven** way of life for those people who practice them.

Your author was taught some yoga techniques by his daughter and saw incredible results in his sacrum and low back from a bad injury 25 years earlier. Yoga is very ancient. Classes are taught at local schools and from video.

"Pilates" (pronounced pee-lat-ees) was developed by

Joseph Pilates about 90 years ago. It involves unique body conditioning moves to tone muscles, increase flexibility and lengthen and align the body.

You author can testify to the unbelievable anti-aging effects that both yoga and Pilates have on older women, who practice them. These women are 20 years ahead of their peers.

**Acupuncture** promotes healing and numbs pain by manipulating energy meridians (pathways). Acupuncture uses tiny needles. It is a modality from the Far East.

**Gua Sha** s a 3000 year old "in home" modality that is easy to learn, very effective and can be used to relieve pain, promote healing and *free* bound ***chi*** energy. Young Again™ offers a teaching video and Gua Sha kit. The technique is extremely effective on whip-lash and neck problems.

**Bio-Magnetics** heals through the use of magnetic energy flowing from *therapeutic* medical magnets. This promising modality has broad application for people who desire *personal* control over their health. It is an inexpensive, in home modality that is very effective.

*Therapeutic* magnets are specific in nature and application. They are particularly useful against stress and they nullify the damaging effects of 110v electrical current. They protect the immune system and stimulate immune response. *Therapeutic* magnets are DC (direct current) energy fields. Their vibratory energy ***awakens*** energy meridians and manipulates pain. Healing follows *repolarization* of cellular organelles and stimulates the production of ATP. These special magnets also stimulate blood and lymphatic fluid movement.

*Therapeutic* magnets balance energy fields in and around injured or inflamed tissue. Millions of people get drug free relief and improved health through magnetic therapy. It is widely used in Japan. In the USA, the medical establishment says magnetic therapy is quackery. The fly in the ointment is the patient who experiences relief. Specifics are outlined in the Young Again™ Source Packet.

**Vibrational medicine** is a composite description that includes dozens of healing modalities that rely on the manipulation of the body's *energy* fields to induce healing. Vibrational medicine recognizes that health and sickness are manifestations of abnormal energy patterns at the subtle energy level of our existence and that healing requires balance to be established **before** a person becomes whole.

Vibrational medicine is a *blend* of Western and Eastern thought that it is rendering wonderful results. Its roots antedate allopathic medicine by many thousands of years.There is no question that this form of medicine IS replacing the Frankenstein we call "allopathy."

A few examples of vibrational medicine are cold laser, photo-luminescence, aroma therapy, flower essences, Network Chiropractic, therapeutic magnets, qi gong, tai chi, DEEP breathing, essential oils, chiropractic, homeopathy, yoga and Pilates, and the use of BEV™ and medical grade ionized waters. All of these, natural techniques that avoid surgical trauma and promote energy flow within the *bio-electric* body.

## Compare The Difference

Allopathic medicine is based on the *Newtonian* view of reality. Sir Isaac Newton saw the world as an elaborate mechanism. Newton so influenced allopathic medicine that for the past three hundred years, the body has been viewed as a grand machine that takes its orders from the brain, central and peripheral nervous systems. This view has been replaced by a new model that sees the body as a flesh and blood biological computer. Nuts and bolts have given way to circuit boards and switches. Both approaches fall short of the reality of life at the **subtle energy level** of our existence and lead us astray.

The Newtonian approach fails to account for energy forces like spirit, intuition, subconscious mental thought, biofeedback, dowsing, etc.—all **subtle** energy manifestations composing our *sixth* sense—a world of metaphysics (*meta-* **beyond** the physical). Strangely, physical is but "frozen light" energy belonging to the Fourth Dimension. Subtle energy CANNOT be measured by length, width and height—the First, Second and Third Dimensions.

## Paradigm Shift

Vibrational medicine (VM) sees the physical body as the *signature* or *footprint* of the invisible "electric" body. VM is based on Einstein's view of matter, which says, "matter will release energy when taken apart." For example, the splitting of an atom in an atom bomb. This is a MAJOR *paradigm shift* from Western medicine's archaic approach to healing. The word ***paradigm*** means *para*-beside, *digm*-an example that serves as a model.

The Einstein model sees the human being as a network of energy fields that co-exist and commingle together, that is, condensed energy resonating at a healthy or sick frequency. (Mother Earth frequency is between 7.8-8.1 Hertz.)

Vibrational healing involves the *manipulation* of opposing energy fields, where allopathic medicine relies on negative energy drugs to overpower **force** the body into submission—thereby bypassing the body's innate intelligence.

Vibrational medicine does not endorse the Germ Theory of Disease. Instead, it recognizes that the TERRAIN of the bio-electric body controls the bacteria and viruses, and not the other way around.

Secondly, present day drug therapy is a mixture of *hoped for* therapeutic effects and KNOWN adverse effects—the good *hopefully* outweighing the bad! Vibrational medicine opts for a less traumatic approach to healing the *bio-electric* body.

Drugs are drugs! They alter body function in negative ways. For example, arthritis medications are extremely potent negative, chemical energy. They do violence to the body and to the liver in particular. They ease the patient's suffering through *palliation* (the relief of signs and symptoms without cure of the underlying causes)—while ultimately killing the patient.

**Health Through Manipulation**

An example of energy manipulation could involve running a magnet over a computer disc or cassette tape. The magnet would neutralize the *energy* stored on the disc by cancelling the other frequency and *erasing* its signature.

If the energy message on the disc were a dis-ease condition in the body, a positive change in one's health will occur when the offending energy field is *neutralized.* Whenever positive energy gains the upper hand, the body returns to a state of "health." Since life is energy and energy is matter, we must conclude that life and energy are manifestations of the same phenomenon. Vibrational medicine's focus is "energy."

**Magneto Hydro Dynamics** (MHD) is a relatively new field of vibrational medicine. Its focus is in the field of dentistry at the "consumer" level through prevention of dental problems.

Plaque formation on the teeth produces cavities. Prevent the formation of plaque and you prevent the formation of cavities, which a poor diet makes even worse. MHD is effective at preventing cavities and treating periodontal gum problems.

MHD utilizes a small counter appliance that pumps water through an ***electromagnetic*** field where hydrogen ions are freed from respective $H_2O$ molecules. These *free* ions carry a positive (+) charge. When this specially treated water is flushed against the plaque on the teeth—or under the gum line—the negatively (-) charged plaque is dissolved and washed away. MHD is an inexpensive ***in-home*** dental modality for your family's teeth—and your dog's teeth, too! Add fresh veggi juices and the Young Again Colon Therapy Protocol™ to MHD and dental problems ease and disappear.

**Radionics** is used by some alternative farmers. It involves broadcasting *energy* frequencies into the surrounding area where it will be picked up by soil, plants, animals and microbes. Compare this practice to a radio station that transmits a melody that is picked up by our radio so we can hear and enjoy it. Properly used, radionics can enhance the production of highly nutritious food while controlling weeds and insects.

**Biodynamics** is *homeopathic* agriculture. It is the *medicine of "similars"* applied to the soil. It involves the use of biodynamic preparations and techniques.

Practical books on the subject are available from Young Again™ Source Packet. *Biodynamic I, II,* and *III, Introduction to Biodynamics,* and *A Biodynamic Farm* are extremely interesting reading and practical information for anyone seriously interested in growing vibrantly healthy food. All "preps" are available by mail, as is a fascinating planting calendar.

*Your author grows a 1 acre garden and orchard and practices these wonderful techniques because they work.*

## Medical Science Challenged

Medical science is threatened by these paradigm shifts because they **conflict** with textbook mentality. They challenge theory that has been elevated to the status of *LAW* by way of the mumbo-jumbo called the *scientific method.* Misuse of the scientific method has gotten us into a lot of trouble. It should be abandoned because it shackles individual creativity. Vision MUST precede inquiry rather than the other way around.

Because vibrational medicine is replacing old dead theories with models that are bringing RESULTS, it behooves each of us to learn as much as possible about these new fields of thought and *apply* them in our daily lives wherever possible. Reversing the aging process relies heavily on the manipulation of *energy* fields within the **"terrain"** of the bio-electric body.

Becoming *Young Again!* involves the application of vibrational medicine at the layman's level. Given the TOOLS and knowledge, we can produce amazing results in our lives and in the lives of our loved ones at minimal expense—and minimal risk!

This book provides a basic overview of the knowledge needed to bring about vibrational healing. Application of the techniques discussed and the response each person experiences will be *unique* to that individual.

## New View

The universe is composed of but two things: *ENERGY* and *MATTER*. Our body is but matter in the form of frozen light. If this is true, then medicines and drugs, which are matter, must also be energy—and they are! However, they are NEGATIVE energy—energy that manipulates illness in the short term at the expense of health and longevity in the long term. No one can deny the advances allopathic medicine has made—especially in the replacement of body parts and in emergency medicine. But there is a negative side also. We must realize that medications and surgical intervention carry *substantial* risk and tradeoffs, and should only be used at last resort.

**Aging is a cumulative process. The *combined* effect of personal neglect, dis-ease and drugs accelerates aging in the youngest of people.**

## Energy Shift

When we choose to live an unhealthy lifestyle, an energy *shifts* occur, resulting in dis-ease and aging. Reversing the aging process involves learning how to manipulate energy forces so negative shifts are minimized and the body is returned to a state of health. When we talk about having an ageless body, we are talking about a body where the positive energy forces are in control—a body that does NOT require perpetual jump-starts with drugs and surgery to keep it going.

Everything we do, eat and drink involves "energy" that influences the *bio-electric* body. We must learn HOW to decipher what is good for us and what is not. By learning HOW to identify these forces, we can also learn HOW to manipulate them *without* the use of drugs or invasive surgery.

**Dis-ease is a manifestation of negative energy forces in the body. Vibrational medicine halts and reverses aging and dis-ease and offers the ordinary person CONTROL over their health and life.**

We *must* recognize that we are more than hunks of flesh and blood, more than biological machines, and more than spiritual beings *trapped* in our bodies during our time on Earth. We are *energy*, and as such, we are part of the cosmos, and yes, we are created in the likeness of God who is also *ENERGY*—positive, beautiful energy!

## Anions & Cations

**An**ions and **cat**ions are usable forms of **"electron"** energy that are released when a chemical reaction takes place—as in our gut and liver when we eat and digest food. The release of energy opposites—one (+) the other (-) produces the electrical activity that grants permission for life.

All matter is a combination of (+) and (-) energy forms. For example, it is the energy *pattern* of anions and cations that gives us steel. When steel is fashioned into a spoon, we identify it as a *steel* spoon. When the energy pattern of matter is altered through fusion, we may get lead or alchemist gold instead of steel. Break the bonds that hold atoms together and energy is released—positive or negative—and often with a big "bang."

### Good & Bad Energy

The terms *positive* and *negative* energy mean the same as *good* and *bad* energy. *Good* energy is "right-spin" energy and *bad* energy is "left-spin" energy. We know good energy from bad energy by its *effect* on our health and the bio-electric body.

**Positive** energy has a particular *spin* of its own—it *spins to the right*, meaning clockwise. **Negative** energy *spins to the left*, meaning counter clockwise.

Solar energy is **an**ionic energy. It is life-giving energy. The Earth's spin is the product of **an**ionic, clockwise, right-spin energy entering the Van Allen Belt (ozone layer). As these energy particles penetrate the ozone layer, they are deflected and bombard the Earth causing it to spin. When Van Allen theorized this belt in 1948, he was laughed down by the *experts*. Later he was vindicated when NASA lost contact with astronaut John Glenn as he passed through this belt (ozone layer) on his return to Mother Earth.

**An**ionic energy can *pass through* matter. It is also very comforting and soothing. Have you noticed the difference in the heat produced by a wood fire compared to the heat produced by gas or electricity? If you have lived in a cold climate, you know that wood heat is wonderful heat and warms you clear to your bones.

Wood heat is **an**ionic energy; it comes from the Sun. Its effect is *right-spin*, and it warms us because the **an**ions released by oxidation (burning) of the wood pass through our body, warming the cells. This is similar to how a microwave oven works—with one very important exception. Microwave energy is left-spin and VERY destructive to living things.

Right-spin **positive** energy keeps you young. Left-spin **negative** energy causes you to become old. The former keeps you on the *anabolic* side of the pyramid as illustrated in Chapter One. The latter puts you on the *catabolic* side. One spins RIGHT; the other spins LEFT. We are interested in the way these energy forces affect living things and HOW they influence the aging process. Please check your understanding by reviewing the following drawings.

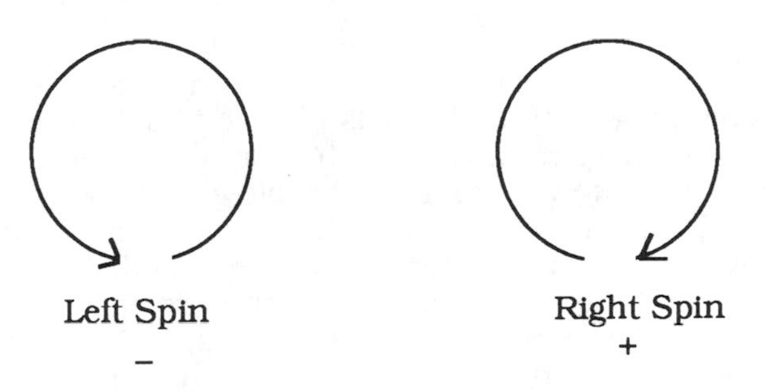


**How To Determine The Spin**

There are several ways to determine the spin and/or predict the effect a substance will have on the bio-electric body.

For instance, look at a bottle of vitamin E and you will see that the word tocopherol is preceded by the letter(s) d or dl. "d" indicates that when infra red light is beamed through the tocopherol, the light is bent to the *right* or clockwise indicating that the vitamin E has life giving energy. The "dl" tocopherol is the opposite and steals life force.

Please note, when "d" vitamin E is carried in SOY or CANOLA oil, its positive energy is converted into a negative substance. (Use only wheat germ oil capsules or dry forms of vitamin E. Avoid soy and canola like the plague.)

Those things that exert a negative influence on the body must be *neutralized*, disposed of quickly, or isolated to minimize its effects. This includes BOTH food and non-food substances like drugs, food additives, colorings, salts and other noxious substances which we will discuss in more depth later.

**Neutralize**

The word **neutral** doesn't mean much to most people. It's kind of a *neutral* word. We must be more specific in its use. When we say that the body must *neutralize* toxic or left-spinning substances, we mean that those substances which exert a negative influence on our body must be **de-energized** by the body. To de-energize something requires energy. Please recall our magnet and cassette tape example. Both are *stored* forms of energy. The magnet's energy neutralized the cassette tape's energy because it had an opposite spin.

The body handles negative energy in similar fashion. Consider a potato—which is a natural form of energy. It is **stored** complex carbohydrate energy put there by the plant for future needs. Depending on how the potato was grown, it may produce positive or negative effects in the body. All potatoes or carrots or peaches or apples, etc. are NOT equal!

A negative energy potato causes the body to forfeit some of its reserve energy in order to process and *de-energize* that negative energy field. If the body is unable to accomplish the task, the toxic energies in the potato circulate in our system doing violence to the vital organs and *bio-electric* body.

A left-spin substance turned loose in the body has **momentum.** It is like a boulder rolling down a hill. Stopping it requires the body to waste *vital* force and creates an energy deficit with a loss in health and vitality. In addition, the body is FORCED to remove the toxic energy from circulation or suffer further damage to the system. When the body is **force-fed** left-spinning energy, vital force is squandered. The effect is *catabolic* and we grow OLD at an accelerated rate.

Back to the *spin.* When we say *right-spin,* I want you to think "good for my body." When we say *left-spin,* I want you to think "bad for my body." It might seem like oversimplification, but that's the way it is.

## Kinesiology

**Kinesiology,** as defined here, relates to body response to "energy fields" and their affect on body physiology. In vibrational medicine, Kinesiology is concerned with the energy dynamics a substance imposes on the *bio-electric* body.

**Kinesthetics** involves "muscle sense." It is known as Dynamic Reflex Analysis, Applied Kinesiology or plain old "muscle testing" and involves gain or loss of strength in the digits and limbs. Some practitioners use it to **diagnose** and **prescribe**. In my opinion, muscle testing is a **crude** form of dowsing that is extremely SUBJECTIVE and of QUESTIONABLE value to the practitioner or the patient—and the same can be said for hair analysis. They are **NOT** reliable.

The primary problem with "muscle testing" is that good, biologically active substances often produce exactly the same response as "known" bad substances. For example, racemized™ products are **VERY** biologicaly active and produce **MAXIMUM** body response. Healing responses are desirable and should be welcomed. The Young Again Protocol™ provides a safe and easy way to "manage" **healing responses.**

Also, muscle testing is GROSSLY influenced by systemic influence of heavy metals on the **autonomic nervous system** which becomes short-circuited in their presence.

Your author does not consider "muscle testing" to be a viable, trustworthy way to diagnose or prescribe. Restore the **"terrain"** and you can forget the *hocus-pocus.* Nevertheless, I will walk the reader through the process.

### How To Test

All that is required is another person and the food, drug or supplement that is being tested. First, form a ring with the thumb and middle finger of your dominant hand. Next, have your friend attempt to gently, but firmly, pull your fingers apart. It is important that he or she note the amount of effort required to *separate* the fingers. In general, if the substance is good for the body, the fingers are supposed to become STRONGER. If it is bad, they will become WEAKER. You can place the item in question in the mouth to test by yourself, but it is more difficult to do. Muscle testing involves just enough voodoo to reach the status of a "warm fuzzie."

**Sometimes,** the body gives false results because it *instinctively* KNOWS that the substance will produce a healing crisis and force the bio-electric body to cope, cleanse and heal. Rejuvenation—like growth—is stressful and the body seeks to **minimize** stress—especially when it **knows** that its owner doesn't really desire healing or is unwilling to cope. I see a lot of this phenomenon. Sadly, these people do not heal.

The above procedure can also be done by extending the dominant arm so that it is level with the shoulder and have another person gently press down while the person being tested holds the substance in question. Do a **before** and **after** test to gauge arm resistance to movement.

### Other Examples

People who drink too much alcohol have a cirrhotic liver (cirrhosis of). So will those suffering from hepatitis or mononucleosis. You can test them easily. Have them extend their arm. Next, pull down on the arm to get a feel of their strength. Then, pull down with one of your hands while at the same time you touch their liver area (just below rib cage on right front). If they have a weak liver, they will LOSE all of their strength.

My friend recently bought some tomatoes at the super market—the kind that grow mold before you get them home. I tested them with a **refractometer**, pendulum and vibration chain. All three tested negative. There influence in his body would have weakened his bio-electric status—and weakened his **"aura"**—a yardstick of body vitality. They were returned to the store for their potential, toxic effects.

### Foucault's Pendulum

A pendulum is one of my favorite ways to measure right and left spin energy. A pendulum is an antenna. It works just like a radio or television antenna, except that here, it is a **moving** antenna. Antennas can send OR receive energy signals. Trees are antennas, too.

All substances emit energy ***spin*** signals! The body issues energy *spin* signals. A HIGH vitality body issues "right spin" signals. The opposite is also true. Body energy is sometimes identified as the body's "aura." Rocks, drugs, food and bodies all have auras. Kirlian photography can capture a picture of these ***subtle*** energy fields.

Suspend a pendulum over an energy field and it will "spin" left or right. Some pendulums are more sensitive than others, as are individual dowsers. Dowsing is highly subjective, hence, variations in interpretation is a problem.

The pendulum's spin reflects the "status" of the energy field of whatever is being checked. For example, white sugar, soy, canola all emit left-spin signals and the pendulum picks them up and spins accordingly. Here, the substances are the transmiters, the pendulum is the receiving antenna, and the body is the interpreter.

Learning to use a pendulum **and** vibration chain requires practice. These are skills that must be "developed." *The Pendulum Kit* and *Vibrations* are very good instructional works on the subject. (See Source Page 384.)

**Other Vibrational Therapies**

**Therapeutic Touch** involves the transfer of positive energy transfer. It is used in the fields of nursing and massage therapy. Here, energy from a healthy person is used to transform the sick person's energy fields.

**Laying on of hands,** a religious practice, and **Qi Gong**, an ancient Chinese modality, are similar to therapeutic touch. We will develop these subjects in a future chapter.

**Scars**

While having my mercury amalgam fillings removed, my dentist noticed a one inch scar under my chin and asked when and how it got there. After I told him, he asked me to do the finger exercise we just described, only instead of placing a substance into my left hand, he had me touch the scar with my left hand. BINGO! No strength!

The EFFECT the scar was exerting was strong because it was directly in the path of a major *energy* meridian that flowed from my abdominal chakra (energy center) to the top of my head. It was *blocking* the flow of that energy.

Scar tissues are negative energy fields. Scars are recorded in the skin's holographic memory (*holo*-light reflected around a central object, *graph*-a record; *ic*-pertaining to). Scars are negative memories—magnetic *energy* messages like those on a computer disc—no difference! Think of scars as "frozen," negative energy messages. (Read *The Holographic Universe.)*

To "temporarily" *erase* the scar **memory**, the dentist injected a homeopathic *remedy* along its length, and instantly *full strength* returned to my joined fingers.

Trauma produces scars—be they internal or on the skin. Scars occur when the system is stressed. My scar resulted from a fall while in poor health at age ten. Had I used SOC™ capsules and lotion I would not have scarred (see box below).

The tissues are composed of *functional* cells called **parenchyma** cells. Scar tissue is *non* functional tissue. Scar tissue in the vital organs alters function and accelerates aging. Altered body function is like a car driving on a flat tire. The further you go, the more damage you do.

**Aging is the CUMULATIVE effect of negative energy forces on the bio-electric body.**

Energy fields are *real!* They underwrite all of our life processes. They are the key to life's mysteries. They control aging. We must come to understand them and learn how to interpret and deal with them in our daily life.

It is important that the reader understand that we live in a world full of energy phenomena. Everyone should learn to dowse (locate, read, measure) and manipulate energy.

We dowse when we use our intuition to guide us in dealing with people, things, and events—so why not in medicine, healing, and dietary choices? You will learn more about dowsing as we progress.

**PREVIEW:** *Our next chapter is an overview about "high-tech" modern medicine and its "magic bullet" promises. It will help you see the futility of relying on medicine's quick-fix techniques and to appreciate the value of good health.*

**Scar Tissue & Stiff Joints**

SOC™ erases scars, clears acne blemishes, softens wrinkles, dissolves internal scar tissue, helps connective tissue disorders, clears arterial plaque, grows hair, stops joint pain, renews cartilage and restores nerve function. SOC™ promotes bilateral movement of nutrients and wastes across cell membranes and carries heavy metals **OUT** of the brain and **OUT** of the body. Limber Life ™ causes the body to become limber, and must be used with Soc™ in order to work. (See Source Page 384.)

**FIR™ Sauna**

A FIR™ Sauna is **NOT** the same as an infra-red saunaand does **NOT** rely on lights, steam or heat for it rejuvenatory effect on old, sick tissues. FIR™ technology leaves you **refreshed**, never tired. People love FIR™ saunas!

- No Water Or Plumbing Required
- Dissolves Acid Wastes in Skin & Tissues
- Improves Blood & Lymph Circulation
- Burns Calories & Reduces Weight
- Eases Aches & Pains Associated With Disease
- Very Inexpensive To Operate (pennies/day)
- Portable • No Tools Needed • Beautiful

**See page 365. Order FIR™ Sauna Brochure, page 384.**

# 6

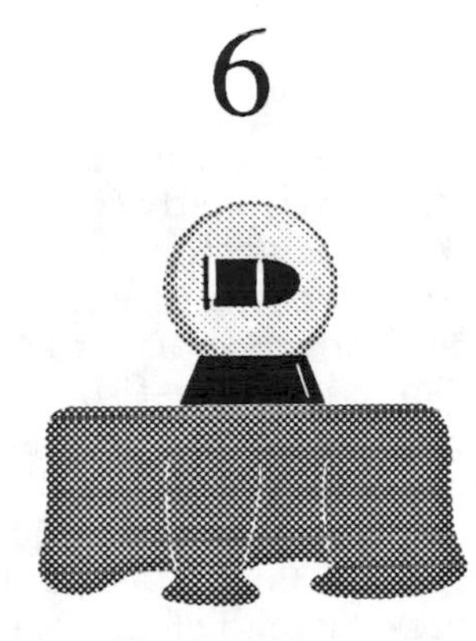

# Magic Bullets

*"We know life only by its symptoms"*
Albert Szent-Gyürgyi
Discoverer of vitamin C

Allopathic medicine is no closer to understanding the *essence* of life today than it was a hundred years ago.

It understands little about basic functions like sleep, growth, pain, aging, and healing. Medicine attempts to manipulate these functions, but it does NOT understand them.

At the same time, we labor under an endless procession of new drugs and high-tech equipment concocted for the treatment of degenerative conditions like cardiovascular disease, cancer and arthritis—just to name a few. These conditions are *technology* driven. They require ever more expensive diagnostic equipment and a long line of *experts* to operate it.

We have **substituted** high-tech medicine for the "take the pill, solve the problem" approach of yesterday. We have **substituted** the dis-eases of *civilization* for the contagious maladies of the past. The problems of dis-ease and aging are still with us despite our passion for "technology."

High-tech medicine has become an extension of our national consciousness. It is the same "magic bullet" approach used in the movies. We wrongly equate medicine's heroic efforts with true healing. Magic bullet technology masks our health problems and allows them to grow worse. Magic bullets blur our vision and numb our reason, causing us to accept life on *marginal* terms under the assumption that the wonderful body God gave us is incapable of healing itself naturally.

## Yesterday & Today

Yesterday, medicine knew us as people. Today, we are but bodies in a cattle line—stripped of our human dignity. The difference is the *system.* The system has quashed the human being on both ends of the continuum. The doctor is denied training in nutrition and vibrational medicine. The patient gets neither. Modern medicine has substituted technology for dignity. It believes in "magic bullets" —and so do the people!

Medicine does NOT understand dis-ease at the subtle energy level. Medicine attempts to diagnose it with tests, X-rays, CAT scans and MRI's. People are **trained** to take refuge in *magic bullets* and *hope* instead of addressing the root causes of degenerative dis-ease.

Daily, newspapers gush with glowing reports of a promising new Flash Gordon therapy. Just as fast, people fill the stalls—like cattle in the slaughter yards—waiting for the *magic bullet* that will cure their misery. Desperate people doing desperate things, ignorant as to the cause of their agony.

## Poor Health • Life Of Simplicity

Poor health isn't a sin, but it's awfully inconvenient and terribly expensive. There's a better way.

A life of simplicity allows you to take control of your life and health. It's the drive for money and things that stands between us and a life of simplicity. We must evaluate what is *really* important and learn to *walk away* from the rest.

If we lose our health chasing a dollar, we lose. Even if we catch lots of dollars, we still lose. When we fail to take care of our greatest treasure—our health—we give our dollars to the doctors and hospitals. When we become desperately ill, money and things mean little. They are a poor trade for good health.

We partake of *magic bullet mentality* because it offers us a quick, efffortless fix to our problems. People like smoke and mirror technology, but it's a **past tense** approach —a fancy band aid at best.

We are confounded by *high-tech wizards* in white coats. We seem unable to see that there is NO difference between empty promises and a bucket full of "empty" hope. *Magic bullets* have become an excuse—a salve for an old body.

Just because you enjoy good health today, it does NOT mean you will enjoy it tomorrow. This is the assumption that people in every generation make over and over again. It is an erroneous assumption. I prefer to regain and KEEP my health.

**It is foolish to squander your good health. Tomor-**

**row is but a few days away. Just ask someone who is old.**

Why experience the hell of old age when you can enjoy **perpetual** good health? TIME stands still when you are truly healthy. So, do whatever you need to do to get your *bio-electric* reference score under .33.When you are *Young Again!* ***YOU*** are in control and you don't need medicine's "magic bullets!"

**PREVIEW:** *In our next chapter you will learn WHY food fails to supply the ENERGY you need to stay young and WHAT you can do about it.*

**The 65% Watery Human Being**

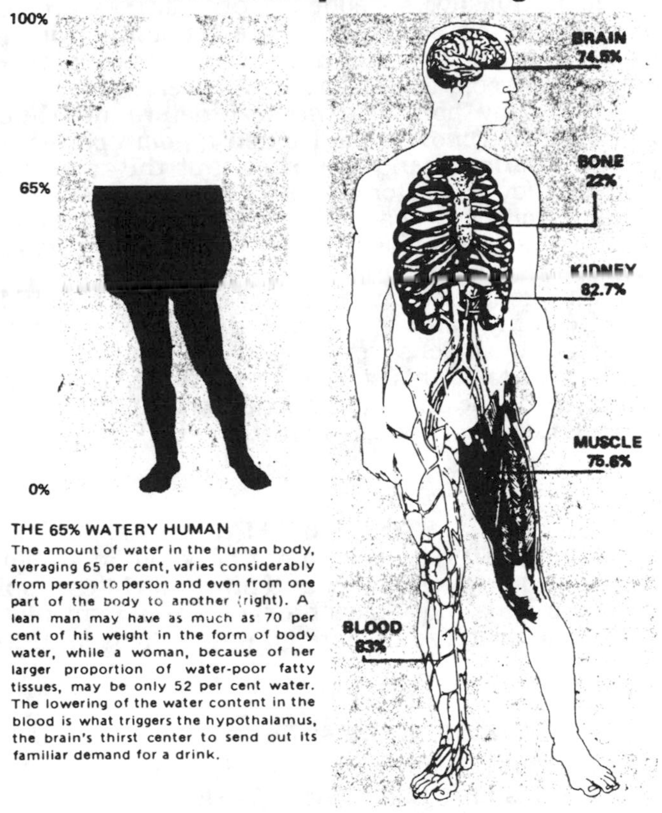


THE 65% WATERY HUMAN
The amount of water in the human body, averaging 65 per cent, varies considerably from person to person and even from one part of the body to another (right). A lean man may have as much as 70 per cent of his weight in the form of body water, while a woman, because of her larger proportion of water-poor fatty tissues, may be only 52 per cent water. The lowering of the water content in the blood is what triggers the hypothalamus, the brain's thirst center to send out its familiar demand for a drink.

**"Pure Water Is The Best Drink For A Wise Man"** – Henry Thoreau

**The "COBALT" Connection**

Cobalt is central to good health, plenty of hemoglobin, strong connective tissues and vibrant energy. The simplest and best way to get enough of it is by using Cobo-12™ skin creme every day—**especially** if you are female!

## Spider Bites • Insect Bites & Stings

Spider bites and insect stings involve "energy" reactions of the body to "foreign" proteins. Some people experience severe reactions, while others suffer loss of body parts. We must come to understand the "nature" of the energy forces that produce these reactions.

In front of me is a story about a lady in Southern California who was bitten by a Brown Recluse spider, went into a coma and awoke six months later missing her arms, legs, nose, and ear. The medical folks don't have any *magic bullets* with which to treat insect bites and stings.

Here is "my" story. I awoke at 2 a.m. with my hand throbbing and swollen. I was in *severe* pain. My hand looked like a balloon! Quickly, I shredded an organic potato, combined it with some Epsom salts and made a poultice with plastic sandwich wrap. The poultice "drew" the poison into two boils. The emergency room doctor had no answers.

I visited my "holistic" dentist. He determined the energy "footprint" of the venom, then located a *homeopathic* remedy that had a **similar** energy footprint, put the remedy in his MORA frequency generator and applied the "invisible" energy to my hand and body—cancelling the spider's venom at the *subtle energy level* of my being. Instantly, the pain was gone. I regained full use of my hand.

Had I depended on allopathic medicine, I could have lost the use of my hand or worse. Fortunately, I was in good health and the spider's venom did not cause permanent damage to my hand. This story is proof of the effectiveness of vibrational medicine and authentication of the "energy" thesis of this book. Future chapters will further elucidate the subject.

## STOP The PAIN!

To instantly relieve the pain of common stinging insects, and in some cases spider and mosquito bites, apply one drop of common laundry bleach or ammonia immediately to oxidize and **de**structure the foreign protein poison. It works!

## Toxic Acids & Wavy Hair

What do chemotherapy, wavy hair, water on the lung and appendicitis have in common? Toxicity!

Chemotherapy causes hair loss because it overloads the skin's waste processing capability. When hair regrows, it usually comes back wavy—even where the person previously had straight hair. "Systemic" toxicity and poor liver function are behind wavy hair, blue and green eyes that become brown or black. Eye color is "symptomic," not genetic.

# 7

## Death By Chocolate Pie

*"Chew your liquids and chew your solids until they are liquid."*
Dr. Paul C. Bragg N.D., Ph.D.

"Death by Chocolate Pie," read the sign. It reminded me that all food is NOT equal.

Some food is *alive* and promotes health, while other food is *dead* and promotes death. We are concerned with the differences in food, and food's influence on the aging process. We are specifically concerned with food's *energy footprint.*

Water has a similar story to tell, but there is a fundamental difference between food and water. Foods are listed in tables and are rated, one against another based on their nutrients, caloric content, carbohydrates, fat and proteins. Water is NOT classified as a food because it does not contain these nurients. But water **does** have an **energy footprint.**

We are told that water is water, but there is MUCH more to the story. Water is more than just "wet." Water's *signature* powerfully influences life and health. Its *signature* is reflected in its spin and measured by its ORP potential.

Water is considered a *necessity* of life because we cannot live without it. Oddly, the *experts* tell us to limit *food* intake. Then, in the same breath, they tell us to drink as much water as we desire without regard to the type of water or its *vibrational* MEMORY or energy footprint, or its ORP potential. Water is food and like solid food, all water is **not** equal!

We pick and choose our food on the basis of taste,

appearance, color and aroma. Yet, we are not concerned about the water we drink. We don't see water as food.

Water IS food. Water is THE most important food we put into our body. Water is not important for the nutrients it contains—it contains none. Water is important for the *ENERGY* that it *should* contain. Extremely pure water with a zero contaminant load, clean vibrational memory, therapeutic bond structure and high ORP can heal a sick body.

BEV™ water is pure FOOD and more. It has right-spin characteristics that people can feel and taste. It is ***body friendly*** because it energizes, hydrates and detoxifies the system. People who drink it will tell you that it is "different!"

## Live Food

Traditional food that is *biologically active* has a right-spin *signature*, and it produces **right-spin effects** in the body. It contains enzymes, charged ionic minerals, vitamins and positive energy that are absolutely necessary for good health. These components of "live" food are the foundation of life itself. Let's discuss enzymes.

Enzymes are biochemical proteins. Enzymes are also *catalysts*. A catalyst accelerates a reaction or causes a reaction to take place that either would not occur or would occur at a much slower rate if it were not present.

Enzymes can be compared to oxygen's affect on a fire. No oxygen, no fire. Without oxygen, fire can neither start nor continue. "True" catalysts are used over and over. They are neither altered nor destroyed in the reaction. An example is the platinum and rhodium used in catalytic converters on cars. These *noble* metals convert toxic gases like carbon monoxide to carbon dioxide and water. They do it through a series of oxidation and reduction (redox) reactions. *(In future chapters, you will learn how to use redox reactions to your benefit.)*

In the body, most biochemical catalysts are consumed, altered or destroyed in the reactions they fuel and must be continually *manufactured* by the body. The liver is our **PRIMARY** enzyme and catalyst manufacturing organ—and therefore, will always be a **major** player in any health disorder.

The constant formation of new enzymes requires tremendous amounts of *right-spin* energy that must come from substances that are "live" and friendly to the bio-electric body. Dead food and dead water are negative energies. They are left-spin energy forces that not only fail to contribute to health, but actually BLOCK the benefits of substances with a right-spin energy ***footprint*** **and** ***signature.***

## Biocatalysts

Biological catalysts cause reactions to occur millions of times faster than what would occur if they were not present. Without biocatalysts, life as we know it could not exist.

Vitamins do not work unless all of the needed major *and* minor (trace) minerals are present in the body in balanced form. In biochemistry, vitamins are called *cofactors* because they work WITH minerals and enzymes. Because most vitamin supplements are synthesized (man-made) despite claims to the contrary on the label, they are useless at best and damaging to the vital organs at worst—creating secondary problems.. Moreover, many supplements are **useless** because they are in elemental form—a form which should be avoided (more later).

Your **BEST** source of biologically active vitamins and minerals is garden fresh food and fresh veggi juices. The **ideal** juice is fresh raw beet + carrot. Juice **MUST** be taken on a fully hydrated body, and should be "sipped" and "chewed," **never** "gulped" or drunk quickly.

When there is **EXCESS** toxins and acids in the system, biochemical reactions slow and blood and lymph circulation becomes difficult. **Excess** wastes and toxins interfere with vital organ function, hormonal balance. Their accumulation leads to "systemic" (whole body) degeneration and rapid aging. The Young Again Protocol™ when followed is the ideal way to do immediate **DAMAGE CONTROL** to stop the aging process dead in its tracks. It is in the aftermath of the damage control that the clock is reversed and youth returns.

## Cooked Food

Cooking denatures enzymes. Denatured enzymes can't do their job because they have LOST the characteristics that caused them to work. Improper cooking **totally** destroys food value and enzymes.

I am not suggesting you stop cooking your food, but I am suggesting that you eat plenty of fresh, raw—and preferably—home grown green leafy vegetables and fruit. *(My favorite source of "auto-grow," no work fresh greens is comfrey. It grows on its own from March to November every year. Roots are available by mail. It can often be found growing locally.)*

Avoid high heat and cook no longer than necessary. Steam instead of boiling. Use stir fry methods. Avoid microwave ovens and table salt, flavor enhancers and dyes. These substances ***zap*** the body's energy fields and block crucial biochemical reactions. When you eat them you **cheat** yourself of good health and you lose vital energy.

## Metabolism

*Metabolism* is a term that comes to mind. It means *biotransformation* and refers to the way food molecules are transformed into energy molecules in the body's energy pathways. Metabolism involves ***fusion*** reactions that join individual atoms into right spin *energy* molecules. This is the opposite of the kind of energy produced by nuclear fission (atom bombs/nuclear power plant wastes, microwave ovens). Fusion reactions are right-spin and **anabolic**—they build up! Fission reactions are left-spin and **catabolic**—they tear down!

*Metabolites* are **by**products of biochemical reactions. Dissected the word looks like this: *meta*-beyond; *bol*-tranformation; *ite*-product of. Hence, a product that is **beyond** transformation. Metabolic wastes are "acid" in nature. Included in this definition are chemicals of organic synthesis—poisons like pesticides, herbicides and food additives—that carry "zeno" estrogen analogs that grid-lock the hormonal system and are stored in the **fat layer** directly **under** the skin.

## Animal Protein

Industrialized man eats high on the hog. He eats too much animal protein and not enough fruits and vegetables. Animal proteins come from the top of the food chain. Healthy animal proteins have a right-spin *signature* and their proteins will sustain us. But if they are not healthy, they will have a left-spin signature causing us to become sick and age prematurely.

Most animal proteins now represent *left-spin* energy in the form of concentrated metabolic and environmental wastes. Sick animals concentrate negative energy. Animals suffering from environmental stresses and excesses (bad food, air, water, and excess metabolites) become sickly just like humans.

**Food energy derived from sick animals brings on dis-ease in man a thousand times faster than does food energy from sick fruits or vegetables.**

Animal proteins can be an excellent source of *energy* and *nutrients*. but they can be a two-edged sword and must be used wisely. The "issue" with animal protein is: the **quantity** eaten, **chewing** of food, **hydration level** of the tissues, **digestive** and **metabolic capability**, **liver efficiency** and **transit time** from the mouth to the toilet. (We will develop these points as the book unfolds.)

In his wonderful book, *Fatu Hiva*, Thor Heyerdahl tells how in 1937 he and his wife lived with the last surviving cannibal of the Marquesas, an island chain twelve-hundred miles northwest of Tahiti. The cannibal told them *"Human flesh is different from other animal flesh. It is sweet!"* And, I would add, so is the flesh from a toxic cow that was in a *catabolic* state and sick when it was slaughtered. Toxic meat and fish have more flavor. Toxins are more concentrated in the animal's fats than in the lean tissues for reasons we will discuss in great detail later.

### The Food Chain

Here is an example of what is meant by the statement, "Animals are at the top of the food chain."

A rabbit eats food that is contaminated with pesticides. The poisonous residues are stored and concentrated in its flesh and fatty tissues. One day the farmer decides the rabbits are out of control and uses a toxic chemical to poison them. Next, an eagle comes along and eats from the carcass of the dead rabbit. Thus the poisons in the rabbit are now in the eagle's body—hence the poisons moved UP the food chain.

When we eat sick meat, fish and fowl, we become the eagle and the poisons and metabolites concentrate in us. If you are going to eat animal proteins, derive them from healthy animals and in limited amounts.

*Negative* energy food from any source—animal or plant—is sick food. Sick food must be dismantled and *neutralized* by the liver. Left-spin food causes the body to squander vital energy that is needed to keep us healthy and young. When we eat sick food, we lose more than we gain!

### Animal Proteins & The Bowel

Animal proteins MUST be eliminated from the intestines within 18 hours, **maximum**. If they remain in the gut longer than this, they putrefy and release extremely toxic, organic poisons. Substances like indoles, skatoles and phenols. These set the stage for dis-ease, premature aging and cancer.

Indoles, skatoles and phenols are WHOLE molecules that are absorbed directly through the intestinal wall—a condition affecting people from infants to elderly. The condition is called **leaky gut syndrome.** Most molecules are broken down into pieces before they are absorbed, thus offering us some protection. Poor digestion is at the root of it!

Potatoes absorb toxic compounds from raw, non composted manure. These toxic molecules pass **directly** into the potatoe's tissues—**whole and intact.** When the potatoes are boiled, a sharp nose can identify the kind of manure that was used to grow them—pig, cow or chicken.

Toxic molecules that are absorbed in this fashion bypass our safety net and are a threat to good health. Undigested food rots in the gut, feeds the parasites, brings on obesity, produces foul gas and leads to colon related problems like colitis, diverticulitis, irritable bowel syndrome, appendicitis, leaky gut syndrome, and eventually cancer, arthritis, diabetes and cardiovascular problems.

**Mastication**

Chewing of food and secretion of saliva is critical to good health. The use of Disorb Aid™ and R/HCl™ further insure complete digestion and absorption of food nutrients. These things will help you to become *Young Again!*

**PREVIEW:** *Our next chapter deals with digestion, junk food, and WHY it causes us to become old.*

---

**Collards & Rhubarb**

Collard greens are easy to grow and thrive anywhere in the USA. You can grow them in pots, in a flower bed or in the garden. They are a "non" hybrid vegatable.

Eaten raw in a salad, juiced or served in plain leaf fashion, they are sweet and crunchy. They promote a healthy colon and will stretch your food budget—and they are loaded with dietary sulphur.

Rhubarb is a easy to grow and produces voluminous stalks that are good food, and a wonderful source of natural vitamin C. To "can" rhubarb, simply wash, cut, fill jar, cover with water, seal and store somewhere cold—like the refrigerator, root cellar, etc. No cooking is necessary to preserve rhubarb. P.S. **Never** eat the leaves! See Comfrey page 284.

---

**Sub-Clinical "Dis-ease"**

Throughout this book, the author refers to health issues as **"sub-clinical"** in nature, as opposed to diagnosable dis-ease(s) which are dependent upon **"SIGNS."**

90% of health issues facing people are **sub-clinical** and are not diagnosable (at least not in the early stages when no once sees the signs. The doctor needs "signs" to diagnose. The Young Again Protocol™ is **ONLY** interested what can be done on a daily basis to maintain the **"terrain"** and avoid dis-ese.

## Water! The *Essence* Of Life!

**Water has memory!** It "absorbs" the *frequencies* of the contaminants it carries—and it **continues** to *vibrate* at those frequencies after the contaminants have been removed—unless their memory is erased.

Contaminants are *energy* fields that leave their *footprint* on water by causing the molecules to ***vibrate*** at frequencies *unfriendly* to the body.

Conventional approaches to water purification are *incomplete.* Methods like distillation, reverse osmosis, carbon block and ceramic cartridges work at the mechanical level only. They are good as far as they go, they just don't go far enough.

The BEV™ process, on the other hand, is a Fourth Dimension approach that delivers water that tastes good and ***feels different*** in the body. People like it because it ***awakens*** natural harmonic frequencies ***at the cellular level and below.***

BEV™ water ***reprograms*** the electrical *rhythm* of the body. It causes body cells to *dance.* Its energy *frequency* is body friendly. Its electromagnetic *signature* is complete. **BEV™ water is liquid *music!***

The BEV™ process "voids" waste energy frequencies in water and alters hydrogen and molecular bond angles so water can **"dance"** and become ***liquid music*** and ***electronic food*** for body and spirit.

BEV™ theory and application *transcends* traditional water testing and comparison techniques. It defies Newtonian physics. BEV™ water must be experienced for its profound significance to human health and longevity. **BEV™ has captured the *essence* of life on planet Earth in liquid form.**

The BEV™ process is a **proprietary** process. A full discussion of the theory and application of BEV™, and its relationship to aging and dis-ease is available in manuscript form (see Source Page 384).

BEV™ water is made from tap water with BEV™ equipment. The BEV™ process focuses on biologically *friendly* **DRINKING** water. Next to the air we breathe, we consume more water than any other substance. ***Make sure the water you put into your body is spelled BEV™.***

**"Water Is MORE Than Wet. Water Is FOOD!"**

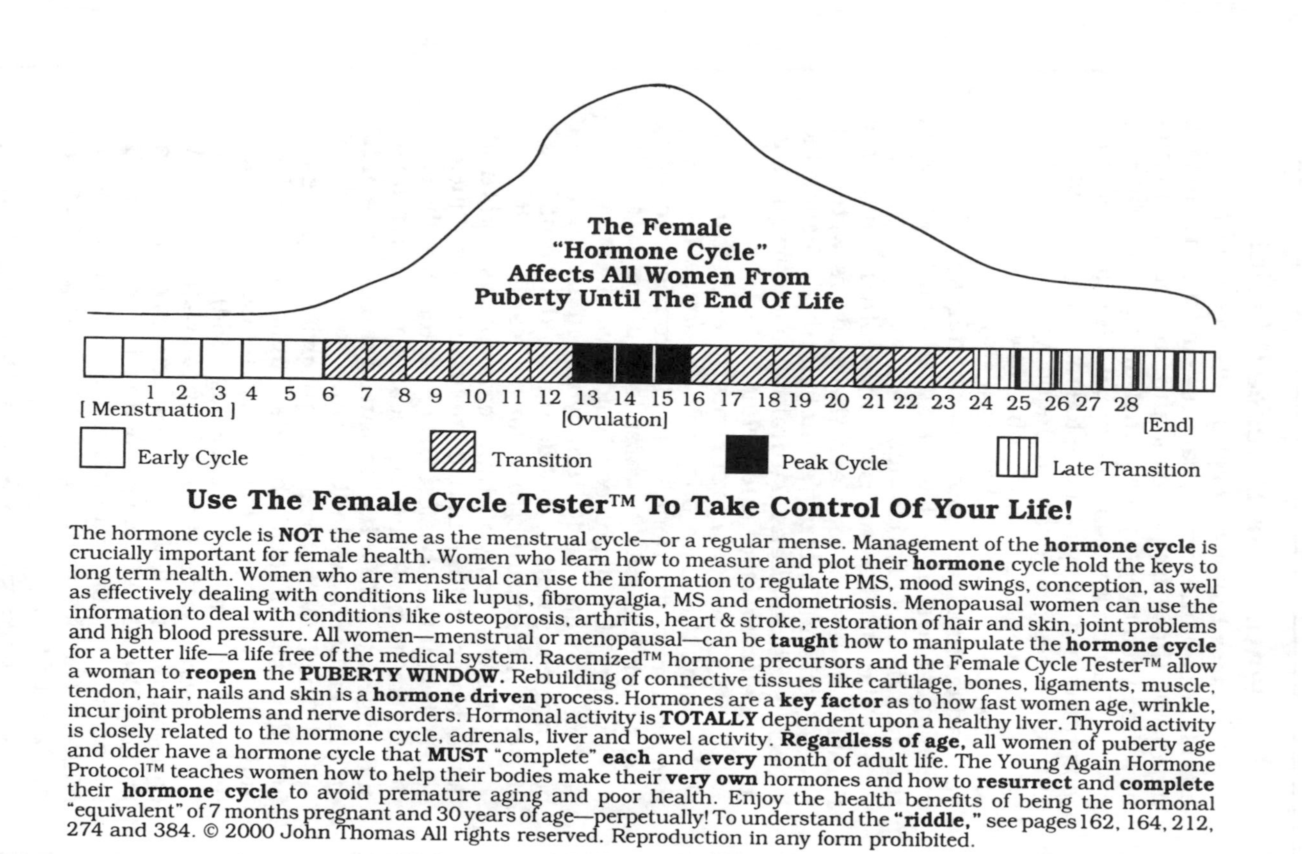


## Use The Female Cycle Tester™ To Take Control Of Your Life!

The hormone cycle is **NOT** the same as the menstrual cycle—or a regular mense. Management of the **hormone cycle** is crucially important for female health. Women who learn how to measure and plot their **hormone** cycle hold the keys to long term health. Women who are menstrual can use the information to regulate PMS, mood swings, conception, as well as effectively dealing with conditions like lupus, fibromyalgia, MS and endometriosis. Menopausal women can use the information to deal with conditions like osteoporosis, arthritis, heart & stroke, restoration of hair and skin, joint problems and high blood pressure. All women—menstrual or menopausal—can be **taught** how to manipulate the **hormone cycle** for a better life—a life free of the medical system. Racemized™ hormone precursors and the Female Cycle Tester™ allow a woman to **reopen** the **PUBERTY WINDOW.** Rebuilding of connective tissues like cartilage, bones, ligaments, muscle, tendon, hair, nails and skin is a **hormone driven** process. Hormones are a **key factor** as to how fast women age, wrinkle, incur joint problems and nerve disorders. Hormonal activity is **TOTALLY** dependent upon a healthy liver. Thyroid activity is closely related to the hormone cycle, adrenals, liver and bowel activity. **Regardless of age,** all women of puberty age and older have a hormone cycle that **MUST** "complete" **each** and **every** month of adult life. The Young Again Hormone Protocol™ teaches women how to help their bodies make their **very own** hormones and how to **resurrect** and **complete** their **hormone cycle** to avoid premature aging and poor health. Enjoy the health benefits of being the hormonal "equivalent" of 7 months pregnant and 30 years of age—perpetually! To understand the **"riddle,"** see pages 162, 164, 212, 274 and 384. 

# 8

## Junk Diets & Stress

*"There is no such thing as 'junk food', only 'junk diets'!"*
Dr. Helen A. Guthrie

All food contains energy. It is the nature of energy and its electrical *footprint* that determines what effect—good or bad—food will have on the *bio-electric* body. To understand the aging process, we must concern ourselves with the "spin" of food energy. The direction of spin as well as the intensity of the spin determines food's ability to satisfy hunger and build and maintain healthy tissues and bones.

Nutritive tables measure nutrients. It is **assumed** that if we eat food listed on the nutrient tables, we will be nourished. It is also **assumed** that ALL nutritive food energy produces positive results in the body. These assumptions are wrong and certainly misleading.

We hear a lot about junk food because we are inundated with it. People identify junk food with quick snacks and fast food. The association is correct. But instead of calling it junk food, let's call it **"bio-junk"** —because that's what it is!

Bio-junk (food) is left-spin energy that greatly accelerates the aging process. If the body cannot eliminate it from the system, it **entombs** it in the **fat layer** under the skin.

*In 1972, 6 billion dollars was spent on bio-junk food. In year 2000, the figure was 110 billion dollars. And that is only* **one** *of many negative factors fueling the acceleration of the aging process. A healthy lifestyle is worth the effort.*

## Dead Is Not Dead

Bio-junk food alters biochemical reactions because of its left-spin ***signature.*** It destroys and blocks critical body pathways and cripples cellular activity. Bio-junk has the ability to multiply its original sphere of influence by transferring its vibratory ***footprint*** to all of the body's tissues. This "transference" takes place at the subtle energy level of our being. Bio-junk is "poison." It has *radiomimetic* qualities—qualities that *mimic* the effect of nuclear *radiation* on the tissues. Eat enough bio-junk and you will eventually see the effects in the mirror.

Bio-junk has the ability to **CHANGE** its *footprint* **after** it enters the body. Its presence in the GI tract triggers *unnatural* reactions that form **free radicals** in the system. Free radicals do severe damage to the vital organs and especially to the liver and kidneys. Worse, they **continue** to interfere with normal metabolism UNTIL their presence is eliminated.

In other words, free radicals have a **life of their own.** It is **impossible** to keep all toxic substances out of our system because they are ubiquitous in our daily lives. And what of the "stuff" we have stored in our fat layer under the skin? The **Young Again Protocol**™ was developed—so the body can safely release the "stuff," and safely transport it through the blood and lymph to be filtered by the liver and sent down the toilet. **"Deacidification"** of the tissues is another way of saying "terrain management." A bio-junk diet insures **"acidification"** of the body's terrain and accelerated old age.

## Kidneys & Liver

The kidneys are crucial to good health, and it behooves us to pay attention to anything that negatively affects them. Bio-junk causes tremendous long-term damage to the kidney's nephrons (blood filters). The kidneys are second only to the liver in ridding the body of waste.

**When you restore the LIVER, you automatically lift the load from the kidneys. The kidneys were NEVER meant to do the liver's job! Kidney issues are liver isues!**

Water affects the kidneys. Taoism teaches that the urinary system (kidneys and bladder) is related to the **Water Element.** Taoists believe that *Jing*—the very **essence** of life—is contained within water. They believe that careful management of the Water Element is the key to youthfulness.

## Digestion & Liquids

If Pavlov's dog is any indication, digestion initiates

through visual and mental stimulation BEFORE we actually eat. In other words, the flow of digestive juices in the mouth, stomach and intestines is linked to **vision** and **thought**.

Digestion begins in the mouth when we chew and mix food with saliva. The flow of saliva and digestive juices is dependent on fluid hydration levels in the body. When we drink plenty of water, we secrete plenty of saliva—which begins the breakdown process we call ***digestion.*** Saliva also lubricates food so it can be comfortably swallowed.

It is important to TRAIN ourselves to drink a cup of water every hour of our waking day. This habit maintains perfect fluid volume levels and moves waste out of the system. Lots of water is key to ***avoiding*** the need to drink liquids with meals. **Drink water throughout the day, avoiding all liquids 1/2 hour before, during and one hour after meals.**

Failure to drink enough water throughout the day creates a shortfall of digestive juices which "limits" digestion, but drinking liquids with meals is very destructive. We do NOT want liquids in the stomach at mealtime because liquids "dilute" digestive juices that contain enzymes and acids.

**COLD** liquids are very hard on the body—and particularly on the stomach and digestive process. Cold fluids taken with a meal **retard** and even **stop** digestion. Correct temperature is one of the necessary prerequisites for chemical reactions like those of the digestive system. Low digestive temperatures promote degenerative dis-ease. Where indigestion, gas or bloating are a problem, DiSorb Aid™, R/BHCl™ and Yucca Blend™ save the day! R/BHCl™ breaks protein and parasitic peptide bonds in the stomach, while DiSorb Aid™ finishes the job on other food nutrient molecules in the intestine. Yucca Blend™ acts as an emulsifier. Women suffer more digestive complaints than do men. **Fact is, for every man who loses his gallbladder, ten women will lose theirs!**

Digestive juices are powerful "right-spin" energy fields. The liver and pancreas secrete their juices through ducts directly into the intestinal duodenum immediately below the stomach. Hydrochloric acid is secreted by cell in the stomach wall as is **intrinsic factor** which **"MUST"** be present for the absorption of vitamin B-12.

By age 30, B-12 absorption dramatically slows in both sexes. But in women, the problem reaches catastrophic proportions by age 40 and older due to loss of blood from menstruation. Cobo-12™ creme is used to solve the problem.

Dr. Franz Morell said, *"[saliva's] purpose is to coat and protect food enzymes so they will neither be damaged by nor do damage to the stomach and GI tract. Exposure to digestive juices at the wrong time during digestion derails biochemical catalysts.*

*Nature designed things such that it takes 5-10 minutes to eat an apple, but only 5 seconds to drink the juice."* Juices are two edged swords. ***Chew*** your juice, do not gulp it!

**Hormones & Hydration**

The **"ductless"** glands secrete hormones directly into the blood for transport throughout the body. Low hydration levels in the tissues also restricts hormonal response.

Hormones dramatically influence aging and vitality. After age 25, hormonal activity slows for both sexes. By age 30, females begin to **lose** the ability to "complete" their **hormone cycle** (see page 72).

The aging scenario is a combination of waste accumulation, under hydration, low hormonal activity and a liver that is in trouble. Excess waste merely speeds the process we politely call "aging." **SIGNS of aging seen on the outside of the body indicate trouble on the *inside.***

We are hormone driven creatures. At conception, hormones dictate male or female. Growth and development are hormone controlled. Hormones bring on phenomenonal change at **puberty** and again at **menopause** and **andropause**. Hormones are **CENTRAL** to aging reversal and rejuvenation because they effect all body systems. The Young Again Hormone Protocol™ is designed to keep the "puberty window" open.

**Racemized™ Hormone Precursors**

A *precursor* is something that precedes something else. For example, we eat carrots to obtain *beta carotene* which is a natural plant food precursor to vitamin A. Dioscoria Macho Stachya is very unique plant hormone precursor. The body converts it into its **very own** corticosteroid hormones when it is in racemized™ form. Use of racemized™ hormone precursors does NOT carry the risks associated with traditional "hormones." Using "actual" hormones means your are playing God—and that includes birth control pills and female replacement hormones. The Young Again Hormone Protocol™ produces wonderful results for women and men of all ages.

Men are concerned with the prostate, sex drive, impotence and balding. Women **should be** concerned with completion of their **hormone cycle** and with KEEPING the "puberty window" open. Please refer to page 72, for a more in-depth discussion of the female "hormone cycle."

In the wonderful book, *Our Stolen Future,* Theo Colborn correctly defined the environmental dilemma the human race faces in relation to "zeno" estrogen analogs and their effect on grid-locking of the hormone receptor sites in the body. The Young Again Hormone Protocol™ is designed to rid the body of "zeno" estrogens and to open the receptor sites. "Zenos" are some of the **excesses** that drive aging and cancer in both sexes. And whether you are young or old, female or male, their effect is there. What you do about them is **THE** issue.

Wild yam creams have been around for many years. Most are a waste of money. In an odd way, the same can be said for "progesterone" creme. Most of the fanfare and hype about this product has to do with "minimizing" the dangerous effects of female replacement hormones commonly prescribed by the doctor. Progesterone creme is NOT the answer to the dilemma women face, but the Young Again Protocol™ is.

Also, **AVOID** the use of over the counter DHEA and melatonin. They have been outlawed in Europe, Canada and Australia. **They are dangerous.** The glowing reports don't tell you these substances are **analogous** molecules not unlike what we have been discussing in this chapter. Consider them similar to anabolic steroids used by athletes and birth control pills used by women.

### Stress • Food • Pavlov's Dog

Stress or unpleasant circumstances grossly affect hormone production as well as digestion and absorption. Sitting down to a *quiet* meal and allowing enough time for casual, pleasant conversation is *vital* to good health. Unfortunately, few people eat this way anymore. Fast track meals are the rule, and mealtime circumstances rarely resemble the ideal. People eat too fast, barely chewing and guzzle **cold** liquids amidst noise and confusion. **The effects of "hit & run eating" on health are *DEADLY* even if you eat the very best food.**

Pavlov experimented on dogs. Dogs are known for their ability to *gobble* their food. Pavlov discovered that the dog's digestive enzymes flowed the moment he rang the dinner bell. And since digestion is stressful to the body, when your dinner bell rings, prepare yourself. A meal should be a *celebration* of physical, mental and spiritual forces. Digestion requires the body to expend energy in an effort to get more energy in return. Bio-junk causes an energy deficit. Undigested food produces gas and bloating, leaky-gut, constipation and **deadly** toxic by-products that give rise to degenerative dis-ease.

### Gas

Gas—particularly *foul* gas—is a GOOD indicator of an out of balance condition in the vital organs and digestive tract.

The fouler the gas, the more you **should be** concerned that things are NOT right. Foul or excess gas is a sign of systemic (whole body) overload and is a SIGN of trouble to come. The Young Again Colon Therapy Protocol™ is an easy solution.

Spoiled animal flesh (carrion) is *necrotic* flesh. Meat is dead flesh, but it is **not** necrotic. In a constipated, airless environment, meat, fish, fowl and cheese become the equivalent of carrion and produce highly toxic by-products and foul gas. High stress meal time environments encourage ***anaerobic*** conditions and accentuate the production of foul *gas*. An anaerobic environment is a cancer environment! **The evening breeze between your knees should NOT smell like cheese!**

Otto Warburg, twice Nobel Laureate, was awarded the Nobel Prize in 1931—over sixty years ago— for documenting a vital factor behind the rise of cancer. He said, ***"Cancer has one prime cause...and that is the replacement of oxygen [aerobic] respiration of body cells by anaerobic cellular respiration."***

Dr. Max Gerson, whom I mentioned earlier, went on to determine the role of sodium (main ingredient of table salt) in cancer. Both Warburg and Gerson agreed that the growth of cancer cells initiates in a low oxygen, high free-radical environment. Cancer does not manifest in an oxygen-rich environment! Mild aerobic exercise followed by lymphatic self-massage with a "lymph roller" does wonders for sluggish, sick bodies.

### Table Salt

It is *impossible* to avoid sodium because it is ubiquitous. It is in almost all prepared foods and it is certainly in municipal water supplies. If you crave salt, you suffer from "salt syndrome." This condition is remedied with Racemized™ ionic sea minerals and BEV™ water. A body that craves salt is a body that is deficient in mineral electrolytes. **De**acidification and restoration of the body's "terrain" is of crucial importance in reestablishing balance in the system.

Table salt must NOT be used to meet salt cravings. It is ***deadly*** to the body's cells and to the mitochondria that produce our ATP energy molecule. Thirst after meals indicates *under* hydration, *over* salted food, and or pancreatic/adrenal stress. Instead of table salt, use **Celtic**™ salt from the Grain & Salt Society (call 800 867-7258 or 828 299-9005.)

### The Water Molecule

The primary function of water is to act as a solvent and as a source of *free* electrons—as measured by the oxidation/

reduction potential (ORP)—of the water.

Water **MUST** carry *energy* INTO the cells, and it **MUST** carry toxic *end products* of metabolism OUT of the body. When we drink low ORP, biologically unfriendly water—like distilled, tap, reverse osmosis, ozonated and common filtered waters, for example—we DENY the body the ability to stay healthy; and we create conditions of **excess** that eventually manifest as so-called "deficiency" dis-eases. **BEV™ water is conception point water. Medical Grade Ionized Water™ is therapeutic water.**

BEV™ water is the foundation water used to create Medical Grade Ionized Water™. Racemized™ sea minerals provide the source of "electrons" necessary to raise the ORP (oxidation reduction potential) to medical status. Special equipment is needed to make this very special water. (Young Again™ has a book and video available. See Source Page 384.)

Below is a drawing of water molecules with their respective bonds. Look at the shape of these "bent" or "polar" water molecules.

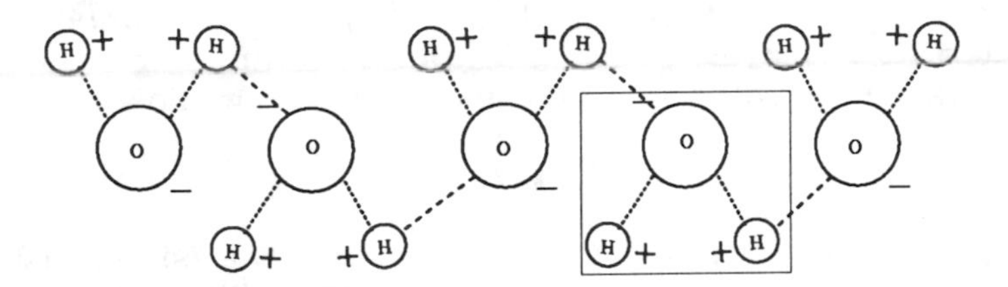


Notice that the two hydrogen atoms on each molecule are off to one side giving each molecule a lopsided appearance. The fine dotted lines indicate "bond" with (+) and (-) charged atoms. The box contains **one** water molecule. The oxygen atom has a (–) charge, the two hydrogens have a (+) charge. The dotted line going from the hydrogen atom in the box to the oxygen to the right of the box is a **hydrogen bond** connecting one molecule to the other. The lines inside the box are **molecular** bonds "within" the water molecule itself.

The strength of bonds holding water molecules together is determined by "free" electrons. The higher the "ORP," the easier water enters the cells and fuels the production of ATP. Bond angle, ORP and pH are what separates BEV™ water and Medical Grade Ionized Water™ from the others. pH (alkalinity /acidity) by itself is a useless factor, despite "hype" to the contrary. "ORP" is **THE** story, pH merely comes along for the ride. Conventional views of water along with so-called testing standards are **useless** yardsticks and "moot" in the arena of BEV™ and Medical Grade Ionized Water™.

## Why BEV Water

BEV water is **biologically friendly** drinking water. It's made in your own home from common tap water. While most water processing units on the market remove some (50-90%) of the toxic wastes in water, BEV™ equipment approaches 99.5% removal of waste and life forms, radioactivity and toxic organic chemicals. Moreover, the process manipulates bond angles while elevating the "ORP" and returning the water to the point of conception—where the egg and sperm were when they joined. The issue is "life force". (Please refer to page 306.)

BEV™ water is highly charged and structured for living systems. It is **different** from other waters, and it is very reactive in the body. By "reactive" I mean it acts like a *magnet* due its strong *right-spin* electrical charge and resonant frequency. A vibration chain or pendulum confirms BEV™ spin and energy footprint. The best test, of course, is to "feel" it in your body.

Other waters do not possess the characteristics of BEV™ water. BEV™ water hydrates the tissues and energizes the cells while removing wastes from the system. Wonderful things happen to people who drink this strange and wonderful water. BEV™ water is both a 3rd and 4th dimension energy substance (we will develop these concepts as we go along).

## Live Food

Home grown food is the poor person's least expensive path to good health. The wealthy can benefit likewise.

If you do not have a yard or space is limited, grow vegetables in pots, plastic buckets and so on. It is amazing how much fresh food can be grown this way. Besides food is a gift from God, and growing some is a real pleasure.

Consider joining an organic gardening club. Many clubs rent garden space where the soil is rich and mellow from other gardeners before you. Or, hire someone to grow food for you and your family. Many older people have the time and would love to grow food for hire. These people are usually gardening pros. Pay them well. Gardening is hard work. They deserve the money and you need the food.

Gardening involves hard *load-bearing* work and is a good way to keep fit. Hard work is good for the body. I suggest a long handled spading fork instead of a tiller. Hand tools are inexpensive, they always start, and they don't burn gas.

For people who cannot garden, fresh live food can be purchased at health food stores and co-ops. Some organic farmers even deliver or have drop points in cities. Farmer's markets are also an excellent source. And if you learn to use a "refractometer," you can assure yourself of getting good food. (Refractometers available from: Pike Labs (207) 897-9267.)

## Composting • Gardening

If you are going to get into gardening, you will want to learn how to compost organic matter. Proper composting technique *controls* the break-down process so you end up with a high energy product. Biodynamic techniques work best.

Aerobic compost catalyses healthy energy reactions in garden soil. Controlled breakdown of grass clippings, weeds, leaves, manure and the like will not generate foul odors ***unless*** the pile becomes *anaerobic.* An anaerobic condition is what produces foul gas in the compost pile and the human gut!

Always use some liquified chicken or cow manure starter to get the pile going. Compost is MORE than old dead things that have turned brown. It is a source of "life force" for your garden. Several wonderful books on biodynamic gardening are available. (See Source Page 384)

Gardening is superb therapy for the body, mind and spirit. Use it to simplify your life and focus your energies on healthful habits. Once you become hooked on gardening, you will be a gardener forever! **Fresh food—and biologically friendly water—are *passports* to agelessness!**

**De**vitalized food is so common in most people's diet that some supplementation is needed. Racemized™ PAC®, Harmonic™ pollen, racemized™ algae and predigested organic liver capsules are superb "whole foods" upon which I **personally** rely. As for minerals, VitaLight™ tablets fill the need nicely. These products do NOT tax the liver and create secondary problems for the body to cope with. Fresh carrot, beet, and ginger root juices provide a wonderful source of **real** vitamins.

## To become *Young Again!*

- Eat "healthy" food
- Grow a garden
- Avoid table salt & MSG
- Use racemized™ minerals
- Get some exercise
- Avoid alcohol & soft drinks
- Juice daily (breakfast)
- Eat RAW vegetables
- Avoid all processed food
- Drink plenty of BEV™ water
- Get plenty of sleep
- Avoid liquids with meals
- Avoid soy and canola
- Do colon therapy

It's what you do 90% of the time that counts. Aging reversal requires focus and commitment because the body is OLD and *SLOW* and you are not young—yet! While all this takes some effort, it is worth it—especially, when you see friends and loved ones are sick and dying. Follow my lead and you will become *Young Again!*

**PREVIEW:** *Our next chapter explains WHY people snack and WHY they become fat and WHAT happens to the body when you eat too much or too often!*

### Harmonic™ Silver Water

Few injuries equal the trauma and pain that burn patients suffer. From a medical viewpoint, the issue is infection. From a social viewpoint, the issue is scar tissue formation. Infection and scars are both ENERGY issues.

To ease pain and prevent infection—even in the case of 3rd degree burns—use Harmonic™ Silver Water. Harmonic™ Silver Water has a vibrational signature & energy footprint that is body friendly. When misted onto burned tissue, gargled or drunk orally, the *energy* signature of the solution speeds healing. (See page 276.)

Industry "hype" says the more parts per million (PPM) of colloidal silver in a solution the better. Not so! The less "silver" the better. It is the "frequency" that is important, and the purer the silver, the higher the energy footprint; ideally .9999 pure. Harmonic™ Silver works similarly to a homeopathic. (See pages 250, and 352.)

### Acne, Skin Scars & SOC™

For **post** emergency and general skin damage from acne blemishes to burn scars, use SOC™ lotion and Racemized™ Skin Creme. These products restore and replace damaged tissue. **One man reduced 65 square feet of 20 year old scar tissue (from burns) to less than 2 square inches by following the Young Again Protocol™.**

SOC™ dissolves **internal** scar tissue, replacing it with functionally healthy tissue. SOC™ transports heavy metals from brain and organ tissues, cleans the arteries of plaque, rebuilds cartilage and nerve fibers and is used to reduce elevated blood pressure. Limber Life™ is used with SOC™ to restore "limberness" to an old, stiff body.

**The 90/10 Rule Of Health**

Strive to live your life doing things 90% correctly, and enjoy your sins (the other 10%) to the fullest—and without guilt!

***"Balance in all things is the foundation of health."***

# 9

# Satiety Blues

*"Everything in Moderation."*
Diane DeFelice

Fullness beyond desire! A primal drive fulfilled! Who can conjure a better feeling than a full stomach after a superb meal? Surely, food is one of the true pleasures of life. Aroma! Appearance! Taste! These are the things for which we live! Yet, in our drive to fulfill a basic physiologic need, we sow the seeds of old age and death.

Food requires a certain amount of time for complete digestion. When we eat too much food or too soon after a previous meal, the body suffers *overload* shock. Shock of any type puts stress on the vital organs (liver, thyroid, adrenals, kidneys, parathyroid, pancreas, pituitary and testes). **Dietary SHOCK** deserves our attention because it accelerates aging.

### Snacks & Food Related Stress

People love to snack. They snack because they are hungry or because it is the thing to do—part habit, part social custom. The *experts* tell us it is good to eat every few hours. They tell us small meals taken more often are less stressful to the system and better for our health. They tell us small meals taken often maintain blood sugar levels and keep us on an even keel. They even tell us that multiple small meals increase productivity. Baloney!

As usual, the experts are WRONG! These things are NOT true. They NEVER were true. Let's stop and analyze what happens to the body when we eat too much or too often, which includes snacking. Snacks are simply small meals!

Food creates stress because it involves digestion. Digestion creates stress by drawing on the body's energy reserves. Food energy molecules must be broken down, transported and reassembled into usable energy forms. Substances that do not promote health must be dumped or stored.

**When we eat, we borrow from our energy reserve account. It takes energy to get the process going; and, if the energy generated from food does not repay the loan, we suffer an energy deficit that is reflected in loss of health and vitality in the vital organs.**

The vital organs have *limited* capacity and resilience. They require rest BETWEEN meals. When they are denied adequate and regular rest, they come under severe stress. Eating between meals and eating more often than every four hours causes the organs and glands to degenerate.

Food related stress results in organ *burn-out.* Burn-out means LOSS of function. The organs age TOGETHER, each following the other. The effect **compounds** itself in chain reaction style. This scenario occurs even if the food is positive energy and nutritious. *Quality, quantity,* and *frequency* are some of the controlling factors.

If snacks and meals are composed of *left-spin* substances, organ stress is greatly increased. When combined with meals that are spaced too close together, the body is left with NO alternative but to shift into OVERDRIVE in an attempt to use, neutralize, dump or store food energy fields.

Food imposed stress creates "involuntary" reactions because the body has NO choice but to process what it has been given—even to its own detriment. The body acts as much out of duty as need when it is fed too much, too often, or when it is forced to process bio-junk food.

*Snacking* and bio-junk food **STRESSES** the organs, upsets hormone balance, destroys vitality, corrupts enzyme function, alters ATP production and promotes aging. Mental and work related stress is no different. Stress is errant **energy.** Remember: **Energy is never lost; it merely changes form. Hence, aging of the body is TIME in motion.**

### "Trophy"

Food related stress brings about *trophy* in the vital organs. *Trophy* means change related to nutrition. If we apply the prefix *hyper* or *hypo,* we are referring to a change in physiologic activity that is above or below the norm. Both hyper and hypo conditions lead to organ burn-out and dysfunction. The terms ***hypo**glycemia and **hyper**calcemia* are good examples of *trophy* type health conditions.

The organs are *interdependent*, and whatever affects one affects all of them. A "condition" is **always** multiple in nature. The word dis-ease is NEVER singular in nature.

### Deficiency Dis-eases & Conditions

**We hear a lot about deficiency dis-eases and deficiency conditions, but there is NO such thing.** The entire concept is but a carry over from the early days of allopathic medicine and the influence of Justus von Liebig's infamous agricultural theory called the *"Law of the minimum."*

Justus von Liebig developed his theory around 1830. He is regarded as the father of the synthetic fertilizer industry and the destructive practices of present day agriculture. His law says, *"the nutrient that is in the **minimum** controls."* To von Leibig, soil was nothing but dirt. He believed that there are only three *essential* nutrient salts needed by plants—nitrogen, phosphorous and potassium commonly referred to as NPK.

Pasteur and von Liebig were contemporaries; and like Pasteur's equally incorrect Germ Theory of Disease, medical science adopted von Liebig's erroneous theory. Clinical nutritionists **perpetuate** von Liebig's erroneous theory when they promote the idea that DEFICIENCIES give birth to dis-ease. The *experts* in the medical arena are wrong—and so are those in the alternative area who perpetuate the lie.

Dis-ease is exactly the *opposite* of what is popularly believed and taught. Dis-ease is nothing but the manifestation of conditions of **EXCESS** within the system. Excesses always manifest as deficiencies. Excesses are **errant** energy.

The presence of **excesses** in the system always rules. A **secular example** is the huge stock market collapse of 2000-2001. It was **excess** liquidity, **excess** debt, and **excess** capacity that wiped out 7 trillion dollars of people's money. The "experts" like to blame everything EXCEPT "excess."

**"Deficiency" conditions appear when excess toxic energy EXCEEDS the body's ability to cope.** For example, medical science teaches that the diabetic suffers from a "deficiency" of the hormone *insulin*. They also classify diabetics as either glucose intolerant or insulin resistant. In actuality, the diabetic suffers from **excess** toxic wastes in the tissues and fluids—along with a good case of "leaky gut syndrome."

The "diabetic" body keeps "carbon" sugars circulating

in the blood to BUFFER acid wastes circulating in the system. **Sugar is a carbon based molecule ($C_6H_{12}O_6$). Carbon acts as a BUFFER, moderating all life on planet Earth.** *To understand more about carbon's role, I highly recommend The Carbon Connection and The Carbon Cycle.* (See Source Page 384.)

In other words, the diabetic's problem hinges on **excesses** in the system, hormonal issues in general, and a good dose of leaky gut syndrome. Restoration of the "gut wall" is crucially important for the diabetic. "Leaky gut" means that the persons intestinal wall is overly porous, allowing poorly digested carbohydrate, protein, fat and "drug" molecules easy access to the blood stream. The results is a body in **TOTAL REVOLT** and sick people. Asthma, allergies and sinus problems go part and parcel with a leaky gut. Sadly, anyone of any age can have the problem. The Young Again Protocol is designed to remedy these issues and more.

Type 1 *early* childhood diabetics problems are LINKED to super antigens delivered via polio and DPT vaccines. A huge body of medical research is available that documents the dangers of immunizations (call **New Atlantean Books** (505) 983-1856 or write P.O. Box 9638, Santa Fe, NM 87504, USA.

Fact is, 75% of children with diabetes and hearing loss suffer from mutant pathogenic viruses, bacteria, foreign serum protein "energy fields" forcefully introduced into healthy children's bodies by mad men and ignorant parents! Please do not fret over poor choices that you made yesterday. The damage is reversable for the most part. Many people feel intimidated by the "system." **Don't! There are ways to beat the game!**

Instead of worrying about microbial "boogie men" getting your child, detox their little bodies, flip their sensory switches and feed them Young Again™ SUPER FOODS to BOOST the child's immune system and transform their TERRAIN so no dis-ease—contageous or otherwise—can find quarter. **Control of the "terrain" is the issue. The Young Again Protocol™ provides results.**

Fifty million people suffer with clinical/sub-clincal diabetes. Science's failure to understand diabetes at the subtle energy level continues the suffering. Independent action, **without** the blessings of higher authority, is a prerequisite to the return of health. **You have to THINK for yourself!**

Let's review. There is no such thing as a deficiency disease—only **excesses**. Aging is a cumulative *condition.* Death is the confirmation of **"excess beyond control."**

The vital organs function like gyroscopes on a ship. They keep us *even-keeled* by dealing with shifts in the body's TERRAIN—that is, if we do not "sabotage" them with incessant snacking, bio-junk , hydration stress and "zeno" estrogens.

How we *feel* is NOT an accurate barometer of our true state of health. Long before the SIGNS of dis-ease become visible, negative energy is building at the subtle energy level. The proof is all the **sub**clinically sick and dying people who "felt" just fine—*yesterday!* **The "lag" between onset, manifestation and the SIGNS of dis-ease is about 20 years!**

### Mental Hype • Body Abuse

*Hype* is taking its toll the world over. People have become skilled in the awesome power of mind over body and drug over mind. They use both to ***drive*** and ***whip*** the bio-electric body. And when asked how they feel, people usually respond "great!" At the same time, over 80% of the US population suffers from sub-clinical illness; 60 % from obesity.

*Hype* and the unbalanced person go together. It goes with unrealistic mental euphoria. Hype drives the body *beyond* its ability to physically respond. Bio-junk, coffee, drugs and popular "magic bullet" supplements are forms of hype.

**Hype WHIPS and DRIVES the bio-electric body into the "twilight zone" of TIME—a warp where aging and the passing of TIME accelerate.**

Symptoms of hype-driven dis-ease are not so plainly visible, but the SIGNS are easy to see if we are paying attention. When the doctor renders a diagnosis of dis-ease, it usually shatters *hype's* hold on us—but by then, we are in trouble.

Dis-ease is the *manifestation* of stress. Dis-ease is a confirmation of aging. Dis-ease is the *manifestation* of Fourth Dimension TIME in man's Third Dimension world. Aging and dis-ease are the result of our failure to square our energy account. Death is energy bankruptcy, while hype is energy inflation. *Hype* is modern man's Achilles Heel because it involves "unrealistic" positive thinking and an "unbalanced" lifestyle. **A simple life void of hype is a life where the passing of TIME slows down.**

### Food Digestion Tables

The following tables indicate the amount of time required for different foods to ***leave*** the stomach. Only *basic* foods are listed. Some common bio-junk is listed because of their prevalence in our society.

Please keep in mind that this information applies to the ***normal, healthy*** stomach without stress or known digestion shortfalls, ulcers, etc. Also note the very small amounts of food used in these examples (1/2 ounce). Large amounts of food take longer to fully digest. If more food is eaten too soon, undigested food is *forced* into the small intestine and colon where parasites and anaerobic conditions produce massive amounts of metabolic poisons. DiSorb Aid™, R/BHCl™ and Yucca Blend™ are used to enhance digestion in general, and specifically to **"lyse"** (break/split) the peptide bonds of incoming incoming parasitic proteins so as to render these food borne passengers harmless be they adult or egg forms.

**One-half to Two Hours**

| | |
|---|---|
| Pure Water | Wine |
| Tea | Milk |
| Coffee | Bouillon |
| Beer | Soft eggs |

**Two to Three Hours**

| | |
|---|---|
| Coffee w/cream | Cocoa w/milk |
| Asparagus (steamed) | Potatoes (mashed) |
| Fish (broiled) | White bread |
| Oysters (broiled) | Butter |
| Eggs (scrambled, fried, hard boiled) | |

**Three to Four Hours**

| | |
|---|---|
| Chicken (broiled) | Bread (whole grain) |
| Carrots (steamed) | Spinach (boiled) |
| Cucumber (raw) | Apple (raw) |
| Beef (roasted) | Salmon (broiled) |
| Tuna | Ham |
| Lentils (boiled) | Beans (boiled) |
| Green beans (steamed) | Lettuce (raw) |

## A Story About Satiety

Dr. Carey Reams told a story that took place during the years he and his wife were raising their large family. As the story goes, the neighbors and their children were over for dinner. When the food bowls were placed on the table, the neighbors made an effort to hide their surprise as their eyes were drawn to the modest size of the various bowls of corn, peas, mashed potatoes, gravy, meat, and desserts.

Expecting just such a response, Reams—in his characteristic style—laughed and predicted that there would be food left over. As you might guess, this is exactly what happened. Everyone had a wonderful meal, a great time, and departed with their gut plum-full!

I tell this story to draw your attention to the *satiety* enjoyed by all with a limited amount of food. What happened at the Reams' home is exactly the OPPOSITE of what occurs today. Today, people are starving to death on FULL stomachs!

Reams' food was alive—chuck-full of enzymes and loaded with bio-active minerals and vitamins. Today's food is

DEAD and EMPTY. It provides minimal *energy* for the body and requires people to stuff themselves in order to *feel* full because positive energy forces are absent. Almost ALL processed foods are *left-spin* energy substances. The body cannot use negative energy and must neutralize it or store it as FAT!

***Did you note those last four words? I hope so, because what we are discussing and piecing together, line by line, chapter by chapter, is going to shed light on the obesity problems that are plaguing 75% of Americans.***

We could surmise that what really took place at the Reams' dinner table was that everyone was courteous and took only small portions of food and all left the table hungry—faking it all the way. But Reams was not a liar. He told the story to make the point that good food, bio-active food, food with a right-spin energy *footprint* is very nourishing! You can believe that everyone at that table left *full and gratified BEYOND desire* which is the correct definition of the word *satiety*.

Few people experience real satiety these days. Instead, they know only the "other" version. *Pseudo* satiety is experienced when the stomach is full, but the body is not nourished. In other words, we quit eating because we run out of space—NOT because we are nutritionally satisfied. **America is full of starving people with full bellies.**

People leave the table hungry, yet too full to eat more! It is impossible to satisfy the body's energy needs with empty, left-spin energy food that is devoid of life giving nutrients!

## The Appetite

Appetite is a combination of *physical need* and *mental desire.* It is controlled by the satiety and hunger centers in the hypothalamus of the brain. It has long been established that the hunger center is ALWAYS active unless it is *inhibited.* The body uses two inhibitory mechanisms to regulate hunger: a **physically** full stomach and a **nutritionally** satisfied body.

The hunger center is a cluster of nerve cells that generate sensations that are a combination of physical need and mental desire. Snacking is a combination of BOTH. Most people meet their body's call for nutritional *energy* (true hunger) with EMPTY calories (physical hype) and cognitive satisfaction (mental hype). These are a deadly combination!

When we are **nourished,** the "I'm hungry" *satiety* center sends a message to the *hunger* center that its needs have been met. This causes the system to shut down and we lose our desire to eat. Real satiety is ***nourishment*** BEYOND desire!

False satiety is different, but the mechanics are similar in that it is based on a FULL stomach which is "bogus satiety!"

When the stomach is full OR when our nutrient energy needs have been met, a message is sent to the hunger center and we lose our desire for food. This is a ***negative inhibition system*** because one system controls the other. It is a system that works flawlessly UNLESS we *sabotage* it with poor choices!

### I'm Hungry Again

Later—after the stomach partially empties—the hungry person's body DEMANDS more nourishment, the appetite returns with a vengeance and the cycle begins over again.

Hungry people in a bio-junk society gain weight when they fail to meet their body's energy needs. The need for nourishment is only one reason ***why*** people become fat. Toxicity is another. Hormonal issues is a third. Poor digestive capability is a fourth reason. Poor saliva secretion, lack of exercise, low water intake, little *load bearing* work, and cobalt shortfalls finish the list.

***Natural*** **weight control involves meeting the body's nutritional and hormonal needs plus DEACIDIFICATION of the tissues, blood and lymph.**

The nervous system is divided into the central and peripheral systems. The stomach is controlled by the peripheral system which is divided into the sympathetic and parasympathetic systems. We have control over the sympathetic nervous system. We control it with our *mental* thoughts. We have NO control over the parasympathetic nervous system. It is involuntary. Both systems communicate with the stomach.

### Load-Bearing Work

Load bearing work is just that—load-bearing! People do not do enough of it. Society has come to view **physical work** as a curse—something to be avoided at all costs! Only poor or uneducated people do this kind of work! They are wrong; the body must be worked! Since people hate the word "work," maybe we should call it **load-bearing *exercise*** which better fits the sports bent of society. Unfortunately, for most people this kind of activity takes place on the couch in front of the boob tube. So let's compromise and call it **load-bearing *activity!***

The body responds to load-bearing activity by building new tissue and repairing old tissue. This kind of activity is called ***anabolism***. When the body is "worked" on a regular basis, rejuvenation accelerates. Aerobic exercise, weight training, and garden work are just a few examples of load-bearing activity to which the body responds with new vigor.

**We are supposed to build a "new" body (bones,**

**cartilage, muscles, ligaments, tendon, skin) every 7 years. Diet, lifestyle, acidification and hormones dictates whether your "new" body will be stronger or weaker than the one you traded in.** The process can be speeded up or slowed down.

As people age, they lose their ability and desire to do physical activity. Part of this phenomenon is the physical inability to perform; part is a lack of desire; part is a lack of energy. A sedentary lifestyle **destroys** the body and precipitates loss of bone and muscle mass—along with loss of mobility. LOAD BEARING activity circulates metabolic waste which explains why people who exercise and work their bodies enjoy better health. **The more sedentary you are, the faster you will age. This is called the *"use it or lose it"* rule.**

### The Dowager's Hump

The dowager's hump is a classic SIGN of total systemic OSTEOPOROSIS, which is **de**mineralization and **de**generation of the bones and connective tissues. The humped-back, bent-over appearance—as seen among older people, particularly in women—is a SIGN that is becoming all too common among younger people, too. It is prevalent in females because of "unopposed estrogen dominance," poor thyroid activity, early acidification and loss of cobalt via menstruation. **Osteoporosis is reversible if the Young Again Protocol™ is followed in every detail. Osteoporosis is a very serious problem.**

Please turn to page 100. Here you see that their spinal column and related connective tissues of the "osteoporotic" person have *shrunk*. Notice that the person has lost *inches* from their maximum height—which they achieved at their ***anabolic peak***. These lost inches occur mostly in the spinal column through deterioration of the vertebrae, tendons, ligaments and discs between the vertebrae. As this occurs, the rib cage *settles* until it eventually RESTS on the pelvis (hip). **This process can take up to forty years to occur fully manifest.**

Settling of the spine and rib cage distorts the visceral cavity and organs. A prolapsed (kinked) colon usually goes with it. The organs are forced OUT of position, and produces massive problems in the bowels. Settling of the spine results in a protruding belly and the *humped* appearance.

**Osteoporosis begins at about age 25 and greatly accelerates after age 35 and again in the forties with the onset of menopause. This sad condition is seldom diagnosed before age 45. Bone density scans only define the problem. What you do about it is what counts.**

When the doctor says, ***"You are in menopause!"***, osteoporosis is already a reality. Turn to page 72 and study it carefully if you are female. The answer you seek is there.

*Dowager is an old English word that described a widow who held property from her deceased husband's estate AND who had the imposing appearance of a humped back and shoulders. Hence—a "dowager's hump." The condition was predominately seen among the wealthy. The poor usually died too soon in life to get the hump. The wealthy dowager did not do any load bearing work because physical work belonged to the domain of the poor.*

The story of the dowager carries an IMPORTANT lesson. Here are a few things every woman (or man) can do to STOP and REVERSE osteoporosis and physical degeneration.

- Reopen the "puberty window" (see pages 72,164,212).
- Use B.T. racemized™ thyroid creme.
- Drink fresh beet and carrot juice every day.
- Follow the Young Again Colon Therapy Protocol.™
- Deacidify the tissues and body fluids.
- Use Cobo-12™ cobalt/vitamin B-12 creme.
- Avoid sugar, soft drinks and artificial sweetners.
- Make and drink Kombucha Tea.
- Do the Young Again Tissue & Liver Protocol™.

***Hanging*** is a simple procedure that s-t-r-e-t-c-h-e-s the spine and joints. Make a trapeze bar or hang from a rafter or tree limb. **Do this twice daily.** Start slowly and increase each day. *Hanging* involves getting your feet off the ground and relaxing the spinal column which increases blood and lymph flow. Anyone with arthritis, osteoporosis or back pain should also take SOC™ capsules to dissolve scar tissue, open blood and lymph flow, and regenerate cartilage.

Use of the L/CSF™ machine can do wonders for people of all ages in helping to reverse body acidification and breakdown of the tissues (see page 366).

## Osteoporosis & Calcium

Women are told to take large amounts of elemental calcium. These include calcium carbonate (oyster shell), calcium citrate, calcium gluconate, and calcium/magnesium tablets just to name a few. Contrary to the *experts'* opinions, these substances should be AVOIDED . They do NOT solve the problem, and they create additional problems. Use only minerals that have passed through the carbon cycle (more later).

Medicine science says osteoporosis in women is the result of insufficient estrogen, but this is a a **BALD FACE LIE!** Osteoporosis is defined as diminished bone density and honeycombing of the bones due to loss of minerals from the bone matrix. **For your information,** calcium's primary job—both in the body and in the soil—is to buffer against toxic **excess** in the system. The osteoporotic person is very **ACID,** and the body is forced to "mine" minerals from the bones to "buffer" the acids in the body tissues and fluids.

Medicine and clinical nutritionists *foolishly* promote calcium supplements to *prevent* and *treat* osteoporosis. They act as if *hypocalcemia* (low blood calcium) is the problem. It is not! Osteoporotic people usually have normal to HIGH calcium levels in their blood (hypercalcemia). These people don't need calcium, they need to **de**acidify their bodies and realize that hormonal activity has caused osteoblast and osterclast activity to dramatically slow. These are the cells that are responsible for renewing the bones and connective tissues.

**If your *present* height is LESS than it was at your *peak*, you need to take ACTION today! (See page 100.)**

### Rouleau-Dowager Hump *Connection*

Deterioration of the bones and connective tissues, in general, is **serious** business—and it plagues millions of people, for sure! But it is only a symptomatic EFFECT, like the dowager's hump and the "Rouleau effect."

Pronounced *roo-low*, the condition is a forerunner of all dis-ease and is seen under the microscope as "sticky" blood, that is, "clumped" red blood corpuscles and slowed metabolism. Rouleau in the blood means less oxygen and nutrients reach the cells, and less carbon dioxide and acid waste exiting the tissues and fluids. The effect is "deterioration" and "calcification" of the connective tissues, hair, eyes, ears and nerves (see page 136). **Rouleau appears 5-20 years BEFORE the doctor can render a diagnosis of a life threatening condition.** Racemized™ liquid sea minerals clear "Rouleau."

**SUMMARY:** Aging reversal is a step at a time project—in REVERSE! If you put to work what you have learned in this chapter, you will be on your way to becoming *Young Again!*

PREVIEW: *Our next chapter looks at the world of "shadows" and commonly held beliefs. Jesus and the Great Pyramid of Cheops have much in common as you will see.*

> **Dietary Fat**
> Hormones are "cholesterol" based and we cannot be healthy by depriving the body of "fat." **AVOID fat free diets**—they kill!

### "Prostate" Inflammation & Pain

Sooner or later, men must deal with their prostate gland. And whether you have problems or want to avoid them, R/Prostate™ is a wonderful answer for men. Pain, inflammation—GONE! And considering men's "medical" options, the debate is mute! For more information, see Source Page 384.

### A Book Worth Reading

*Your Body's Many Cries For WATER* details how water cures a multitude of dis-ease conditions. In fact, chronic **under hydration** fuels rheumatoid arthritis, allergies, chronic fatigue, asthma, angina and hypertension—all of which are **symptoms** of hydration stress.

The author believes "advanced" cultures are ***trained*** to ignore thirst signals; and that we are ***taught*** to **substitute** coffee, soft drinks, tea and alcoholic beverages for water. It is NOT possible to meet the body's hydration needs with liquid **substitutes** that merely contain water. We take water for granted because it is inexpensive and available. The author's findings are astounding and the his research is impeccable. Yet, the man is shunned and his work ignored by the American medical "establishment!" (See Source Packet, page 384.)

### Racemized™ Asparagus

Racemized™ asparagus is good for heart arrythmias, lung and bronchiole congestion, and stuffy sinuses. Aspar-Max™ was developed to assist older people who suffer with multiple conditions like: kidney and bladder, cancer, eyes, diabetes, bowel disorders, insomnia, and nerve conditions just to mention a few. As it turned out, Aspar-Max™ also helps attention deficit and hyper active children. Kids also respond to fresh veggi juice given daily as part of the Young Again Protocol™.

**Hormones, lifestyle and dietary habits control aging!**

### Old Body, Young Body?

Women experience menopause and men experience andropause. BOTH sexes must attend to their hormonal needs if they hope to "stay" young. The Young Again™ Hormone Protocol™ reopens the PUBERTY WINDOW. The miracle of puberty was MORE than "sexual" in nature. Hormones **fuel** the building and restoration of body tissues and bones. B.T.™ thyroid creme boosts metabolic rate so that the female body can regenerate easier and faster. (See pages 72, 164, & 212)

# 10

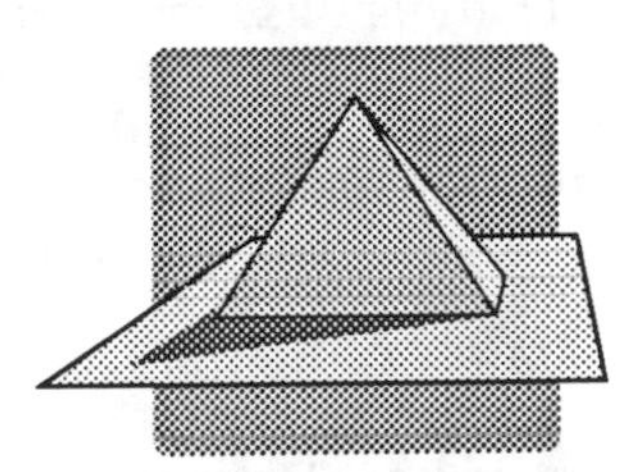

# Shadow Land

*"Most people would rather swallow lies than truth, especially if the liar has authority and the dis-information is soothing, like a fine liqueur."*
Charles Walters

As Pontius Pilate passed by the side of Jesus at His trial, it was reported that he asked the great teacher: "What is Truth?" The Roman propounded a timely question that went unanswered, at least from the lips of Jesus. Pilate posed his question to Jesus, not as an interrogatory, but a statement about the Christ.

Socrates maintained that Truth could neither be proved nor disproved. Rather, it formed the basis of our beliefs by the reality of its existence. The Great Pyramid of Cheops is a present day TRUTH. It cannot be denied because it is THERE.

Earlier we posed the question, "Why do people like experts and expert opinions?" We also asked, "How could anyone trust their most prized asset, their health, to the throw of medical science's dice?"

The answer to both questions is that the individual is relieved of personal responsibility when the decision process is given over to the experts. Forfeiture of responsibility gives an excuse and someone to blame if things go sour. Unfortunately, blaming others will NOT keep you young—or alive!

### The "Expert" Syndrome

Medical science all too often tells us to do exactly the *opposite* of what we should do. Today, it treats its theories as gospel. Tomorrow, it casts them aside for new ones. In the process, it issues the proclamation, "magic bullet!"

An unsuspecting public buys into THEORIES that were

never true in the first place—like fluoridation of water and toothpaste, the Cholesterol Theory of Heart Disease, the Germ Theory of Disease, the idea that menopausal women are estrogen "deficient," the need for calcium to prevent osteoporosis, the benefits of soy and canola oils, vaccinations and immunizations and so much other hogwash.

We are trained to ACCEPT and NOT THINK and IGNORE our instincts and rely on *experts* in medicine, government and industry—who are "experts" at **manipulating** us.

## Mass Delusions

In 1850 MacKay wrote, *Extraordinary Mass Delusions and the Madness of Crowds*. In it, he showed how unbelievably gullible we are, and that the more desperate the circumstances, the greater is our propensity to make unsound decisions *in mass*—usually with the help of the *experts*. **People go crazy in mass, but they return to their senses one at a time.**

People seek the health care *experts* because they hope to solve their health problems. They don't know where else to turn. The are in trouble—and they want a fix.

If people would learn to ***read*** their body's SIGNS and ***listen*** to the body's SYMPTOMS, they could prevent health problems and save a lot of pain, suffering and money.

An ENDLESS supply of money—**like medical insurance**—allows the experts to keep their hooks in us. Few people escape medical science's tentacles, expect under only three conditions: when we are healthy, have no money or when we are dead! Medical "decisions" should **NEVER** be based on "who" is paying the bill. The better your insurance, the worse it is for you. "Experts" get the money, and we get a "bone" in exchange—if we are alive when they are finished with us.

By definition, an expert is someone from more than fifty miles away. Our fascination with EXPERTS convinces me that this is the SAME phenomenon that makes the Law of Bureaucracy work flawlessly. This law has NO exceptions. It says: ***"Regardless of the intended result, exactly the opposite will result."***

We CANNOT rely on the experts. It is the experts who have taught us to *doubt* our intuitions and ignore good sense. The experts practice tunnel vision; that is why they are called experts. **We live in a world of shadows—where most of what we see and hear only *looks like* the truth. Where the more something is believed to be true—and the greater the number of people who believe it to be so—the better are the odds that it is NOT true.**

Allopathic medicine is in trouble. So are people who

rely on it to save them from their choices and bad lifestyles. Medicine science's model is based on the Germ Theory of Disease and the Scientific Method. Neither are valid.

Consider the difference between conventional medicine's approach and vibrational medicine's approach to solving the hearing problem for the deaf. At the age of fifteen, Dr. Patrick Flanagan invented the neurophone—a device to help the deaf hear. Flanagan sensed that the brain is a hologram and that it has different areas that are capable of performing **multiple** OR **duplicate** functions. Consequently, Flanagan used the skin as both a pathway to the brain and as a hearing organ. The deaf person's "brain" could now hear through the "skin."

Flanagan solved the hearing problem through visualization vs. surgical intervention. The brain is **not** hard wired as taught in the medical schools. The body can **regenerate** new brain cells. We **do** have the ability to grow new limbs, bones, cartilage, nerve fibers, skin and connective tissues. Flanagan had **vision.** He understood the Creator's handiwork.

**Cause & Effect**

Earlier we referred to something called single factor analysis, which translates: For every effect there is **single** cause; for every disease there is a **single** pathogen that is responsible. This kind of academic tunnel vision has gotten us into a lot of trouble. It is unrealistic and it is NOT true. Whenever we attempt to FORCE the facts to fit a pet theory, TRUTH becomes secondary, ***legitimate*** science suffers, and trouble results. So it is with the hallowed "scientific method."

Charles Walters summed-up the problems inherent in the *scientific method* when he stated, *"Most of what is generally called the scientific system is not science at all, but merely a procedural aspect that calls for setting up experiments that eliminate other possibilities or it deals with making instruments that enable the investigator to find what he/she is looking for.*

*"There is a second scientific method that, although unwritten, has far greater impact on scientists and their findings. This is the reality of project funding, "peer" review and the publishing of scientific papers.* **Walters went on to say,** *"The backbone of the scientific system has to do with asking the right questions, and a scientist can only ask the right questions after his/her life has absorbed the experiences that lead to a vision of the Creator's handiwork, hence the right question.* Also,....*discovery is accomplished by the mind and soul of the whole person and cannot be reduced to a mechanical scientific (by-the-numbers) procedure. It stands to reason that you can't get the answers if you don't know the questions [to ask].*

### The Double Helix & The Germ Theory

It was this second process that caused James D. Watson, one of the discoverers of the DNA molecule, to rock the scientific world when he disclosed the behind-the-scenes power plays, jealousy and fights for "funding" in his book, *The Double Helix.* Watson also offered an antidote—the observation that scientific discovery involves human thought and vision *more* than test tubes, procedures and microscopes.

The Germ Theory of Disease (GTD) is tremendously important to the aging process because it influences the way we **perceive** dis-ease. It so completely colors our thought processes that we are blind to the subtleties and cumulative effects of bad living habits and poor diet. Medical Science does **not** understand that the battle for life and health vs. death and disease is fought, won or lost, on a playing field that has absolutely **nothing** to do with the GTD. They are like **blind men** with fat egos stumbling in the dark—fearful of the light of TRUTH.

We cannot rely on medical science to solve our problems because they don't know what the problem is. They don't understand the phenomenon of life at the subtle energy level nor the manifestation of dis-ease. The proof for this statement is contained in the following fact.

**Experts suffer from the same problems as the rest of the population. They grow old. They succumb to the same dis-eases. Their "magic bullets" do NOT save them!**

The GTD is a theory, yet medical science treats it as holy writ. It is the cornerstone of the archaic medical model under which medicine labors. It is a stone around its neck! The GTD is so *accepted* that 99.99999% of the medical community own "stock" in it and "live" by it. Perhaps you do too. All conventional medical modalities—from diagnosis to treatment—are based on this **false** theoretical dis-ease model.

The model says we are nothing but a bundle of chemicals, proteins, fats, water, nucleic acids, flesh and blood. It says that dis-ease results when the body is "invaded" by a bug and this causes us to come down sick. It says that dis-ease erupts out of *nowhere!* These things are not true. Loyalty to the model stands in the way of change.

Regardless of medicine's bullheadedness, we are moving into an era where the reality of the 3rd dimension *physical* body and the 4th dimension *energy* body are beginning to be recognized and brought together for total healing.

**A healthy bio-electric body is a synthesis of energy fields vibrating in *concert* with Mother Earth.**

## Things Are Changing

Lancet and the New England Journal of Medicine now carry "alternative" medical care articles. This is a calculated move. The press is signalling the BIG "players" to position themselves for **control** over of the transition from allopathic to vibrational medicine. The driving force behind these moves are the pharmaceutical companies. They are the "forces" behind the GATT (General Agreement on Trade and Tariffs) Agreement which is already stifling competition in Europe, Canada and Australia by hobbling the health industry via "mandatory" prescription of supplements. The FDA in the united States of America would love to implement "CODEX" provisions of GATT.

*We have a way of fighting back. It's called the* ***Foreign Soverign Immunity Act*** *which is useful in going after any official or bureaucrat, who, with knowledge and through neglect, under color of law, coerces, extorts, racketeers against, deprives or perpetuates a FRAUD against a sovereign "Citizen." To learn how to assert yourself and defend your liberties and have access to alternative health, order the Yellow Fringe Flag 12 hour tape course and the UCC Connection.* (See Source Page 384.)

The movie, *The Medicine Man* is a ***futuristic*** movie. It was aired for a reason. It officially signaled the shift away from bogus organic chemistry and allopathic medicine to more natural modalities. Alternative medicine is growing at an exponential rate. It's no accident that our present medical and economic system is being systematically dismantled. Consider in 1994 40% of the people in the United States sought help through some form of *alternative* medicine. People are beginning to realize that conventional medicine has limits.

Natural healing is "the" thing to be into these days. Conventional doctors are authoring books and issuing newsletters that "trumpet" their charade. Few physicians can think outside the confines of their discipline or training. Licenses and bruised ego's are not conducive to alternative healing.

The experts can ignore TRUTH, but they cannot deny it, for TRUTH is there—like the Great Pyramid of Cheops—etched in stone and timeless. Becoming *Young Again!* involves the recognition and application of TRUTH *beyond theory.*

**PREVIEW**: *Our next chapter looks at HOW water functions in the bio-electric body. It is a foundation chapter in reversing the aging process. Elixir Of The Ageless provides answers to questions seldom asked.*

***"You want the truth? You can't handle the truth!***
Jack Nicholson (from *A Few Good Men*)

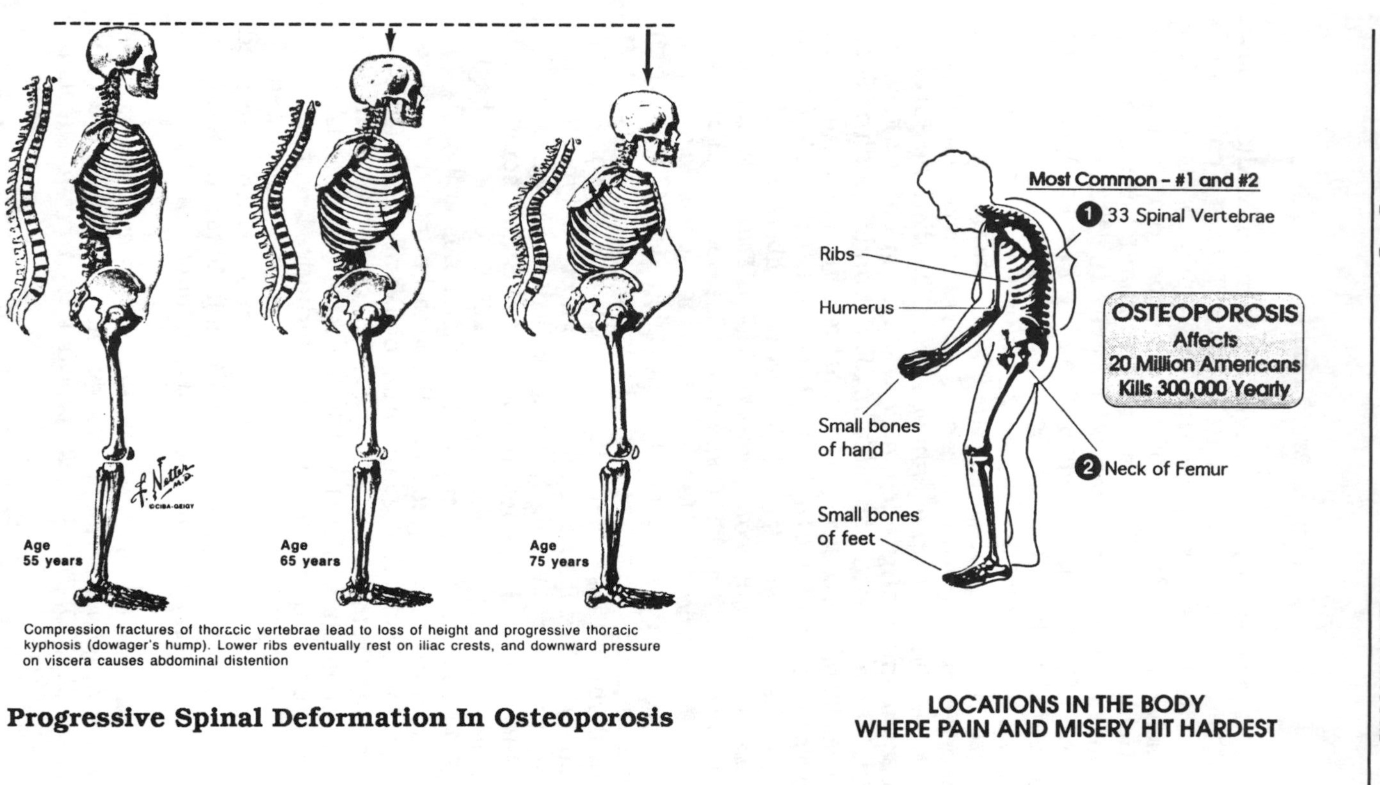


Compression fractures of thoracic vertebrae lead to loss of height and progressive thoracic kyphosis (dowager's hump). Lower ribs eventually rest on iliac crests, and downward pressure on viscera causes abdominal distention

**Progressive Spinal Deformation In Osteoporosis**

**LOCATIONS IN THE BODY**
**WHERE PAIN AND MISERY HIT HARDEST**

# 11

# Elixir Of The Ageless

*"In health and in sickness, pure water is one of the choicest blessings. It is the beverage given by God to quench the thirst of man and animal, and to cleanse the poisons from our system."*
*Byrne*

At birth, the human body is over 90% water. By age 3, *average* body hydration level **should be** 75% water. Adult hydration levels often dip to 65% in men and 52% in women. At death, hydration level can be 5-10%. Fat holds 55% water and muscle 75%, and the brain 75-85%. These figures have meaning because they impact the aging process. They partially explain *why* we age and they ***hint*** at what we can do about it.

The *bio-electric* body requires water to function. When we are water deficient, it is called *neglect.* When we drink contaminated water, it is called *abuse.* Most people's bodies suffer from both abuse and neglect. The *bio-electric* body can bounce back from abuse and neglect, but it can't do it without the help of *biologically friendly* water!

Water has many faces: some wet, some dry, some heavy, some structured. Water has different names. There is distilled water, reverse osmosis water, deionized water, carbon block and ceramic filtered water, hard water, soft water, tap water, ionized water, Grander water, Ludwig water, Ange water, Pi water, Living water, Miracle water, Willard water, Medical Grade Ionized Water™, saline water, electrostatic water, and BEV™ water. Some waters are pure and wholesome, while others are the harbinger of dis-ease and death.

**Water underwrites health and vitality. Water is a controlling dietary factor in the aging scenario.**

### Water Questions

Some water is so dry, you can hardly get wet, while other water is very *wet*. Many factors affect water's qualities: ORP (oxidation reduction potential), pH, mineral load, chemical load, bond angle, vibrational memory, smell, feel, hardness, softness, molecular size, hydroxal load, etc.

Why does some water taste good and some not? Why does some water quench the thirst while another water satisfies so poorly that we avoid it? Why do some religions erect shrines around *certain* waters? Why are certain water holes around the world called *health* spas? Why is water used in the rite of baptism?

Why do plants grow better when it rains than when irrigated? Is all rain water the same? Why is water used as the transport medium for fluorine and chlorine? Why is water the carrier of choice for pesticides and herbicides? Why do we add poisons (like fluoride and chloramines) to drinking water? Why do people like to camp near lakes and rivers? Lastly, what does water have to do with reversing the aging process?

### Water In The Body

There are TWO fluids in the body —blood and lymph— and water is the foundation of both of them. We need water to sweat, bleed, blow our nose, breathe, menstruate, spit, cough, and defecate. Without water the mucous membranes that line our air passages and gastrointestinal tract cannot function. All four excretory corridors—SKIN, LUNGS, KIDNEYS and BOWELS—rely on water!

**Water is the ONLY dietary substance over which we can exercise *complete* and *total* control.**

### BEV™ Water

Water interfaces every system in the body at the most fundamental level of human existence. "Choice" in drinking water is of immense importance. My choice of **drinking water** is BEV™ water beacuse its ORP potential is close to where the egg and sperm were at conception (see page 306) which gives the word **WATER** new meaning. My choice of "therapeutic" water is Medical Grade Ionized Water™ because if its extremely high ORP, **not** because of its pH.

*Experts* like to talk about "pure" water, but they can't agree on exactly what *pure* water is. Chemists will tell you distilled water is pure water, but it's not so. Distilled water is purer than tap water, but it's not *pure*—and it's not healthy!

Pure water is void of ALL substances except one oxygen and two hydrogen atoms and their respective electrons. Pure water should be FREE of the vibrational memories imposed on water by the contaminants the water once contained.

BEV ™ water is pure, "restructured" water that has its "memory" of toxic waste "erased." It is a right-spin energy substance that acts as a liquid magnet in the body.

Please refer to the water molecule diagram on page 79. Notice the hydrogen bonds connecting the $H_2O$ molecule in the box to the adjoining molecules outside the box. These are *hydrogen* bonds and they cause water molecules to **stick** together. The effect is referred to as ***cohesion.*** The stronger the hydrogen bonds, the more cohesive the water. The more cohesive water is, the more ENERGY it possesses and the better people feel when they drink it. BEV™ water is VERY **cohesive.**

Water with a high energy *footprint* likes to **coat** things. The phenomenon is called ***adhesion.*** The stronger the hydrogen bonds, the greater the adhesion qualities and the greater the water's affect on the body. BEV™ water feels and tastes nice, while its ORP gives it some buzz and a high energy ***signature.*** BUT THERE IS MORE!

The qualities discussed are further enhanced by manipulation of the *hydrogen* and *molecular* bond angles within and between water molecules.

Please refer to the drawing on page 79, and note that each hydrogen atom is connected to an oxygen atom at an **angle.** So called "normal" bonding angle is $104.5^0$ at room temperature and $109^0$ when frozen. The BEV™ process enhances the energy footprint and signature of water by manipulate the **angles** *within* and *between* the water molecules and drives up the ORP—giving BEV™ water more ***life!***

Water containing inorganic minerals, toxic chemicals, viruses, bacteria, radioactivity, etc. has POOR cohesion and adhesion qualities and WEAK hydrogen and molecular bonds. But contaminant removal alone isn't enough. Waste's memory MUST also be erased and the ORP potential elevated. Traditional water processing units are **primitive** in comparison to the BEV™ proprietary system. People who drink BEV™ water will tell you, ***"This water feels different in my mouth and body. I feel good when I drink it!"***

Pollutants that hitch a ride on the $H_2O$ (water) molecule alter bond angles, weaken water's *magnetic* footprint and diminish its *electrical* signature. The end effect is water that has LITTLE energy to donate to the body and even LESS energy to transport wastes out of the system.

BEV™ water should **NOT** be left exposed to air or held in metal or common plastics because it's ORP potential "pulls" contaminants from these substances trading off its load of high energy electrons in the process. BEV™ water is stored in its own system, in glass bottles or in inert BEV™ containers.

It is not unusual for people who drink BEV™ water to experience easing of sinus and lung congestion. For certain, they feel better and have more energy. Bowel habits also change. **Non water drinkers become water lovers!**

Tap, distilled and conventional reverse osmosis waters are NOT particularly good for the body. They are not pure and their ORP is low. The body must "restructure" these waters BEFORE it can use them. They are energy consumers instead of energy donors. Certainly, they can be improved and made better by using racemized™ sea mineral ions in them.

ORP stands for oxidation/reduction potential. Translated, this means the water has extra ENERGY available in the form of "free" electrons. Oxidized water is dead water. Reduced water is "live" because it contains extra electrons that the mitochondria use to produce ATP, the body's energy molecule. ORP is the issue. pH is **NOT** the issue!

## Skin • Sweat • Lungs

The skin is a mechanical barrier to infection from bacteria. When we fail to drink enough water, the skin becomes stressed. Bathing in polluted, highly oxidized, low ORP tap water stresses the skin and causes it to age. Drinking it weakens the skin from the inside out and stresses the organs.

Failure to drink enough water denies the body the opportunity to **shed** its wastes through sweat. When we sweat, we secrete toxic waste energy out of our body.

The ability to **freely** sweat is a good SIGN. Otherwise, the waste builds-up in the subcutaneous tissues, closing a major waste exit portal and forcing the load onto the kidneys, lungs, and bowels and liver. Wastes that cannot be **exported** from the body are **stored** in FAT the body ***manufactures*** for this purpose. Failure to drink enough water greatly accelerates aging. Low hydration level cripples respiration, diminishes blood and lymph fluid volume, decreases available oxygen and raises blood pressure and pulse rate.

## Water & The Lungs

The lungs also rid the body of waste energy. The lungs are VERY dependent on mucous secretions to protect delicate tissues from airborne contaminants. Mucous production is dependent on water intake. Low hydration levels in the tissues cause the mucous membranes that line our mouth, throat, respiratory system and GI tract to come under severe stress. Mucous lubricates the nasal passages, airways and vaginal canal, and it transports airborne wastes OUT of the body. Mucous coats and protects the lining of the stomach and intestines. Conditions like colitis, diverticulitis, leaky gut and irritable bowel syndromes have their **roots** in "stressed" mucosa lining. Many dis-ease symptoms vanish when water intake increases, as documented in the wonderful book *Your Body's Many Cries For Water* (see Source Page 384).

## More "Cries" For Water

The term **hypo**volemia comes to mind. It refers to a condition of low fluid (blood and lymph) volume in the body. People who are sick, immobile or bed ridden often suffer from hypovolemia because they do not drink enough water. Sexually impotent men are usually under hydrated, toxic, acid and are hormonally messed up and at risk. Men with "male" problems are NO different from a woman with "female" problems. Impotence, be it male or female, is a forerunner of trouble, as is adult diabetes Type II—and water is a factor in all of these.

Fluids like milk, juice, soft drinks and beer are **liquid foods.** And while these "foods" contain water, the water they contain stresses the system because it is **not** body friendly. Fact is, food (even good food) imposes stress on the system, so it is very important to eat good food and avoid bio-junk.

Underhydration is a problem of EPIDEMIC proportions for much of the population and particularly among the elderly and sick. Both are notorious for not drinking enough water, and their health problems are a direct reflection of it.

Prescription drugs, weak livers, poor bowel function, tap water "laced" with toxic chemicals and under-hydration, in general, are a perfect recipe for a population of sub-clinically sick, cranky and **depressed** people. Do not drink city water because the chemicals in it DESTROY the mucous lining of the gut wall and seriously stresses the microbial matrix of the gut.

**AVOID city water for bathing and colon therapy.** Use an oxidation/reduction filter to remedy the problems associated with toxic, city water (see pages 383, and 384).

## Illness • Colon Therapy

Production of bile and bile flow are dependent on water. Liver and gall stones develop and indigestion problems manifest without enough water. Arthritis, fibromyalgia, gout, lupus, leaky gut syndrome and dozens of other conditions respond when proper hydration levels are maintained.

Colon problems "go with the territory" when water intake falters—and bowel problems respond well to the Young Again Colon Protocol™ and fresh veggi juices, too. People have all kinds of hang-ups about this "unamerican" health regimen. People **think** colon therapy is a *pain in the butt*, but it not a big deal, just a new experience. Whether it be general body and health rejuvenation or a life threatening dis-ease, colon therapy is a wonderfully simple and inexpensive answer to people's health problems. **Everyone** should be practicing it!

*Most cleanse programs are better at stirring-up the waste, than MOVING it OUT of the body. The Young Again Protocol™ has perfected the process.*

**Both fat AND skinny people hold large amounts of mucoid matter in their colon. I often hear people say, *"Oh! I don't need colon therapy! I go every day!"* Regularity is NOT a reliable yardstick. Build up of mucoid waste begins as early as age two and gets progressively WORSE with age. Count on it!**

When the most popular cowboy in movie history died (his name was John Wa...), over seventy (70) pounds of **mucoid matter** was removed from his colon upon autopsy. The odor was *beyond* description! The great actor's transverse colon—the part that hangs over people's belt lines—was almost **12"** in diameter! YET, the lumen (opening) through which his waste flowed was only one inch in diameter! Elvis suffered similarly. The lumen of a "healthy" colon should be totally open and should not "sag." If you want to tighten-up your waistline, get into fresh veggi juicing and the Young Again Colon Protocol™.

**When you see a man's belly hanging over his beltline or filling a women's pelvic area, you are seeing a VERY engorged and prolapsed (i.e., sagging) colon—full of waste!**

## Colonic In A Bottle

Herbal cleansers are helpful, but they are **NOT** capable of reversing the aging process. Aging reversal can ONLY be accomplished through restoration of the "terrain." You will **NOT** become young or stay young if only "play at it"—and that is exactly what the world is doing. Terrain management is "total." The consumption of 14 day old Kombucha tea defats the liver and increases bile flow. Hair regrows, sex life improves, aches and pains ease, gray hair disappears and for some—*"Like me!*—brown eyes turn green! **Wonder what I was full of?**

**Deep Breathing • Aerobic Exercise**

Deep breathing and aerobic exercise in moderation lead to good health. These therapies are a simple and effective way to increase oxygen levels in the blood and tissues and stimulate the immune acitvity through accelerated release of toxic energy from the lungs and stagnant lymphatic fluids. Deep breathing also builds mental focus and a sense of well being. Both Yoga and Pilates include breathing techniques.

"Use it or lose it!" sums up the issues of body movement and lymphatic circulation. Weak lungs do not process enough oxygen. Blood movement is dependent on a strong heart. Lymph circulation is TOTALLY dependent upon physical "movement." The L/CSF™ machine was developed to do all of these things with little effort—especially for sick and older people.

**Soft Drinks**

Soft drink consumption is epidemic, and the problems that spring from it are as SERIOUS as the effects of alcohol usage. Soft drinks upset the body's calcium:phosphorous ratio. They are LOADED with phosphoric acid, sodium, and aluminum ions (from the can), and they damage the kidney's nephrons (filters) while upsetting body fluid pH. The sugar in soft drinks **steals** the body's minerals and artificial sweetners like aspartame (think of the "red and white swirl") destroy the liver. **It takes 40 glasses of high ORP Medical Grade Ionized Water™ to offset the effects of just one can of soda** (more on page 220). The nick name *"soda pop"* derives from the high amounts of sodium contained in soft drinks.

Soft drinks are socially acceptable and are believed to be safe to drink. **They are not!** They are viewed "differently" from cigarettes, coffee, drugs and alcohol because their effects manifest over very long periods of time—NEVER in a "real time" relationship to their consumption. Soft drink addiction is no different than any other addiction (food drugs or alcohol). **Soft drinks greatly accelerate aging—especially in females.**

**Energy Production & Water**

The body uses the oxygen in water for respiration at the "cellular" level. Cellular mitochondria use oxygen to burn (oxidize) our glucose sugars during the Krebs Cycle and glycolysis. These "flameless" processes are catalytic in nature. They "free" hydrogen ions via the electron transport chain which takes place in the mitochondria where "cellular respiration" occurs and our energy molecule ATP is produced.

BEV™ water—and especially high ORP Medical Grade Ionized Water™—supply large amounts of free electrons that fuel cellular metabolism. That is why people who drink these waters say, "WOW!" Purity, ORP and molecular size are the issues here. Restoration and management of the "terrain" is the goal—that is, if you wish to stay young and healthy.

## Ionized Water

Medical Grade Ionized Water™ is used in special Japanese clinics to heal people suffering with diabetes, cardiovascular problems, nerve and connective tissue disorders (arthritis, fibromyalgia, lupis, etc.) and cancer.

In Japan, VERY expensive CLINICAL equipment is used to raise the "ORP" of water to medical status. It is now possible to create this wonderful water in the home using laboratory equipment that is easy to operate.

To make "medical grade" water, you must first produce BEV™ water. Next, racemized™ minerals are used to raise the resistivity level of the solution to proper levels. Then the equipment is activated for 10 minutes. When done, you have one gallon of water, one-half is oxidized, the other half is reduced. One is drunk. The other is used on outside of body.

The process involves "stripping" electrons from the racemized™ acid elements (sulfur and phosphorous) and super bonding them to alkaline elements (calcium and magnesium). Sounds complicated, but the process is simple to do. This process has nothing to do with trying to create "alkaline" and "acid" water. We are after the "ORP" which is a measure of the electron load the water is carrying. The ORP is what does the trick in the body and helps restore health.

**Medical Grade Ionized Water™ defies all the laws of physics, chemistry and valence. It is "strange" stuff!**

## Medical Grade Oxidized & Reduced Waters

Medical Grade Ionized Water™ CANNOT and should NOT be made from tap water! Tap water is too polluted and its frequency is wrong. It is bad to **concentrate** and **activate** the pollutants—and the ORP falters.

pH is a measure of acidity and alkalinity. ORP is a measure of free electrons in solution. When you drive up the <minus> ORP potential of BEV™ water, you drive up the pH as well, giving the water has wonderful healing qualities.

We want to create **medical grade** "reduced" water with a pH between 10-12 and an ORP potential between <->800-900. Without the ORP, pH is meaningless. Promoting water's "pH" is useless rhetoric. Unfortunately, that is all you hear throughout the "alternative" industry. Same for the idea that we want to be "alkaline." **No,** we want to be "less acid." These sound like flip sides of the same coin, but they are not. But combine pH and ORP and you have **"something of value"** to share with your family and friends!

"Oxidized" acid water is for external use, with a pH between 1.5-2.4 and an ORP above (+) 1200. Despite its very low pH, it does NOT burn delicate tissues like the eyes. What it does do, however, is destroy **ALL** pathogenic bacteria, viruses, yeast and fungi on contact. Nothing gets past it.

High ORP oxidized (acid) water creates beautiful skin, heals wounds and infections and promotes a youthful appearance. A video showing a Japanese man growing a new FOOT with **water** is available along with scientific manuscript documenting the water's effect on microbes.

High ORP alkaline water is the exact **opposite** of high ORP acid water. Where acid water has been *oxidized* i.e., stripped of its electrons, alkaline water is highly *reduced* and is loaded with massive amounts of extra electrons.

***Reduction*** is an organic biochemistry concept and term indicating a substance **GAINED** electrons and its positive valence is increased. With the marriage of BEV™ water and Medical Grade Ionized Water™, wonderful benefits are available to anyone—right in their own home.

**The ability to create therapeutic water allows people to UNPLUG from the medical system and TAKE CONTROL of their health.**

This water does NOT cure dis-ease. Rather, it returns control of the body TERRAIN to its proper state and to its rightful owner—YOU! ***Control of the terrain*** is the guiding principle behind the development of BEV™ theory as documented in the BEV™ **manuscript** and in this book.

*Let there be no mistake. If I had a degenerative disorder of* ***any*** *kind, I would STOP destroying my liver with medications and begin the process of* ***de****acidification and restoration and prove the experts wrong. I would teach them a lesson by outliving every last one of them!*

### Fatigue & Water

Fatigue is a SIGN that the body has accumulated **excess** acids in the system and ATP reserves are low and metabolic rate is slowing. When we *overdo* we experience muscle *soreness*, because acid wastes have overloaded the system. Lactate formation occurs when there is a **shortfall** of available oxygen at the cellular level leading to **incomplete** oxidation of blood glucose sugars. Lactate is the salt of lactic acid,which is the waste byproduct of **fermentation**. Lactate—like carbon monoxide from automobiles—is the result of **incomplete** oxidation. During the sleep cycle, the body attempts to rid itself of lactate and other wastes. Failure to do so results in fatigue, soreness, dis-ease and aging. Drinking Medical Grade Ionized Water™ reverses the aging process.

***The FIR™ sauna rejuvenates the body similarly by neutralizing acid wastes in the tissues and speeding metabolic activity.*** ***(See pages 159, and 366.)***

### Urine

Urine is the metabolic waste byproduct of the kidneys. An examination of urine produces clues as to what is happening in the body. pH is an extremely important indicator. An alkaline pH (above 7.0) indicates one set of circumstances. An acid pH (below 7.0) means something altogether different.

Most people's urine pH is below 6.0. According to a nurse friend of mine, 90% of the people she checks have a pH between 5.0 - 5.5 which she says is "normal." If her patients are indicative of the rest of the population, she is prophesying a nation of people whose health is in SERIOUS jeopardy. My urine has finally stabilized at pH 6.8. This is ideal!

Low urine pH is a RED FLAG for cancer. Cancer manifests itself when urine pH drops to 4.5. Blood and saliva pH and **resistivity** should also be factored into the diagnosis in order for urine pH to be meaningful.

Body fluids with a low pH are not desirable, **unless** the body is "cleansing." It is common for urine and saliva pH to "go acid" for several years when following the Young Again Protocol™ because it takes YEARS to reverse 30, 50, 70 or more years of life and waste accumulation during one's life. Eventually, the "terrain" and the pH normalize. Only then does aging reversal **accelerate** in a **"big time"** way. *As your author has put on more years, he has become noticeably younger.*

### Water pH • Sodium

Most tap water is between pH 7-9 and is highly *oxidized* state (no life force and very toxic) despite that it is "potable."

For each number you move up or down the pH scale, the acidity or alkalinity is ten times greater or weaker. At a pH of

8, tap water is ten times more alkaline than at pH 7. But at pH 9, it is one thousand times more alkaline. This is a logarithm ic scale. It takes a LOT of pollutants and dissolved minerals to raise water from a pH of 7 to 8. Lime (calcium carbonate), sodium, aluminum and potassium all raise pH. Cities use all of them, but especially sodium hydroxide (lye) to manipulate pH. Sodium hydroxide (NaOH) is **extremely** alkaline (pH 12), but sodium is toxic to the cells. People with cancer must NOT drink tap water—nor should YOU if you want to stay healthy and live a long life.

Tap water has a huge load of contaminants attached to its molecules. The more "passengers" water carries, the less energy that is available to the body. The more waste entering **INTO** the body in drinking water, the less waste that can be transported **OUT** of the tissues. Water pollutants have a left-spin and negatively impact the *bio-electric* body.

### Casts & Albumin In Urine

Casts are sometimes found in urine. They are aptly named. Casts are deposits of mineral salts (like the ones in drinking water), hyaline and plasma proteins (albumin) that have taken on the shape of the kidney's tubules.

The tubules collect urine and any wastes it contains. Casts are a RED flag! They're indicative of pH imbalance, underhydration, **excess** metabolic wastes and mineral salts.

Albumin is a blood and lymph *plasma* protein. It does NOT belong in urine and its presence spells trouble (see a/g ratio, page 179). Carbamide is also lost in the urine. When urine is drunk, it is the "carbamide" that causes healing.

Urine tells a story. If you drink plenty of water, it should be straw colored between meals and bright yellow after meals. The doctor usually wants a urine sample from the first urination of the day. The first urination is usually dark with strong odor and cloudy. Failure to drink enough water will give a similar effect. Too much table salt and a bio-junk diet combined with poor digestion compounds the problem. If you sweat heavily and don't offset fluid and electrolyte loss, strong, dark colored urine appears—and urination may even be painful!

Go on a "strict" 3 day lemon juice and honey fast and the first urination on the second day will be **extremely** dark. If you collect it in a small, clear bottle and set on a shelf, it will form dark brown diamond shaped CRYSTALS of plasma protein waste byproducts such as uric acid. Read *The Miracle of Fasting* to learn more about this process. Also, the book *Your Own Perfect Medicine* (dealing with drinking your own urine for healing purposes) is available. (See Source Page 384).

## Kidneys & Heart Connection

The blood is filtered by the kidney's nephrons at the rate of 250 gallons a day or 1000 quarts every 24 hours. However, poor heart function equates to poor kidney function and the build up of **excess** waste in the lymphatic fluids and tissues.

When you hear someone is dying of *"congestive heart failure,"* **KNOW** that the heart is **giving out**, waste and fluids are **overloading** the system due to poor kidney function, and the lungs are **filling** with fluids. Restoration of kidney function is accomplished by **lifting the load** from **THE LIVER.** The Young Again™ Tissue/Liver and Colon Therapy protocol(s)™ accomplishes this task.

## The Bowel

When we are young and healthy, we experience regular bowel movements because bile flow is stronger and muscle tone is better, and we get adequate and regular exercise. As we grow older, the story changes—and so does our health.

Visit a doctor who thinks "basic;" and one of the first questions he will ask is, ""*How often do you move your bowels?"* The answer tells a story.

The word *bowel* comes from the French and Latin. It means *sausage* (intestines resemble sausage). Next time the question is asked, your response should be, "I move my sausage, ..........." Better yet, stay away from doctors.

Freud said we are obsessed by **defecation** in our early years of development. He called it the "Anal Stage." Gandhi was once described as a man who had been "over potty trained." Daily, he asked each of his wives if they had moved their bowels. Perhaps great people are "anal retentive?"

Even Lawrence Welk had a thing with constipation. He always pushed a laxative on his show. The laxative company had a smart marketing team. They knew that people over forty were the **target** audience! Today the target audience is people 5 years and older. The problem is real! (See pages 46, 150, 234.)

**Bowel problems are linked to poor liver and gallbladder function, marginal diet and under hydration.**

Follow the Young Again Protocol™ by doing the Tissue & Liver program, drinking fresh veggi juices **every** day of your life and by making colon hydrotherapy a fundamental part of your life. **Do these things and you will get your wish.**

## Water Therapy

Water has many uses beside drinking and bathing. It

can be used to break fevers, relieve constipation, cleanse the colon AND stimulate the flow of bile from the liver. The first thing my mother would do when we children were sick was to give us an enema to empty the lower bowel. We hated it, but the results could not be denied.

*In 1983 I pushed myself too hard and became very ill with the flu. My temperature reached 106° F. I was in serious trouble. At two in the morning, all I could think of was to crawl into the bathtub and turn on the cold water. It didn't help! In desperation, I gave myself a "mini colonic" and emptied my bowel. Within 15 minutes the fever dropped to 100° degrees F. I used no medication of any kind, and I recovered quickly.*

### Hemorrhoids • Constipation • Prostate

Hemorrhoids and appendicitis are first cousins. So are colitis and diverticulitis. Each sets up house for the other, and together they make a *miserable* pair. Constipation always **precedes** the others. Constipation is **SERIOUS** business.

Water keeps the stool moist and soft. Lack of water results in hard, dry stools. Dietary fiber holds water and acts as an intestinal broom and lubricant during defecation.

People claim hemorrhoids are caused from sitting on cold tree stumps, hard chairs and the like, but these things are NOT true. Truck drivers say they result from poor seats, vibration and road bounce. These things are **NOT** true either. Ask a hundred medical doctors what causes hemorrhoids, constipation and rare is the one who will mention WATER!

If you are constipated, drink 3 BIG glasses of water immediately upon rising in the morning. Thereafter, drink water every time you urininate. Throughout the day, HOLD your bladder—and you will experience more bowel movements! **Frequent urination robs you of your bowel movements.** A full bladder puts *pressure* on the colon, stimulates peristalsis (rhythmic movement of the intestines) and produces the gas and cramps that often go with a bowel movement. Other natural remedies are the use of Colon Prep Formula™, eating plenty of raw vegetables, apples, dried prunes and heavy consumption of Kombucha tea.

50% of men over forty-five years of age have sub-clinical prostate symptoms. Eventually, all men will have to deal with this "male" issue. Obesity, underhydration and poor diet are factors. The major problems are dysfunctional liver, hormonal imbalance, constipation and insufficient intake of essential fatty acids. A backed-up bowel causes the colon to swell and push against the prostate allowing bacteria **to migrate** from the colon into the prostate. The inflammation and swelling is called *prostatitis.* An enlarged prostate in a man is the male equivalent of an enlarged thyroid in a woman. Stress on the ovaries, testicles, bowels, liver and adrenals are at issue here.

Older men are known for "dribbling" their urine because an enlarged prostate restricts urine flow through the uretha. In other words, these men can't make water!

***When a man is young, all he thinks about is making love. In his middle years, all he thinks about is making money. When he becomes OLD, all he thinks about is making water!***

Become *Young Again!* and you can have it all!

**PREVIEW:** *In our next chapter you will learn how to save thousands of dollars in dental bills and how to feel good!*

---

### Stones & Nails

"Stones" in the gallbladder and "nails" in the liver BLOCK the flow of acid waste laden bile from exiting the body. The result: premature old age and poor health.

Acids accumulating in the body's tissues eventually settle in the joints and connective tissues producing pain, stiffness, deterioration and eventually a diagnosis from the doctor. The **MOST TOXIC** waste resides in the **fat layer** under the skin. Acne, wrinkles, psoriasis, graying hair result because the waste has no where else to go.

Gall stones are actually liver stones that form in the liver and settle in the gallbladder. They range in size from B-B's to golf balls. "Nails" take their characteristic shape from the biliary ducts they block within the liver itself. Nails only appear in very sick people. When they exit, they "clink" against the toilet bowl or tub floor. Poor bile flow ALWAYS results insub-clinical illness, dis-ease, stones and nails.

**All people—including children—have stones in their gallbladder. The way to get them "out" of your body is to do the Young Again Tissue & Liver protocol."**

Necessary preparations and instructions come with the package. Adults do a series of six purges over a two month period. Waste exiting the tissues exits the body via the bowels. A **"normal"** life is followed during the process. Epsom salts are toxic and are **not** used. Stones appear in the toilet in colors of green, brown, black and red. OX™ and R/C™ control cleansing reactions, restore gut wall integrity while boosting blood immunoglobulins, antibody levels and protecting the immune system from overload.

# 12

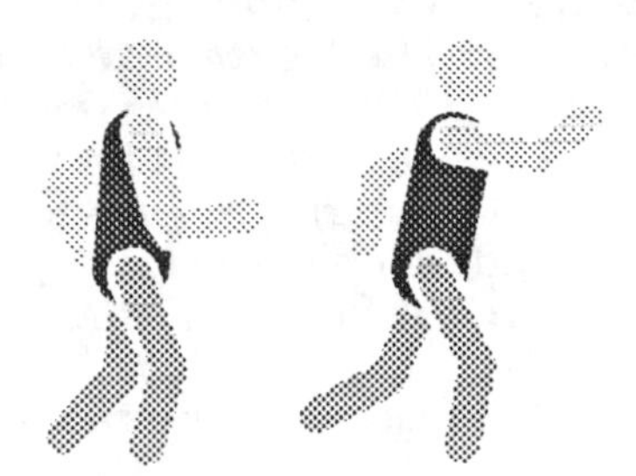

# I Feel Good

*"Stress is like a chicken. It always comes home to roost!"*
*John Thomas*

We describe the way we feel in terms of black and white. "I feel good!" "I'm sick!" People don't like shades of *gray* when it comes to the way they feel.

If we substitute the word *aerobic* for good and *anaerobic* for sick, our descriptions shift from black and white to *gray*. Our words no longer *appear* to carry the same meaning, but they do help us to better understand WHY we feel *good* or *sick*.

## Breathing • Respiration

When we are **aerobic,** we are "with air." When we are **anaerobic**, we are "without air." Both of these states of being are influenced by the way we breathe.

Shallow breathing encourages the accumulation of wastes in the tissues and accelerates aging, while deep breathing causes the body to shed its wastes and rejuvenate itself.

Shallow breathing creates an oxygen starved body, windedness, low energy and poor focus. Deep breathing produces an oxygen surplus, endurance, high energy and a steely focus. Breathing is central to the yoga experience.

Exercise and strenuous activity promote deep breathing and endurance. Endurance **implies** that a person is in "aerobic" state—mentally and physically.

Respiration (breathing) takes place on two levels: external and internal. **External** respiration is somewhat of a mechanical process that occurs in the lungs, while **internal** respiration is more esoteric because it takes place IN the cells.

**The exchange of carbon dioxide ($CO_2$) and oxygen ($O_2$) in the lungs is called *external respiration.* The exchange of $CO_2$ and $O_2$ at the cellular level is called *internal respiration. Both processes must be in balance.***

Glucose (blood sugar) is burned (oxidized) at the cellular level, and the production of the energy molecule ATP is the result. ATP is why we eat food and drink water.

## Clinical vs. Subclinical

Aging occurs at the cellular level **BEFORE** it appears in the mirror. And while we think of aging on the physical (Third Dimension) level, we need come to understand that aging is really an energy "concept" rooted in other dimensions. Aging transcends Third Dimension reality where we live out our lives.

The doctor uses SIGNS to diagnose dis-ease. SIGNS are observable and ***clinical*** proof of dis-ease. Symptoms, on the other hand, are *not* observable, but they are ***subclinical* evidence** that something is amiss.

When you are clinically ill, you are usually under a doctor's care, in the bed or perhaps in the hospital. **Clinical illness is OFFICIAL!** "Clinical" means you are in trouble!

***Subclinical*** illness is the "occult" or hidden stage of dis-ease. It takes place at the ***subtle-energy level*** of our existence. It is a ***gray*** state of being, often described as "feeling a little off." People tend to ignore these *off* feelings, hoping they will go away. In time, however, symptoms take **form** and give way to clinical **SIGNS** and an official diagnosis from the doctor.

Most people live out their lives at the ***SUBCLINICAL*** level, that twilight zone ***between*** true health and official disease. Here, ***abnormal*** is viewed as **normal**, and black and white are lost among shades of *gray!*

## Microbes

*Aerobic* and *anaerobic* states of being greatly influence health and dis-ease. The *aerobic* state is a right-spin condition, while the anaerobic state is a left-spin condition. These energy "states" dictate the **type** of microbe (bacterial, viral, yeast or fungal) that **develops**, **inhabits** and **prospers** in the body of man and animal.

***Pathogenic* microbes LIKE an anaerobic environment. They are blamed as the cause of dis-ease, but they do NOT cause dis-ease. Instead, they are only actors fulfilling the roles that YOU and I dictate to them as a result of our chosen lifestyle and the "state" of our terrain.**

If we dissect the word pathogenic, we get: *path*-suffering, disease, *gen*-producing, giving rise to; *ic*-pertaining to.

When a condition is described as pathogenic, it is a "diagnosed" condition that displays certain **agreed upon** SIGNS. SIGNS elevate it to a "CLINICAL" condition.

Pathogenic conditions are described as *morbid* conditions, hence, the term ***morbidity*** as used in life insurance company morbidity tables to predict death rates among a population. A ***pathologist*** is a specialist in *pathology* which is the study of the nature of dis-ease, its causes, processes, effects and alterations of tissue structure and function.

### Microbes

**Microbes "change" form according to THEIR environment and the terrain of the host.** Hence, they are referred to as being "poly" or "pleo" morphic because they adapt to their environment and only "appear" to be different species of organisms, medical opinion to the contrary not withstanding.

A body with a healthy energy *footprint* relies on non-pathogenic aerobes to maintain peak health. **Aerobes** are usually non-pathogenic microbes that like an oxygen RICH environment. As the body's energy *footprint* becomes left-spin, aerobes mutate and become **an**aerobes (microbes that prefer *oxygenless* environments) (the prefix *an* means without), or facultative **an**aerobes (microbes that can tolerate oxygen, but don't require it). A constipated colon is an **an**aerobic environment where pathogenic microbes set up shop and do their job.

Pathogenic microbes were once "friendly" organisms that turned against the host with a vengeance. These include bacteria, viruses, yeast and fungi, all of which exist and live in the blood which is NOT a sterile medium as we have been taught. From the moment of conception, our blood carries the SEEDS of our own destruction. ***"The sins of the father shall be with us to the tenth generation [and beyond]."***

Microbes common to the human body include: *staphylococcus* —an **aerobe** that is often involved in skin infections, *clostridium* is—a **facultative anaerobe** that produces **entero**toxins (*entero:* related to toxins of intestinal origin) that are responsible for deadly botulism, *E. coli* is a VERY important facultative anaerobe that is found in the colon.

The job of pathogenic life forms is to **"attack"** the host when the host is weak and under stress and remove the host from the Earth. People who exercise enjoy better health because they move their blood and lymph, increase oxygen levels and circulate more nutrients to the liver for filtration and disposal via increased bile flow and bowel activity.

### Cavities • Dental Plaque

Cavities and periodontal conditions like gingivitis, pyorrhea and bleeding gums are indicative of microbial activity in the mouth and an out of balance body fluid pH. Bacteria that produce cavities secrete a protective substance to shield themselves from air (oxygen) while they dissolve tooth enamel. These *facultative* bacteria **create** their own environment to do their dirty work. They can *only* do their work in a low pH saliva environment. Periodontal problems are easily treated with a Bio-Magnetic™ dental irrigator. The Young Again Protocol™ "deacidfies" the terrain and raises the pH environment.

Stagnant, low pH saliva, blood and urine is a bell weather of trouble in the making. Body fluid pH outside the norm **translates** to subclinical illness or clinical dis-ease.

When the hygienist removes "plaque" from the teeth, it alters the bacteria's *anaerobic* environment—but it does NOT stop new plaque from forming again. In time, you must return and have your teeth cleaned again. Some hygienists and dentists coat the teeth with plastic to discourage the bacteria from taking root on the teeth. This is helpful, but it does NOT address the **fundamental issues** of decay. Coating the teeth with plastic is the dentist's version of *palliation.*

Proper dental hygiene and "terrain" management means no plaque and means no decay. Plaque, gingivitis, bleeding gums and pyorrhea are easily TREATED with a simple, inexpensive device called a **Bio-Magnetic**™ dental irrigator that uses plain water to do the job (see pages 204 & 384).

Instead of having your teeth cleaned twice a year, equip your home with a *bio-magnetic irrigator* and wash your problems down the drain. This simple appliance can save a family a fortune in dental bills. You can even use it to clean your dog's teeth—that is, with the animal's own cleaning tip, of course. Veterinarians charge $100 to clean an animal's teeth. My teeth are clean and bright and they haven't been cleaned in over 8 years! Here's how the dental irrigator works and why every family should be own one.

### Magneto-Hydro Dynamics

Plaque is a negative energy field. The coating bacteria

secrete to protect themselves has a negative (—) electrical charge on its surface. The hydrogens on the $H_2O$ molecule have a positive (+) charge ( please review diagram on page 79).

Magneto-hydro-dynamics (MHD) is the *process* used in Bio-magnetic™ irrigation. MHD uses an electromagnet to free the hydrogen ions (H+) in the water so they can react with the negative (—) surface of the plaque as ions wash against it. Positive charged H+ protons **oxidize** the plaque's negatively charged protective coat by ***stealing*** electrons—a process referred to as **oxidation.** As the plaque loses its "protective shield" the bacteria disappear down the drain! Instead of " pic" type devices that are only fancy squirt guns, a Bio-Magnetic™ irrigator **converts** water into a special substance that really cleans the teeth and gums—a **therapeutic** approach instead of the usual methods that are marginal at best.

***The process just described is an electrical event not unlike the rusting of iron or disappearance of aluminum window screens in a salty, ocean air environment. Transference of electrons is the name of the game. Medical Grade Ionized Water™ also involves shifting of electrons.***

Magneto-hydro-dynamics is a blend of vibrational medicine and technology. The process is acclaimed worldwide. The reason you have probably not heard of it is that the dental industry will suffer a huge loss of revenue once people wake up and realize that they can enjoy FEWER dental problems and save a lot of money with a bio-magnetic irrigator in their home.

I found that when I used my irrigator I could not detect the smell of decay when I flossed my teeth. The bio-magnetic irrigator is vibrational medicine's answer to dental problems!

### Birds Of A Feather "FLOCK" Together

***Dis-ease is an expression of negative energy dominance! Contrary to conventional thought, LIKE energy attracts LIKE energy. The sick body tends to become MORE sick unless action is taken to "create" a healthy environment and break the dis-ease cycle!***

Low vitality reflects a negative energy state, and negative energy *activates* microbes that "FEED" on toxic energy. An acid body **cannot** restore itself unless toxic wastes are neutralized and flushed from the system. **De**acidification is as fundamental to restoration of health as good food and water. ***In an acid body, positive energy is hijacked and used to support and promote dis-ease!***

It is the terrain of the *bio-electric* body that ultimately determines the EFFECT an energy field will produce. It is the "terrain," NOT the microbes that determines **when, where** and

**how** dis-ease will manifest itself in each of our lives. If you "tune-in" to your *bio-electric* terrain, your bio-electric clock will rewind itself while you enjoy *limitless* energy and a young body.

### Stress & Attitude

Place a person under mental or physical stress and dis-ease often **erupts** onto the scene—not because of the presence of microbes and "bugs," but because stress is an energy condition that caters to the NEEDS of pathogenic life forms. In other words, **stress seeks an outlet**—and it uses the *course of least resistance* to express itself. Stress usually attacks an old injury or settles into an area of the body where there is a weakness. Conditions like hepatitis, chronic fatigue and leaky gut syndromes, asthma, arthritis, lupis, MS, fibromyalgia are antagonized by stress, only "seeming" to appear out of no-where. But they have their roots in a sick body TERRAIN. *The latter three conditions are* ***hormone driven*** *conditions affecting deterioration of the myelin sheath that protects nerve fibers and the disappearance of Schwann's cells located at nerve synapses along the axons (see page 248) Schwan cells are specialized cells responsible for keeping the receptor sites of the neurilema open for nerve signal transference.*

Dis-ease often appears in the **wake** of high stress circumstances or chronic negative thought. People can "handle" stress when they are under fire, but when the heat is off, illness appears out of nowhere to settle the score.

**The point is this:** body, mind and spirit are irrevocably linked. Thoughts and attitude are **potent** forces in dealing with dis-ease and maintenance of good health. A good attitude, however, **cannot** overcome physical problems created by a toxic, hormone unbalanced and underhydrated body.

### Under Siege: *Fever*

There are two kinds of fever conditions: local and systemic. An infected finger is a localized condition, while a systemic condition places the WHOLE body under siege causing it to *react!* Systemic conditions bring on things like vomiting, runny bowels, phlegm, chills, fever and horrid gas.

Fever that accompanies dis-ease is the body's reaction to the presence of a morbid condition and should NOT be considered bad. Contrary to popular belief, fever is good and serves a useful purpose. Fever is the EFFECT of an accelerated metabolic rate. Fever is a condition of ***hyper*** *thermogenesis* (*thermo:* heat producing; *gen:* origin of; *sis:* condition).

*Mucous that accompanies colds and flu is the VEHICLE*

*that carries toxic wastes from the body. Mucous is one way the body expels waste. Illness erupts onto the scene when toxicity levels EXCEED the body's ability to maintain homeostasis.*

If fever is not allowed to go above 106° degrees and the victim is FULLY hydrated, fever does a wonderful job of denaturing and destroying bacterial and viral proteins by altering the body's "terrain". A FIR™ sauna [page 60] provides similar benefits. These **therapeutic** saunas penetrate deep into the tissues dissolving acid wastes that provide perfect conditions for the manifestation of dis-ease. A FIR™ sauna uses FIR energy instead of steam and hot lights to work.

Fever destroys the microbes' "breeding" grounds — particularly in the colon and appendix. Fever is the body's way of ridding itself of toxic "waste" energy. If a fever rises too high (above 110°F), however, it can denature enzyme proteins in the brain and can be deadly.

*Medicine authority and society have held strange views about the nature of fever over the years. For example, at the time of the American Revolution, people associated body lice with health. When fever got too high, the lice would leave and the person usually died. People came to associate the presence of lice with health. Lice=life. No lice=death. Obviously, this is wrong, but it's a good example of the problems incorrect thinking produces. Relying on "symptoms" to diagnose and prescribe a "cure" is an endless cycle.*

## Denatured Proteins

If you drop the contents of a raw egg into boiling water, you will see the egg's proteins change form. The egg will become firm and solid. Heat denatures egg protein enzymes, alters their form and causes the egg to harden. This is what a *febrile* (fever producing) condition does to pathogenic bacteria. Fever alters their **protein** based enzymes and structure causing bacteria to die.

## Muscle Tone

When mineral **electrolyte** levels collapse—as in heat stroke or heat exhaustion—the effect is similar to a high fever and severe under hydration. Fever weakens protein enzymes and debits the mineral electrolytes that are responsible for maintaining **muscle tone.** Muscle tone allows us to stand, hold up our head or maintain a position. Without tone, we would function like a jellyfish.

The muscles controlling the vital organs receive their orders through the *involuntary* parasympathetic nervous system. Loss of tone stresses the vital organs. When high fever occurs, colon therapy is mandatory if you wish to end the suffering sooner. In hot weather or during physical exertion, use of racemized™ sea minerals gives instant relief. **Colon therapy is direct, physical intervention designed to restore balance to the terrain by removing toxic wastes.**

### Medications

Antibiotics, aspirin and other drugs are forms of **chemotherapy.** All of them alter body function and accelerate aging. Despite the *apparent* positive results they produce in the short term, their long term effect on body terrain is disastrous.

Despite all the propaganda put out by the pharmaceutical companies, drugs are not safe. ALL drugs have **known** side effects. Drugs are prescribed on the same basis that is used to justify the chlorination of public water supplies and the spraying of food crops with "known" poisons. It reads like this: *"If the benefit outweighs the risk, a drug is prescribed."*

What is NEVER talked about is the long term effects of drugs on the vital organs and glands. Many older people take as many as FIFTY (50) pills a day! The short and long term side effects of these left-spin energy substances is beyond comprehension. One look at the CONTRAindications in any drug *reference* manual (i.e. Physicians Desk Reference) ought to be enough to cause any thinking person to opt for alternative measures in the treatment and cure of their condition.

"NEW" drugs are constantly pushed by the pharmaceutical companies to replace those drugs where patents have expired. New drugs are MORE expensive, and each new generation of drugs carries an ever increasing risk.

People are taught to differentiate between "prescribed" drugs and illegal drugs. There is NO difference between them.

### "How To Stay Healthy Until It Is Time To Die"

Personal survival requires that we learn to live our lives in harmony with nature so we have NO need for drugs!

Do you know anyone who has suffered from the side effects of drug therapy, or maybe someone who walked into the hospital or clinic for testing and was carried out—feet first? If you apply the lessons in this book, you will have NO need for the medical system nor will you become a medical statistic.

Drugs diminish liver function and burden the kidneys. They do violence to the kidney's nephrons. They destroy the liver's hepatocytes—the cells that perform the thousands of *bio*chemical reactions that keep us alive and healthy.

A dis-eased body is a body that is under siege. Drugs

destroy organ function—particularly the liver. A healthy liver is so fundamental to health that any treatment modality—conventional or alternative—that does not make provision for restoration and maintenance of the liver is doomed from the start. We must never forget that 75% of the waste exiting the body leaves via the LIVER in the form of bile and bowel flow.

## Colon Therapy

An enema is a "quick" but incomplete version of a colonic. A colonic is sometimes referred to as a DEEP enema, but it is more, much more. A properly executed colonic flushes mucoid waste from the sigmoid, descending, transverse and ascending colons. Mucoid is a combination of mucous, drugs and fecal matter. It can accumulate for years. When it becomes excessive, the ileocecal valve locks in "open" position.

The **ileocecal valve** controls fecal flow between the small and large intestines. It is located in the cecum, a fist-sized pouch from which the appendix hangs (see page 46). A properly executed colonic reaches the cecum, which is six feet up from the rectum.

The small intestine (the gut) ends and the large intestine (colon) begins at the cecum. Undigested food and bile from the liver enter the colon by way of the *ileocecal* valve. **People with cancer usually have their ileocecal valve "locked" in the OPEN position.** The Young Again Colon Therapy Protocol™ and the Tissue & Liver Protocol™ clear the colon and free the ileocecal valve. The process is not difficult to do.

Colon therapy stimulates peristaltic activity and increases bile flow from the liver and gallbladder. The process duplicates the effect of a MASSIVE acupuncture treatment over every square inch of the body because colon therapy done properly **stimulates** the complex of nerves that flow from the colon wall to ALL of the organs and tissues of the body.

An enema is NOT a substitute for a colonic, but enemas are very useful when traveling. Enemas empty only the lower part of the colon—which is six feet long. Every person should own a "good" enema bag—not be to confused with a "fleet" device—and should take it with them whenever they **travel** (available from the Source Packet, see page 384). A women's douche bag doubles as an enema bag and comes with both a vaginal and rectal syringe. Water, a hook or wire to hang the bag, an enema bag and a motel bathroom are all that are needed to avoid appendicitis, ease constipation or break a flue related fever. For Montezuma's revenge, use R/C™ and Microbize™, and drink lots of fresh lemon juice.

Colon equipment is the ultimate health management

tool. I've had mine for 25 years! It is easy to use and nicer than lying on a towel covered floor. The Young Again Colon Protocol ™ package is inexpensive, easy to use and effective.

It's especially nice to do your own "colonics" in the privacy of your own home. Clinics are costly **if** you can find a therapist in your area. Done at home, colon therapy is private, easy, and inexpensive. Besides, the Young Again™ protocol calls for colonics 2-3 times a week for **life.** I am serious!

Colon equipment is **CHEAP.** Every home should have it. In the case of severe illness, colon therapy can save your life. The process may seem un-American, but I am here to testify that it is a **fast track** to vibrant health. Begin today and you will ***SHOUT,"*** I feel good!" as you become *Young Again!*

**PREVIEW:** *Our next chapter deals with the HIV virus and its alleged progeny, AIDS. There is an important connection between "weeds" and viruses.*

---

## People & Pets

Dogs and cats are people with four legs. They suffer from the same metabolic problems that humans do—and their bodies respond and rejuvenate similarly, too!

Because pets live shorter lives, they age faster than humans, but they also respond faster, so we often can see them come back to life much faster, also.

Hormones maintain health. Acid "excesses" destroy health. Diminished liver function is central to both. Treat your pets like you would treat yourself.

Give your pets these products to keep them healthy. Pac's, OX™, R/C, Algae, predigested liver caps, Yucca Blend™ and racemized™ sea minerals. Also, rub their abdomen with F/G™ or Maxgest™ creme and Cobo-12 creme. These products work miracles in people and they can do the same for your pet! It is easier to keep your pets healthy than to treat them after they are sick. TIP: In dogs, look for constant licking and chewing of the paws.

---

➥ ***If I can practice what's in this book, so can you!***

---

## The Golden Years

The "golden years" come earlier than they used to, and anyone who is honest will tell you they are NOT golden! Aging is the socially correct way of describing the ultimate dilemma. Growing old is NOT my idea of a "golden" future. Having **"control"** of one's health is as golden as it gets. If you will call John thomas, ask for help and apply the lessons in this book **you will get your wish!** (See page 352.)

**Statistics & Palliation**

It's difficult to discuss "health" with people who have been schooled in the scientific method. It's not that they are anti-health—they are not. Rather, their world is built upon medical statistics and studies. Theirs is a world of numbers—numbers that prove something is or isn't so. The *passwords* into their world are "statistics show" and "scientific proof."

Medical science sees health and dis-ease in terms of single problems that demand single answers based on "findings." Medical science demands that "health" minded people play their statistical games or suffer the ridicule of *"no scientific proof!"*

Anyone with a lick of sense knows that you must take care of yourself or good health falters and dis-ease results. Health minded people know that if you eat nourishing food, drink plenty of pure water, get enough exercise and rest, entertain positive thoughts, keep your bowels clean, and do the things we discuss, you greatly improve the odds of a better life. **"Our" PROOF is *healthy* human beings living in accordance with nature's laws.**

Medical science sees "health" as a numbers game. Their game is designed to keep the public confused by dazzling them with skewed studies and statistical gymnastics. **"Their" PROOF is millions of subclinically sick people who *bear witness* to medicine's "findings."**

*Palliation* lends itself to the numbers game called "statistics." *Palliation* (see glossary) is a powerful tool of *manipulation* in the hands of medical science. *Palliation* allows science to state its case in the short run with little worry that the public will ever discover they were duped.

Medical science **knows** the risks that accompany drug usage. However, drugs provide credibility and "scientific proof." Without tools of manipulation, medical science would lose its **strangle hold** on the people and the endless flow of money would STOP!

Health minded people do not live in fear of medical science's statistics and studies. Rather, we **ignore** them. For us, their game is an exercise in futility. We ACHIEVE health and vitality, and we try our best to live according to nature's way. Nature rewards our efforts with PEAK health instead of statistics and illness. **We measure results in years YOUNG. My goal is 250 years YOUNG! And you?**

---

**Food additives and colorings have the same effect as rogue, zeno estrogens found in the environment!**

---

## BEV™ Water

BEV™ took its name in honor of French Professor Louis-Claude Vincent who developed the theoretical standards for **biologically friendly** drinking water for the body.

**Consider these points about BEV™ water:**

•BEV™ water promotes cellular metabolism. Its molecules cause the body to "dump" cellular waste and fuels mitochondrial production of the high energy molecule "ATP" within the electron transport chain.

•BEV™ water is a naturally potent biological solvent of body wastes and toxins.

•BEV™ water STOPS the flow of waste minerals, trihalomethanes, bacteria, viruses, chlorine, chloramines, fluorides and toxic chemical wastes into the body.

•BEV ™water is VERY aggressive and acts as a liquid magnetic transport system to the tissues and cells.

•BEV™ water effectively hydrates the tissues due to its bonding angles, conception point "ORP" and low resistivity. It's ORP is very close to where the egg and sperm were when life was conceived (see page 306).

•BEV™ water uses the homeopathic principals of *resonance* and *transference* to bring "life" into the body.

•BEV™ water processing units do not require electricity and there are no elements to clean.

•BEV water helps maintain control of body "terrain," and it is enjoyable to drink. Non water drinkers become water drinkers with their very first glass.

•BEV™ water is the ultimate biologically friendly drinking water and is the basis for the creation of Medical Grade Ionized Water™. (See pages 220, 306 & 384.)

## Alzheimers

Over 50,000,000 people are expected to have this dreaded condition by year 2005. Sad, but true!

The best way to treat this horrible condition is to AVOID it in the first place by following the Young Again Protocol™ BEFORE it affects your life. Once the condition is diagnosable, it is too late. Don't allow yourself or your loved ones to slip away. Restore your **"terrain"** now, while there is still time. Doing it on "your" terms now is better than on the doctors terms later. Besides, it saves a lot of heart break for families.

**Soft drinks are loaded with "toxic" heavy metals.**

# 13

# Viruses & Weeds

*"There is no difference between plant and animal."*
Dr. Guenther Enderlein, 1898

Medical science knows little about viruses. The average person knows almost nothing about them. Most folks think a virus is like a bacterium—a "bug" that you somehow "catch!"

Antibiotics hold no power against viruses. If you are sick with a viral infection, you are usually told to stay warm and drink lots of fluids, okay advice, but there is a better answer.

The *informed* person will perform COLON THERAPY, and take a hot Epsom salt, ginger and hydrogen peroxide bath along with a shot of whiskey and a handful of SOC™ capsules. **The informed person does NOT wait to be told to clean the bowel and flush the body of its poisons and viruses.**

In college little time is spent discussing viruses. They are poorly understood by the student and often by the instructors, too. NOTHING is taught about where they come from or how to deal with them.

### Viruses Today

We hear a lot about AIDS, influenza, herpes, Hepatitis, Chronic Fatigue Syndrome and mononucleosis. These are *here and now* viral conditions afflicting millions of people.

The best cure for any type of viral condition is prevention—and the best way to accomplish the task is to focus on the the "terrain" and the **conditions** under which viruses prosper. We need to understand the link between these "fringe" life forms and the aging process from an *energy* perspective.

The virus is an anomaly, a paradox and a slave master. The virus is the point man of nature's garbage crew. Science does NOT consider viruses to be life forms—but they are NOT dead either. Viruses cannot reproduce on their own. They are **OPPORTUNISTIC** organisms—as are bacteria. When we create a suitable environment and lose control of our terrain, viruses appear, *seize* control of cellular machinery and take control of life at the subtle energy level.

Viruses are energy fields and they have an energy *footprint*. A virus is a strand of either DNA (deoxyribonucleic acid) or RNA (ribonucleic acid) that is protected by a protein capsule (energy shield), but this is an incomplete picture.

Viruses exist in the *grey* area between living and non-living things and can neither reproduce nor perform normal life functions on their own. Viruses are *entirely* dependent on energy generated INSIDE the cells of the target host's body. Viruses are classified based on their composition (DNA or RNA), origin, mode of transportation, reproduction methods and where they first manifest themselves in the host.

Viruses are so small that it used to require an electron microscope to view them, a problem overcome with a Nassens condensor microscope. Because viruses are ubiquitous, there is NO avoiding them. Yet, in a healthy body viruses do NOT threaten the host because the **"terrain"** is unsuitable for their proliferation. Consequently, viruses *cannot* access the host's cellular machinery unless control of the "terrain" is **forfeited**.

When we are under mental or physical stress, our energy fields are disrupted and the body's protective systems are sabotaged. The immune system is one of those systems.

The immune system can overcome viral activation and restore homeostasis, but only IF we provide the a terrain environment that supports such a process.

**Viruses—like their cousins bacteria and fungi—— have a job to do. Their job is to rid the Earth of weak life forms—be they plant, animal or human!**

### HIV & AIDS

HIV (human immunodeficiency virus) is the virus that is associated with the manifestation of AIDS (Auto Immune

Deficiency Syndrome). HIV uses an enzyme called *reverse transcriptase* that allows it to infect the host in *reverse*. This is why HIV is called a **retrovirus** (*retro* means after the fact, in reverse). As the HIV virus mutates, it is given other names like HTLV 1, 11, or 111, etc. HTLV stands for human T-cell **lymphotrophic** virus. Dissected, *lymphotrophic* means: **lymph**-the watery, clear fluid in the blood minus the blood corpuscles (think of the clear fluid that oozes when a wound is healing); **troph**-a change or a turning; **ic**-pertaining to. A lymphotrophic virus causes a *change* **within** the **lymphatic** fluids.

### The T-Cells

The HIV virus has an affinity for the T (helper) cells which are lympho**cytes** that originate in the *thymus* which is the center of the immune system. ***Cyte*** means cell. So a lymphocyte is a cell in the lymph fluid. In this case, we are speaking of the T-cells. Viruses wage war in the plasma proteins (lymph fluids) long BEFORE they appear in the blood. This explains why blood samples often test negative for the presence of HIV virus. As plasma toxins accumulate, the body's energy fields shift from right to left spin as the immune system weakens. This is the body's equivalent of the star ship Enterprise dropping its defense shields. A bio-junk diet—including soy and canola—further weaken T-cell function.

### AIDS Not A Virus

AIDS is not a virus. It is a ***syndrome*** of secondary conditions brought on by a weakened immune system. HIV is an **adeno**virus (*aden*-a cavity as in the lungs or chest). This class of viruses is OPPORTUNISTIC and usually results in death from infections of the chest cavity, as in *pneumonia*. We do not die from AIDS, but from secondary complications like pneumonia. (Actually, we die when the mitochondria within the cells fail to produce sufficient ATP to keep us alive.)

As HIV infects the system, a "syndrome" of problems called AIDS develops. Contrary to popular belief, AIDS is not a dis-ease of homosexual origin. Little of what the public has been told about AIDS is true. Most is ***disinformation*** purposely disseminated to keep the public confused.

***NOTE:*** *People who "drink" Medical Grade Ionized Water™, bath in it and douche with it can kiss their infectious diseases good bye. If you suffer with herpes, syphilis, strep throat, hepatitis, athletes foot, gangrene, pink eye, ring worm, insect bites, yeast infections, etc., here is a wonderful solution.*

### Sabotage

Retroviruses—like HIV—sabotage the cell's genetic information base (DNA or RNA), then siphon away the ATP energy produced by cellular mitochondria and take control of the body's energy reserves while they multiply exponentially.

The process just described is predictable and should be expected in a toxic body terrain. The virus' job is to kill the host and rid the Earth of weak organisms. **Viruses are NOT the enemy!** They and their cousins—the bacteria, fungi, and yeasts—are present the moment the egg and sperm join. They are polymorphic "mutant" life forms that **ONLY** manifest into their pathogenic form when **control of the terrain** is lost.

Viral infection is a *confirmation* that things are not right and should cause the THINKING person to deduce that their terrain must be *"au fait"* (favorable) or the viruses would not manifest and stir up trouble.

Viruses **only** attack people who are acid and toxic; who eat dead food, who do not digest well, who have poor liver function and who are constipated and anaerobic. **The Young Again Protocol™ of drinking enough water, doing colon therapy and tissue & liver purges goes a long ways in restoring the body's terrain.**

### Blood NOT Sterile

Contrary to medical teachings, the blood is NOT a sterile medium. Medical science has perpetuated this gross mistruth in the face of irrefutable evidence to the contrary, as discovered by Dr. Guenther Enderlein and Gaston Nassens and documented in *Hidden Killers* and *The Prosecution and Trial Of Gaston Nassens.* (SeeSource Page 384).

***"All life contains the seeds of its own destruction within its own fluids."*** That is what Dr. Enderlein meant when he said, *"There is **NO** difference between plants and animals."* He discovered that when the energy balance of the terrain is lost, the microbes **automatically** break out of their "healthy" 3 stage CLOSED loop into a 21 stage loop that leads directly to the grave yard.

The pharmaceutical companies and the medical system stand to lose trillions of dollars if the above information was taught in medical schools. **Recognition that the blood is NOT sterile is tantamount to open refutation of the Germ Theory of Disease and allopathic medicine as we know it.**

Pride and greed prevent medical science from refuting its false theories. Millions of people have suffered and died needlessly because medicine labors under the shadow of many other big lies and withheld information. As Christ said in Luke, *"Woe be unto you lawyers, scribes, Pharasies. You hold the keys of knowledge. You yourself will not enter AND you prevent those who would enter from entering."* Life was meant to be a celebration, not a requiem. Unfortunately, as Hosea said, *"My people perish for lack of KNOWLEDGE."*

## Cell Electrical Charge

Strong, positively charged cells and tissues are not affected by viruses. "Acid" tissues are waste stressed tissues and are in an "anaerobic" state. Such a body is "compromised" with a weak enzyme system and insufficient oxygen. Under these conditions viruses take over the cell's machinery and replicate (reproduce) themselves.

Rogue viruses *steal* the body's production of ATP and use this energy to multiply and form cancers. Cancer tumors and masses are HUGE fields of *negative* energy that control all metabolism within their sphere of influence. **Cancer viruses proliferate in a body that is anaerobic AND whose cells are loaded with sodium.**

An *anaerobic* body is an OLD body. Old bodies are unable to rejuvenate for lack of sufficient ATP. Dis-eases are energy wars and the bullets they shoot are negative energy bullets. Conventional medicine's "magic bullets" are worthless in the cancer arena. The PROOF is all the dead and dying people! The solution is a healthy lifestyle, immediate **de**acidification of the tissues and restoration of hormone imbalances.

## Useful Oxygen Forms

Hydrogen peroxide ($H_2O_2$) and "medical grade" ozone (triatomic oxygen or $O_3$) are useful products. Their effectiveness is related to the amount of available oxygen present and their molecular instability. Instability allows them to give up oxygen atoms freely. Oxygen is a highly magnetic element, which accounts for the bent shape of the water molecules on page 79.

Oxygen therapy can be useful in the treatment of cancer **masses** and **tumors.** Skilled healers sometimes inject $H_2O_2$ or $0_3$ directly into cancer masses with good results. Given intravenously or by water infusion in the rectum or vagina, ozone therapy can be effective.

In the home, a "medical grade" ozone generator purifies the air and eases respiratory problems. Emphysema patients respond well to ozone therapy, partly due to oxidation of "in house" environmental pollutants, but also due to the elimination of microbial breeding grounds such as carpets and drapes.

Medical grade ozone destroys pathogenic molds, fungi, yeasts, dust mites and viruses and oxidizes (burns-up) the food supply that these organisms feed on. Cigarette odor disappears from your clothes, house and car, AND they are GOOD protection against winter illness. Every home should have one.

Ozone equipment is easy to use. However, only a very few pieces of ozone equipment on the market can produce "medical grade" ozone. Please UNDERSTAND that ozone in the WRONG form irritates the mucous membranes of the sinus cavities and lungs. Industrial grade units are superior to "home type" models commonly available. (see Source Page 384.)

### Exercise & Viruses

Aerobic exercise is crucial to long term good health. Exercise increases lymph and blood fluid circulation and raises plasma and cellular **oxygen** levels. Exercise revitalizes the body's organs by speeding **de**acidification of the tissues. **People who exercise regularly experience less sickness, too!**

Much has been written on the benefits of aerobic exercise. Recently, however, the press is parroting the idea that we don't really need aerobic exercise. A recent article read, *"The benefits of aerobic exercise have been overstated. People can get all the exercise they need cleaning the house, or walking out to dump the trash."*

Nothing could be further from the truth! This is a *disinformation* campaign at the expense of the public parroted by "experts." If people buy into the NO aerobic exercise idea, they will suffer and grow OLD! Equally bad are those who promote ***hyper*** aerobic exercise. Ignore them all. Instead, seek *moderation* and *balance* in your exercise program. ***Extreme* anything translates: *abuse!*** Good circulation is a prerequisite to good health. Blood and lymph movement reduces waste build-up in the system and creates an environment that is hostile to pathogens. A "rebounder" and a "lymph roller" greatly improve fluid and tissue waste circulation.

### Rebounding

A rebounder (see page 367) is a simple piece of health equipment. The "correct" way to use a rebounder is to stand flat footed on the mat, gently swing both arms to the front and then the rear **together** as you add a little "flex" to your knees and develop a slight "pulse" sensation in your head. Your feet should **NEVER** leave the mat. The "pulse" sensation is produced by the movement of lymphatic fluids. The body depends on MOVEMENT to circulate these fluids, where the heart "pumps" the blood. An L/CSF™ (lymph/cerebral spinal fluid) machine is far superior in every respect and can be used by elderly and bed-ridden patients, and by those who want to AVOID abusive exercise or by those with busy schedules.

Increased lymphatic circulation is helpful in restoring hair, hearing, eyesight and improving skin tone. "Movement" prevents stagnation of plasma protein wastes—particularly in the legs. Edema (water retenstion) is a SIGN of fluid stagnation. Do NOT ignore it! Edema is linked to hormones and waste. Many women "puff" prior to their period—NOT a good sign!

The head receives 40% of the blood and wastes leaving the heart. In time, the VERY fine capillaries of the scalp, eyes, and ears become clogged followed by the SIGNS of old age—balding, gray and thinning hair, wrinkles, deafness and eye problems. These SIGNS are reversible, but you must do your part if you wish to see the miracle unfold.

After "rebounding" or a L/CSF™ workout, use the Young Again™ Biogenic™ body roller to stimulate subcutaneous nerves and break-up cellulite and circulate waste so the liver can remove it from the body. **Kombucha Tea** helps **de**acidify the body and is most useful and inexpensive to make at home. Many professional football and hocky players take a gallon of it to their games for increased energy and stamina.

**Viruses & Molds On Foods**

Have you noticed the vegetables and fruits in the grocery store are growing strange molds and fungi? Molds tell a story. They are the lowest level of parasitic growth. Their color indicates the toxicity level of the "food" it is growing on. White is the least toxic, red the most toxic, green, gray, and black are in between. Fuzzy, smooth, and shiny tell a similar story.

The *experts* have been in charge of our food supply for a very long time. They have convinced the farmer to use hard chemical fertilizers, pesticides and herbicides—the latter two contain VERY potent "zeno" estrogen analogs that foul the planet and create "hormonal" complications for women and men alike. (Read *Our Stolen Future;* see Source Page 384.)

The *experts* have upset nature's balance and in so doing have brought marginal health and dis-ease upon us all. People are aging faster and are becoming subclinically sicker because we eat what the experts "call" food! These are the same *experts* whom Rachel Carson vilified in her 1959 blockbuster book, *Silent Spring.* The book is must reading if you want to better understand the nature of the dilemma we face. *Silent Spring* is more pertinent today than when it first appeared.

The fruit in the stores has little flavor because mineral

are almost non existant and the "energy footprint" of the food is SICK! Is it no wonder the people are sick, also!

The *experts* tell the farmers to use chemicals to ward off the bugs and weeds. The more they use, the stronger they come back! Nature will NOT be mocked, and mankind is paying the price.

### Weeds & Aging

Look at the weeds! They proliferate in the face of voluminous amounts of herbicides. Each year, the weeds grow bigger. They are **mutating!** They have a job to do. They are getting ready.

Leonard Ridzon is a farmer. He is close to the Earth. He is a living Wizard and one of the most original thinkers I know. He authored *The Carbon Connection* and *The Carbon Cycle.* Both are must reading.

**Ridzon has recorded ragweed over forty feet tall!** Weeds are to the soil what pathogenic life forms are to the body. They proliferate and take over. They **appear** to be the problem, but they are only reacting to changes in the "terrain"—the soil and air in this case. Their job is to protect Mother Earth and to reclaim abused soil and air with the help of the microbes. The weed's job is to **absorb** the toxic energy fields in our atmosphere and soil and make them available so the microbes can break them down and return the soil and air to a healthy state.

Weeds are not plants out of place. The proliferation of noxious weeds is no more an accident than the molds and fungi on our food or the viruses in our body. They are SIGNS. Signs give rise to the diagnosis of dis-ease. Dis-ease unchecked amounts to a death warrant. Dis-ease at the subclinical level means a population of sick people and escalating violence.

### Answers & Overview

Asking a question implies that there is an answer. But incorrect questions generate incorrect answers. There are plenty of CORRECT answers to the questions we have raised thus far, but you will not find them in the press, scientific literature or college texts. You will only find pieces—and incomplete answers. Science asks piecemeal questions—usually the wrong questions—and *pontificates* piecemeal answers.

When we use poisons against the Earth, we wage war! When we poison plants that God put on this earth and foul our air, we wage war! We are at war with every living thing on this planet—including ourselves—and we are paying the price!

Rachel Carson, author of *Silent Spring,* died shortly

after her book was released—saving her from immense hatred by those who came to hate her. She came from *within* science's camp and science proclaimed her a **witch**. They burned her at the stake for the TRUTH she heralded. They are still trying to burn her memory from our consciousness, but TRUTH does not go away. Like the Great Pyramid, it is there!

Anyone with a lick of sense knows that things are not right. The hole in the ozone layer is no accident. The hurricanes are not accidents. The floods, crop circles and crop disasters are not accidents. These things are the direct result of science and money turned to EVIL purposes—and all of the inhabitants of the Earth are paying the price.

### Mother Earth Is Vomiting

Mother Earth is deathly sick! She is vomiting her guts out. She is fighting back the only way she knows how—with viruses and bacteria, abnormal weather patterns, floods and weeds. She will overcome the arrogance of our attacks.

The abnormal pressure created by negative energy forces cause the Ozone Layer to periodically open and close. In this way, deadly energy is released into space before every living thing on the planet dies. Industrialization as we know it is incompatible with Earth. Man's toxic energy fields alter life at the *subtle*-energy level of our existence. These abnormal energies produce mutations in our children. **Earth and Her inhabitants CRY OUT—*"Dear God, we are sick!"***

**A Word from the Author.** The aging process has many pieces. Camouflaged pieces. Odd pieces. Pieces found in odd places. Pieces that fit together so precisely that when we come to understand why we age, it sometimes **appears** to be oversimplification—but it is not. TRUTH is simple, and straight is the path and narrow is the gate that leads to TRUTH. Few people find the path—**especially** "experts" in the fields of science, nutrition and medicine. They have knowledge without understanding. Follow the path of TRUTH and become *Young Again!*

**PREVIEW:** *The next chapter deals with the transfer of energy. Laying on of hands, microwave ovens, carpal Tunnel Syndrome, radiation and irradiation of food.*

---

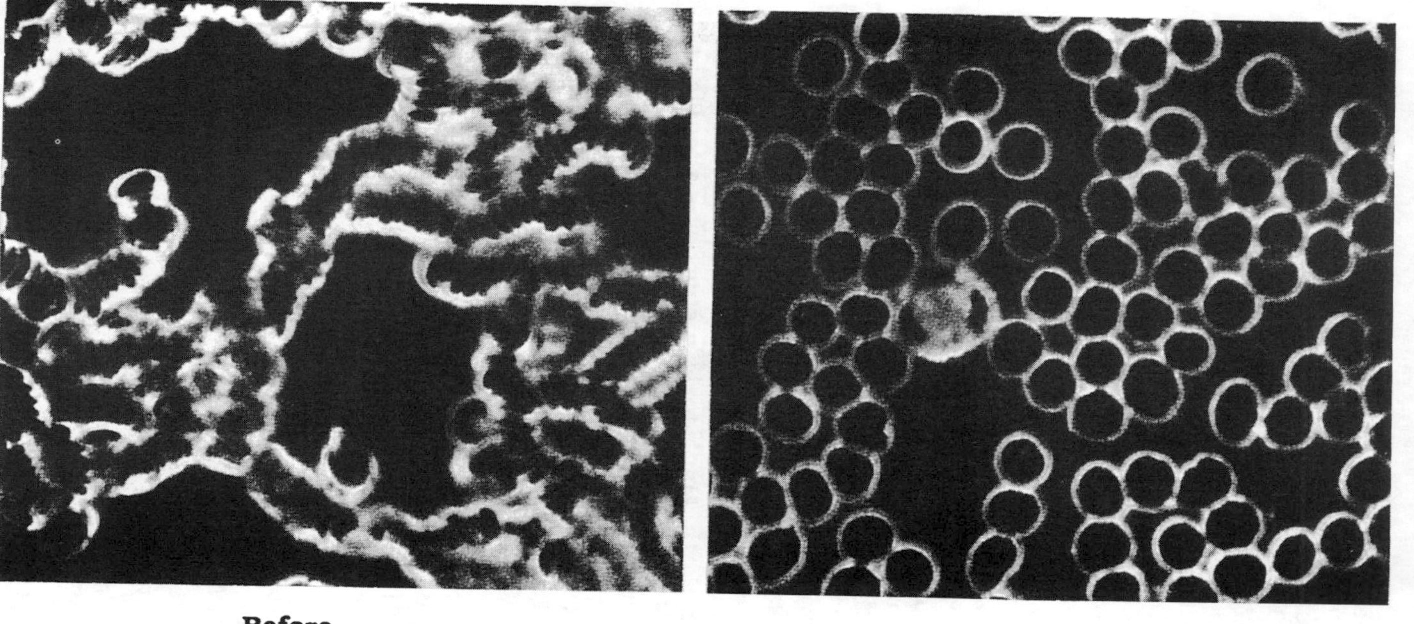

**Before** **After**

Elimination of ***Rouleau*** from *live* blood one hour after drinking water with racemized™ ionic sea minerals. "Sticky" blood looks like rolls of pennies stacked together. The effect is due to negative energy "acid" wastes in the blood. Healthy blood does not stick together and is free to access the fine capillaries of the body delivering oxygen and nutrients and removing toxic wastes. Photos are of "live" red blood corpuscles (red blood cells without a nucleus). Medical grade magnets produce a similar effect on body tissues and fluids accounting for their therapeutic effect. Taken on a Nikon Opithat microscope with a 100 watt lamp and a Naessens condenser at 15,000 magnification.

## Water Comparison

**Medical Grade Ionized Water™:** Uses BEV™ water as foundation water; ORP potential **beyond** conception point; *oxidized* type water used to treat/prevent topical skin infections, eradicate venereal infections (syphilis, herpes, warts); *reduced* type water helps reverse arthritis, diabetes, heart attack/stroke and cancer; fuels the production of mitochondrial ATP; costly to set up; cheap to operate; long term health implications beyond description; documentation available; a good investment. (See page 306.)

**BEV™ Water:** Biologically friendly to body; extremely pure water (up to 99.5% contaminant removal, including parasites, viruses, bacteria, heavy metals, radioactivity, toxic organic chemicals); flushes contaminants as it works; superb flavor; feels "silky" in mouth; conception point ORP; energizes body; uses principle of *resonance* to raise ORP potential; and principle of *transference* to raise body metabolism; hydrogen and molecular bond angle restructuring; cost per gallon about 5-10¢. No electricity needed.

**Distilled Water:** Biologically dead water; partial purification; water unfriendly to body; concentrates volatile gases (PCB^s^, THM^s^, TCE^s^, chlorine, chloramines); microbe growth problems; consumes lots of electricity; very slow; requires continuous maintenance; flat taste; negative ORP potential; water structure destroyed; diminishes body vibratory rate; zero carbon exposure time; cost per gallon approximately 50-80 cents; high parts replacement cost.

**Reverse Osmosis:** Partial purification (75-90%); quality and flavor better than distilled water; incomplete removal of bacteria, viruses, and parasites; does not provide BEV™ restructuring; okay taste; *resonance* and *transference* zero to poor; limited carbon exposure time; cost per gallon 15-20 cents; ORP below that of BEV™; wide variation in quality of water produced.

**Carbon Block/Ceramic Cartridge:** Purification fair; not self-cleaning; microbe & toxic waste build up; cost per gallon about 15-40 cents. **Ceramic Cartridge:** Marginal purification; fair taste; not self cleaning; cartridge subject to fracture and leakage; expensive; poor ORP.
**Bottled Water:** Questionable purity; expensive to use.

***"Water is MORE than wet! Water is FOOD!"***

**Hormone "Analogs"**

*Radiomimetic* chemical substances are everywhere around us. Pesticides, herbicides, plastics, food additives and dyes are good examples. These "zeno" hormones act like the real thing, but they are NOT the real thing. And once they attach to the body's receptor sites you become a prisoner unto yourself—unable to monitor and regulate your own system.

Radiomimetic chemicals *mimic* nuclear radiation. DDT is a good example of a radiomimetic free radical chemical. Chemical analogs raise holy hell in the body, and the ONLY way to free yourself and become whole again is to "polish" the receptor sites and oxidize these chemicals from the body by following the Young Again Protocol™.

Colon therapy and the Tissue & Liver program begin the process. Receptor site polishing and removal of zeno estrogens follows. Fresh juices like carrot, beet, and ginger are very important. Depending on age, sex, and state of health, other Young Again Protocols are followed.

**180° Off Course**

We are told to stay out of the sun because it causes cancer, that soy and canola are good for us, to take aspirin, that liquid foods are acceptable substitutes for water, that science's version of a balanced diet is good for us, that routine work from house cleaning to dumping the trash is as good as aerobic exercise, to not eat butter, to avoid eggs, that there is no difference between "synthesized" vitamins and those in real food, that tobacco and second hand smoke are behind the proliferation of lung cancer, to take calcium supplements to avoid osteoporosis, that red meat is bad for us, that chicken is good for us, to eat fish in lieu of both, that healthy processed foods are just as good as fresh food, that soy products are good for us, that dis-ease is the product of microbial invasion, and that genetics controls all.

None of these things are true. Follow the experts advice, and you will grow old fast and die early. All of the above is *disinformation* and *misinformation* emanating from the halls of science, medicine, and the media.

If you want proof that what I am saying is **true** and what *they* are saying is **false**, take a good look at the "experts." They are old and sick because they live the **LIE!**

# 14

## One Day At A Time

*"The highest [energy] form of hostile organisms are fungi that are always present in the tissues of a corpse, and often in the tissues of sick patients."*

Dr. Guenther Enderlein 1916

We live in a physical world and we perceive dis-ease to be a "physical" process because we can *see* and *feel* and *measure* dis-ease's EFFECT on the "physical" body. We know that the *bio-electric* body is a *composite* body—part physical, part energy. We know that dis-ease is the *manifestation* of conflicting energy fields where left-spin energy has dominance.

The conflict between energy fields occurs in the invisible world—a world that we do NOT see even though it is there. The process we call **aging** occurs in that invisible world, also. It occurs **one day at a time.**

### Laying On Of Hands

An example of *positive* energy flow between the visible and invisible is the practice of **Laying On Of Hands.** Most religions have some version of their own.

Laying On Of Hands (LOH) couples the power of prayer with the physical body. It involves the *transfer* of positive energy from *healthy* people to the body of the sick person. It is a practice that demands tremendous focus.

Laying On Of Hands can spontaneously heal the sick person. Although it is not a science, it is a religious healing ***modality*** that involves the transfer of energy!

LOH often fails to produce positive change in the sick person. No results sometimes elicits skepticism and mockery when the event should be recognized for what it is—people with good intentions trying to help an ailing fellow traveler. Few participants understand the electrical phenomena involved, but they devoutly care about their friend or loved one.

LOH is a phenomenon that involves the ***manipulation*** of electrical ENERGY. The principles involved are no different from those used when dowsing for water or using a pendulum to determine left vs. right-spin substances or measuring energy fields with an aurameter—except LOH takes place in a religious setting where "energy," intense focus and love are the controlling factors. Positive results are called *miracles.*

In the religious arena, people accept healing at face value and without explanation because the end result is beneficial to them. We must also learn to accept the benefits that derive from other energy manipulations because they, too, can be beneficial to us.

If we could heal with a **black box** that had bells and flashing lights, no one would question it. We need the same openness when considering energy phenomena and paranormal healing where the manipulation of energy, good intent and focus are involved, be it in a church, a hospital or in the presence of a healer.

An example of the **exact opposite** of energy used for good purposes is "black magic," only here, energy is used for EVIL purposes. Sticking pins in dolls should not be dismissed. It is good example of "dark side" manipulation of "energy."

## Therapeutic Touch

The phenomenon known as *therapeutic touch* is used in nursing. It is similar to LOH and is taught in nursing schools and practiced by cutting edge nurses.

Touch is our most highly developed sense. A baby's response to touch is indisputable. Combine touch with loving care and a nurse can "open" congested energy centers in the body and redirect the flow of energy to promote healing.

First, the nurse assesses the person's energy state using *gut* instinct and by "reading" energy auras. The nurse then opens the body's energy meridians so ***Chi*** can flow. Chi is what the Chinese call the **force** of life. It is also spelled Qi. Therapeutic Touch heals! Think of someone in whose presence you feel loved and whose touch—a hand, a hug—can make you feel safe, healed and free of fear. Both parties must "focus" their mental and spiritual energies for healing to occur. Disbelief, negative thinking or contempt can BLOCK energy flow.

We are talking about the use of ENERGY manipulation in healing. Science pronounces it quackery, but it has practical value to vibrational healers. Therapeutic touch, dowsing, LOH, use of a pendulum or vibration chain, magnetic therapy and Network Chiropractic are facets of the phenomenon.

**Manipulation of energy for good purposes can be a good thing. Learning when, where and how to use the skill is another. "Gut" instinct is the healer's compass.**

### Energy Abuse

The proliferation of *negative* electrical energy pollution is a serious problem. Electrical pollution has subtle effects and disastrous consequences on people's health.

Consider the microwave oven. It is very popular throughout the USA and the industrialized world. I remember when it first appeared on the scene. A lot of fluff and excitement accompanied its introduction to an unsuspecting public. It was touted as *the* answer for the mother on the run and the conservation of energy. We were told of its "health" benefits!

Oh, how I remember the power companies making their case for the marvelous benefits of *microwave age* cooking. Where I lived, they even assigned an "expert" to assist people in the transition from the old way of cooking to the new. Microwave recipes appeared in the *food tips* bulletin that accompanied the power bill.

### Few People Questioned

Few people questioned the idea of the microwave oven—except the usual "cranks," and everyone already knew they were nuts. Objections were ignored.

Microwave ovens initially made their way into the schools and government operations in the name of *efficiency*. They soon appeared in restaurants across the country. Owners and cooks alike loved them because they were so *people-friendly*. Food and plates would be piping hot when served. Preparation became easier too.

Today, you are considered in the stone age if you do not own and use a microwave oven. These *electrical* appliances are now considered a necessity for people on the run. People love them because they equate nourishment with a hot meal.

Microwave cooked food is neither alive nor life supporting. It should be avoided because of its NEGATIVE effects on the body's energy fields. Its effects are the exact OPPOSITE of homeopathic principles used to heal sick bodies. **Avoiding** the use of a microwave oven is something over which we have TOTAL control—if we choose to exercise it!

### Effects Of The Microwave

Microwave ovens produce left-spinning energy frequencies. They are dangerous to people and children who are in the same room. They ZAP the immune system. They are DEADLY to your nutritional health!

Microwave energy destroys food enzymes by altering their molecular structure. These devices produce energy frequencies that are ***anti-life*** and incompatible with living things. When healthy people are exposed to **freak** energy frequencies, they become *subclinically* ill and suffer from symptoms often described as "syndromes." It is a serious form of STRESS that accelerates aging by altering body rhythms and enzymes.

Enzymes make life possible! In their natural state, food enzymes are right-spin energy. The body uses them to build and repair tissue (anabolism). But when microwaves *zap* living molecules, they become scrambled and useless and biochemical reactions FAIL to occur and aging accelerates. The effect of scrambled enzymes is **catabolic!** Use of racemized™ digestive enzymes like DiSorb Aid™ and R/BHCI™ helps tremendously. Adequate hydration and **thorough** "chewing" of food produces heavy saliva secretion. Avoid liquids with meals.

### Two Seconds

Food cooked in a microwave oven for as little as two seconds takes on the pall of death. When eaten, the body attempts to these process and **neutralize** "freak" energy molecules before the body can get on with the business of life and health which we call ***anabolism.***

All microwave ovens leak energy despite opinions to the contrary from the "experts." Microwave energy is, of course, *invisible;* and it alters body frequency in the *invisible* realm. When you eat microwaved food—and water—the homeopathic principles of *resonance* and *transference* drive down the *life force* to such a low energy state that the "food" draws-down energy reserves and weakens us.

### Microwaved Blood

Microwave ENERGY destroys the structure of the water molecule—turning what should be a life giving substance into something antagonist to life. Microwaved water denatures enzymes in the blood since blood is 90% water. It also stresses the immune system via the lymphatic fluids.

*It was reported that in a hospital in Oklahoma, a nurse used a microwave oven to warm blood. When the blood was given to the patient—he died! Blood is a living substance. As little as two seconds in a microwave is all it takes to destroy the life force in blood. I doubt any "expert" will use microwaved blood to prove this statement wrong!*

### Police • Carpal Tunnel Syndrome

Lawsuits have been filed throughout the country by policemen who used RADAR guns for traffic control. No one told them of the cancer causing effects of *microwave* energy fields. Eye cataract formation and joint and connective tissue disorders are a predictable outcome of microwave exposure. Microwave created degenerative dis-ease has MANY faces that take form in the invisible realm—quietly and slowly.

*Do not expect the courts to protect people from microwave devices. Doing so means biting the hand of powerful interests. Faceless experts with* ***credentials*** *can always be brought forth to testify that there is "no scientific evidence!"*

Carpal Tunnel Syndrome ( CTS) is a big problem for tens of thousands of people. Repetitive activity is often blamed as the controlling factor. Yet, whenever microwave radiation is present, the problem becomes exaggerated. That is why CTS is especially prevalent among supermarket checkers and computer operators—people that are exposed to small but continuous amounts of microwave energy.

Microwaves antagonize nerve fibers and connective tissues (bones, gums, ligaments, tendons, muscles and cartilage). Some people are affected more than others and develop "syndromes." We are concerned with the LONG TERM effects of microwave energy. Short term effects are hard to measure and provide the *experts* with a cover.

### Computer Terminals

We hear little about computer induced health problems—except for eye strain. But have you noticed how you feel after several hours in front of one? Tired! ***Drained*** is a better word. Computer operators often have carpal tunnel syndrome and immune system problems. A Biogenic™ Super Magnet™ worn around the neck and over the thymus gland provides protection and is very beneficial. (See pages 233 & 384).

Super Magnets™ protect you from the effects of 110v,

60 cycle alternating current. Super Magnets™ are 12,000 gauss "permanent" fields of DC energy that neutralize the insidious effects coming from fluorescent lights, TV and computer terminals. Screen filters help with glare and screen radiation, **but they do NOT block the energy field.** The source of errant energy is the electric motor in the unit.

Like microwave radiation, not everyone experiences the same problems from exposure to alternating current energy fields—at least not in the beginning. For most people, the effects are *subtle* and *slow* to manifest. When the *bio-electric* body can't take any more, SIGNS of dis-ease magically appear out of nowhere and the doctor provides the diagnosis.

Symptoms of electromagnetic pollution are usually *sub*clinical. Degeneration occurs quietly and slowly—under cover—until dis-ease announces itself. In the meantime, life comes under a cloud of symptoms, low energy, sleep disorders, mental lethargy and marginal existance.

*[I am wearing a Super Magnet to protect my vital organs and immune system while I process these words. I sleep on a medical grade magnetic mattress pad and use a magnetic pillow. Women use Super Magnets to ease menstrual pain by taping them over the ovaries (front and rear). Cancer and Alzheimers patients sleep better. Sinus problems and head cold congestion also respond well (see Source Page)].*

## FOOD: Radiation & *Irradiation*

The word "radiation" paints the picture of energy radiating outward from a central point—like light from a light bulb, but it also describes energy as a **"substance"** and as a condition or state of being.

*Fission* energy is *radiation* that comes from nuclear devices or their radioactive wastes. Fission energy does violence to living tissues and speeds the aging process.

People are afraid of fission (nuclear) energy for good reason. Fission energy *ionizes* living molecules. Another word for ionization is *scramble. Scrambling* of living molecules makes life impossible and produces suffering.

***Irradiation*** is another term often touted in the media. It describes the *act* of applying *ionizing* radiation to living things. It also **infers** that energy is "substance" and therefore MUST have a "footprint." In the case of food irradiation, negative ionizing energy scrambles food energy molecules making them worthless. Eat irradiated food and you will grow old and die early. Radioactive isotopes and waste products from the nuclear industry are the source of the *fission* energy that is used to "irradiate" America's food supply.

The word "irradiation" is a *bastard* term. It has little meaning, and it confuses people who are not wise in the ways of crafty wordsmiths. It is a *quasi-scientific* term used to disguise a lie and distort TRUTH.

Irradiation focuses on the *act* involved, rather than on the *effect* the *act* produces. People think nuclear when they hear ***radiation.*** When they hear ***irradiation*** they don't know what to think. In the public eye, *irradiation* does NOT mean the same thing as *radiation.* The word irradiation is neither black nor white. Rather, it is *grey!*

The wise person avoids microwave radiation, refuses to eat "freak" food and avoids subjecting their body to the effects of 110 volt, 60 cycle alternating current energy radiating from computer terminals and fluorescent lights. In the book *Vibrations* (see Source Page 384), Owen Lehto offers his readers practical ways to "neutralize" a home at the power panel. Everyone should take a **defensive** posture on this subject if they want to live a long and healthy life.

Irradiated food has NOTHING to offer the *bio-electric* body. For certain, it diminishes vital force, so why eat "things" and do "things" that promote slow suicide.

**Radiation • Irradiation • Genetically Engineered Food**

The term "genetically engineered" is a **new** synonym for irradiation. It is acceptable to the public because it sounds scientific and does not hint of "radiation." In future chapters on hair loss, balding and blindness, you will learn that genetically engineered food is no different than irradiated food. Both are sources of FREAK energy.

The **experts** talk of the wonders of food preservation through *irradiation.* They talk of bacterial contamination of food and water from microbes like E. coli 0158.H7 and Cryptosporidium and scare us with bogie man stories. What they forget to mention are the *real* reasons behind the drive to irradiate America's food. They *know* that chemically grown food has poor shelf life and must be ***treated*** to keep it from spoiling on the store shelves, so they give us the"industry's" version of a **forever** shelf life. Eat their processed food and you will experience the **graveyard** version of forever.

Irradiated food has a "forever" shelf life. Whatever *living* enzyme molecules the food may have had are destroyed during *irradiation.* And the **proof** is that the bugs and microbes will NOT eat food whose molecules have been *scrambled.* They can "read" the energy signals given off by left-spin foodstuffs. Insects and microbes follow their instincts. People do not.

**Don't buy *irradiated* food. Don't eat *microwaved***

**food. Learn to use a pendulum, vibration chain and brix meter to check the food BEFORE you buy and eat it! Developing your defense skills is a matter of "survival" in a hostile world. Count on it!**

## Measuring Energy Fields

It is easy to verify the presence of stray energy fields emanating from electrical appliances and equipment. The following method measures *SOME* negative energy frequencies, but there are many.

For example, connect a radio to a long extension cord and locate a spot on the dial *between* two stations that is *silent*. Next, turn-up the volume to maximum, and with the radio held in front of you, approach your computer monitor, TV or microwave oven. When the radio begins to buzz, you have entered that device's *field of electrical influence*. Remember, you are only measuring SOME of the stray frequencies. Our concern is the *length* of time spent in the negative energy force field as well as the *strength* of the field.

When using 110 v alternating current electrical devices like a computer, stay ***beyond*** its "field" and wear a Super Magnet™. The EFFECTS of these anti-life energy fields are subtle—like the effects of microwaved food on health. Their short term effects go unnoticed, but they do rob us of LONG TERM health and vitality and ultimately our life!

**Alternating current energy fields have an extremely invasive "presence" because they surround us "24/7."**

A two inch thick slab of LEAD can block nuclear radiation, YET it **cannot** stop 110v energy fields from damaging the body. *Never* use an electric blanket. If you are cold, solve the problem with some exercise, rebounding, BT™ Thyroid Creme, a hot bath or a cup of Yucca Blend™ herbal tea.

## Medicine & Radiation

*Radiation* therapy and *radioactive chemo*therapy used in the treatment of cancer are devastating to the body. The public believes allopathic medicine's propaganda and forms a line at the medical clinic. People are confused and fail to differentiate between diagnostic X-rays and the overkill effect of radiation therapy. Radiation is not a "therapy" because it is anti-life. It is ***palliative*** (treatment of signs and symptoms without cure of the underlying dis-ease). Patients are taught to focus on HOPE of cure instead being told of the violence *ionizing* radiation inflicts upon the body. Likewise, we are TRAINED to "welcome" *irradiation* of our food instead of being told of the plethora of symptomatic complaints, dis-eases and death that follow in the wake of "poor choices."

**Ask The Experts**

If the things we are discussing regarding microwave radiation, irradiated food and genetic engineering are true, why are the *experts* not telling you about it?

The answer is because these areas of risk are NOT being funded for study by the *experts*. The corporate and government GRANT SYSTEM is not about to study anything that might quash the two biggest monopolies in history: electrical power generation and the pharmaceutical industry of which allopathic medicine is a part. **It is up to you to protect yourself.**

Ignorance is a lame excuse, and it most certainly will NOT keep you young. Aging is the TOTAL of all the *negative* influences in your life. You become young the opposite way that you grow old. You become *Young Again!* one day at a time.

**PREVIEW:** *Our next chapter looks at wrinkled skin—WHY it occurs and WHAT you can do about it. It also discusses body odor as it relates to aging.*

**Sex Drive • Male • Female**

Loss of sex drive indicates deterioration and atrophy of the internal vital organs. The problem is systemic, and goes *beyond* just sexual malaise and should be seen for what it represents.

Conditions like obesity, skin disorders, thinning hair and balding, thinning of the vaginal wall resulting in painful sex and "dryness", yeast infections, bowel disorders, digestion problems in general and acid reflux in particular, sagging facial tissue, diminished muscle mass and wrinkles are "first cousins" to low sex drive. Impotence in men is a dead give away that **prostate** trouble is on the way along with **diabetes** that will one day announce itself. Behind all of these health complaints are "terrain" and hormonal issues.

To restore health and sex drive, the reader should juice and follow the Young Again Protocols™. Liver function absolutely MUST be restored. Thyroid function in women must be addressed. Finally, the puberty "window" must be reopened. Once the "terrain" is deacidified and the hormone cycle is restored, the symptoms of old age fade away. (See page 72, 164, 212 and 384.)

**Protocols includes:** Juicing, colonics, Tissue and Liver program, male or female hormone programs, Women's Comfort™, Cobo-12™ and B.T. Thyroid Creme™.

**Understanding Diabetes**

Diabetes plagues millions of people in industrial societies. Yet, in third world countries—where people eat traditional diets—the incidence of diabetes is very low.

Medical science blames genetics for the rise in diabetes. They are wrong. The problem is fivefold and **genetics is NOT one of them.**

Diabetes is the product of toxic **excesses** within the system, loss of the gallbladder, hormonal imbalance, IMMUNIZATIONS and a generous dose of leaky gut syndrome.

Diabetes is **proof** of vital organ **stress** and hormone imbalance. DHEA production drops off beginning at age 24 and is soon followed by a drop in progesterone production. As hormone production slows, metabolism slows and **excesses** accumulate in the system.

Type II diabetes is the most common type. It occurs between ages 35 and 50. **These are the years** when women AND men *ease* their way into old age and the window that **opened** at puberty officially CLOSES. The hair thins, energy slips, sex drive falls, fat accumulates, cancers manifest, thyroid symptoms exaggerate, nerve deterioration proliferates, skin wrinkles and muscle turns to flab.

Type I diabetes (AKA "juvenile diabetes") is a *severe* condition where the child's immune system attacks the pancreas cells responsible for insulin production. It is an *"autoimmune"* condition brought on by the introduction of **SUPER antigens** into the body. A superantigen is a foreign protein that makes the immune system go crazy.

DPT (diphtheria, pertussis, tetanus) and polio vaccines contain **SUPER antigens** that bring on Type 1 diabetes, autism and deafness. These children suffer from ***mutant*** SUPER antigens in their poor little bodies!

*Associated Press* recently confirmed that *attenuated* strains of the polio virus ***"can and do mutate once inside the body!"*** And so do hepatitis B, DPT, and flu vaccines! AVOID VACCINATIONS AT ALL COST!

Loss of the gall bladder is a 99% guarantee of diabetes within 20 years—**unless** the person takes protective measures against it. Worse, 10 women to every man suffers gallbladder surgery. Sadly, these ladies continue to have the same complaints after the surgery. Worse, 8 out of 10 women did NOT need the surgery in the first place. Gall bladder surgery is very BIG business. The Young Again Protocol™ remedies the need. It's a matter of choice.

Many children become diabetics at **puberty** due to stress on the liver. Acne is a "liver" issue. Children and teen health issues are both avoided and remedied through active participation in the Young Again Protocols™.

***"The TERRAIN is the issue!"***

## Biogenic™ Skin & Body Toner

Look in the mirror. Do you see sagging skin hanging from your arms and jaw line? Are you sporting "Howdie Doodie" lines from the corners of your mouth to the sides of your chin? Are those tell tale lines forming on your upper lip? And do you see crows feet around your eyes?

And what about your torso? Does it bear excess fat or cellulite? Has muscle mass given way to flab? Do you have a pot belly or saddle bags on your hips? Drooping breasts? Do you remember when your body was younger?

When you were developing in your mother's womb, you were fed a steady supply of "**ante**genic" protein and balanced hormones. **Ante**genic protein is very special stuff that normally is only available to the unborn. The body uses antegenic protein to grow "new" cells, tissues and organs—like heart, brain, bones, muscle, liver, skin, etc.

When racemized™ **ante**genic protein is supplied to aging adults, the body transforms itself into a more youthful appearance—like when **you** were young. The combined effect of Biogenic Skin & Body Toner™ & Biogenic™ hGH is dramatic, but it's the long term **cumulative** effects we are after.

Central to the aging reversal process is a healthy liver and a non-acid "terrain." Fresh veggi juice and colonic are fundamentals if you want your "wish" (see Source Page 384).

## Prostatitis • Thyroid • Sex

Behind prostatitis, thyroid issues and loss of sex drive are liver and bowel issues. Prostate issues in men are the equivalent of thyroid issues in women. Loss of sex drive and thinning of the vaginal wall come are common. The Young Again Protocol™ provides answers for these problems. Don't allow them to cheat you of your life (see Source Page 384).

## Smoke-Out™

Why put up with the effects of second hand smoke—be at home or at the office—or carbon monoxide fumes from automobiles when you are stuck in traffic and can't avoid them? Now you can **remove the residues** of these airborne pollutants and carcinogens from your body tissues with Smoke-Out™. Works equally well for children and adults, alike.

## Bleeding Gums • Periodontal Disease

The Bio-Magnetic™ dental irrigator solves problems like gingivitis, bleeding gums, periodontal dis-ease and the need for constant teeth cleaning. This simple appliance **transforms** water molecules into an effective dental modality, and goes far beyond a "Pic" type devices which are nothing but a fancy squit guns. See pages 79, 204 & 384.

**Stool Analysis**

**Bear Poop**-the "ideal" stool should resemble a pile of mush and should pass in 2-3 seconds. Sit down, stand up, its over. **Maximum** transit time from mouth to toilet should be: 12 hours.

**Normal Stool (so called)**—formed stool; medium brown color; easy passage; little taper; ends with gas pocket.

**Floaters**—stools that float in the toilet. Indicative of poor fat metabolism; poor bile flow; poor digestion.

**Stringers**—stringy stools that are both narrow and fat. Indicative of a spastic and kinked colon, poor muscle tone in colon wall; high stress personality; negative thinking; poor bile flow.

**Pelleted Stool**—Indicates slow transit time; poor bile flow; under-hydration; poor diet; inadequate fiber and/or lack of rhythm in life and bowel habits.

**Pale Colored Stools**—Indicative of liver malfunction, poor bile flow, viral activity (white stools are seen with hepatitis). Stools should be medium brown.

**Bloody Stools**—Indicative of hemorrhoids, diverticulitis; colitis, irritable bowel and leaky gut syndromes; under hydration; stressful life or personality.

**Dark Colored Stools**—Sluggish gut and bowel; old blood from ulcers and colitis; under-hydration; dietary influence of prunes, beet juice, and greens.

**Fat Headed Stools w/Tapered End**—"Pooling" at rectum; under-hydration; ignoring nature's call; lack of fiber and exercise; incomplete evacuation; poor bile flow.

**Complete Stool Evacuation**—characteristics of "bear poop" stool with nothing *held back*. Bowel movement often ends with distinctive pocket of gas.

**NOTE:** Drink 1 gallon of water daily to improve your "poop" characteristics. Drink **one quart** of water with a freshly squeezed lemon immediately upon rising, a glass of water with racemized™ sea minerals at each urination. Take one tablespoon of Yucca Blend™ 2X daily. Eat fresh veggies and dried prunes. Do colon therapy 2-3 times weekly. Drink a large glass of beet, carrot and ginger juice daily, preferably for breakfast. Get some exercise.

# 15

## Grandma's Lye Soap

*"Oh, little Herman and brother Therman,*
*Had an aversion to washing their ears.*
*Grandma scrubbed them with lye soap,*
*And they haven't heard a word in years."*
Dr. Roger Lent

The **integument** (skin) is the largest organ of the body in surface area. It includes the **hair** and **nails**, and it is one of FOUR exit portals for the elimination of toxic wastes.

Like its siblings—the bowel, kidneys and lungs—a functioning integument helps prevent the build-up of acid wastes that would otherwise take the form of acne, psoriasis, wrinkles, skin ulcers and boils—just to name a few. The skin is the body's first line of defense against dis-ease. When the skin becomes stressed, regardless of the underlying cause, dis-ease soon follows in the wake.

The skin functions much like the lungs. It breathes. It absorbs. The skin **releases** wastes through **perspiration**, secretion of **oil** and **fats**, and the growth of **hair** and **nails**. The blood and lymphatic fluids provide the moisture given off as sweat. Sebaceous glands secrete oil and fats.

Waste that cannot escape through the skin become trapped in the **dermis** (surface layers of skin) and **subcutane-**

**ous** tissues (below the dermis) and eventually appear as acne or blemishes and pave the way for wrinkle and sag.

The body stores metabolic waste in the fat layer **under** the skin, in the joints and in the "soft" tissues causing them to calcify, lose their elasticity and break down. Wrinkled skin, sagging facial tissues and sagging breasts are examples of collagen, elastin and reticular fiber deterioration. Joint pain, inflammation, immobility, arthritis, and feet problems are examples of an acid "terrain" and deterioration.

Collagen comprises about 30% of the connective tissues (skin, bones, ligaments, muscles, gums, tendons and cartilage). Collagen omprises about 90% of the body, including the bone's **matrix** which is filled with minerals.

**Connective tissue can be restored and scar tissue can be dissolved by using *racemized*™ carbon and sulphur "sulfhydryls" as found in SOC™.**

Accumulation of **acidic** body wastes promotes **calcification** of the tissues. Osteoarthritis involves calcification of the joints; tuberculosis involves calcification of the lungs; cancer tumors often calcify as the body's way of **isolating** highly toxic energy and rendering the tumor moot.

Aging involves the build-up of acid wastes in the fluids that circulate BETWEEN the cells within the soft tissues. These **extracellular** fluids are called "lymph" fluid. **Extra**cellular fluid is not the same as **intra**cellular fluid which is found **inside** the cells. We will discuss both in more detail later.

### Waste • Hormones • Slowdown

DHEA, pregnenolone and melatonin are some of the "magic bullet" **SYNTHETIC** hormone analogs available over the counter. No one tells the public that there is **"NO"** difference between "them" and anabolic steroids, birth control pills and estrogen replacements. Avoid them because they "lock-up" the receptor sites in the body and prevent regulatory centers in the brain (hypothalamus, pituitary and pineal) from doing their job. Worse, these analogs have a "forever" life and don't break down. Marketing claims of *natural* are **bogus!** Crafty chemists have moved the "—R" group on the molecule so they can "patent" it. The real stuff cannot be patented. **REAL** DHEA is made in the body by the adrenals, and its production slows beginning at age 24 followed by other hormones like progesterone, pregnenolone and melatonin.

In women, thyroid **malaise** is a given; and after age 40, thyroid function simply crashes. Blood and lab tests will never confirm "malaise," but the symptoms are easy to spot and easy to remedy with B.T. Throid Creme™—a racemized™ transdermal product that is the real McCoy and **NOT** analogous. Symptoms of thyroid malaise are: cold hands and feet, increase in fat, falling and graying hair, memory complaints (brain fog), low energy and sagging and wrinkling skin.

Once analogous hormones attach to your receptor sites, you become a prisoner in your own body. The Young Again Hormone Protocol™ is designed to clear hormone analogs from the body. Please refer to pages 72 and 384.

**The following conditions are hormone related RED FLAGS for women: thyroid dysfunction, fat, thinning hair, yeast/bladder infections, depression, diminished sex drive and deterioration of the skin and joints.**

## Skin & Scar Tissue

There are only TWO classes of tissue: healthy **functional** tissue and **scar** tissue. The body builds scar tissue in response to trauma and the inability to produce new, healthy tissue. Scar tissue can be internal or external. When biologically active carbon and sulphur are in **short** supply, the body is unable to build strong, healthy tissue which is why I highly recommend the use of SOC™ capsules. They are VERY rich in racemized™ **carbon** and **sulfur** "sulfhydryls"—and helpful for anyone with arthritis, weak joints, cartilage degeneration, nerve disorders and heavy metal toxicity.

Wrinkled skin, thinning and graying hair and arthritic joints are hardly signs of youth and vitality. They are symptoms of deterioration and metabolic slow-down, build-up of tissue waste and exhaustion of cobalt-12.

Wrinkles bother people who want to look young. The beauty industry tries the "mud against the wall" approach by putting collagen in their products, but topical collagen is NOT the answer, nor is condroitin or glucosamine.

## Movie Stars • Skin • Hair

As we age, outer skin layers become tightly bonded, stiff and leathery. Cracking and bleeding occurs on the chafe points as conditions worsen—especially with the elderly.

Movie stars resort to face lifts to remedy their wrinkles. They understand that a young face pulls better at the box office. The stars also understand that the "younger" you look and feel the longer you will be a movie star.

Face lifts help, but they are very expensive and they do NOT solve the problem. Your author's vanity secrets are simple. Fresh carrot, beet, and ginger root juice, colon therapy, SOC™ lotion and Racemized™ Skin Creme. SOC™ lotion softens outer skin layers and increases capillary blood flow **beneath** the skin in the fat layer. It also dissolves scar tissue and clears skin blemishes while R/Skin Creme™ encourages the body to lay down "new" skin.

When SOC™ lotion and R/Skin Creme™ are used regularly, the skin becomes unbelievably soft, wrinkles fade and the face takes on a healthy glow that people love. These products are **food** for the skin—NOT cosmetics. I use them religiously and my skin is 58 years YOUNG. Their combined effect is **awesome!** Another personal secret for no gray, full color, thick hair is Kombucha tea and $GH_3$+. Colon therapy and tissue and liver purges are a crucial part of the story because they **de**acidify the tissues.

**Society is strongly biased AGAINST the aged. People who look and feel young enjoy a big advantage!**

### Urine & Your Face

The term **acid** is a chemical term. An acid is a hydrogen donor. Natural vinegar contains natural organic acids that taste sour. Natural acids like those in raw apple cider vinegar and Kombucha tea, lemons and sauerkraut rejuvenate the body through **de**acidification **despite** the fact that they are acid in nature. These foods help us to be **LESS ACID** not more alkaline. There is a world of difference between the two.

Natural acids heal. Urine contains acids that beautify the skin. Some Scandinavian women wash their face in their urine because the **uric acid** in it keeps the skin smooth and young looking. Some people drink their urine to rid themselves of cancer and heal their bodies of dis-ease.

The body's ability to produce STRONG digestive and absorptive enzymes diminishes rapidly after age 30. Digestive issues are always linked to poor liver function and leaky gut syndrome. Inadequate protein metabolism increases protein metabolites in the urine. As the body grows older, it cannibalizes its own tissues through "auto" digestion in an effort to meet its protein needs. Cancer patients and starving people are classic examples of this sad condition. Vegans and vegetarians suffer a modified version of the problem.

Poorly digested food fuels uric acid levels and the growth of parasites. Poor digestion is a **BIG** issue. There are many good digestive products available. Your author relies on a combination of DiSorb Aid™, R/BHCI™ and Yucca Blend™.

Digestion of proteins is done by breaking of the peptide bonds in the stomach in a HIGHLY **acidic** environment. The balance of digestion and the absorption of food energy occurs in the small intestine (gut). After age 30, *intrinsic factor* production collapses and absorption of vitamin B-12 drops-off, **regardless** of how much is in the diet. The Young Again Protocol™ calls for the use of Cobo-12™ cobalt, metabolite creme applied to the skin. Oral B-12 is useless. Vegans and vegetarians (especially females) are **forever** "at risk" for anemia.

### Rich Man's Dis-ease

People who eat **too much** animal protein and who have poor digestive systems, often suffer with gout. Historically, gout was known as a **rich man's dis-ease.** The rich suffered from inflammation of the feet, toes and hands because they overloaded their systems with too much animal protein which produced excess uric acid waste. Waste stresses the system and causes the **liver** to form STONES which block the flow of bile. Bile is both a fat emulsifier and the **vehicle** by which the body rids itself of 75% of its wastes.

Social pressure makes it difficult for people to maintain a healthy lifestyle, and the wealthier you are the more difficult it is. Alcohol and late evening meals of animal protein bring on gout. Eating HIGH on the hog is a carryover *cliche* from centuries past. Rich food overloads the body with **purines** (protein waste molecules from nitrogen rich meat, fish and fowl) and overworks the kidneys causing a sharp rise in **excess** blood and tissue uric acid levels. Excess fuels aging!

**Excess** uric acid in the blood and lymph combines with alkaline mineral bases like calcium and forms salt crystals. Waste crystals settle in the joints of the toes and extremities and cause inflammation and misery. Gout is a classic SIGN of old age. Gout medications treat only the symptoms and fail to address the issues behind the manifestation of gout. Palliation is the word that best describes science's approach to gout. No one tells the patient that gout medication destroys the liver. **Patients are often more concerned about who is paying the bill (insurance) than long term loss of their health. Dumb!**

In the past, gout was not a problem for middle class and poor people who traditionally did hard, physical, load-bearing work. A sedentary lifestyle belonged to the domain of the wealthy. Today with the advent of the "service" society and the computer, **sedentary** life styles are epidemic. Wealth and opulence are no longer gout's domain. The middle class and poor also share in the misery.

**Precipitates** like uric acid crystals, gall, liver and kidney stones and bone spurs are ABNORMAL. They are SIGNS of aging. The body does not handle *precipitates* well. It expresses its dissatisfaction with *inflammation* and *pain.*

In the case of **gall stones**, death occurs if a duct becomes blocked and the stone is not removed within 24 hours. Systemic shock follows waste accumulation from a blocked duct resulting in "toxemia" (*tox*-toxic; *emia*-of the blood). Toxemia is the pregnant woman's ultimate threat!

Poor quality drinking water compounds the problems elucidated thus far. Tap water is full of toxic chemicals and useless minerals.

*[Grandma mixed and heated animal fats with lye (sodium hydroxide) and got lye soap through the process of* ***saponification****. But when her soap was used in* ***hard mineral tap water,*** *she got soap scum in the tub. The scum comes from a reaction between the soap and the hard minerals in the water. This is called "precipitation." The scum settles out of the solution. Precipitation of dietary oils like soy and canola oils mixed with waste produce similar effects in the blood and lymph.]*

Clogged and hardened arteries (**athero**sclerosis and **arterio**sclerosis) are filled with "plaque" like the scum in grandma's tub. Plaques are a combination of chlorine, fluoride, chlor*amines*, oils and fats, metabolic waste and minerals.

**Plaque formation** in the arteries is a SIGN of impending trouble. It's also the product of a careless lifestyle and poor dietary choices. Soy and canola oils play a crucial role in plaque formation and clogging of the fine capillaries. We will discuss these devilish oils in great detail in future chapters.

## Calcium & Fats

Despite medical opinions to the contrary, elemental calcium and magnesium pill supplements, taken for arthritis and osteoporosis, are **worthless!** They fail to solve the problem and they create new and different ones in the process. Doctors prescribe them because they **think** calcium is deficient, especially in females above age 40 where osteoporosis manifests. They try to to FORCE the body to accept minerals in elemental form, that is, minerals that have not gone through the carbon cycle (more later). Elemental minerals precipitate OUT of body fluids and join with other metabolic wastes to form plaque in the arteries and bone spurs. When taken with meals, elemental mineral forms upset the stomach environment, shutting down the digestion of proteins. Proteins **MUST** have their peptide bonds broken in the stomach or they are **not** processed and assimilated downline in the intestine. Unprocessed proteins **rot** in the gut, **poison** the body and **feed** the parasites. Eventually, **leaky gut syndrome** develops.

Loss of bone mass is called **osteoporosis**. It is particularly prevalent among WOMEN. **It is considered a problem for**

**post menopausal women, but ACTUAL onset begins in the "pre" menopause years (25-40).**

For women, the early "symptoms" of menopause are: fat/cellulite, thyroid troubles, low energy, depression, mood swings, PMS, painful periods, swelling, bloating, excess gas, bowel problems, mental confusion, yeast/bladder infections, arthritis, cysts on ovaries, tender breasts, vaginal infections, loss of sex drive, fibroid tumors, thinning/graying hair, etc. These symptoms appear years ahead of the ceasing of the "menses," therefore, "regular" periods often mislead women.

In other words, these symptoms signal that the window that opened at puberty and changed a little girl into a woman is beginning to close. This process is not "medically" acknowledged until menopause manifests. In the meantime, women suffer and see their life and their beauty and joy slip away.

The good news is that there is **no justifiable reason** for women (or men) to hormonally slow down and grow old. The process is reversable and the puberty window can be reopened. The middle years between puberty and menopause can be extended indefinitely. Please review page 72 in detail, as it provides a clue about how the Young Again Hormone Protocol™ teaches women **HOW** to measure and map their **hormone cycle** so aging can be reversed and youth can return.

## Body Odor

Body odor (BO) is a **symptom** of a *polluted* body. BO is experienced when toxic wastes build up to the point that they spill over into the subcutaneous tissues and feed the bacteria that live on those wastes. BO is more than socially offensive. It is the **shadow** of old age. When you smell BO, you are smelling toxic aromatic molecules evaporating from the body.

We first become aware of body odor at puberty. It is usually related to hormonal activity and increased **STRESS** imposed on the **liver**—the same stress that occurs at menopause. The liver is **central** to every function in the body, and especially to hormonal issues.

In adults, teens and children, BO signals tissue acidification liver and bowel issues, slow-down in vital organ function and hormonal imbalance. The stronger the BO, the more toxic the person. **Strong BO should not be ignored!**

You do NOT have to be old to have foul body odor. If you are *old in body* and *young in years*, you will have strong BO. If you are old in years and old in body, the odor will overpower the best of deodorants. A healthy, clean body has little, if any, BO.

Children have a good sense of smell. They are quick to detect toxins escaping from their grandpa's or grandma's body.

They are smelling old age! Take note of older people's skin, color, pallor and lack of vitality. These things paint an unfortunate and sorry picture as to why BO is often strong among sick and older people. Children smell sweet and fresh because they are YOUNG in years; for sure in body. BO is symptomatic of *catabolic* activity. People with potent BO can shower five times a day with grandma's lye soap, use the best of deodorants and get zero results. BO "oozes" from the body as fast as it is washed off. ***The problem is internal.***

The quickest way I know to rid a body of BO is by following the Young Again Colon and Tissue and Liver Protocols™. there was a time when your author believed like the rest of the world that the waste we want to dislodge from the body is stored in the liver and colon. **Wrong!**

Acid waste is stored in the **"fat layer"** under the skin. The Young Again Protocol™ helps the body to **safely** release and transport those wastes through the system and down the toilet. Only then do "you" get out of jail and the aging reversal process begins in earnest.

As the "terrain" of the body changes, so do the life forms that inhabit it. Everything we have discussed thus far in this book relates to CONTROL of the "terrain."

### Deodorants & Menstruation

Anti-perspirant deodorants should NEVER be used. They BLOCK the sweat glands, load the body with heavy metals and strangle the flow of wastes in the lymphatic system. Most antiperspirants contain toxic ALUMINUM ions that are involved in degenerative conditions like *Alzheimers*.

Please note the areas of the body where sweat is heaviest. They are areas of high lymph node concentration—like the groin, arm pits, breasts, neck and head. Limited ability to freely sweat is indicative of a sluggish lymphatic system which is **crucial** to good health. Cancer originates in and travels the lymphatic system. Moreover, it is impossible to rid a body of cancer if the lymphatic system is in trouble.

Medical Grade Ionized Water™ has the ability to rid the body of BO and cancer. It does NOT cure cancer, but it does alter the "terrain" sufficiently to cause it to "disappear."

Hormones affect body odor. A good example of hormonal influence on body odor is menstruation. When the female body is flushing itself, hormonal shifts accelerate the escape of aromatic molecules. Humans don't detect subtle odor changes, but animals like the bear can. They have attacked women who are menstruating.

Men also experience a monthly hormonal shift in body

odor. They obviously don't have a menstrual cycle, but they do have a monthly "hormone cycle," and their equivalent of menopause is called **andropause** (*andro*-refers to androgens which are **male** hormones; *pause*-cessation of).

*Menopause* and *andropause* follow loss of function in the vital organs, and especially in the testicles, ovaries and **liver**, hence the term "the change."

*Your author has learn how to measure and map his hormone cycle, just like he teaches women to do their own. When the **LIVER** is making lots of hormones, the aging process stops and reverses.*

At the turn of the century, menopause was called "the climactic" because it is the "official" SIGN of approaching old age. Menopause and andropause are **"past tense"** terms because they begin 15-20 years **prior** to manifestation. The good news is that the "effects" of of both are **reversable.**

**We are supposed to grow a "new" body every 7 years or sooner. Whether your NEW body is stronger or weaker than the one being replaced depends on the path YOU "choose" and your ability to control your hormone cycle.**

### No Sweat

People sweat. Some people sweat profusely. Other people hardly sweat at all. Sweat is a good indicator of how efficiently the skin is functioning as a waste portal.

If you sweat heavily, it's a very good sign, providing you keep the body adequately supplied with plenty of water and mineral ions. If you do not sweat easily, you must ASSIST your body to do so.

Until recent years, your author did not sweat easily. Now that I am healthier, I sweat much more freely. My solution was simple. Fresh veggi juices, colon therapy 3 times a week, some yoga and Pilates, a little aerobic exercise and the use of the L/CSF™ machine. L/CSF stands for lymph/cerebral spinal fluid. The machine moves massive amounts of body fluids with little effort. It is ideas for anyone who wants the **benefit** of all exercise: lymph and cerebral spinal fluid circulation.

If you don't sweat easily, your system is toxic and congested in the fat layer under the skin. The Young Again™ protocol is designed to free you from your self-imposed prison.

### FIR™ Sauna Is Here!

FIR™ technology has **ALL** of the benefits and **NONE** of the problems associated with hot tubs, steam rooms and dry heat. Water is not needed. Cost to operateis a little as 15¢/day.

This new technology rids the body of massive amounts of acid waste. Older people and anyone with arthritic problems or degenerative nerve conditions find wonderful relief from regular use of a FIR™ sauna (see pages 60 and 365).

### Skin: A Two Way Door

In Dan Skow's book *Mainline Farming for Century 21*, he mentions a question that was once asked in the medical literature. *"Given two quarts of water that is contaminated with a volatile chemical at 7 parts per "billion," would it be better to bathe in it for fifteen minutes or to drink it?"*

The experts answered, *"Drink it because four times more chemicals will enter the body by taking a bath in it than from drinking it."*

There is no question that we absorb large amounts of poisons via the skin. Yet, the mucous membranes that line the mouth, throat and GI tract have a combined surface area that is 600 times greater than the skin AND they absorb more efficiently, too. **The experts were wrong!** It was a dumb question because two quarts isn't enough water to bathe in anyway. The response options should have been "neither!"

The skin functions **bi**directionally. It vents and absorbs. The Young Again™ approach utilizes the skin's fast and efficient absorption for racemized™ transdermal products like F/G™ (female) creme, B.T.™ (thyroid) creme, and Maxgest™ (male) creme and Cobo-12™ cobalt creme because they are absorbed directly into the blood bypassing the oral route.

Few people realize the massive amounts of environmental poisons that access the body through the swinging door called *skin*, which includes the lining of the bronchioles and lungs (external respiration) and the cells (internal respiration).

Most man-made chemicals are toxic to living things—including the body. Ask a beautician if it is possible to become toxic through the skin and lungs. Many grow old and suffer dearly due to chemical exposure in their line of work.

If chemical toxicity is severe enough, the body will break out in a rash, hives, develop asthma or degenerative dis-ease. The body was not meant to deal with the barrage of poisons that bathe it daily—particularly environmental "zeno" estrogens.

Because toxic exposure to environmental poisons is **unavoidable**, it is **VERY** important that the body be assisted in "dislodging" such poisons on a regular basis rather than losing control of the body's "terrain." **Terrain management is the underlying principle of the Young Again Protocol™.**

The body has **ONLY** two options when it comes to

dealing with toxic chemicals: flush them from the system or store them in body fat. Without our active participation, the body grows sick and old by **default**.

**Time Bombs**

Absent the Young Again Protocol™, sick and old is the menu for everyone. Your author hopes that the reader will opt to follow his lead and enjoy a long and wonderfully healthy life.

Otherwise, we can only "hope" to pospone our day of reckoning. **When that day arrives,** you notice a lump in your breast, abnormal discomfort, sore bones or bleeding from the vagina or rectum; and the doctor says, **"YOU HAVE CANCER!"**

And all you can think about is, "Why me? What did I do to deserve this? This is not possible. I'm NOT old enough to have cancer. Surely, the diagnosis is wrong." BUT, you did have a hand in this story, didn't you? Don't bother with excuses. They don't count! Claims of ignorance won't ease the hell you face! Wouldn't it have been better to take responsibility earlier?

**Imprint these thoughts in your memory and LIVE by them. Prevention is far better than a cure. Neither government nor science can protect you. In matters of health, never blame others. You alone are responsible.**

The "health care" industry is a financially healthy **oxymoron**. It protects its own health and economic interests. Learn to protect YOUR health and economic interests by taking care of yourself. Be willing to do **whatever is called for** in your drive for good health and longevity. Becoming *Young Again!* is a matter of **choice!**

**PREVIEW:** *Our next chapter is about "wildcats." It was a favorite of those who reviewed this book prior to publication.*

**Prostate trouble is an easy problem to solve!**

**Deadly "Word" Games**

**Hydrolyzed vegetable protein** (HVP) is used in hundreds of foods—including health foods! HVP is a *trade name* for MSG (monosodium glutamate). MSG contains glutamate + aspartate + cytoic acid—known poisons. **Aspartame** is the chemical name for a popular sweetener with the red, white and blue swirl. These **SOY** derived **excitotoxins** destroy nerve/brain cells. Public outrage ended the use of MSG in baby food, so they changed the name to HVP and added a pretty little swirl!

**HAIR: What To Do About It!**

Fourteen day old Kombucha tea is a very powerful body rejuvenator that has the ability to clear acid waste from the system, ease aching joints and improve bowel activity. But where Kombucha really shines is in helping people regain "natural" hair color, and regrow hair.

Loss of hair color, thinning and balding are **SIGNS** that the body's terrain is in **trouble**. Hair problems are one of the first aging signs to appear and must not be ingored.

We "gray" from the top down and we lose body hair from the top down. If you are fifty or older and your axillary (arm pit) hair or pubic hair is gray, realize that loss of body hair is the next step. Medical science ignores the importance of hair, but hair has purpose!

Hair draws off toxic waste energy from the tissues **beneath the skin** where the most toxic waste in the body is stored. Fast growing hair is a good SIGN. Hair that comes back to full natural color or returns after years of absence is a good SIGN—and Kombucha tea and $GH_3$+™ help make it happen. Hair problems in women, especially over age 38—the menopausal years and beyond—are unquestionably linked to diminished thyroid activity. Blood tests are next to useless, here. Younger women also suffer from low thyroid activity. B.T. Thyroid Creme™ works wonders and addresses bone mass formation, cartilage regeneration, joint, memory and "brain fog," and skin and hair issues.

Use of Kombucha Tea and $GH_3$+™ are part of your author's regimen for "jet black" hair at calendar age 58. Racemized™ hormone precursors, liver and tissue purges, colonics thrice weekly and fresh veggi juice, too.

Kombucha tea is VERY **inexpensive** to make at home—so no one can complain they can't afford it! Approximate cost per gallon is only 50 cents. The Kombucha organism reproduces itself perpetually with a little care from **certified** healthy "starts".

If you want hair OR natural full color hair, Kombucha tea and $GH_3$+™ will help. B.T. Thyroid Creme™ for women is a must. Cobo-12™ creme is fundamental. Reopening the "puberty window" is critical. First comes the "terrain." Then comes hair with color followed by nice skin, good muscle mass and sex drive.

---

Hormones are the keys to the "middle years" wondow. Keep your window "perpetually" OPEN by following the Young Again Hormone Protocol™ for both sexes. See pages 72, 164 & 212.

**Colon Therapy Book**

Forty wonderful color pictures is why this book is a "must read," and why it is included in the Young Again Colon Therapy Protocol™.

Experience the fun of learning how to STOP THE AGING CLOCK by following the Young Again™ way. Having done colonics for over 25 years, your author finally discovered the secrets about this simple and inexpensive therapy—and those discoveries are critically important to anyone wishing to experience the miracle of agelessness.

**Ileocecal Valve & Cancer**

Six feet up from the anus is the beginning of the colon (large intestine) and the end of the small intestine, (the ileum). Between the large and small intestines is the ileocecal valve that **controls** waste movement and nutrient absorption in the intestinal tract. People with cancer almost **always** have their ileocecal valve "locked" in the open position causing cancer patients to **starve to death.**

Colon therapy "restores" ileocecal valve function and stimulates nerve activity of the nerve complex feeding from the colon wall while increasing bile flow.

Children2as young as 5 years have colon and bowel issues that need addressing; adults without question.

So take the leap and call John Thomas for guidance in this very simple health technique. Consultation is available without charge. Please see that you have your Source Packet before calling John Thomas for help.

**Enhanced "PAC$^s$"**

Enhanced PAC$^{s}$™ are an awesome complement of biologically acitve **proanthrocyanidins** —all in racemized™ form. PAC's™ buffer the body from acid wastes released into circulation during the **Tissue and Liver Protocol™**. Without them, the body will **NOR** release it's most toxic of wastes. Taken daily, PAC's™ strip the arteries and veins of plaque, lower blood pressure, help heart and stroke problems, ease eye problems plus aches and pains—all of which are "symptoms" of toxicity manifesting in the "terrain." PAC$^{s}$™ are **both** *fat* and *water* soluble . **They are a one of a kind product without equal, containing 24,660 activity units per bottle** and a racemized™ energy footprint and biological activity rating of 10/10. Activity and value in one bottle.

**Female Issues**

"Polycystic" ovaries is a common diagnosis given to women. The problem is that diagnosis does NOT tell the patient why she suffers and what to about the problem.

Multiple cysts on the ovaries are INCOMPLETE ovulations; that is, multiple eggs never burst through the wall of the ovary, hence, "poly " cystic.

Whenever women experience female complaints, you can be sure that "yeast" is a player in the story. You can also bet poor sugar metabolism and Insulin Growth Factor-l (IGF-l) are involved, also.

So called adult diabetes type ll goes along with polycystic ovaries. So does leaky gut syndrome, a sluggish bowel, poor bile flow from a congested liver, poor diet, and a shortfall in vitamin B-12.

A vitamin B-12 shortfall afffects everything about female metabolism and can appear at any age from puberty to old age. Women run short of this critical compound due to poor diet, insufficient secretion of "intrinsic factor" from the stomach wall and loss of blood due to the menstrual cycle.

Vitamin pills won't solve the problem, and neither will sublingual tablets under the tongue. B-12 shots are band-aids at best. The Young Again Protocol™ call for the use of Cobo-12™ cobalt metabolite creme applied to the skin for quick absorption into the blood, bypassing the oral route. The results can be miraculous, especially when racemized™ algae and liver capsules are taken with it.

The ingestion of fresh beet and carrot juice for breakfast each morning helps women deacidify their tissues. The Young Again Colon Therapy Protocol™ speeds the deacidification process.

Thyroid issues like cold bodies, dry skin, wrinkling skin, thinning hair, low energy, brain fog and memory complaints, slow metabolism and fat bodies are always part of the female story. It's just the way it is. Women of all ages can benefit from the Young Again Hormone Protocol™.

Please refer to pages 72, 212, 274 and 384.

**Female Cancer**

Female cancer is NOT genetic, but it has everything to with lifestyle, hormones, birth control pills and "zeno" estrogens. Follow the Young Again Hormone Protocol™ and you can remove the word "cancer" from your vocabulary.

# 16

## Wildcats

*"The skin is to the body what the soil is to the Earth."*

John Thomas

The halogens are known as the "wildcats" of the earth's elements. They are gases, and chemically speaking they are *extremely* reactive. The term *"halogen"* can be dissected: *hals*-Greek for salt, *gen*-to produce. When a halogen atom (acid) combines with a alkaline metal atom —like sodium, calcium or magnesium—it forms a salt like sodium chloride. When a **halo**gen combines with **hydro**gen it forms an acid, like the fluoride in tooth paste.

The halogens are IMPORTANT to the aging story.

When the halogens are part of a naturally occurring mix of mineral ions—as found in sea water or soil—they do not pose a health problem because they are not in a toxic form.

But when man isolates the halogens and creates out-of-balance waste byproducts, the aging process accelerates. Consider rock salt (halite) which is sodium chloride (table salt). Nature isolates this compound and stores it in the earth. Man comes along, mines it, and puts it on the dinner table in defiance of nature's dietary laws, speeding the aging process.

Chlorine and fluorine are HALOGENS. They are also gases. When these gasses are dissolved in water, they change their nature by binding with the metal ions and contaminants in the water. Chlor**ine** becomes chlor**ide**. Fluor**ine** becomes fluor**ide**. They have become salts in solution.

Halogen gases are **extremely** unstable and VERY chemically active because they need only one electron in their outer valence shell. To counter halogen instability, industry stores them as salt "solids."

In LIVING systems, the chemical bonds that bind fluorine gas are broken by hydrolysis (*hydro*-water; *lysis*-to cleave or break). Fluorine then bonds to components in the blood and lymph forming **unpredictable** compounds that are hostile to delicate life processes. Fluoridated water and tooth paste are **deadly** and the experts know it. Yet, "corporate" government throughout America continues to force it upon citizens under the "yellow fringed" national "war" flag that flys on every court house and public place in the union.

### Chlorine

Chlorine is a bactericidal. It indiscriminately kills bacteria and is very effective as a disinfectant (laundry bleach is a good example). Chlorine is also used to treat public water supplies. It is VERY toxic to the liver.

Use of chlorine in public water supplies is justified on the basis of what medical science calls the "benefit to risk" ratio. Applied to the population, this means the benefit to the population as a whole outweighs and justifies the damage done to individuals within the whole (vaccines are promoted on the same basis). ***This type of thinking keeps the hospital stalls full! It's your job to avoid this trap!***

Chlorine's carcinogenic characteristics are well known and are expressed in the body in many subtle ways. "Subtle" is the word, since no one dies from drinking chlorinated water.

For instance, chloroform is a byproduct of chlorinated drinking water. Chloroform is extremely toxic. It is a broad spectrum poison that indiscriminately kills both good and bad bacteria in the gut and tissues. Chloroform replaced ether as a general anesthetic in surgery rooms at the turn of the century. Both have been replaced by other safer, "less toxic" substances. **Safe** is a relative term, however.

There is a strong relationship between chlorine's introduction and use in public water supplies (1908) and the statistical emergence of heart attacks and cardiovascular disease. The relationship is **more** than happenstance.

**Prior to 1920, coronary heart disease was not a statistically recognized problem in the United States.** *Atherosclerosis* (build-up of plaque in the arteries) is directly linked to chlorination of public water supplies.

Chlorine's initial popularity must be understood in the

wake of the epidemic of waterborne dis-eases that ravaged the United States between 1910 and 1920—infecting or killing tens of thousands of people. In those days, there were few alternatives, but this is no longer the case.

**No one wants to drink water that is contaminated with pathogenic microbes. At the same time, those of us who are concerned with health and longevity dare not rely on officialdom to protect us. Most people in the USA rely on municipal water as their primary water source. More and more people are buying bottled water, but this is NOT the answer to the dilemma. The correct response is to "make" and drink BEV™ and Medical Grade Ionized Water™ and "unplug" from the system.**

Due to recent outbreaks of pathogenic *E. coli* and *cryptosporidium* bacteria in public water supplies, the Feds are squeezing local "corporate" governments and water districts to use toxic chemicals, chlorine, mercuric acid, etc.

Chlor**amines** are extremely toxic to the liver. The BEV™ system removes these as well as fluoride, flagellates that trigger amoebic outbreaks, viruses and bacteria, radioactivity and junk minerals. Once removed, the vibrational memory of these contaminants is "erased" and the water is restructured. Now, you have **biologically friendly** drinking water.

For bathing and colon therapy, use a 3 stage oxidation/reduction filter—a long lasting, high volume filter. Young Again™ Colon Therapy Protocol™ calls for 15-20 gallons of non-toxic, warm water per session, 2-3 times a week (see page 234). The process is very easy, safe and fast to perform—and it will save or give you back control of your life!

### Sodium Hypochloride

Chlorine is dissolved into public water supplies from a stable **salt block** form. The reason chlorine is used in salt form has to do with pH, which we will discuss momentarily.

A salt is a combination of an acid (halogen) and a base (metal), hence, "sodium fluoride," as disolved in tooth paste. Water treatment protocol calls for the use of sodium hypochlorite containing fluorine. Sodium is an alkaline metal **base** and hypochlorite is an extremely **acid** form of chlorine. Together they form a solid—a salt compound called **sodium hypochloride.**

When the Jekyll and Hyde sodium hypo-chlorite compound is dissolved in water, it separates. The chlorine kills the bacteria and the hydroxide raises the pH so the water will be palatable. The pH of most tap water is between pH 8-9. Biologically friendly drinking water—like BEV™—is a combination of pH, reactivity and ORP potential. These are the things that heal sick bodies and return control of the "terrain."

### Terrain Problems

Toxic chemicals enter the body **bonded** to *waste* mineral ions. In the body, acidic chlorine and fluorine bond with metabolic wastes and oils (like soy and canola) and form *hybrid* toxins that ALTER the terrain. The change appears in the **"electrical STATE"** of the blood as "Rouleau." Rouleau manifests as clumped red corpuscles and is a "marker" condition, a red flag of dis-ease in the making and a confirmation that the "terrain" is in trouble. **The word "aging" hints at the problem. The word "degeneration" says it all.**

Sodium is a player in the above scenario. High sodium levels in the tissues often manifests as hypertension. As excess sodium invades **interstitial** fluids BETWEEN the cells, it upsets the sodium/potassium balance in the body which in turn sets the stage for cancer.

The body requires a **constant** supply of organic potassium to maintain its sodium/potassium balance. Fresh veggi juice and home grown, organic green leafy vegetables are the very best sources of organic potassium. The body attempts to offset dietary deficits of potassium by taking it from the inside of the cells in trade for sodium. The process is **"invasive."** Sodium invasion slows mitochondrial activity and converts an aerobic environment to an anaerobic one. The mitochondria **cannot** function in a high sodium environment.

Chlorinated tap water is high in sodium is weakening the entire population. There are better and safer alternatives, but powerful industrial interests support chlorination. Our situation today is not unlike the outbreaks of Childbirth Fever in Dr. Semmelweis' time. Chlorine, fluoride, and chlor*amines* are good for business. They keep the cattle lines at the clinics and hospitals "full."

**"Corporate" government is a BOGUS foreign "state" operating under the "yellow fringe flag". It has a vested interest in keeping people sick. Sick and dead people are good for litigation, probate, estate taxes and other legal mewings. See Source Page 384.**

Think of the effects that safe, biologically friendly food and drinking water would have on organized medicine, the legal system, society, and the government school system.

### Public Mentality

Fluoride is an American Institution, second only to hot

dogs and apple pie. Americans have a love affair going with their sweetheart "halogen" fluorine (fluoride in its salt form). The question is WHY? This book provides the answers for those who care to displace ignorance with KNOWLEDGE.

Industry, medicine, dentistry and the pharmaceutical companies have done a magnificent job of *brainwashing* Americans on the benefits of fluoride.

Fluorine is THE wildcat of the halogens. It is numero uno—**number one**—on the list of atomic elements for reactivity. God put fluoride under lock and key by isolating it in underground water and mineral deposits. When man discovered fluoride's industrial uses, he opened a Pandora's Box.

Fluorine is toxic to all living things. Fluoride poisoning (fluorosis) of the tissues manifests itself as hundreds of symptoms. Because it is a "systemic" poison that takes *years* to manifest, fluoride escapes blame—along with the **criminals** that promote it. Medical science's challenge of "no scientific proof" is an effective cover for the industrial poisoning of the world's population. **Fluoridation of public water is a crime!**

### HARD (Teeth-Bones-Skin ) HEADS

Fluoride hardens the teeth—and the head. The experts forget to mention the toxic side effects—effects that grossly outweigh any conjured benefit. Fluoride has a subduing effect. It "slows" the brain and makes us docile—and easier to manipulate. Fluoride is easily absorbed through the skin and mucous membranes of the mouth, respiratory system and intestines. Fluoride is a perpetual money machine for the medical system.

**Good medical insurance creates the "illusion" of security. Reliance on it causes people to forfeit personal responsibility for their health.**

*A certain toothpaste introduced in the late 1950's received the endorsement of the American Dental Association. It uses fluoride in stannous form. Stannous fluoride is a tin-containing compound. Tin is a element and a metal. When you mix an acid (fluor***ine** *gas) with an alkaline metal ion (tin), you get a SALT—a crystal. We know that stannous fluor***ide** *is a salt because of the -***ide** *on the end of the word. When you convert stannous fluoride—a waste product—from the status of waste to the status of a medically endorsed and publicly accepted drug, you have really accomplished something. The profits to be made in a deal like this are beyond the dreams of avarice.*

Fluor**ine** is widely used in thousands of industrial processes. Fluor**ide** is the industrial spin-off. Stannous fluoride is the waste product of the tin industry. Fluorine-containing compounds are VERY powerful left-spin energy fields. Their signature and footprint is anti-life and very biologically active.

In a living system, fluoride **dis**associates and becomes EXTREMELY unstable. It looks for something to bond to—like our ***protein enzymes.*** It bonds with the proteins in the bones and the minerals in the body and slows metabolism.

Fluoride "attacks" the collagenous protein fibers that give the bones, skin, muscles and ligaments their *resiliency.* **Wrinkled skin** is a good example of a fluoride side efect. **Acidification** of body tissues is another. Fluoride is **ACID!**

**People are concerned about wrinkled skin, brittle bones and failing hair. Yet, most American's use fluoridated water and toothpaste. They just don't get it!**

If you dissolve a bone in an acid, the minerals will go into solution and leave a rubbery like substance that resembles a piece of spaghetti. This substance is the protein collagen matrix into which the osteoblasts deposit minerals for the construction of bone tissue.

Fluoride acts similarly to the hormones in birth control pills, estrogen replacements and "zeno" hormones in food and water. These molecules interfere with the osteo**blasts** (bone building cells) and osteo**clasts** (bone dissolving cells) by slowing the repair and reproduction of bones and connective tissue. Fluoride causes collagen proteins to turn **hard and brittle.** The bones should be **rigid** and **flexible**—like a healthy tree.

Over a period of years, people who use fluoridated water and toothpaste build-up **excess** fluoride in their tissues, and serious degeneration develops. The *experts* blame osteoporosis, scleroderma, lupus and exposure to the sun. *Connective tissue syndrome* is the latest "in" label. Broken bones AND weak joints are common among adolescents and older people. Why? Something has changed! One of the somethings is fluoridated water, toothpaste and that innocent little cup of poison from the school nurse and the dental hygienist.

*Despite the damage caused by fluoride in the diet and lifestyle choices people make, the aging process is* ***reversible****, if a person are willing to follow the Young Again Protocol™.*

Medical science has endorsed the use of fluoride and is too stubborn and proud to admit its mistake. Please consider what Sir Arthur Edington once said about the scientific mind.

***"Verily, it is easier for a camel to pass through the eye of a needle than for a scientific man to walk through an open door."***

The public does not know that the famous fluoride study about natural fluoride in well water and the absence of dental caries (cavities) was bogus. What the experts fail to mention is that man-made *sodium* and *stannous* fluorides are

FAR more reactive and hostile to living tissues than is naturally occurring fluoride. "Living" systems are DYNAMIC. People are not sterile, laboratory test tubes. Fluoride **reacts** when heat, pesticides, food additives, soy and canola oils and metabolic wastes are present in the metabolic dynamic of the body.

Powerful interests in dentistry, medicine, and the pharmaceutical houses influence public policy in regard to issues like fluoridation of drinking water supplies. The insidious *"grant system"* decides WHO gets public monies and WHAT projects science will study—money dictates!

These same powerful interests determine what is taught in the medical and dental school curriculums and see to it that text books are heavily biased. Private interests use "corporate" government and the "yellow fringe flag" court system to shield them while they foist their deadly industrial wastes—like sodium and stannous fluoride—onto a trusting and unsuspecting public. Experts act as rubber stamps by providing **new** labels and **new** drugs for **new** dis-eases in an effort to to keep the public confused. Five years ago, there was no such thing as "acid reflux." Ten years ago, fibromyalgia and lupus hardly existed. Twenty years ago, Alzheimers didn't exist, etc.

## Synergy & Synthesis

*"Synergy"* is a term that refers to the "combined" action of two or more chemical agents. Synergy produces positive OR negative consequences for human beings.

*"Synthesis"* is a closely related term. It refers to molecular structure and the location of the "—R group" which identifies the molecule and dictates its effect on living systems.

A healthy, youthful body is the result of *anabolic synthesis* (positive *bio*chemical synergy). Healthy food, fresh vegetable juices, colon therapy and water are fundamental.

Fluorides, chlorine, vaccines, pesticides, mercury, toxic air, food dyes and additives, soy and canola oils, chlor*amines* and free radicals "trigger" chain reactions in the body. If the immune, digestive or hormonal systems are stressed, negative synthesis reactions destroy cells and produce waste byproducts in the form of toxic ACID wastes.

## Free Radicals • Antioxidants • Organic Food

Toxic substances are "free radicals." Free radicals trigger uncontrolled oxidation of the cells and tissues. The actions of free radicals can be HALTED by the use of potent racemized™ products called Enhanced PAC'sTM. PACs stop uncontrolled oxidation. Oxidation involves the addition or loss of electrons between molecular substances. Uncontrolled oxidation is catabolic activity that kills cells. **Catabolic activity involves free radicals and self-cannibalization.**

Pesticides are another example of free radicals. They are man-made **"organic"** chemicals—a term that is a misnomer. I prefer to call them poisons! Pesticides are organic by definition. The word **"organic"** is used to describe them because these deadly molecules contain CARBON (atomic element #12). Carbon is the essence of life on Earth. Industry's immoral use of the word *"organic"* confuses the public.

Crafty wordsmiths and bogus science jumble terms so that their **poisons** will APPEAR to be to friendly to Earth and Her inhabitants. Confusion is the tool. *Unholy* profit is the goal. Sick people, animals, and plants are the result! This is why I keep reminding the reader to ignore the recommendations of the "experts." **Their advice will seal your grave!**

When the term *organic* is applied to food, the implication is that poisons are not present and that the food was raised using natural fertilizers as opposed to commercial, NPK salt fertilizers. Organic food is generally better than non-organic food, but home grown food is the very best!

**Everyone should grow some fresh vegetables—be it in pots or a section of the yard. Even small amounts of "live" food have a powerful affect on health.**

## Doctors & Dentists

The entrenched scientific, medical, and pharmaceutical establishment is at odds with personal health and longevity. They have a vested interest in keeping things status quo so they can bilk the people of their money and freedom.

Professional people often suffer from **professional myopia.** Most are the product of their training, and few think outside if it. At the same time, professional people are **"watched"** by their licensing boards, i.e., the "state." Those who step out of line or put the patient's best interest first are at odds with their fellow practitioners! Doctors and dentists who act on TRUTH must be very careful and keep a very low public profile.

**It's good to know an alternative health care professional in your area. But remember, healthy people have little need for medical care.**

Recently, I moved from a city that had over two-hundred dentists. All of them—except two—use fluoride and mercury amalgam. That's TWO out of two-hundred! The rest claim ignorance. They quote chapter and verse from the medical literature in their defense. They refuse to seek alternative training and to learn to care for people in a humane manner. Most REFUSE to think or act outside of the "accepted" protocols of their profession—even when they know better! They are caught between profits, insurance companies, an ignorant public and the medical review boards.

***Many medical insurance carriers decline to insure people who work in dental offices because of the inordinately high incidence of sickness and dis-ease. The mercury and fluoride they use are Trojan Horses in their own camp—and they pay with their health and lives—just like their patients.***

**Mercury • Fluoride • BEV™**

Heavy metals—like mercury, cadmium, and lead are serious business. They interfere with brain and nerve activity and MUST be purged from the tissues. SOC™, racemized™ algae and Yucca Blend™ will remove them from the tissues.

The West—and the USA in particular—are experiencing huge increases in neurological BRAIN disorders like Alzheimers, multiple sclerosis and tumors—conditions that were unknown or seldom seen thirty years ago. Today they are common and you better believe that fluoride, heavy metals and hormone analogs are at the root of them!

Fluoride hardens cell membranes and the "sulfhydryl links" that compose protein based connective tissues. When fluoride combines with mercury residues, the immune system takes a hit and the Schwann cells at the nerve synapses (see page 248) diminish resulting in nerve disorders.

Mining and smelting operations are notorious for pouring fluoride dusts into the air. Third world countries suffer miserably from the uncontrolled use of industrial fluorides. The faces of the people are OLD! **Fluoride is a systemic poison. Ingestion of fluoride is in conflict with the desire to stay young or become *Young Again!***

**PREVIEW:** *In our next chapter, you will discover WHY sex hormone production shifts as the bio-electric body ages.*

***"What is the hardest task in the world to do? Think!***
Ralph Waldo Emerson

**Think!**

Did the cancer patient *always* have cancer? No! Was the diabetic *always* a diabetic? No! And did the lady with arthritis *always* have arthritis? No! These people LOST CONTROL of their body "terrain" due to:

- Failure to understand the "fundamentals."
- Failure to remove wastes from the body's tissues.
- Failure to restore the hormonal system.
- Failure to drink biologically friendly water
- Failure to eat right-spin, high energy food
- Failure to live a disciplined life

FAILURE to make correct choices dictates health and longevity. Failure is a "self imposed" CHOICE! If you want God to do miracles, you have to do your part first!

**Mind & Body**

Never underestimate the power of the mind. Daily, I talk with people who **cannot** be helped because they **refuse** to control their thoughts, and who labor under gross misconceptions about the source of their problems, be they social, family, financial or health in nature.

There are many good books written about the power of the mind. Let's summarize a few points.

1. Negative, unhappy, critical, angry, fearful, depressed and misguided thoughts—and words—affect the production of brain chemicals, hormones, depress the immune system and bring on dis-ease. **Thoughts and words are energy bullets!**
2. The aura diminishes in size when we "think" negative thoughts. **Dis-ease manifests as "thought" in the flesh.**
3. A healthy outlook promotes healing. A poor emotional/ mental attitude hinders healing—no matter how good our food or lifestyles. **Guard your thoughts.**
4. Bowel and liver function are affected by our emotions and thoughts. **Good thoughts are better than laxatives.**
5. Positive image visualization brings good results. **What we think, we experience. What we voice, we create.**
6. Beliefs about oneself, life, the future and others affect us and those around us. **Refuse to harbor bad thoughts.**
7. Exercise is as good for the mind as it is for the body. **Exercise daily. Walk, pump iron, calisthenics, yoga.**
8. Good thoughts, kindness to others and self love all speed healing and rejuvenation.
9. Learn to forgive. Do not hold grudges. **Release yourself and the other person's hate.**

**Read:** ***Your Body Believes Every Word You Say***
(See Source Page 384.)

# 17

## Diagnosis Or Post Mortems?

*"The organs of the body can be likened to towns on a map, each being a unit unto itself, yet each is connected to the other and ultimately to the composite body."*

Dr. Arnold Lorand

The Golden Age of Medicine extended from approximately 1840 to 1930. It was a period that saw an explosion of new knowledge in all fields of science.

The clinical observations of the doctors of this period are of particular interest to us because of their impact on the aging process. Their observations *precede* the advent of modern man's environmental mistakes.

The Golden Age of Medicine was a period of "low tech" drugless medicine. Doctors relied on astute observation to guide the patient. They also spent more time with patients, often getting to know them better than they knew themselves.

Uncommon good sense was the guiding rule. There was no place to shift the blame if the chosen modality (therapy) failed to cure the patient. The patient was viewed *in camera*—as a unit—rather than as separate parts. The word "syndrome" was not in fashion. Cause and effect, diagnosis, and prognosis were anchored in observation, rather than endless tests.

### Modern Medicine

Present day medical technology is a mixed blessing. It excels in diagnosis "after the fact," organ transplants and in emergency medicine. Beyond this, it is a never ending process that produces ***isolated snap-shots*** of the process we call dis-ease—each picture but a *glimpse* of the suffering patient.

High-tech modern medicine suffers from a severe shortcoming: doctors and nurses are **NOT** trained to diagnose **subclinical** illness. Observations of yesteryear are considered to be "dated"—even primitive—for lack of hype and high tech smoke and mirrors.

Allopathic medicine has an ***unholy*** reliance on high tech gadgets and high-powered, left-spin chemical drugs. It views people as flesh and blood machines composed of "parts." Medicine doesn't understand ENERGY is lost at the "invisible" level before dis-ease is seen in the "visible" realm. They don't see people as *energy* dynamic beings and they don't understand the dynamic energy forces that **interface** the vital organs and **dictate** true health in the body's terrain.

**Diagnosis Or Post Mortems?**

If it were possible to examine the vital organs of the body, particularly the ductless glands—the pituitary, thyroid, parathyroid, adrenals, thymus, pancreas, and gonads (testes and ovaries)—the effects of our living habits would be plainly evident. But we cannot make such an examination and must therefore learn HOW to assist the *bio-electric* body through a healthy lifestyle and common sense.

Dr. William Albrech, a brilliant professor of soils at the University of Missouri, once commented that we no longer know what healthy animal organs look like because we see only ***abnormal*** organs. That's the way it is in medicine today.

There was a time when the physician could examine both healthy and *pathogenic* organs and compare them. By knowing what healthy organs looked like, the doctor could identify dis-ease in its "formative" stages, and if a good observer, pick up on *subclinical* symptoms before they became SIGNS. Subclinically sick people are now the norm, and the vast majority of medical science's efforts goes towards "naming" the dis-ease. The "label" is **meaningless** unless you come to understand the progression that led to the dis-ease.

**Strange Meanings**

To compensate for the universality of a subclinically sick population, the medical schools have rewritten the STANDARDS by which they define health and dis-ease. This is similar to what is occurring in "government" schools, where today's "A" is yesterday's "C," and in the financial markets where people are forced to rely on "lies" spewing from government bureaus and corporate financial reports based on "pro forma" balance sheets i.e. the Enron disaster, et al.

For example, BOGUS holistic medicine, as taught in "traditional" medical schools, defines **illness** as an abnormal condition where the present level of function has declined compared to a *previous* level. By this definition, *neither* the present level nor the previous level of function meets any defined STANDARD. Traditional definitions are moot and no longer define "illness" as the absence of health and "health" as the absence of dis-ease. **Illness is neutral!**

Today, health and illness are defined in terms of the individual's *personal perception* of their state of being; in other words, how one *feels* about oneself. Trying to make sense out of all of this reminds me of the Chinese journalist who exclaimed, *"Explain please, strange words and meanings."*

**Approximately 85% of the population suffers with Rouleau in their blood. Rouleau is the harbinger of dis-ease in the formative stage of acidification.**

Reversing the aging process requires that we become enlightened as to WHY we age. We must not assign responsibility for good health to a medical "model" that ignores the root causes of illness, dis-ease, and aging.

### The Endocrine System

To further understand the aging process, we must look at the **endocrine** system of the body. This system is one of two regulatory and communication systems that transmit and coordinate messages to various parts of the body. The other is the **nervous** system. *(Medical science* ***ignores*** *the lymphatic system which is the body's protein "communication" system because it involves the movement or stagnation of the plasma proteins that "leak" from the capillary walls into the spaces between the cells to provide nourishment.)*

The *nervous* and *endocrine* systems are ***irrevocably*** linked to each other. The nervous system transmits electrical impulses (energy) that originate in the neuron's cell body and are relayed via dendritic fibers that are composed of axons. The signal is transmitted in picoseconds faster than the speed of light—moving along the axon from synapse to synapse by specialized cells called Schwann cells (see page 248). Schwann cells are **critical** to a healthy nervous system, but the "experts" don't want to talk about an issue that affects all women.

As we age, the neurilemma (myelin sheath) covering the nerve fibers deteriorates paving the way for degenerative conditions like Alzheimers, MS, peripheral neuropathy and lupis. The use of F/G™ creme, Cobo-12™ creme and SOC™ capsules has been useful in moderating these conditions.

Once nerve degeneration progresses enough for the doctor to diagnose it, the person is in deep water. Yet, give the body the opportunity and it will **regenerate** an entirely new and functional nervous system. The body can regenerate missing limbs, grow hair on bald heads, exchange fat for muscle and grow new cartilage in the joints. These miracles require a functioning endocrine system, **de**acidified tissues and fluids—and some PATIENCE!

The endocrine system makes its wishes known using chemical **and** hormonal messengers. Chemical messengers are chemical *energy* that causes a *fast* response in the body.

Hormone messengers are *different.* They often take hours to produce a response. Hormone response, however, can last for hours, days or weeks. *(Think of the effects experienced in the aftermath of an emergency situation where large amounts of adrenalin were produced to help you cope with the situation.)*

Restoration of our hormonal systems is **fundamental** to good health and longevity. The Young Again Protocol™ puts you in control of your body. See page 72.

### Exocrine & Endocrine Glands

Most exocrine glands secrete into *ducts* which in turn flow into body cavities like the stomach or intestines. Some exocrine glands, however, like the sudoriferous (sweat) and sebaceous (oil) glands, secrete to the skin's surface.

The *ductless* glands of the endocrine system secrete their hormones directly into the **extracellular spaces** around and between the secreting cells, instead of into ducts. The extracellular spaces—between the cells—are filled with extra-cellular fluid and house the blood and lymph capillaries.

Some hormones are transported *by the blood* to their destination(s), which may also be another gland. Hence, the ductless glands depend on each other and act in *concert* with the entire body terrain via the "receptors." If the receptor sites "lock up," as in women who have used birth control pills. estrogen supplements, or steroids including DHEA, cortisone, and melatonin, the ability to monitor their system is lost and they become their own prisoner. Synthetic hormones do **NOT** release from the receptor on their own. The Young Again Hormone Protocol™ provides a way to deal with this dilemma.

Stress in the ovaries, bowels, liver or adrenals affects thyroid function and visa versa. Once the party starts, it doesn't make any difference who started it, hence, the all inclusive approach used by Young Again™.

Some endocrine glands are **both** duct and ductless glands. Examples are the pancreas, ovaries, testes, kidneys, stomach, small intestine, skin, heart, and placenta.

Hormones maintain health by changing the *rate of activity* in the body. The amount of hormones released into circulation is based on need, the gland's ability to produce them and the body's ability to utilize them. **Hormonal excesses manifest themselves as deficiency conditions.**

Some hormones are carried "free" form in the blood. Others require blood plasma *carrier proteins* to bind and transport them—for example, insulin. Blood plasma carrier proteins are made by the liver, hence, a stressed **liver** creates additional stress on the other organs and glands. The multitude of problems associated with menopause says it best.

When the receptors on the target cells respond to a hormone, a message is relayed back to the gland that produced the hormones to STOP production. Excess hormones are degraded (oxidized) and disposed of by either the target cells themselves or by the **liver** and removed from circulation.

### Old Age Symptoms In The Young

Some of the SIGNS of early senescence (aging) as seen in young adults are obesity, graying/thinning hair, balding, wrinkles, connective tissue issues and lethargy.

Symptoms that serve as **markers** of poor health are amenorrhea (irregular menstruation), low sex drive, impotence, accelerated pulse, cold in the extremities, a tendency to constipation, edema, fading memory, mental depression, excess albumin or the presence of casts in the urine.

Albumin is a blood protein that has escaped through the capillaries of the kidney's glomeruli (filters). Albumin in the urine is a SERIOUS indication of loss of kidney function. Since the kidneys are one of the primary waste organs of the body, the presence of excess albumin spells trouble.

Casts are composed of salt, hyaline, protein, and chemical and mineral wastes. These wastes take the shape of the kidney's tubules. Their presence indicates *catabolic* activity and degeneration. Weak kidneys are a *prerequisite* to cancer and viral infections. Weak kidneys allow the establishment of clandestine outposts throughout the body and cold war maneuvers by viruses and bacteria fueled by the build-up of acid wastes in the system. Acid wastes are left-spin energy.

Cold in the extremities indicates thyroid disfunction, stressed ovaries and hormonal excesses. All of these are linked to a stressed **liver**—the body's furnace. An accelerated pulse indicates a systemic condition where the body is overworking to make up for shortfalls or **excesses** in the system.

Constipation is a "systemic" condition that greatly influences ALL body functions. Constipation is usually defined as not moving the bowels "regularly"—whatever that means. Bowel activity **SHOULD** be the **result** of bile flow from the liver. Just because you move your bowels is **not** the same as a bowel movement as a result of bile flow into the intestine from the liver and gall bladder.

Having worked with 65,000+ people over the last 10 years, your author has come to the stark realization that frequency of bowel movement is only part of the story. While there is no question that it is better to have 2 or 3 bowel movements a day instead of one, the quiestion is, "As a result of what?" Water intake, fiber content of the diet, physical activity, juicing, etc. all affect bowel activity level. **The most critical issue to human health is "bile flow."**

Herbs and laxatives can **"make"** your bowels move without increasing bile flow. Bile carries the "acids" out of the body. The flow of bile is the **primary** issue in **de**acidification of the body. **De**acidification is the **primary** issue in maintaining and regaining control of the "terrain." The Young Again Protocol™ teaches people how to increase bile flow, speed **de**acidification, and as a result, see increased in bowel activity.

The so-called "acid stomach" is a symptomatic condition experienced after a meal. It is NOT an acid condition at all, but a digestion, liver, gut and bowel issue.

Insufficient production of digestive enzymes in the stomach and intestine is a "given" after age 30. The older you are, the worse the problem. Hence, the need for racemized™ products like DiSorb Aid™, R/BHCl™ and Yucca Blend™.

But there is **more** to the story. These days, everything related to indigestion is "acid reflux syndrome"—a condition no one ever heard of until the pharmaceutical companies came up with a new "magic bullet." The condition has **nothing** to do with acidity or stomach regurgitation even though these factors are involved. It is a liver, bowel, enzyme and gut issue.

Acid reflux syndrome, leaky gut syndrome, irritable bowel syndrome, diverticulitis, colitis, Crohn's, constipation and hemorrhoids are all birds of a feather. The **solution** is simple enough if the **Young Again Protocol**™ is followed. Yucca Blend,™ DiSorb Aid™, R/C™, Microbize™ and R/HCI™ provides both relief and healing. Restoring the gut wall and ending "leaky gut syndrome" along with some digestive help ends so-called food allergies. The flow of fully digested food deprives yeast and parasites of the food energy they need—gas and bloating being a side effect.

Proper digestion and absorption also prevents edema

and further acidification of the tissues because of the accumulation of toxic plasma proteins in the tissue spaces. Edema (water retention) is linked to **excess** plasma proteins in the fluids that surround and bath the cells. **Edema is a sign of toxicity** and often accompanies loss of body hair. Drugs and plasma protein wastes settle in the legs of older people compounding swelling and nail fungi, loss of body hair and deterioration of the feet. Use of the L/CSF™ machine to circulate lymph fluids and move waste out of the legs.

### Oxidation/Reduction

As early as 1903, it was demonstrated that the **ductless** glands control **ALL** the processes of oxidation and that the diseases of metabolism like diabetes, obesity, gout, arthritis, heart dis-ease, etc., are the direct consequence of *alterations* in the function of these important glands.

Oxidation is another word for aging and **acid**ification of the tissues. Oxidation is the opposite of "reduction." In a broad sense, oxidation amounts to a slowing of the metabolic rate and marked slow-down in the production and storage of the ATP energy molecule. B.T.™ Creme accelerates metabolism.

Hormones play a key role in glandular metabolism and are a driving force in the production of ATP. The adrenals, pancreas, thyroid and ovaries stress whenever the body is UNABLE to rid itself of **excess** waste due to a shortfall in **liver** activity. Central to all dis-ease is the liver and linked to the liver are the ovaries and testicles, adrenals, pancreas, thyroid and other hormone related sites throughout the body.

**Sluggish thyroid is epidemic among women in general, and among women over 40 years, in particular.**

### Scar Tissue • Alcohol • Cirrhosis

When functional (parenchyma) cells die, they are replaced by dysfunctional (stroma) cells which become **scar** tissue. Liver parenchyma cells are called hepatocytes (*hepat*-liver; *cyte*-cell). Stroma cells cover and protect the liver. As the hepatocytes die, the stroma cells invade and scar tissue forms.

**Alcohol is a POISON!** It kills the hepatocytes in the liver. That is why a drunk person is said to be in**tox**icated. **Tox**—as in **tox**in—means poison. When you drink alcohol you are **poisoning** yourself. If you want to REVERSE aging, you are going to need a healthy functioning liver. Avoid the use of alcohol if you want to see your wish fulfilled. For your information, the alcohol industry (like the dairy and ice cream industry) is not required to list the toxic ingredients added to its brew.

If you know someone who drinks, perform this liver test on them. First, have the person lie on their back on the floor and raise their knees to relax their stomach. Then, gently but deeply, push down on the person's right side, just below the rib cage. You will feel a *firm to hard* mass—the LIVER! Be careful, it may be very tender and massaging it harshly can cause the person to become ill! The liver should be soft and somewhat hidden under the ribs.

Here is another test. Have the alcoholic person stand and extend their right arm. Next, gently pull down on the arm while your other hand touches the liver region. People with limited liver function will lose their strength and their arm will fall. Some people become **nauseated** and have to lie down because of the *surge* of electrical energy into their sick liver.

People with hepatitis, mononucleosis, or chronic fatigue syndrome and Lyme dis-ease usually have a distended, swollen liver. These *conditions* stress the liver and impact all of the other organs and systems.

### Atrophy Of Sex Glands & Obesity

Atrophy (deterioration) of the sex glands goes hand in hand with systemic toxicity, obesity, thyroid, and liver problems. Obesity is a SIGN of metabolic slow-down and hormonal imbalance. Atrophy of the ovaries (which includes the ova and follicles from which the egg springs) and testicles takes years to manifest. Loss of the ovaries slows the metabolic rate. Many doctors think nothing of removing a woman's female organs (uterus and ovaries). **Removal of a woman's ovaries is the equivalent of castration for a man. How many men have you seen standing in line to be castrated?**

Women MUST learn HOW to stay healthy if they expect to avoid female problems. See page 72 for an in depth discussion and diagram of the female hormone cycle, which is **not** the same as the menstrual cycle. Women should NOT wait until problems start. A problem avoided is a problem SOLVED.

Detoxification of the tissues goes a long way in keeping a woman young and vibrant and provides the foundation for effective prevention or treatment of female problems. Women MUST learn to manage their own health and not depend on medical "experts." Sadly, OBGYN physicians—even female ones—don't have any answers other than the usual "stuff" that does NOT work, and all but guarantees a woman will develop uterine or breast cancer. If you don't believe your author, look at the risks and contraindications that go with this "stuff."

Unopposed estrogen dominance and closure or failure to "complete" the hormone cycle underwrites every female condition known. The problem is that women don't even know there is such a thing, and they have not been taught how to measure and map the cycle and relate it to what is transpiring in their bodies.

**Osteoporosis**

Osteoporosis (honeycombing of the bones) involves vascularization (invasion) of the bones by the blood vessels. The blood vessels are the body's front line troops. Their presence precedes bone formation as well as bone *dismantling*. Osteoporosis is a symptomatic EFFECT. It is not the cause of loss of bone mass, but it is related to hormonal imbalance and **excess** toxicity in the form of acid waste build-up within the system AND reduced bone formation by the osteo**blasts** which are responsible for building new bone and cartilage. Osteoporosis is common in older people—and especially in post menopausal women due to the collapse of the female hormone cycle (see page 72).

Osteoporosis is **preventable** and **treatable** if a woman understand the rules of the game. The rules have **nothing** to do with calcium intake, despite all the fairy tales in the magazines and on television. Acidification of the system and collapse of the hormone cycle with some help from a slowing thyroid and you have the picture. What you do about it is the issue. That is what the **Young Again Protocol**™ is about.

**Tissue Types & Beautiful Skin**

**Connective tissue** is one of the four basic types of tissue in the body. It performs the functions of binding, supporting and interfacing other tissues. It consists of relatively few cells in a sea of "intercellular substance."

*The four basic types of tissue are **connective** (elastic, collagenous, reticular), **epithelial** (skin), **muscular** (muscle) and **nerve** tissue.*

The last two words of the definition of connective tissue (intercellular substance) are of particular importance to aging. ***Intercellular substance*** is the material between the cells.

If we are speaking of the skin, we are talking about the dermal and subcutaneous layers which are composed of CONNECTIVE tissue. This area is served by the blood and lymph capillary systems. It is here, in the basement membranes of the skin that the body stores **excess** acid wastes, mineral salts and FATS. These wastes are deposited by the blood capillaries and lodge in the spaces "between" the cells.

Deposition of **excess** acid waste causes "cross-linking" of collagen fibers that make up the connective tissues of the body. Wrinkling and sagging skin is the result. The most toxic "stuff" the body possesses is stored in the fat **under the skin.**

Waste causes *hardening* and *thickening* of the outer skin with LOSS of *elasticity* and resiliency. SOC™ lotion softens outer skin and helps dissolve topical scar tissue. SOC™ capsules dissolve internal scar tissue and encourages new tissue formation **from the inside out.** Racemized™ Skin Creme hormonally stimulates the formation of "new" skin.

### Venereal Disease • Sexual Excess • Goiter

Sexually infectious dis-ease is on the rise. The increase **transcends** the issue of promiscuity by what is says about people's poor state of health—particularly the young.

Few people reach adult age as virgins. These days contracting some sexually transmitted venereal (*venus*-love, *al*-pertaining to) dis-ease (STD); statistically, **3 out of 5!**

A healthy body is immune to STD just like measles, hepatitis, small pox, etc. Venereal infections can only occur when the body's "terrain" is ripe for infection. From genital herpes and sexual "warts," to syphilis and gonorrhea to chlamydia involve more than "exposure." The issue is the **"terrain."**

Medical Grade Ionized Water™ that is "acid" has an extremely high (-) ORP potential and does wonders on STD. As an aside, your author had a buddy in the army who visited brothels regularly. When asked how many times he had contracted STD, he responded, *"Never! I always take a fresh lemon and wash down immediately afterwords!"* The highly acid breaks the peptide bonds that form the protein structure of the dis-ease organism. Perhaps fine for men, but the delicate female mucosa would never tolerate lemon. Women should use diluted raw apple cider vinegar douches. **Herpo-Max**™ provides **relief** from herpies outbreaks (see Source Page 384).

Sexual excess alters thyroid function as noted by the ancient Hebrews who examined the neck of the newly married bride the morning following the wedding night. A swollen neck was a SIGN of marriage consummation and heavy sexual activity. Young adults, who sexually abuse their bodies, lose their youthful appearance early and age faster—especially females—because of the stress on their ovaries and glands.

A man's inability to get an erection or frigidity in women are hormone and terrain driven (poor blood flow, low hydration levels, thyroid and bowel driven issues, plus borderline diabetes, liver stress, and *atrophy* of the ovaries and testicles).

Soy and canola oils play a part, too. In fact, A test lab found that canola oil caused sterility in rabbits, and it definitely messed up milk cows. In the book, *Our Stolen Future*, the soy

**myth** is EXPOSED for the damage it does in BOTH sexes by loading the body with *analogous* "zeno" estrogens that warp the system. **Ah yes, those scientific myths!**

Too frequent pregnancies, prolonged lactation accompanied by a poor diet can precipitate **goiter** in women. The female body needs at LEAST two years of rest and nourishment between each child. Over stress of the liver fuels menstrual and ovarian disorders, obesity and thyroid problems. Coldness in the feet and hands, low energy, brain fog (poor memory), sagging skin, joint problems and falling/graying hair are all "red flags" for a lagging thyroid—especially if you are female.

**Diabetes**

Diabetes and obesity are first cousins. Adult onset diabetes (Type ll) is the most common type. Buildup of metabolic waste, slow-down in organ function and systemic stress bring on adult diabetes. When waste levels EXCEED the body's ability to cope, symptoms **appear** out of nowhere.

As for juvenile diabetics (type l), there is **NO question** that polio and DPT vaccines mutate and bring on at least 75% of the cases. Hearing loss and autism in children are **CLOSELY** linked to vaccinations. The "problem(s)" appear in the hours, days, weeks, months and years that follow. Just because the child doesn't die in your arms—and thousands of babies have done just that—doesn't mean there is no connection to the damage done. The Federal government even established a "fund" to **insulate** the pharmaceuitcal companies and doctors from any liability related to vaccinations, be it death, disabilities or diabetes Type l. If you must vaccinate, wait until the child is **AT LEAST** 5 years old. Call for guidance.

ETVC™ helps with blood sugar management and fat metabolism. Obesity and sugar are **closely** related. Leaky gut syndrome is a **HUGE** issue for diabetics and obese people—and R/C™ works well for IGF-1 (insulin growth factor) issues. Reduce weight, restore the "terrain" and adult diabetes often disappears. The liver is **THE** central organ of "terrain" management, while colon therapy is a **fundamentally** critical protocol.

**The way to avoid serious health problems is also how you treat those problems after you have them. This concept should come as no surprise to the reader.**

Sugar is a **carbon** molecule. The diabetic uses carbon sugars to BUFFER acid waste, just as the soil in the garden does. Control of the "terrain" is the issue.**The goal is always the same: RETURN the terrain to a non acid state.** Terrain management is what the Young Again Protocol™ is about. Aging and dis-ease are only abberations thereof.

### Iodine

Oral iodine supplementation is the traditional health approach for hypo (low) thyroid conditions; and synthetic or glandular thyroid pills for the medical folks. Iodine (a halogen, like fluoride and chlorine) as found in kelp tablets is a powerful *stimulant* to the thyroid—but it does **NOT** solve the problem. Iodine can **cause a goiter (swollen thyroid) to form** by over stimulating the thyroid gland (hypertrophy). Stimulation of the thyroid in the face of **dietary and hormonal insufficiency** is futile. Traditional thyroid medications (pills lymph Synthroid™ and Armor Natural™) don't work. Alternative sublingual and oral supplements accomplish little. At best, they are *palliative* in nature. Racemized, biologically active, B.T. Creme™ works wonders directly through the skin—especially in "females."

### Let's Review

The organs become stressed from **acid**ification, over activity, waste build-up and malnutrition. Stress compounds the symptoms. **Excesses** then manifest as "deficiencies" causing a NEGATIVE energy shift and the manifestation of dis-ease. Reversing this process requires commitment and patience—**two qualities that most people need more of.**

Healing "crises" experienced during **de**acidification are a direct reflection of the person's toxicity level. **De**acidification is not fun, but it is a necessary step that lays the foundation for healing and aging reversal. **Healing "crises" are the price you must pay for your sins. I can assure you the price is little compared to growing old and suffering!**

The body is a DYNAMIC living energy field that succumbs to the process we call aging through our own mistakes. You cannot escape death, but you can reopen and keep the puberty window open for a very long time. **Post-mortem examination is a poor way to discover that your "chosen" lifestyle and belief system were fraudulent.** When you assist your body—instead of sabotaging it—you become *Young Again!*

**PREVIEW:** *Our next chapter discusses HOW the body "manufactures" what it needs by way of the bacteria and how mineral energy fuels our life processes.*

**It's Your Choice!**

**You don't have to feel and look old** and lose control of your life unless you are simply unwilling to take personal responsibility for your life.

Young Again™ products and protocols were developed to help people get control of their lives. The programs are NOT hard to follow. You do NOT have to take time off work. Suffering and discomfort are NOT a problem considering what most folks labor under most of the time.

Your author knows of **NOTHING** that feels as good as **NOT** having a personal physician and **NOT** having to swallow red, purple, blue and pink, doctor "pills" each day.

It is a **wonderful** feeling to get up each day and know you will feel better than you did yesterday—and that your tomorrows will be healthy and happy. When you feel "good," you are happy and glad to be alive—and you are a **blessing** to people around you.

So **WHAT** is holding you back? Money? The Young Again Protocol™ was designed for people on frugal budgets, too, so money is only an excuse. Fear? You can only **improve** the quality of your life by following John Thomas's advice and doing the program. Fear is just another excuse.

Most folks **appreciate** help and guidance in trying to put their life back together again. There is no need to order "everything" offered in the Source Packet. All you have to do is call and ask for "help!" and you will receive it **without** cost. The Young Again™ program, by necessity, is preceded with a "cost free" consultation. It is important to find your "comfort" zone.

**Gas Lady "Gloria"**

In March, 1994, in Riverside CA, Gloria Ramirez (age 32) checked into the emergency room—her body a "balloon." When the doctors and nurses cut her open, her blood became white crystals and poisonous gas filled the room as the entire medical staff collapsed on the floor—some in critical condition. Gloria was a customer of my brother. She drank heavily and did drugs. Her body was a "cannister" of metallic nitrogen and she was ready to **spontaneously** burst into **"flames."** Her body was a ***extreme*** example of toxicity and acidification.

**Alternative DENTAL Care**

The VERY best way to take care of your teeth and gums is with a Bio-Magnetic Dental Irrigator™. This device manipulates the hydrogen ions in water so plaque and calculus are **"oxidized"** from the tooth's surface and gum lines. **Do not confuse** a vibrating tooth brush or "pic" type squirt gun with this device! There is NO COMPARISON. My teeth are beautiful and my gums are healthy and I haven't had my teeth cleaned in **over 8 years!** No plaque means no decay, no gum disease and no dental bills. See pages 79, 204, and Source Page 384.

### "False" Readings

Positive energy can ***stir*** the system to the point of illness. This type of reaction is called a "healing crisis." It often occurs in people who are very toxic.

The body has *innate* intelligence. It ***knows*** and can ***anticipate*** the effect a positive energy substance will produce. Hence, the bio-electric body often rejects therapy and supplements that it needs. Sometimes the body "rejects" because it ***knows*** what it is going to have to go through to heal, and it knows the **owner** does NOT truly desire to be healed.

Often, the body "tricks" its owner by giving ***false*** muscle tests or false pendulum or vibration chain responses. To be useful, dowsing practices require the novice and professional alike to sharpen their skills and ***clear*** their minds so "gut" instinct can manifest.

Muscle testing is questionable at best and NOT accurate in the presence of heavy metal tissue contamination which skew "readings" derived from the autonomic nervous system . Muscle testing is mostly "hocus pocus" and useless for diagnosing or prescribing. "False" readings are all too common among practitioners.

Racemized™ products **do not** lend themselves to dowsing because their energy footprint is **beyond** the testing "dimension."

As the "terrain" improves, the body settles down so healing can take place on an accelerated basis. First, it's damage control. Then, aging reversal follows.

### The Pendulum

If you would like to learn how to use a pendulum and vibration chain, I recommend the books *The Pendulum Kit* and *Vibrations* because they have proven to be the best and least expensive way to teach people how to plug into the *invisible* world of "energy fields" surrounding us.

*The Pendulum Kit* comes complete with a nice bronze pendulum and a beautifully illustrated book, while *Vibrations* comes with a vibration chain. The tools and techniques learned are unique and useful. Dowsing teaches people how to access the big Internet in the sky.

"Dowsing" is a phenomenon and a GOD given gift that's available to anyone who desires to come to grips with the reality of life on planet Earth. See Source Page 384.

# 18

## Biological Alchemy

*"Since Einstein, Physics has been relegated to Mathematics, the former having lost all contact with reality. Your magnificent discovery of weak energy transmutations should have marked a scientific turning point, (but instead it) encountered a wall of stupidity."*

Ren de Puymorin

***...speaking of the work of Professor C. Louis Kervran and his discovery that the motion of life derives from the continuous transformation of one mineral into another or—"transmutation."***

**"Alchemy!** *Impossible! This is a good example of just plain old BAD science!"* So ended my official inquiry at the college level—but it did NOT end my inquiry.

What sparked the explosive outburst was the trigger word "transmutation" which means ***alchemy***. The *attacker* was a superb college chemistry instructor who did not like the implications of the questions I was raising, questions like... *"How* do you explain food plants that contain minerals not present in the soil? *How* does the cow produce milk that contains minerals far in excess of her dietary intake? *Where* does the hen get the minerals for her egg shells when they are not in her diet? *Why* does horsetail herb thicken and harden the nails, yet we derive NO such benefit from calcium supplements? *How* can organic manganese produce an increase in blood serum iron levels when it's not iron? *How* is it that a dried prune has more minerals than a fresh one? How, indeed? The answers to these questions derive from unrecognized genius (WIZARDS) and compromise ignored and forgotten knowledge.

Asking these type of questions is like proclaiming the invention of a perpetual motion machine. They can get a person in a lot of trouble, especially when put to the wrong person.

In our world of neatly packaged chemicals and defined LAWS of chemistry and physics, these questions have no answers. But, make no mistake, these ARE valid questions—just the kind Professor Kervran liked to ask. The problem isn't the questions posed, but the implications they suggest.

Some people of science are intimidated by questions for which they have no answers. Daring to ask them is an assault on DOGMA and enough to get a person branded *"science heretic!"*—and instant burning at the stake!

**Mineral Energy**

The life work of Professor C. Louis Kervran (1899-1990) has startling implications for reversing the aging process.

Kervran surmised that the energy *phenomenon* we call LIFE is related to the transformation of one mineral into another. He called this process *"transmutation."* Science calls it alchemy. We will refer to it as biological alchemy.

Alter the energy forces within an element and a new and different element results. In the process, energy is released. Kervran believed this energy fueled metabolic processes and was the "life force" upon which life manifests. Transmutation, as he described it, would require a change in elemental structure at atomic and subatomic levels and the rearrangement of **an**ions and **cat**ions. In other words, COLD fusion!

Kervran's discoveries came from **inside** Science's camp. Kervran was a member of both the French and American National Academy of Sciences, the most prestigious watering holes of modern science.

Professor Kervran *dared* to ask the right questions. He *sinned* against Science and dogma when he offered God's answer to his fellow man. He broke the rules because he failed to submit his findings for "peer" review. Great Wizards have NO peers! They see visions of God's handiwork and proclaim the great news, **while science curses in contempt!**

Like Copernicus, Kervran's peers *attacked* and *ridiculed* him as they have done to so many other Wizards before him. They tried to ignore him, but they could NOT deny the TRUTH he heralded. When a vessel of TRUTH is opened, it can NEVER be closed again. Truth is a Pandora's Box for those who live in ignorance and who are afraid of it—**especially those who egotistically "bask" in degrees and credentials.**

## Visions

Kervran suspected that minerals contained concentrated energy fields within their bonds. His vision of the Creator's handiwork was not unlike that of his contemporary, Dr. Carey Reams. These great men of science never met. Each developed his own vision independently. Each talked about the same phenomena from their own perspective and interpretation of the phenomena they observed.

Reams called his vision, *The Biological Theory of Ionization.* Kervran called his, *The Theory of Biological Transmutation.* Both spoke of energy forces that grant permission for life. Both spoke of energy as a "footprint" or "signature," the same phenomenon described by Vincent and incorporated in BEV™ and Medical Grade Ionized Water™.

Reams talked of positive energy ions called **an**ions, and negative energy ions called **cat**ions. Kervran spoke of the rearrangement of energy forces and the fusion of these forces at the atomic and *sub*atomic levels.

Reams spoke of left and right-spin energy and the release of cosmic forces trapped in mineral bonds (ionic bonds). Kervran talked of mineral ***transmutation*** in the gut of animals and in the skin and lymph of the Earth—soil and water.

The Sun was a central fixture for both men. They saw plants, animals, and microbes as **mediators** between Sun and Earth. Both men sought the answer to the "Why?" of life that we raised in chapter two—the mystery of life and death, health and illness. God answered both men with living examples of the importance of biologically "live" food, high ORP water and disciplined lifestyles. He answered Reams in English and Kervran in French. Our version will be a translation of both.

## Plants • Animals • Microbes

The plant is the link between the Sun and the animal world to which man's body belongs. The plant converts solar energy into carbon sugar molecules with the help of the microbe. Plants bring life and energy INTO the Earth.

The animals—with the help of the microbes—process plant tissue and live off the electron energy released during the digestion process. Animal waste becomes part of the Earth's "skin" and provides a catalyst for new life—plant, animal and microbe.

To Kervran, mineral energy fields in a living system were forever dynamic—shifting and changing one into the other. For example, in HEALTHY multiple stomached animals (called ruminants), calcium limestone is "transmutated" by bacteria in order to meet the animal's needs. Humans have but one stomach. To be effective, minerals must be in the biologically active form—"ionic" form, **not** colloidal form!

Kervran saw "life" energy flowing from a potpourri of mineral elements. To him, health was a manifestation of a microbial *fiesta* in the gut and liver of man and animal! In order for Kervran's *fiesta* to occur in man's body, the "terrain" must be electrically **balanced**. The microbe is at the center of the *alchemy* process we call *fusion*. Cold fusion allows life to express and maintain itself. It involves the transmutation of one energy field into another. **Transmutation of mineral energy fields slows aging and maintains peak health.**

### Cows & People

The cow utilizes the transmutation process. She eats plants (compounds of carbon, hydrogen, sulphur, nitrogen, sugars, fats, proteins, and minerals) and converts them into NEW and DIFFERENT energy forms—like muscle and bone.

The cow does this by way of the enzymes and microbes in her liver and GI tract. The bacteria that share her system have a *symbiotic* relationship with her. She provides them room and board; they provide her with energy and vitality. Without the microbes and enzymes, the fantastic biochemical reactions Kervran called *transmutations* CANNOT take place. Without the microbes, the cow is unable to nourish herself. Without the microbes, man grows old and dies early.

**The microbe is man's passport to a continued presence on the Earth. However, man's disobedience is causing the microbe to turn against him.**

Sick cows have much in common with sick **people**. Both are UNABLE to effectively use the transmutation process. Health and vitality in man is a reflection of the ***terrain*** and the processes Kervran and Reams called transmutation and ionization. The requirements for a healthy life are nutritious, right-spin, high energy food, ionic minerals, biologically friendly high ORP water, exercise, and a clean *internal* environment.

When the cow drinks chlorinated water, the chemicals create an energy imbalance that causes the microbes to mutate into *pathogenic* life forms. The result of this energy shift is a slow-down in metabolic activity in the gut and liver and loss of vitality and health.

Antibiotics cause a similar effect. They upset the balance of intestinal flora by changing the ***terrain*** of the body. So called "good" microbes live off right-spin energy, while pathogenic microbes live off left-spin energy present in a toxic environment. Anaerobic environments are left-spin environments. Aerobes (friendly bacteria) cannot live in an anaerobic environment, and they **forfeit** their "terrain" whenever such a condition develops. A sick cow—or a human being—is the reflection of a sick internal environment.

### Fusion & Fission

Life is a tug of war between opposing energy forces. Transmutation and ionization are involved in both positive and negative biological energy shifts—fusion and fission.

**Fusion** involves the joining of atoms to form larger molecules. Under normal biological circumstances, it is a positive energy activity and represents the build-up process we call *anabolism.* Fusion occurs on the surface of the *Sun,* in the *soil,* in plants and in the gut and liver of man and animal.

An example of *abnormal* biological fusion would be cancer. Cancer results from toxic waste build-up, hormonal imbalance and the introduction of *radiomimetic* substances. Examples would be irradiated food, microwaved food and water, prescription and over the counter drugs and food laced with hormone analogs. The process produces tissue oxidation and free radical formation. Oxidation accelerates aging into FAST FORWARD. The Young Again™ protocol can stop these uncontrolled processes and reverse the damage.

**"Fission"** breaks down molecules and atoms. Normal, biological fission activity is good. But once we lose control, the fission process becomes *catabolic* in nature. Examples of destructive fission reactions are nuclear reactions, irradiation, radiation therapy, microwave cooking, etc. Fission reactions orchestrated by **friendly** microbes are beneficial. But, when we lose control of the *terrain* (acidification of the tissues), we usher in negative fission reactions and dis-ease orchestrated by mutant pathogenic microbes.

### Skin • Dirt • Soil • Lymph

The Earth has skin. Her skin is called soil. Some folks call soil "dirt." Dirt, however, is *dead* unless it is *energized* with microbes, organic matter and carbon. The microbes *transform* dirt into soil. Soil is biologically *alive.* Soil has *life.*

Water is the essence of life. Water is the Earth's lymphatic fluid, and it is capable of transporting massive amounts of energy. Soil energy and soil depth are controlled by carbon. Carbon underwrites Mother Earth's aura.

When the Earth becomes stressed, her skin forms boils, her lymph becomes toxic, the plants become weak, the animals suffer and man experiences dis-ease. The condition of Earth's skin and lymph dictates the quality of life AND which life forms live or die. Fundamentally, life is a microbial affair that involves transmutation and ionization of mineral energy.

**The microbes and the minerals are man's ticket to longevity —if he has the wisdom to recognize their importance and follow nature's rules.**

### *Synchronization*

Synchronization can be the end result of a chemical reaction—like mixing vinegar with baking soda—one acid, the other alkaline. When the reaction has run its course, two things have occurred. Energy has been released (heat) and synchronization has occurred between the original reactants. Here, in an inorganic chemical example, the reaction stopped. The dynamics of the human body are not quite so simple.

The body's **ability** or **inability** to digest and process food energy (potential energy), and break the molecular bonds holding that energy that **dictates** the outocme. Food's energy "footprint" and the "terrain" **govern** the outcome of the reaction as much carbohydrate, protein and fat composition.

Where an *anaerobic* gut and a toxic liver are involved, even right-spin energy food can synchronize or convert to a left-spin energy condition. That is why leaky gut syndrome and chewing of "good" food, digestive enzymes and liver function are so **fundamental** to a healthy "terrain." In the end, it is the terrain that governs the maintenance of an aerobic "state." **An *anaerobic* gut is the perfect terrain for a negative energy takeover—like cancer.**

Synchronized energy is energy that is on hold. It is energy that is NOT available to the body. People in poor health are in energy **gridlock.** They are unable to neutralize *negative* energy fields and too weak to free potential positive food energy. Negative energy neutralizes positive energy. Sick bodies produce lots of negative energy. Dis-ease is the end product of a left-spin *anaerobic* take over—a *catabolic* state.

**Tissue and liver deACIDification along with colon therapy "free" a toxic, gridlocked terrain.**

When the *bio-electric* body suffers *systemic* synchronization, OLD AGE goes into FAST FORWARD and life becomes impossible! As we approach total synchronization, we lose our "radiance." The aura diminishes and dwindles until it ceases to be and the physical body dies. The ghost is gone! Yet, synchronized energy remains in the form of a cadaver which Earth reclaims. Ashes to ashes! Dust to dust! **Energy is never lost, but it does change form and recycles again.**

## Energy Takeover

When the chemical bonds holding synchronized energy under lock and key are broken, energy can go EITHER way. If the bonds are broken in a predominantly *anaerobic* environment, the energy can become a negative force—even if it was originally positive in nature. This is what I meant earlier when I said right-spin energy entering a left-spin environment can be diverted and used to promote dis-ease. The "terrain" is key.

**Cancer lives on the negative energy available in a sick, anaerobic body. Learn HOW to manage your TERRAIN and cancer will never be a threat.**

A person suffering from bowel disorders is under stress—*anaerobic stress*. Gut and bowel problems slow ionization and transmutation of mineral energy and create the perfect "parasite" situation. Gas and bloating are PROOF of incomplete digestion and a "terrain" that is out of balance.

Cancer follows in the wake of years of personal abuse. It likes an anaerobic environment where it can divert positive energy to negative purposes—like the growth of a "mass." People with cancer should NEVER be given large amounts of high protein foods—be it meat, fish, fowl or beans. Moderation is key along with racemized™ digestive products designed for a body terrain that is our of control. The cancer patient is literally starving to death and at the same time fighting to hang onto life. **TIME** is not on the cancer patient's side. The use of Taoist™ products and the L/CSF machine are crucial, here.

## Cancer—A Different Set Of Rules

The rules of life are different once a person is under cancer's pall because cancer is a *catabolic* state and the cancerous person is very fragile.

Alternative approaches often fail because the doctor/patient fail to understand that the rules have **changed**. Clinical nutrition doesn't work here—the rules are NOT the same! Cancer hijacks the body's energy. Cancer masses are **black holes** that draw-in and subvert all available energy and then EXPORT it to outlying colonies. Cancer uses biological alchemy to BREAK **synchronized** bonds to fuel its growth.

There will NEVER be a "magic bullet" cure for cancer. Cancer defies the rules and complies with none of the LAWS of normal health. Cancer has but one purpose: to kill the host and rid the Earth of weak organisms. **Cancer is NOT the enemy, but it is the perfect double agent. First it kills the host. Then it kills itself. SYNCHRONIZATION!**

When you are in control of your body terrain, YOU are

in control of your life and the *magical* processes that Kervran and Reams described so eloquently.

Health and vitality are the **effects** of the process we call *biological alchemy.* The process depends on our microbial friends and the "terrain" environment we provide for them. Water is part of the terrain story. BEV™ water is fundamental. Medical Grade Ionized Water™ should be viewed as "frosting on the cake." First comes **damage control**, then **restoration** of the **terrain**. Aging reversal occurs as a natural result in the wake of these. To learn more, order the BEV™ manuscript and the water book and video (see Source Page 384).

Kervran and Reams discovered a vital piece of the process we call aging. Their life's work points the way to total body rejuvenation and good health if we understand the rules of the game and are willing to take **personal responsibility** for ourselves. Only then can we become *Young Again!*

**PREVIEW:** *Our next chapter is about the gut (small intestine) and the E. coli bacteria infections that killed many people and children during 1993. You will also learn what's behind Montezuma's revenge.*

---

### Cancer "Craps!"

Conventional cancer therapy has more than a little resemblance to the game of "craps."

You have stakes—your life. You have rules—*house* rules. You have the dealer—a *house* dealer that wears a white robe and who is controlled by the licensing boards and pharmaceutical industry. You have the *house* support team—they wear uniforms and they have licenses and are trained to do as they have been trained or are told. You have the other players—who appear to be winning enough to justify your joining the game. You have chips—called insurance, life savings, a farm, a house. You have dice—weighted in the *house's* favor. You have liquor—called radiation and chemotherapy. You have the *house* bouncer—his name is Fear. You have the *house* preacher—his name is Hope. You have odds—the **75%** the house *dealer* gave you during your "consultations" prior to joining the game.

All games have an end. When you play cancer craps, the game automatically ends when you run out of money, or when you die—whichever comes first.

The *house* always wins when people play *their* game, on *their* turf, by *their* rules. Is there a solution? You bet! **Don't play!**

Instead, clean up your body. **LAUGH!** Don't cry "poor me!" Don't dwell on hate, anger and fear. Use your mind to create a new body. Never entertain negative thoughts. Got it?

What you say your body believes! What you think, you get! It took me fifty years to get this straight, and I am here to tell you that your mind has the ability to create or to destroy! Use it to create a better life and world.

**Celebrate!** You're ***ALIVE*** and if you do what you need to do, you will continue to celebrate life and see your great, great grand children mature; and you will get to experience the many wonders the future holds for those who love life MORE than those who fear death.

**The Game Of Cancer Craps Is A "Crappy" Game!**

### Herpies • Shingles

Herpeis and shingle complaints can be "fixed" with Cobo-12™ and Herpo-Max™. Both involve stressed nerve tissue, in people at opposite ends of the age spectrum for similar, but different reasons. For help, see Source Page 384.

## *Young Again! Pyramid*

(+) **Peak** (-)

Life — Death
Good — Bad
Strong — Weak
Aerobic — Anaerobic
Right-spin — Left-spin
*Slow* Time — *Fast* Time

*anabolic* — *catabolic*

**Young** — **Old**

| **Life is a scrapbook of lessons—never mistakes!** |
|---|

## pH Scale

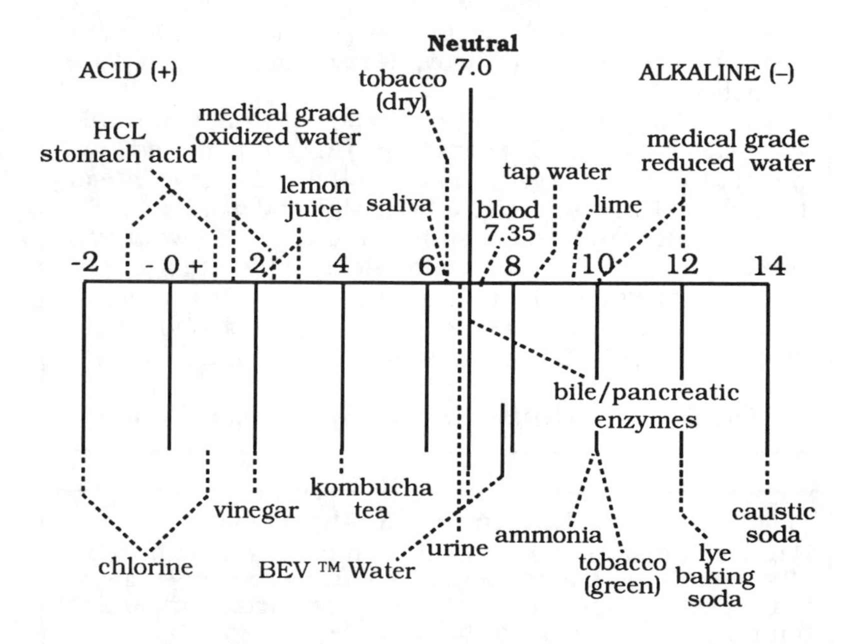

# 19

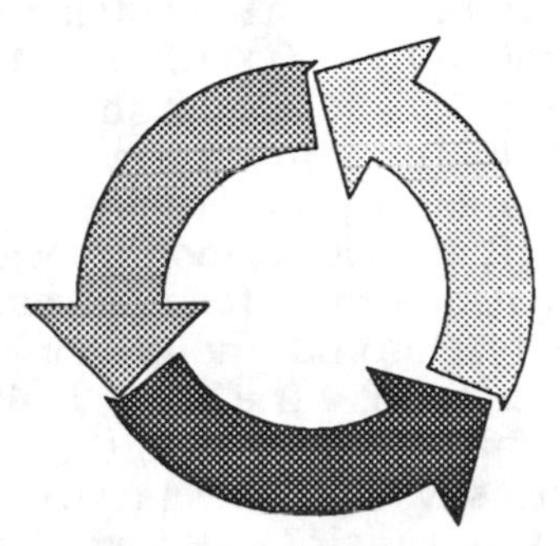

## A Tube Within A Tube

Dr. Spot: *"There's always scissors!"*

*Earlier we described some of the characteristics of the integumentary system (skin) as it relates to health, Now, we will consider our "inner" skin and see what part it plays in the process we call aging.*

Man's body is a tube within a tube. The skin is our *outer* tube and the mucous membranes form the *inner* tube. The mucous membranes are the soft tissues that line the mouth, nasal passages, respiratory tract, stomach, gut, colon and vagina. With the exception of the vaginal canal, the body's "inner" tube begins in the mouth and end at the anus. The vaginal canal is not part of the GI tract, but the importance of the health of the mucosa to this part of the female reproductive system is **immense.** The mucous membranes have tremendous significance to the story of aging and dis-ease.

The tissues lining the mouth, nasal passages, respiratory system, and mucous membranes are classified as *stratified epithelium* and their primary job is to **protect** underlying tissues, secrete fluids, and to transport waste.

The remainder of the inner tube is the GI tract. Its membranes are made up of *simple epithelium* whose job is to **ABSORB** nutrients, **PROTECT** underlying tissues, **SECRETE** mucous and enzymes, and transport food and waste.

Our outer tube, the skin, has a combined surface area of about 30,000 square inches. The pores (openings) of the skin are called *stoma*, and there are as many as 3,000 of them per square inch. By comparison, the mucous membranes have an approximate surface area of 18,000,000 (million) square inches or 600 times greater. One inch on the outside equals 600 inches on the inside or a ratio of 1:600. THIS IS IMPORTANT!

In the healthy person, eating should cause digestion, absorption and elimination. But beyond age 24, these VERY BASIC functions diminish and eventually become major health issues in the years that follow. Food imposes stress on the body, even good foo. Undigested food putrefies in the gut and fuels parasitic activity. Gas and "indigestion" are confirmation of digestive and bowel trouble. The latest "fashion" condition in style is **acid reflux** which is nothing but the side effect of a toxic terrain and liver, digestive and bowel issues rolled into one.

**The longer the transit time from the dinner table to the toilet, the more toxins we produce and absorb.**

The mucous membranes are a favorite conduit for drug chemotherapy. Medications in the form of suppositories, sublinguals and aerosols are easily absorbed through the membranes of the rectum, vagina and respiratory system. A doctor dares not prescribe the same dosage of medication via the mucosa as would be given orally or by subcutaneous or intramuscular injection because of the absorption rate.

### E. coli & The Gut

Most nutrient absorption takes place in the intestinal mucosa. This is the body's most **vulnerable** and most important "terrain." An infection in the gut causes the natural sloughing action of the mucosa to increase. Normal sloughing occurs at the rate of approximately twenty million cells a day. These cells provide an important source of intestinal enzymes (the enzymes are contained in the sloughed-off cells) which act as the vehicle of delivery. *Pathogenic* infection increases sloughing to such an extent that digestion and absorption of nutrients and fluids fail to occur resulting in diarrhea and malnutrition.

The infamous **E. coli 0157.H7** bacteria that contaminated hamburger in the USA in early 1993 produced severe sloughing of the intestinal mucosa and "bloody" diarrhea followed by dehydration, starvation and electrolytic shock in hundreds of children and older people. What was "really" going on here was a classic case of **SEVERE** leaky gut syndrome.

E. coli 0157.H7 produces an **exotoxin** (*exo*-to export, *toxin*-poison) that severely STRESSES the functional tissues of the liver and kidneys. Dead (necrotic) cells MUST be removed immediately or their acid wastes will putrify and produce systemic toxemia and even gangrene. A "dead" body left unattended, swells like a balloon due to the gasses produced by gangrene; hence "gas gangrene." Such a condition **overloads** the liver which then **overloads** the kidneys, forcing the need for kidney dialysis (artificial filtering of the blood). Dialysis is required to prevent systemic shock (toxemia).

### Old & Young

Elderly people are grossly affected by E. coli infections because their organs and glands are weak and their metabolism is sluggish. Moreover, their ATP energy reserves are low and toxicity levels are high. Their bodies are catabolic and usually anaerobic. Lack of resiliency is their Achilles heel.

Children are at the other end of the continuum. They are highly resilient, but their immune systems are not fully developed and they are often malnourished and toxic because they eat the *usual and customary* American diet. At the heart of any major illness in a child is the **LIVER**, bowel issues, diet and underhydration. A stressed body terrain is a **made-to-order** environment for bacterial infections like E. coli 0157.H7. Not all E. coli are alike! Friendly, non-virulent strains live in the gut. Life is IMPOSSIBLE without their help. It is the "terrain" that dictates response and ability to handle pathogenic forms. Antibiotics and vaccinations create "perfect" environments for virulent microbes to proliferate. Avoid both of them.

### Not Everyone Died

Over a million pounds of E. coli contaminated beef found its way into fast food restaurants, yet only a few hundred people became sick and only 6 died. The question is WHY? The answer has to do with the vibrational frequency of the "terrain" of the sick and dead people.

Pathogenic organisms "feed" on negative energy fields produced in a TOXIC environment which explains why, in a family with three children—all of whom ate contaminated beef—only one child died. No mystery is involved here.

**The body's energy field—the TERRAIN—determines sickness and death or health and vitality.**

The contagious dis-eases that plagued mankind throughout history—bubonic plague, smallpox, typhoid, etc.—did NOT kill everyone. Those who die have stressed TERRAINS. The same can be said about the so called "anthrax" attacks following the 9/11 disaster in NYC (September 11, 2001).

These points raise serious questions about the absurdity of immunizing against dis-ease—a **sacred cow** in the USA. A healthy terrain is the correct answer.

*The panic seen in the recent movie Outbreak IS understandable in light of the general level of ignorance regarding contagious dis-ease. Clean up your act and Ebola plague, Hanta virus, Cryptosporidium bacteria, necrotizing facitis (flesh eating bug) and their likes will pass you by.*

**A clean body is equivalent to the blood on the lintel stone over the doorway of the Israelites. Death passes by.**

### Lack Of Understanding

People of science have difficulty understanding discussions like this because of their training. Scientific thought embraces the "scientific method" and the "Germ Theory." Our discussion does NOT fit their "model" or their false theories, and conflicts with their *pusillanimous mewings*.

***Whenever the phone rings and the caller asks, "What are your credentials?" I know I have an "expert" on my hands, or someone who wants to defend something. Credentials are for the ego and the licensing boards. The modest professionals have their ego and prejudices in tow and don't care about credentials which are proof of the ability to regurgitate the "party line" and not think. Credentials are nice—IF they don't get in the way. Got it?***

Vibrational medicine asks square questions and it provides square answers. It approaches health related problems from an ENERGY vantage point. It is not hindered by the Germ Theory of Disease and other theoretical artifacts.

Remember, healthy bodies are nourished bodies. Healthy bodies are clean bodies. Healthy bodies are bodies in good physical condition. Healthy bodies produce and store massive amounts of ATP energy. The healthy body will not support proliferation of pathogenic microbes.

### It's The Pits

The small intestine is lined with convoluted folds called the *plicae circularis*. These folds are lined with *villi* (little fingers) and *microvilli* (hair-like structures) that increase the surface area of the intestine to 600 times that of the outer skin. The microvilli contain the cells that absorb and transport food nutrient energy. The spaces *between* the villi are known as the **Crypts of Lieberkuhn.** The Crypts are lined with cells that secrete digestive enzymes and mucous.

As we age, the valleys that make up the intestinal ***pits*** become shallow. The villi and microvilli atrophy. Transit time of food—from mouth to anus—slows. Constipation manifests. Parasites appear. As these alterations occur, the pits, villi and microvilli become smothered in slow moving fecal matter, mucoid substances and acid metabolic wastes.

**Anaerobic** conditions in the colon produce serious changes in the chemical make up of the fecal matter interfacing the intestinal walls. Fecal matter *transforms* into a rubber-like, **mucoid** material that thickens and narrows the opening (lumen) of the colon—like an occluded water pipe—through which the body's wastes must pass. During serious cleansing and fasting, the mucoid lining "forms" and sheds.

Earlier I mentioned that the colon of a very famous Hollywood cowboy had grown to almost twelve inches in diameter at the time of death, yet the lumen for waste movement was only one inch. The rest was mucoid matter.

Fully **85%** of the population needs colon therapy to get their house in order. The *Rouleau* effect (see page 136) seen in the blood of 95% of the people. There is a connection, here!

The combined effect of limited digestive and absorptive capability, poor liver function and congested skin means the average person **forfeits** over 75% of their waste processing capacity! The waste exit portals remaining—the lungs and kidneys—are NOT capable of handling the load. Toxic overload of the "terrain" **accelerates** aging of the *bio-electric* body.

**A CLEAN bowel and healthy liver are the difference between youth and vitality vs. old age and death.**

Colon therapy may be unAmerican, but it should NOT be dismissed. The Young Again **Colon Therapy** Protocol™ is the **fast track** to good health. Yet, despite my doing colonics over an 18 year period, the Young Again **Tissue & Liver** Protocol™ produced over 1600 stones from my body. Following the stones, came MORE dumping of mucoid matter. **It takes 5-10 YEARS to clear the terrain of "stuff!"** Please read it again.

A great book on the subject of colon therapy is *Tissue Cleansing & Bowel Management.* I highly recommend this book because it shows the reader —in forty full color pictures— exactly what people are up against in when it comes to restoration of the body's "terrain."

## My Story

By 1977 I had reached a plateau in my personal health. I visited a lady who had been trained by Dr. Reams in the Biological Theory of Ionization. Dolly took saliva and urine readings and read the sclera (whites) of my eyes. The results showed I had mucoid build-up in my colon. Subsequent colon therapy confirmed this as I saw hard, compacted fecal material exit my body. The event caused my health to reach NEW heights as my body immediately ***surged backward*** to more youthful days. **This was in the old days BEFORE the Young Again Protocol™ was researched and perfected.** Colon therapy can be done at home. It is safe and easy to do. In times of severe illness, colonics can save your life.

UNPLUG from the medical system and follow the path outlined in this book and you will enjoy a wonderful life. That's what this book is about. I did it! And so can you!

A *live testimony* from your author—and you can believe it, for I am ***Young Again!***

**PREVIEW:** *Our next chapter is about YOUR aura. Why do people climb rock mountains? HOW could Jesus pass through the wall of the temple?*

**The Bio-Magetic™ Dental Irrigator**

## Oxidation = Aging

Enhanced PAC's prevent uncontrolled cellular oxidation. Uncontrolled oxidation causes the body to cannibalize itself. **Oxidation** is another word for aging.

As we age, the tissues oxidize faster and faster. The cross-linking that occurs in "skin" collagen and causes wrinkles is an example of tissue oxidation. A massive heart attack is another example. "Aging" sums it up, nicely. SOC™ Lotion and capsules reverse scar tissue formation, wrinkled skin and aging, in general.

A *free radical scavenger* is a chemical compound that **bonds** to "free radicals," which are highly reactive chemicals that are short or long on electrons. PAC's prevent rapid oxidation and destructive chain reactions from occurring. PAC's are "proanthrocyanidans" with both **hydro**philic and **lypo**philic racemized™ qualities.

We ingest massive amounts of free radicals every day. They come from air, water, and food. The body also *manufactures* them in the process of *metabolism.*

Once toxic substances enter the body, they **metamorphose** and become even more toxic. Examples would be food additives, fluorides and chlor**amines** in tap water, soy and canola oils, pesticides, microwaved food, vaccination induced viruses and bacteria and animal serum proteins that transport them.

PAC's neutralize wastes released into circulation during the "**de**acidification" process of the Young Again Tissue & Liver Protocol™. They minimize acid waste from reabsorption as the waste works its way down 20 feet of intestine on their way to the toilet.Without PAC's and Yucca Blend,™ the body will **NOT** release the acids.

All dis-ease conditions respond favorably when PAC's are incorporated into the diet. Sickly children and kids with ADD and ADHD show marked improvement. Older folks find them very easy to use.

PAC' possess 24,660 activity units per bottle—enough to easily offset the damage done by BOTH over-the counter and prescription drugs. Pac's eliminate the need for less effective antioxidants like vitamins A, E, C and zinc. Anyone on medications should be using Pac's.

Aging reversal is a very TALL order and the older or sicker you are, the TALLER is the request. We live out our lives inundated by "stuff." The easiest way to avoid tissue oxidation is to incorporate PAC's into your regimen. Try some and find out for yourself (see Source Page 384).

**STOP Those "pesky" PERIODS**

The medical folks and their cronies in the pharmeceutical industry have officially admitted "defeat" in helping women with menstrual difficulties enjoy a normal female life. Their latest answer is to force the body to STOP menstruation altogether. The side effects of birth control pills are bad enough, but can you imagine the side effects of this asinine proposal? Madmen in white coats fixing what God could not. I think this is a good example of "playing" GOD!.

Helping women with menstrual and menopause problems is easy when the "model" represents the reality of female physiology rather than symptomatic complaints. The Young Again™ model and female protocol is a better and safer path that allows women to avoid the hassles associated with a female body "terrain" that is out of control.

---

**Cell Phones**

Lots of folks spend a lot of time on cell phones these days. Since these devices are now part of the social and business "fabric", your author STRONGLY suggests cell phone users invest a few dollars in a simple, TV advertised device that "blocks" brain radiation generated by cell phones. The bones of the sides of the skull are very thin where cell phone energy generation is strongest. A few dollars is better than a brain tumor or Alzheimers—or death!

---

**High Blood Pressure & Chelation**

Blood "chelation" (not to be confused with chelation therapy, as in cancer) with the agent EDTA is a very safe and viable procedure that really works.

The medical folks don't like the modality because it "mocks" their faulty medical model. If you have serious blood pressure problems, find a practitioner who offers "chelation" and get "fixed."

And if you will follow Young Again Protocols™ prior to doing chelation, you will enjoy even better results—and you will be astounded to discover a "new" life that's worth living.

---

**Where Does All That "Stuff" Come From?**

80% Of stool "bulk" is Bacteria! Is takes 5-10 years to totally clear the human body of acid wastes. Maintenance of the "terrain" is a **forever** issue—and it's worth the effort!

# 20

# The Aura Effect

*"Man's mind stretched to a new idea never goes back to its original dimension."*
Oliver Wendel Holmes

The injury had occurred the night before, but Jerry was not aware of any specific damage. As Jerry and I walked into the shop and began browsing, the lady who owned the shop approached Jerry and said,

*"OOOH! You must be hurting pretty bad?"*

He looked at her blankly and asked what she meant.

*"Oh! Your aura! You have a very BIG hole in it in your groin area. Did you injure yourself?"*

Jerry was hurting. He had torn a hernia in the connective tissues of his pelvic region the night before.

What was so intriguing about the encounter was that this lady was a total stranger. She knew nothing about Jerry, yet she was able to vividly see his body aura and the hole in it. We had heard of people like this lady, but neither of us had witnessed the phenomenon before.

### The Glow Of Health

The body has a radiation field surrounding it. This is an established fact. Kirlian photography can capture the aura on a photographic plate—its size, shape and color in direct relation to the overall "condition" of the person.

Jesus was reported to have a *glow* about Him. Whenever He is pictured, the halo or aura effect is always seen around His head. The halo and aura are right-spin energy. Many people believe the greater your aura, the more advanced a human being you are. Perhaps. For certain, each of us has an aura, and the greater it is, the **healthier** we are!

When people suffer with dis-ease, the electrical charge of the *bio-electric* body shifts from one that is right-spin and healthy, to one that is left-spin and pathogenic. Whenever we notice the sickly pallor of another person, we are taking note of a diminished *aura*, though we may not recognize it as such. We also recognize when the person has returned to health—by noting their pallor and energy "state" by way of their aura.

### Energy Drain

Some people are exhausting. I am not speaking of the person who runs in *hyper drive*, but the person who drains your energy and leaves you feeling very tired. These folks are energy sinks! They may be nice people, but the *effect* of their presence is less than refreshing. A whole lot less!

Sue owned a massage therapy and iridology clinic for many years. She once commented that certain people drew so much energy from her that she could not work on them. Later, I learned that my wife had severed her friendship with one lady Sue would no longer treat. The reason was that the lady was *exhausting!*

Sue was an interesting person. She had the uncanny ability to *see* and *feel* things about people who came to her for treatments. They call people like Sue "healer." Sue definitely was a healer. Sue was also a superb organic gardener. Sue had a green thumb and the plants produced abundantly for her. Her plants were "vibrantly" healthy and never required any form of poison to control bugs or weeds.

One day I asked her, *"Sue, what is your secret?"* She just smiled. As I came to know her, I realized that she knew how to speed up body frequency—through the laying-on of hands. In her case, it was called massage therapy. Sue could speed up the electron flow in the body of the patient to such an extent that the person walked out of her clinic TOTALLY refreshed and happy to be alive.

By accelerating the flow of energy, Sue strengthened the positive energy fields in the body and "drew off" negative energy forces. The effects were seen immediately in the patient's *aura* and vibrancy. Sue had mastered the skill of energy manipulation. She understood that **life** is a field of competing energy forces. Sometimes she would shake her hands, walk barefoot in grass or sand or hug a tree barefooted to dissipate the negative energy she had taken on from her sick patients.

**Energy & Auras**

The world is composed of but one thing: energy! When energy condenses, it is called matter. Matter has three states: gas, liquid, and solid—every substance is a variation of energy density and vibrational molecular frequency.

Rocks are hard and solid. Skin has texture and can be stretched. Rocks and skin are not *really* solids, we just "classify" them as solids. Solids are energy fields joined together in such a way that they take on the shape, feel, and smell of something we learn to identify as rock, skin, tomato, etc.

All things living and non-living have an aura. A rock's aura—and the effect it exerts on things near it—can be positive or negative. If the rock's energy state is positive, it will have a therapeutic effect on plants and visa versa.

If we increase the flow of electrons around the nuclei of the atoms in a rock, it will change form. For example, if we heat sulphur, it will change from a solid, to a liquid, to a gas. Water does the same—ice to liquid to steam.

**Rocks & Mountains**

In the Bible, rocks had particular significance in matters of health. Rocks have a sacred place in most religions. Rocks are not *live* in the animal sense, but they do possess *life*. A rock's life is expressed in its energy footprint and signature.

People like rocks. Some people like them so much they have a head full of them. People who climb rock mountains are often asked, "WHY?" The answer usually given is *"Because they are there!"* There is a more accurate reason. People climb rocks because they find it ***invigorating***. Climbers absorb fantastic quantities of ENERGY from rock mineral formations. Rocks radiate ENERGY that syncs the climber with Mother Earth. Climbing rocks is one way for people to tap-into nature's energy bank. So is swimming in sea water or walking bare foot in sand or grass or hugging a tree or eating food grown on healthy soil. Energy is released and "absorbed" when mineral ion "bonds" are broken—and that energy makes us feel good!

**Jesus & The Wall**

It is recorded that when Jesus was about to be stoned in the Temple, He passed through the wall and disappeared to the frustration of his enemies. As a child, I accepted this story, but I never believed it because anyone with a lick of sense knows that you cannot walk through a wall.

Today, this story delivers a different message—one that is both factual and explanatory. Christ possessed the knowledge and ability to accelerate the flow of electrons in His body. In so doing, He was able to pass through the wall of the temple. By speeding up His electrons to the point of disintegration (think of ice becoming steam), He squeezed between the atoms of the stone wall and vanished. Neither He nor the wall were solids! Both were made up of energy "particles." Christ did not violate natural law, rather He knew how to manipulate it.

Life is a STATEMENT of positive (+) and negative (–) energy forces. Man gives them different names and classifies them in ways that are more easily understood. For example: good and evil, light and dark, right and wrong, left and right, YOUNG and OLD and so on. Regardless, we are referring to the phenomena we call ENERGY!

### Reflections

The body's aura is a reflection of our inner state of health. We can measure our aura with a pendulum, vibration chain or aurameter, but does require the dowser to clear the mind so as not to interfere. **(*The Pendulum Kit, Vibrations,* and *Map Dowsing* is a trilogy of books to teach you how to effectively dowse.)**

A pendulum is nothing but an antenna that sends and receives electrical energy. Our mind receives the information and "interprets" it. Measuring your body aura establishes a **reference point** that we can use to measure change or determine the effect a substance is likely to have on the body. The "hitch" is learning to clear your mind and asking valid questions. What will be the immediate effect of this product? The long term effect? Can I expect a healing crisis? And so on.

Use a pendulum or aurameter to check food substances. Identify left-spin or right-spin apples, carrots, etc. Whatever is being measured is like a radio station that is sending out ENERGY signals. In this case, the pendulum is the receiving antenna. It can also be used to transmit signals.

We send and receive electrical signals when we "follow" our intuition—which is a kind of sixth sense. We will discuss these Fourth Dimension concepts in a future chapter.

As you reverse the aging process, your aura expands and your physical VITALITY increases. When your aura has returned to the level it was before you began the descent into old age, you have returned to your *anabolic* PEAK. In the process of getting there, the passage of TIME slows until it STOPS altogether. When this occurs, you have achieved agelessness and you are *Young Again!*

**PREVIEW:** *Our next chapter deals with energy and numbers. Did you know that big can mean small, and weak can mean strong?*

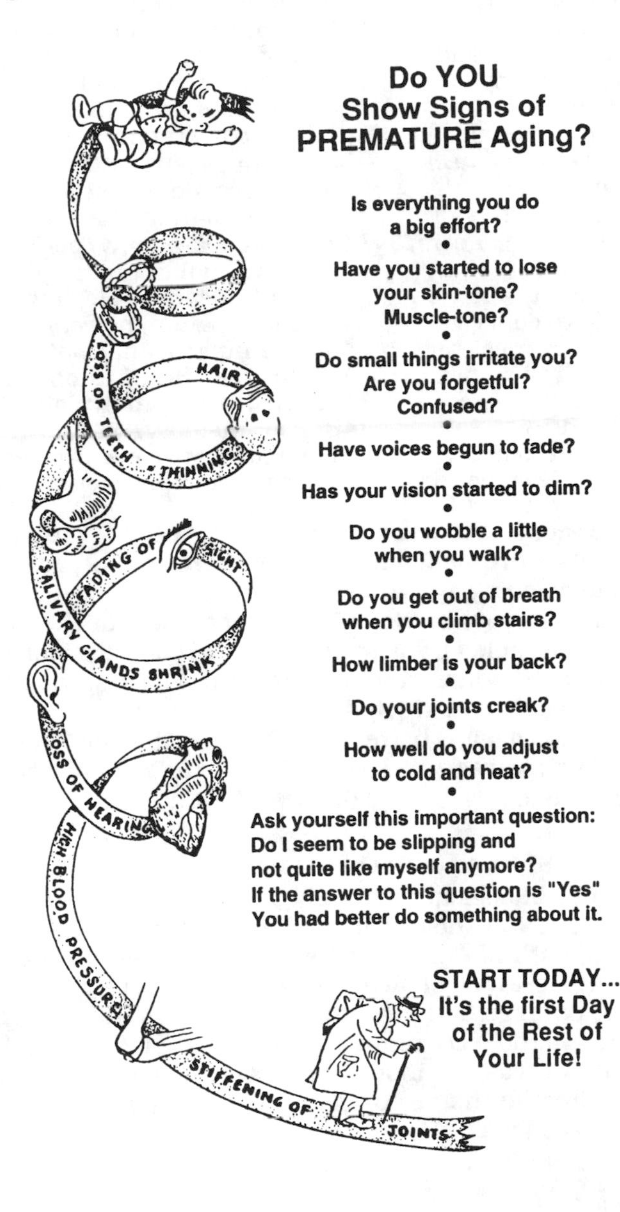

## Hormone "RELATED" Conditions

1. Asthma/emphysema
2. Excess fat/poor figure
3. Thyroid problems
4. Hearing loss
5. Menstrual PMS
6. Prostate troubles
7. Thinning hair
8. Gray hair
9. Cold body/feet/hands
10. Low energy/drive
11. Impotence
12. Bladder/yeast infections
13. Sagging cheeks/neck
14. Skin wrinkles
15. Joint pain/stiff body
16. Female/male cancers
17. Osteoporosis
18. Spontaneous abortion
19. Inability to conceive
20. Cysts on ovaries
21. Loss of physical height
22. Knee/hip problems
23. Low sex drive
24. Painful sex (females)
25. Edema in legs/hands
26. Loss of muscle mass
27. Cellulite (hips/thighs)
28. Irregular menstruation
29. Painful periods
30. Fibroid tumors
31. Painful breasts
32. Endometriosis
33. Depression/gloominess
34. Body painful to touch
35. Nights sweats/hot flashes
36. Loss of muscle tone
37. Arthritis/rheumatism
38. Allergies/sinusitis
39. Fibrocystic breasts
40. Gas/bloating after meals
41. Low back pain w/period
42. Menstrual crankiness
43. "Out of control" feeling
44. Constipation/bowel prob's
45. Thinning vaginal walls
46. Dowager Hump/stooped over
47. MS/lupis/fibromyalgia
48. Poor memory/brain fog
49. Degenerative eye problems
50. Low iron, pernicious anemia

**The common denominator to ALL of the above SIGNS and symptoms is "hormones" grid locked receptor sites and an acid body "terrain."**

Follow the suggestions in this book and in the Young Again™ Source Packet if you want control of your life. Hormone "issues" are easily addressed if the "terrain" is restored and the "hormone cycle" is resurrected.

It doesn't get any better than 30 years old and 7 months pregnant. If you want to understand the **"riddle,"** call and ask for guidance. See pages 72, 162, 164, 274 and 384.

---

### Shower & Bath + Colon Water

Bathe in safe, biologically friendly water with a three stage oxidation/reduction shower filter that goes far BEYOND common shower/bath filters. A "redox" shower filter makes your skin and hair feel and look healthier while protecting your liver for chemical damage. These are "full flow" filters that are VERY long lasting and do NOT require cartridge replacement. They are inexpensive, easy to install and provide wonderful water "perfectly suited" for home colon therapy. See pages 196, 368, 383 and Source Page 384.

# 21

Carbon
12.01115
**C**
6

## Avogadro's Number

*"The health of the people is the foundation upon which their happiness depends."*
Benjamin Disraeli

It was a hot August day in 1975—the mercury had reached 95⁰ Fahrenheit. Out of nowhere came what looked to be a hippie carrying a clip board. He said, *"I'm from the City of Madison and I'm checking all buildings for proper placement of address numbers, and you don't seem to have any!"*

*"Do too!"* I retorted.

*"Well, I looked and I didn't see any and I want to know what you are going to do about it?"* he rattled as he flashed a copy of the local business ordinance in my face —expecting to cement his authority and intimidate me.

*"Do too!"* I said again, *"And I can prove it!"*

As we proceeded to the front of the building, I motioned to Dale to follow my new found acquaintance and me.

There we stood, the three of us, facing a 4x4 **"blank"** post that formed the door frame, and I said;

*"Dale, this fine gentlemen is here from city hall and he says that we are not in compliance with city ordinances regarding having our building properly posted with our street address."*

*"Right there!"* I said. *"See! It says, 505 S. Main. What's wrong with that?"*

The man looked at me and said with a strange look on

his face, *"There is no address there! It's blank!"*

"Hmmm!" I buzzed, as I turned to Dale and said,

*"Dale, do you see 505 S. Main posted here on this post?"* Dale look at me and fired back, *"Sure do! Right there on the post!"*

With that, the man looked at me, then at Dale, shook his head, **gave up,** and just ***walked away,*** unsure who was nuts, but completely unsure about what had just taken place.

### Things Not What They Seem

Things are not always what they seem. Sometimes **nothing** can be something. Something small may actually be big. Something weak can be strong. We cannot always trust our eyes and sometimes logic does not make sense of conflicting circumstances or experiences. Sometimes we must follow our instincts or we lose our direction, go insane or just ***walk away.***

The man in our story knew when to ***walk away.*** Science does not. Instead, science tries to make natural energy phenomena comply with its LAWS, and in the process it misses nature's lessons. So do MANY religious folks.

In homeopathy, something weak is actually strong. Something that should not exist actually does exist. Something that is nothing can be made into something.

These *apparent* "contradictions" cause science and medicine to ridicule instead of inquiring with an open mind. They demand *scientific* proof backed by a body of "literature" when they should be interested in RESULTS. They get caught up in theory and method and forget that their **double blind "studies"** and discoveries are **riddled** with contradictions.

### Phenomena

Here are a few examples of electrical phenomena. Let's see if they shed light on the aging process.

**Biodynamic** agricultural practices *transmute* raw cow manure into a potent, yet *different* substance. It mixes a "pinch" of the *potentized* substance in twenty gallons of high energy water and *transfers* the energy from the new substance to the water through convoluted stirring procedures that elevate and concentrate energy. Applied to hundreds of acres of dead soil, the *energized* solution creates an energy *explosion* in the soil and life bursts forth. *Science cannot explain this phenomenon because it does not fit its model.* Science wants proof, when it should be interested in results.

**Homeopathic medicine** uses the principle of *dilution, succussion, resonance,* and *transference* to create energy substances (called remedies) that effectively treat dis-ease at the Fourth dimension energy level.

If you were to add one drop of black paint to one gallon of white paint, you would have a MIX of both colors. The black paint would, of course, be very diluted and would exert little influence on the white paint. The more white paint added, the less influence the black paint has. However, black paint is still there, albeit in smaller amounts each time more white paint is added. This is a "physical" dilution, and this example deals with the **physical** influence of the black paint on the white paint.

Homeopathic medicine is concerned with the influence of invisible energy fields upon each other, rather than the physical influence in our paint example above.

### Potentiation

Remedies work on the basis of "similars." Homeopathy starts with a substance that has a ***similar*** vibrational frequency as the dis-ease energy field. The substance is then ***diluted.*** At each dilution, the remedy is pounded (successed) so that it will absorb various frequencies (10x, 20x, 50x, 100x, 200x, etc.). This process is called ***potentization,*** and the remedy is referred to as a "potentized" solution.

The idea is to create multiple dilutions of different vibrational requencies that, when taken into the body, will "cancel" the dis-ease's frequency. A *potentized* remedy treats the patient at a Fourth Dimension energy level. In homeopathy, dilution and succussion add power, where in our paint example, the black paint became less influential each time we added more white paint.

Homeopathic dilutions are different from physical dilutions. They are electrical phenomena instead. Remedies are CONCENTRATED energy fields that are derived from the vibrational frequencies of "physical" substances. The more the remedy is *diluted* and the more it is *succussed,* the more energy the remedy contains and the more effective it becomes. Logic says a remedy should NOT exert any influence because the original substance is weaker—almost non existent. Energy transference through *succussion* pushes the "scientific" mind too far. Logic, however, is faulty here because it is based on Third Dimension physics instead of taking note of Fourth Dimension natural energy phenomena. Homeopathy **manipulates** and **transfers** the electrical ***signature*** (frequency) of one substance to that of another, hence, *resonance* and *transferance.* In homeopathy, something that should not exist DOES exist. *Science cannot explain this phenomenon because it does not fit* *its model, so science ridicules and expresses contempt!*

**MORA** is a spin off from homeopathy, just like the word processor is a spin off from the typewriter. MORA electronically duplicates energy *signatures* and electronically *transfers* them to the patient INSTEAD of using the actual *remedy* itself.

The *remedy* is placed into a scanning "well" where its frequency is *duplicated*—much like a computer scanner reads a typed page and converts it to codes and signals so the computer can work with it. The **duplicated** frequency is then *transferred* to the sick person's body and the desired healing takes place. The process can be repeated over and over without consuming the remedy itself. In homeopathy, something that doesn't appear to exist does exist and does work.

**Whether or not a healing modality "fits" accepted medical theory, models, dogma, or the LAWS of science doesn't matter. The only thing that counts is results!**

### It's In The Numbers

Amadeo Avogadro (1776-1856) was the Italian chemist who saw big numbers in small things. He developed a method to estimate the number of atoms that exist in a substance by comparing it to a known reference substance whose number of atoms were known—at least in theory. This reference number is called Avogadro's number or [N], in his honor. Like Reams, Pauling, Caisse, Semmelweis, Carson and Gerson, Avogadro was ridiculed by his "peers" for his vision and the TRUTH to which he bore witness. *(Avogadro was a wizard, and wizards don't have peers. Often, they are surrounded by copy cats who want to put their names on someone else's discovery.)*

Avogadro's reference substance was 12 grams of carbon-12. The carbon atom is extremely small. The number of atoms in 12 grams of carbon-12 is *extremely* large! It is estimated to be approximately 602, 000, 000, 000, 000, 000, 000, 000 atoms!

In homeopathy the most powerful remedy is one where a substance has been ***diluted*** and ***potentized*** to a point that NONE of the original substance remains. Physically, a substance no longer exists once it goes *beyond* Avogadro's number or *twenty-two (zeros) places*. Logic says that when the original substance ceases to exist—you have reached NOTHING! Yet, a homeopathic remedy has an enormous energy "footprint" for something that supposedly doesn't exist.

A 9x remedy equals 1 part per **billion** (ppb); at 30x it's beyond Avogadro's number with 30 zeros, and so on. Homeovitic remedies are **combinations** of 9x, 20x, 30x, 100x, 200x and provide broad spectrum bioresonance to meet a sick body's changing electromagnetic requirements.

### Aging & Avogadro's Number

**Avogadro's number is VERY important to the aging process.** If the positive energy contained in a highly diluted homeopathic remedy can cause MASSIVE change for the "good," then the negative energy **transference** of a poor lifestyle, bad food and dead water should be equally DISASTROUS to health and longevity. The same reasoning holds true for **negative *actions* and *thoughts*** that produce effects millions of times greater than the actual event. Like ripples that are created when a rock is tossed into a pond—each negative thought and action creates an exponential reverse effect on health that manifests with negative consequences.

### Dr. Samuel Hahnemann

Samuel Hahnemann (1755-1843) is considered the father of "modern" homeopathic medicine. He was a brilliant German physician. The electrical phenomenon he discovered is known as the medicine of **"similars"** or homeopathy.

Let's compare homeopathic medicine to allopathic medicine and see if a contrast of the concepts involved can help us to understand the aging process.

**Allopathic medicine** (conventional medicine) attempts to treat dis-ease with drugs and chemicals that are *antagonistic* to the symptoms being treated. Drugs induce a **pathologic** reaction that stresses the system with an **"opposite cures opposite"** approach. A pathologic reaction is one where pathology (dis-ease) is "induced!" Drugs are prescribed based on the benefit to risk ratio discussed earlier. Pharmacology recognizes that all drugs carry **RISK** and all drugs **DAMAGE** the vital organs. Allopathic medicine attempts to ***overpower*** dis-ease with drugs that SHOCK the body into a condition of *subclinical* illness. Allopathic medicine uses powerful, *left-spin* energy fields (drugs) and shoots their negative energy bullets (magic bullets) into the vital organs, tissues and glands. Allopathy is the medicine of "opposites."

**Homeopathy** is the exact opposite of allopathy. It is the medicine of *similars,* and it uses energy fields with *similar* vibrational frequencies to CANCEL offending dis-ease energy frequencies. Homeopathy is "legitimate" holistic medicine that relies on **like cures like** reactions that don't offend the body.

**How Homeopathy Was Discovered**

Hahnemann was extremely disillusioned with conventional medicine. While treating patients for yellow fever, he discovered that if he gave a healthy person—who did NOT have yellow fever—a tea of cinchona bark—which was known to be effective against the fever—intermittent fevers would spontaneously develop as if the person actually had the condition.

Hahnemann further discovered that a *diluted* substance is more powerful than a *concentration* of the same substance. He further refined his new method of treatment and eventually included the physical, emotional and mental disturbances of the patient. Remedies were developed by *trial and error* based on their ability to *produce* a response similar to the sick person. If a trial remedy produced a **similar** reaction, it was further tested on a sick person to see if it would produce a healing. *(Present day homeopathic remedies do NOT bring on actual illness or dis-ease in a healthy person. They can* ***only*** *cancel offending energy fields that* ***exist*** *in the patient and they produce NO side effects.)*

Hahnemann experienced much success applying his *remedies*, but noticed that their effectiveness increased in direct proportion to **dilution** and **potentization**. In other words, the MORE he *diluted* and *successed* the remedy, the more effective it was on the patient! His findings were in serious CONFLICT with the orthodox medical dogma of his day. The conflict continues to this day!

*Dosage-related effects—as practiced in modern pharmacokinetics (the study of the dynamics of chemical drugs in the body) looks at the action of drugs on body metabolism with emphasis on the time required for absorption, duration of action, distribution in the system, and method of excretion from the body. These things determine the activity level—that is, the* ***saturation level*** *of the drug in the blood and tissues.*

Allopathic medicine is acutely aware of the problems brought on by drug usage. It walks a tight rope between short term benefits and short term damage to the vital organs. **Long term damage is NOT an issue because it cannot be proven.** New names are "conjured" for long term dis-ease effects.

Hahnemann got wonderful results using remedies that *exceeded* Avogadro's number. His findings conflict with Newtonian physics which states, *"where there is an action, there is an equal and opposite reaction."* Newtonian LAWS are the basis of modern drug chemotherapy mentality. Pharmacology and medicine as we know them, rely on "saturation effect" to produce an ***activity level*** that can be MEASURED. Medical science uses a "sledge hammer" approach based on *opposites;*

homeopathy uses *gentle* remedies based on *similars.*

**Allopathic medicine loads you up with drugs to a point BEYOND the ability of the kidneys, liver, lungs and skin to excrete them.** The cells and tissues are "forced" to accept drugs by default! Damage to the *bio-electric* body varies with the *type* and *quantity* of drugs used and the *duration* of time they remain in the system.

Homeopathy is the modality of **preference** for patients and physicians who are interested in "healing." Remedies *interface* the subtle-energy level where dis-ease has its roots.

### Homeopathy & Agriculture

Modern agriculture uses SUPER *potentized* poisons to try to stop insects and weeds. Until recently, large amounts of poison was called for. Now, VERY small amounts of poison is mixed with huge amounts of water. The principles involved here are homeopathic in nature. Agricultural and pharmaceutical companies have **cloned** Hahnemann's principles of *dilution, potentiation,* and *transference* and have turned them to **EVIL** purposes. The *experts* are at war with God's creation.

This is why I encourage the reader to plant a garden and grow some food. Home grown food makes up for a plethora of poor choices and mistakes in personal lifestyle. Live, fresh food is a gift from God. It causes the cells to resonate "healthy!"

### Think Small

Americans like to think big—big cars, big houses, big meals, big surgeries and big bottles of pills! In fact, the "big" syndrome is so prevalent that people complain and feel cheated when they pay a lot of money for a small bottle of pills!

In health related matters, we must LEARN to think *small* as in terms of the HUGE side effects created by the negative energy substances we put into our bodies. We must understand that the body is altered by both positive and negative energy forces and that "tiny" amounts of a toxic substance exerts massive **long term** effects on health.

We are surrounded with toxic chemicals everywhere. The prudent person who thinks in terms of Avogadro's number has the best chance of becoming *Young Again!*

**PREVIEW:** *Our next chapter looks at our multi-dimensional body. It looks at the "terrain" of the bio-electric body and reconsiders Pasteur's obsession with "bugs" and the Germ Theory of Dis-ease.*

## Medical Grade Ionized Water™

This is a special class of *therapeutic* water used in special Japanese clinics to treat everything from diabetes and nerve disorders, to cancer, heart and stroke problems.

In Japan, this special water is made with very expensive equipment designed for **clinical** settings. In the USA, tap water is seriously polluted in the process of making it "potable" (safe). BEV™ water is the water of choice for people who want biologically friendly water.

**Medical Grade Ionized Water™** (MGIW™)is made from BEV™ water and racemized™ liquid minerals. Raw tap water is **NEVER** used. It is important the reader understand that water pH (acidity/alkalinity) has nothing to do with the healing qualities of this special water. Rather, it is the "ORP" (oxidation/reduction potential) that carries the extra load of electrons for production of our energy molecule, ATP which is produced by the **mitochondria.**

Dis-ease has its roots at the cellular level which is where Medical Grade Ionized Water™ does its job. The benefits of high ORP water derive from a combination of purity, ORP, resistivity and pH. Highly ***reduced*** acid water and highly ***oxidized*** alkaline waters have pH values of 1.5-2.4 and 10.5-12 respecitively, and ORP potentials of -900 and +1200 respectively. High ORP water is composed of "tiny" water molecules that easily cross cell membranes for delivery of electrons to the mitochondria for production of ATP within the electron transport chain of the Krebs cycle.

**Oxidized** water is used externally to heal infections, for douches, treatment of genital herpes and for beautiful skin. **Reduced** water is taken orally. It neutralizes acid wastes. A FIR™ sauna **de**acidifies the tissues in a similar way WITHOUT the use of heat, steam or lights.

Medical grade Ionized Water™ is a big health advance and should be considered **"frosting"** on the cake. It is the Young Again Colon Therapy and Tissue & Liver Protocols™ that help create the "cake." Depending on age and sex, racemized™ hormone precursors, B.T. Thyroid Creme™ and COBO-12™ creme assist in the process.

Now that it is possible to make Medical Grade Ionized Water™ "in home," people are discovering what Japanese clinics have known for a long time.

The **ONLY** health issue facing people today is the restoration and management of the body's "terrain!" MGIW™ is another quantum leap in terrain management.

**(See pages 107-110 and diagram on page 306)**

# 22

# Change The Terrain

*"No tree has branches foolish enough to fight among themselves."*

*"Watashi Wa"*

The great French bacteriologist, Pasteur, said, *"Le microbe c'est tout! The microbe is everything!"* A contemporary, Claude Bernard retorted, *"Le microbe c'est rien. Le terrain c'est tout! The microbe, that's nothing! It is the terrain that's everything!"*

When we look *beyond* the microbe, we see that they are only participants in a grand scheme. Microbes take their cues from the body's "terrain." Microbes cannot prosper unless the *terrain* is conducive to their growth. **Microbes include bacteria, virus, fungi, yeast and parasites.**

It is the *terrain* that must concern us. The terrain is the doorway through which dis-ease appears and old age expresses itself. Body terrain is multidimensional and goes BEYOND the Third Dimension world in which we live.

### Multi-Dimensional Body

Humans are *multi-dimensional* creatures that experience life on mental, physical and spiritual planes—but life goes beyond these. We learn early to perceive and interpret our world in physical terms and geometric concepts we call length, width and height—the First, Second, and Third Dimensions,. But there are other dimensions—higher dimensions—that we experience from time to time like intuition, telepathy, dowsing, and maybe even the ability to see holes in another person's aura—things that belong to the 4th dimension and beyond.

## Aging & The Fourth Dimension

The higher dimensions are *invisible* for all but a few. Aging **occurs** in the higher realms before it is **experienced** in our Third Dimension world, where it is seen in the mirror. Vitality and health are controlled by the electrical energy forces of the Fourth Dimension. Anything that impacts the Fourth Dimension electric body affects the Third Dimension physical body and visa-versa.

**Health and dis-ease are expressions of the "energy" tug-of-war constantly going on in the *invisible* world of the Fourth Dimension.**

When we die, the tug-of-war is over. The negative energy forces won! Simultaneous with death, vital force (spirit) leaves the body. We *"give up the ghost!"* The spirit returns from whence it came. It returns to a *higher* energy level, perhaps the Fourth Dimension. Maybe higher. No one knows for sure. Call it heaven, hell, hereafter. Suit yourself.

The Fourth Dimension body goes by different names like—**subtle energy** body, **soul, astral** body, **spirit, invisible** body, **bio-electric** body, **etheric** body, **Chi, Qi, Prana**. They all refer to the same thing, depending on your belief system.

Our Fourth Dimension existence is generally invisible, but it is there nonetheless. Some folks try to deny its existence, but doing so does NOT change the reality of it or alter its influence on our earthly journey.

When we attempt to heal the physical body, but ignore the spirit body, healing is marginal. If we allow the electric body to become old, the physical body follows suit. If we experience death in the physical realm, but maintain our hold on our spirit, we are NOT really dead and we return to our physical world with tales of ***after death*** experiences. If death occurs in the Fourth Dimension realm—where our spirit body resides—we experience physical death and life on Earth ceases.

## Vantage Point

**The electric body should be viewed as an *extension* of the physical body, and the physical body as the *expression* of the electric body. The multi-dimensional body interfaces dis-ease and health, life and death.**

**Try to become comfortable with the above concepts. Understanding them will help you to understand our earthly experience.** To get a wonderful overview and "feel" for this area of thought, read *The Holographic Universe.*

Long before dis-ease manifests itself in the physical realm, the electric body is undergoing *vibrational* changes that set the course for the physical recognition of illness. This is what Bernard meant when he said, ***"The terrain is everything!"***

Before we can learn how to *manipulate* the energy forces that interface the physical AND electric body terrains, we must adopt a ***vibrational*** view of health and dis-ease.

In order to understand the forces of aging, one must understand the idea of an "invisible" world of *antagonistic* energy fields. We feel the influence of these invisible forces when they appear in our physical, *visible* world in the form of SIGNS confirmed by the doctor's diagnosis.

The *invisible* world is poorly understood. Yet, this is the arena where the war for health and dis-ease is fought. We are concerned with the terrain of BOTH worlds—the *visible* and the *invisible*—and the energy force fields that influence and govern them. Examples of these energy fields are a bio-junk diet, toxic water, negative thoughts and words, drugs and bad living habits and their effects.

### Food Plants & Insects

Chinese Taoism teaches that humans are a reflection of the universe and that **all life** is of the spirit of the creator. Man has much in common with plants and insects because they also have a ***dual*** existence.

Plants have many functions. Two functions are the production of food energy and the infusion of solar energy into the soil. In the process of synthesizing food molecules, plants take CARBON from the atmosphere and *infuse* it into Mother Earth's dermal *skin* layer (the "soil") through their roots.

The plant is the **mediator** of solar energy. Plants capture it and use it to form complex organic food molecules. Organic food molecules contain carbon, oxygen, nitrogen, hydrogen, sulphur and "ionic" minerals. These molecules are biologically active, and they participate in anabolic activities we call *growth and repair.*

**The body needs sulphur and carbon in sulfhydryl form. When sulfonyls are present in sufficient quantity, the body automatically dissolves scar tissue and restores elasticity to unhealthy tissues. SOC™ capsules supply massive amounts of sulfonyls so healing can occur.**

### Mediators

Plants **mediate** energy. They receive solar and cosmic energy and convert them into new and different energy forms—like food, wood and carbonaceous matter in the soil. **Energy is never lost; it merely changes form!**

Plants are living ANTENNAS. They receive energy constantly—by day from the Sun and by night from the cosmos. By day, plants convert solar energy into hydrocarbon sugars (*hydro*-water, *carbon*-atomic element #12.) with the help of mineral ions and enzymes supplied by the soil bacteria. At night, plants use the sugar molecules and earth minerals for growth. The "dew point" is the **peak** of the plant feeding period when sufficient sugar is burned and heat is given off to cause the formation and condensation of sweet "dew."

**Early Viking adventurers who landed in New England reported tasting early morning "sweet" dew from the blades of grass.**

Plants CANNOT create by themselves. They need the trillions of unpaid workers in the soil—the microbes—to perform the miracle of **photosynthesis** which is the **same** as metabolism in humans. All higher life forms—be they plant, animal or man—require help from the microbes for their continued existence.

The microbes live on cosmic energy as well. They consume the carbon sugars that plants manufacture. Their roots eat the energy released in the breaking of covalent bonds when carbon based cellulose (carbonaceous matter, like leaves, stems, manure, etc.) is broken down in the soil.

It is the microbes that are responsible for breaking the bonds that hold earth minerals and rocks together. Plants and animals live on that energy and so do humans.

Plants submit their order for nutrient energy at the *root level.* The bacteria receive and fill the order IF the soil is in a POSITIVE energy state. Unfulfilled orders **stress** the plant and cause an energy shift to the left. Stress related changes in the plant's "terrain" lower vibrational frequency causing plants to TRANSMIT negative energy signals to nature's garbage crew—the insects, fungi, bacteria and viruses.

**The health minded person must learn to MANAGE "stress" if he or she expects to enjoy good health and endless vitality. Techniques like yoga, deep breathing, prayer, Qi Gong, Tai Chi, walking barefoot in sand or on grass, sleeping under the stars, exercise, laughing, meditation, positive thoughts, etc.—ALL neutralize stress.**

NEVER forget, *stress* seeks an outlet, just as electricity seeks ground. Be alert and PROVIDE a safe outlet for it to dissipate. When you fail to dissipate stress energy, it will take physical form. Neck and spine problems are good examples.

### The Carbon Connection

The body is built of proteins. **Sulfonyls** are amino acid proteins that contain sulphur and carbon in their structure. These are organic molecules by definition because they contain carbon. Carbon is number 12 on the chart of atomic elements.

Carbon is UNIQUE because it can *bond* with so many different elements and *participate* in millions of different reactions—all of them *unique* unto themselves. It is this characteristic that allows toxic ***organic*** poisons to *hitch* a ride on the carbon atom. The R-group (stands for *reactive* group, usually desiganted "—R " on a molecular diagram) and its location on a carbon molecule determines whether something is DDT, malathion, or dioxin. All are **organic** poisons!

Toxic organic chemicals are POTENT left-spin substances. When used on plants, the health of the plant suffers greatly. Animals and humans that eat poisoned food suffer too. In only a few decades, man-made organic poisons have spoiled life on Earth. Poisons rate high on science's agenda—the agenda of "yellow fringe flag" interests of the "corporate" state—an agenda which says *"cheap food at politically popular prices is desirable."* **There is an implied threat in the words, *"Cheap food is better than no food."***

Plants are more than green things. They are living miracles. The *experts* tell us plants only need NPK (nitrogen, phosphorous and potassium) to produce food that will sustain life. This is NOT true! It is a **covert** effort to mislead and confuse to keep the "misery" line at the clinics full of sick people.

Agricultural practices control nations. A gut full of poisoned, empty calories CANNOT produce or maintain a healthy human being or a happy nation. When we eat left-spin food, violent crime soars. Violent people suffer from **excesses**, hormonal imbalances and slowdown of the vital organs. Eventually, these changes are confirmed upon post mortem examination. **Too soon old, too late smart is a sorry excuse for a premature death.**

### Explosions

Carey Reams did most of his life's work in the agricultural arena. He believed that plants and animals live on the energy released from the breaking of mineral bonds. He referred to these reactions as "explosions!"

Explosions occur when WATER reacts with soil—especially rain water! Rain accelerates plant growth—grass leaps; the corn jumps! Rain water is biologically active water. It reacts with soil minerals and acids and releases energy so plants can grow. Rain water has a slightly acid pH.

**High ORP Medical Grade Ionized Water™ does similar things in human beings by providing massive amounts of extra electrons for growth and healing.**

From the air, plants extract carbon and then secrete carbonic acid (hydrogen+carbon) from their roots so as to dissolve and free mineral ions from rock with the help of water. Soil bacteria absorb mineral ions into their bodies, digest them and then hold them in solution or secrete them mixed with sugars as a kind of glue-like substance. It is this secretion that gives healthy, "organic" soil its crumbly texture and causes it to flocculate, hold together and not "leach."

Carbon-rich soil is **young**, **active** soil that is **anabolic** in nature. It's ***alive*** because it is high in what Leonard Ridzon calls "biogenic carbon" in his book *the Carbon Connection.* Soil rich in biogenic carbon will NOT leach. It holds minerals and nutrients as colloids for the plants.

The yardstick of measurement for soil fertility is known as the "cation exchange ratio" (CEC) which is a measure of the amount of freely "available" mineral ions the soil particle can provide the plant. Ionic mineral ions are held in colloidal form until the plant places an order for them. If the plant orders ions that are *different* from what is on hand, the bacteria use the *alchemy/transmutation* process described earlier to **transmute** minerals into elements the plants need. This process can be best described as "cold" fusion.

**Carbon acts as a bridge in cold fusion reactions—be it in the soil or in the gut and liver of man or animal. Carbon underwrites health and aging. The body obtains biogenic carbon from healthy food grown in healthy soil, not from white sugar ($C_6H_{12}O_6$). In the long term, sugar is deadly.**

## Transmitters & Receivers

Plants grown as nature intended have a healthy aura that radiates "healthy" energy signals. Plants grown with commercial fertilizers and poison sprays radiate signals in the ***"I'm sick, come and eat me!"*** **band.**

Phil Callahan discovered how insects use their antenna to pick up these distress signals and navigate by them—like an enemy war plane homing in on the target. Insects eat ***sick*** plants, but they do NOT wage war. Insects and microbes comply with nature's mandate to remove the weak from the Earth. In the human arena, acid waste buildup stresses the *bio-*

*electric* body and weakens vital organ function. Microbes detect stress in humans. They operate like insects by tuning into our ***"I'm sick; come and do away with me!"* signals.**

Insects have antenna on their heads and cilia (tiny hair like projections) on their body. Both structures are tuned to vibrate in the "sick" band—where stressed crops broadcast "signals" indicating their energy "state."

Insects **know** exactly which plants represent a meal and which ones do not. Different insects are tuned to different frequencies. You won't find Colorado Potato Beetles eating sweet corn. Nature tunes each insect's antenna to its own *"I'm sick, come and eat me!"* frequency. Signals are transmitted in the near and **far infrared** spectrum of light which are neither audible nor visible to man.

White light contains all visible color frequencies and is part of our Third dimension experience and world. Light is electrical in nature which means anything electrical in nature is related to light. Color therapy, cold laser therapy FIR™ sauna therapy and ultrasound are applications and variations of **therapeutic** light frequencies that stimulate healing. Microwaves and radar are also light based frequencies, but they are anti-life energy frequencies. **Dis-ease belongs to the world of invisible energy frequencies.**

When a plant is sick and stressed, you will see the insects gorging themselves. When farmers have to spray insecticides to produce a crop, you can bet the food crop will ***sicken*** the people and animals that eat it. Both sick and healthy food plants can be measured brix meter.

Crops requiring poisons to keep the insects at bay are sick. Eat and absorb **freak** food energy and you will become sick, too. Food and water **impose** their energy footprint upon the animal or human eating it, much like a homeopathic.

### Organic Poisons • Refractometer • Terrain

Organic poisons are **potent** negative energy fields. They work like a homeopathic remedy, only in **REVERSE** and their effect on the body of man or animal is beyond comprehension.

**The use of organic poisons is NO different from medical science's insistence on mass immunization of the population. Healthy crops don't require poisons. Healthy people don't need—and should NOT have—immunizations.**

If sick plants attract predatory insects, viruses and molds, can we assume that healthy plants repel them? The answer is a big YES! The same rules apply to the *bio-electric* body. A positive energy **terrain** repels dis-ease, but negative energy attracts more of the same UNLESS a concerted effort is made to break the cycle by the sick or aging person.

Dr. Carey Reams discovered a unique way to determine the health and nourishment level of food plants. **He discovered that healthy plants have a high level of dissolved mineral solids in their juices.** He determined this with a refractometer, which is a simple, hand held device that refracts light and measures the *"brix"* level of natural sucrose sugars in plant juice.

The higher the "brix" level (brix is a unit of measure—like a foot or a pound), the higher the mineral content of the juices. The higher the level of sugar and minerals, the healthier the plant and the more the food satisfies. *(Do you remember the story earlier in chapter nine about satiety and Dr. Reams' dinner party for his neighbors?)*

When sugar levels are high, plants do NOT radiate negative energy in the *"I'm sick; come and eat me!"* band. Moreover, if an occasional insect stops by to have a bite, it promptly dies because high sugar levels—which the insect is not equipped to handle—quickly turn to alcohol in the bug's system and it dies! **Instant and fatal intoxication!**

*Alcohol is a toxin (POISON) to living systems. Yet, when sick, it is often helpful to take a hot bath containing 2 C. of Epsom salt, 1 qt. of 3% hydrogen peroxide and a pulverized fresh ginger root, followed by a shot of whiskey before going to bed. The alcohol kills multiplying organisms and SHOCKS the system. The alcohol serves as a drug and the effect is palliative, but it often brings relief. A better solution is colon therapy, followed by the above bath water mix and a shot of Harmonic Silver Water or Medical Grade (acid) Ionized Water™.*

Plants grown in highly mineralized high carbon soil that is loaded with microbes will have high brix readings. "Brix" are a "marker" of the level of dissolved minerals in the plant's juices. The higher the brix readings, the MORE nutritious the food and the greater is its "life force." Protein level is another way of gauging life force, but this method fails to account for the footprint and signature (SPIN) of the proteins, fats or carbohydrates. Soy protein is a classic example of this.

The refractometer scale is 0-32 brix, "0" is the bottom and 32 the top of the scale. **The lower the number, the more insect infestation and plant dis-ease that will be seen.** In the case of sweet corn, nature's garbage crew back-off at 18 brix and will cease to be a problem above 24 brix. The insects will not be seen at maximum brix levels. High brix means NO disease and food that is extremely nourishing for man and animal. Crops raised by conventional means will be **low brix** and insect infested. The "experts" and the chemical companies—and their "yellow fringe flag" friends don't like the simplicity of this.

99% of the crops grown in the USA are low brix, low vitality food that spoils easily. Low vitality food breeds violence in children and adults. **This is the perfect food for perpetuating a militaristic society that will do as it is told by the forces behind the "yellow fringed" U S flag.** Sick food, weak minds and violence are part of our obsession with sports. Rome took a similar path—that is, AFTER desecrating its flag and flag poles with an "adornment" similar to the yellow fringe, ball, eagle and/or spear that has imposed foreign state "corporate" jurisdiction over Citizens of all countries worldwide.

***"In a nation whose legions once commanded the known world, the people cry but for two things: bread and more games."*** -Pliny

Civilizations deteriorate because nature's dietary laws are ignored with reckless abandon. Poor nutrition manifests itself in a plethora of ways. Populations under nutritional stress are weak. Sick food and water spawns social EXCESS, not the other way around. Birth defects are part of the "terrain" story and are linked to poisoned food and water. The pregnant woman's liver—and unborn baby—labors under additional stress when mom consumes "stuff" that is not good for her.

**Eat Your Vaccinations, Dear!**

Inferior food with a short shelf life is behind the drive to *irradiate* America's food supply. Ditto for the genetic manipulation of food crops. Did you know that **madmen** scientists have begun gene splicing Hepatitis B and dozens of other disease organisms into plant DNA.

If historical myth has any substance, I would remind the reader that Atlantis and its people were destroyed for genetic cruelties and cross breeding of life forms. Genesis says, *"Kind begets kind."* Home grown food solves the problem.

**I predict that people who eat genetically manipulated food will sicken faster, suffer miserably and die early. Furthermore, their offspring will experience gross pathologies with no hope of cure. Darwin's "survival of the fittest" will take on new meaning (see page 369).**

We are breaking the rules when we cross species lines. Like with like. Kind begets kind. Cross breeding of species produces offspring whose vibrational ***signatures*** and DNA are "freak" beyond comprehension.

We are making another horrible mistake by classifying animal fats and liquid oils together just because they have similar characteristics. The difference between them is more than just a matter of liquid, solid, saturated, unsaturated, short chain, long chain fatty acids, omega this and that, etc.

Vegetarians and meat eaters alike MUST strive for MORE balance in their diets or their bodies will break down. Real food offsets dietary mistakes which is why your author recommends the inclusion of racemized™ SUPER FOODS in every persons diet—even if you grow a garden and eat organic.

## Parenteral Nutrition

Food energy is metabolized into glucose sugar energy in the **liver**. Glucose fuels ATP production via the Krebs Cycle in the electron transport chain of the mitochondria that live in our cells. ATP is our energy molecule and the end product of the food we eat. Glucose is **stored** in the liver and muscles as "glycogen". Lactic acid accumulation—and sore muscles from strenuous activity—are a byproduct of poor liver function and gylcolosis—the production a ATP in the **absence** of oxygen.

It is standard medical procedure to add a few minerals and vitamins to glucose solutions if a person is on any form of parenteral nutrition. Parenteral nutrition is **any** form of nutrition administered other than by way of the mouth. For example, intravenous feeding or the use of a feed tube inserted directly into the small intestine.

Parenteral nutrition is a crummy way to keep someone alive. It's a **glimpse** of the future for those who "think" they can eat a bio-junk diet and drink soft drinks and consume toxic water and IGNORE nature's laws!

## The Terrain Of Weeds

Weeds are a yardstick of soil fertility. They tell a story AND their presence holds meaning. For sure, weeds don't have to be a curse to the farmer or gardener.

The popular definition of a weed is "something growing out of place." This definition is based on ignorance. Weeds grow where they choose because they have a job to do. Their job is to *absorb* negative energy from both the soil and the atmosphere for the benefit of all life. Their job is to *rejuvenate* the soil. **Weeds—like bacteria and viruses—only grow where the "TERRAIN" is to their liking!**

We bought a home with large yard that was infested with quack grass. The neighbors laughed when we said we would get rid of the quack grass and have a nice garden. They stopped laughing when we shared beautiful vegetables with them. Change the soil TERRAIN—and no more quack grass!

Quack grass grows on soil that is low in organic matter

with a high in pH, an unbalanced decay system, and an excess of aluminum. The solution was simple. We "hand" dug, shook and piled the quack grass. We then built four or five compost piles around the garden site using organic matter of all types —including quack grass, leaves, fresh manure, grass clippings—plus chicken manure as a "starter," granite dust, gypsum, soft rock phosphate, and red wigglers (worms). We turned the piles biweekly. After two months, we spread the finished compost and dug it into the top four inches of soil.

After this process, we could NOT get quack grass to grow. The reason? We changed the TERRAIN of the soil. We helped Mother Earth energize her skin. Every weed has a place and a time. If you change the environment, that weed will cease to be a problem because you have altered the terrain. Some weeds grow where food plants cannot grow. Some weeds also grow along side food crops. Their job is to maintain energy balance.

I remember a story an acquaintance of mine told me about how the pioneers abused the soil as they came west. They found virgin soils high in life giving energy and nutrients. They would move on as soon as the soil had "burned itself out." Later, after the deserted farm had sat for eight or ten years, Tex's father would come along and buy the farm up for next to nothing and presto, the soil produced! Tex's father understood that weeds play a very important part in life on this planet. Weeds ONLY proliferate when the *terrain* dictates their presence. **Weeds, insects, bacteria and viruses are our friends. Understand them and you will enjoy a better life.** The food supply is sick because the soil is sick. We should not be surprised that man, who eats sick food and water is also sick!

## Hybrid Food

The advent of the hybrid seed has particular significance for the health minded person. The hybrid was heralded as a wonderful thing. Bigger crops, sweeter corn, better germination and more control at harvest. Some of these things are true, but there are serious trade-offs—like unbalanced enzymes and vitamins, "freak" proteins and poor mineral uptake.

It should be noted that **hybrid crops** better withstand the salt fertilizers and poisons presently used to force food crops to produce on sick soils.

Hybrid seeds came into "fashion" because seed companies can ***patent*** them. The farmer—ever dependent on bank loans—was *persuaded, and often strong armed* into using these new seeds. **The "ag" schools and government "experts" said, *"Hybrids are the wave of the future!"* And a poor**

**future it has turned out to be.** In the words of one farmer, *"We traded open-pollinated seed left over from the past harvest—which was a FREE gift from God—for these damnable hybrids that we have to buy every year!"* Powerful commercial interests operating behind the "yellow fringed" US flag took control of the people's food supply. High vitality food from healthy soil was traded for empty calories and poisoned crops from sick soil. **The Earth and her inhabitants are now paying the price.**

### Native Wisdom

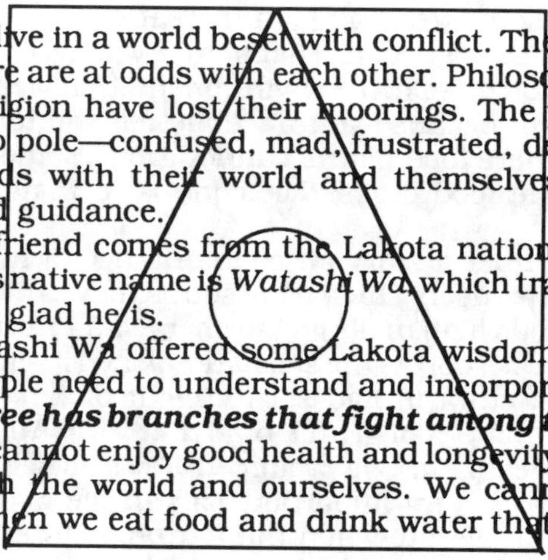

We live in a world beset with conflict. The four corners of the square are at odds with each other. Philosophy, science, law and religion have lost their moorings. The people gyrate from pole to pole—confused, mad, frustrated, depressed, violent—at odds with their world and themselves. They need wisdom and guidance.

My friend comes from the Lakota nation of American Indians. His native name is *Watashi Wa*, which translates *"I am here!"* I am glad he is.

Watashi Wa offered some Lakota wisdom that health-minded people need to understand and incorporate into their lives. ***"No tree has branches that fight among themselves."***

We cannot enjoy good health and longevity when we are at odds with the world and ourselves. We cannot fulfill our destinies when we eat food and drink water that is *anti-life.*

### Hybrid Inferiority

When we eat food grown from hybrid seeds, we are eating food that is genetically weak. Hybrids do not reproduce true to their own kind. They *defy* the ultimate test of viability for any living thing: offspring that duplicate the parents.

Hybrid seeds are the freak offspring of controlled breeding techniques. They are *inbred* and they are inferior. Their energy spin is LEFT! **Hybrid food is INFERIOR food.**

Food crops grown from hybrid seed play into the hands of the yellow fringe flag "devils" who CONTROL commodity prices and markets—and the food supply of the whole world.

Remember these points when *experts* in the "media" **hype** the wonders of genetically engineered crops and irradiated food. Behind the rhetoric, you will find sick food and **gross** human suffering.

**Food is a gift from God. It was NOT meant to be a plaything. Eat good food and drink biologically friendly water. Do these things and you will enjoy health and vitality as you become *Young Again!***

**PREVIEW:** *Our next chapter is about "OBESITY." Learn the "real" reason for obesity. Whether you are thin or not, the chapter contains VALUABLE information that you will need to understand the remainder of this book.*

**Magnetic Health**

**Depolarization** of body tissues occurs when people are exposed to extraneous microwave radiation and chemical pollutants everywhere present in the world we live in.

Computer usage is a big source of ionizing radiation. Microwave cellular phone transmitters and dishes account for MASSIVE amounts of low frequency energy that interferes with cellular balance and body physiology.

Here are a few examples of how you can protect yourself and even reverse the effects of radiation.

**Super Magnets™** "kindle" cellular activity by stimulating mitochondrial activity and nerve flow while **BOOSTING immune activity**—a key ingredient in health. Super Magnets™ are helpful for **carpel tunnel** syndrome, **sleep** irregularities, and HELP in **emergencies** like a bad fall, a mashed finger, broken bones, head injuries, etc. by slowing histamine response and accelerating blood and lymph flow in and around the traumatized area.

There are ONLY a few magnetic products that are practicable for people to incorporate into their lives. The **Super Magnet™ pendant** is suspended from the neck directly over the thymus area (upper chest) and is used to neutralize energy radiation and boost immune activity. A **medical grade** mattress pad "**re**polarizes" body tissues. **Shoe inserts** stimulate nerve reflex points in the feet.

Medical grade magnetic mattress pads **MUST** possess six characteristics to be of benefit. They are: quantity of magnets, gauss rating, placement, thickness, surface area and field direction. **Biogenic™ Super Mattress Pads are constructed to meet ALL six requirements.**

Modern medicine classifies magnetics as *witchcraft*, but users of Biogenic™ magnetic products will tell you they work. Energy has "polarity." We live in sea of energy. The **issue** is management of that energy.

**Colon Therapy**

Colon therapy speeds **de**acidification of the tissues, blood and lymph. The reader should consider colon therapy as a "given" in the battle to get well, stay well and stop the aging clock. Colon therapy is as **basic** as you can get in regard to management of the body's terrain. Many people are unjustifiably *squeamish* on this subject. Your author has taught thousands of people how to "proper" do colonics. Those who make the effort, "see" their lives transformed. The Young Again Colon Therapy Protocol™ teaches people to effectively do colonics. The process is a "pain-in-the-butt," but it sure works wonders. If you prefer to have colonics professionally done, doing your own between sessions will help your colon therapist, too!

**Call John Thomas @ Young Again™ for guidance.**

**Parasites In "YOUR" Body**

Parasites are a monumental problem, but they are **NOT** the enemy! Rather, they merely reflect loss of control over the body's "terrain." Let me assure the reader that you are **loaded** with parasites. How do I know? Because every time food or water enters your mouth, parasite eggs and adults come along for the ride.

**If** your digestive system is working at peak level—and few are—the *peptide bonds* joining the proteins that form the parasites are broken and the parasites and their eggs are "digested." Digestion of parasites and their eggs is only one reason to use Yucca Blend™, DiSorb Aid™ and racemized™ hydrogen chloride **after** meals. This combination even works wonders for travelers to India and Mexico! No sickness. No diarrhea. Fresh lemon at meals also helps.

Parasite Purge™ I & II kill parasites in the brain, heart, lungs, spleen and other "vital" organs. Intestional parasites are driven out of the body. It takes 60 days to "clear" your vital organs of parasites and to dismantle and shed the debris that was once living organisms feeding on YOUR acid tissue wastes. See pages 316 and 377 for more information on parasites.

# 23

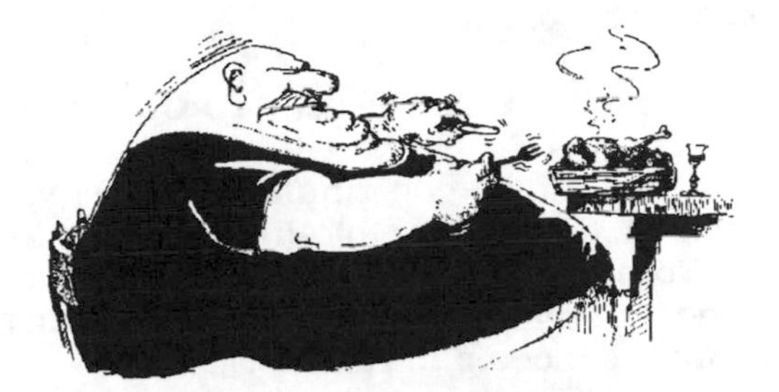

## Fat Falstaff

### Shakespeare's Prince Hall to grossly overweight Falstaff:

*"Leave gormandizing; know the grave doth gape?*
*For thee thrice wider than four other men!"*
Shakespeare

Obesity is the **curse** of the industrialized world! We eat the wrong things instead of the right things. We live to eat, when we should eat to live. We eat much, when we could eat little. We dig our grave with our teeth.

Obesity is an EFFECT. It has little to do with inheritance and everything to do with incorrect living habits. We are concerned with the **causes** of obesity and its influence on the aging process.

Obesity is dis-ease. It is a forerunner of more serious conditions! Lifestyles that precipitate obesity involve *under activity* (not enough body movement) and *over activity* in the vital organs. Hyper-activity stresses the vital organs, causing them to exhaust themselves, while lack of movement weakens the connective tissues and leads to degeneration.

Fat bodies respond *differently* once they become fat. Obesity has its own rules—like cancer. Traditional dietary approachs to obesity fall short because they ignore the issues of liver function, digestion, **de**acidification, hormones, colon therapy etc.—the list goes on.

Obesity is confirmation of metabolic "slow down" and loss of vitality in the body "terrain." Obesity is the most obvious SIGN of aging. It is **not** something that just happens to people—it is a self-imposed condition brought on by ignorance, lack of self-love and poor choices. **Obesity is maintained through ignorance, reliance on conventional beliefs,and "experts" who perpetuate the problem.**

### Factors That Contribute To Obesity

Excess food intake contributes to obesity, but so do many other factors. Obviously, a bio-junk diet is the equivalent of "sabotage." Hormonal imbalance slows the system and poor digestion provides a steady flow of putrified food and poisonous byproducts into the blood and tissues.

As body fat increases, vitality and organ function slow. Fat does not *cause* the body to slow down, but it is a confirmation that slowdown is in progress. Obesity gives way to diabetes, hypertension, gout, poor self-image, frustration and a wardrobe full of unusable clothes.

As waste levels increase, the aura dims. The aura can be compared to the defense shields on the Star Ship *Enterprise*. A *vibrant* aura works like a defense shield—nothing can penetrate it. If it is weak, dis-ease manifests.

A fat body has LIMITED electrical capacity which is reflected in low energy and drive. As body fat increases, the fat person's body slows down even more. Hence, the fat person gets fatter, and the path to a youthful existence becomes ever more difficult and further out of reach.

Obesity is a vicious cycle. Sluggish blood and lymph flow slows cellular respiration (mitochondrial production of ATP) and movement of waste to the liver where bile wastes are carried to the intestines and eventually to the toilet.

The obese person often fails to understand that because they are obese, they will have to go the extra mile to get their health back. Colon therapy is **mandatory!**

**De**acidfication of the fat person's body produces **many** healing crises. Healing crises occur when toxic waste energy is released into the **blood**, **lymph** and **intestines**. These wastes must be quickly flushed from the system or headaches, gas, cold sweats, dizziness, etc. result. That is the purpose of following the Young Again Colon Therapy and Tissue & Liver Protocols™.

The liver dumps its bile wastes just two inches below the stomach's outlet—or about twenty feet UP from the anus. Anything that impedes the flow of waste and bile from the body, causes the poisons to be "reabsorbed." Wastes must LEAVE the body for healing to occur. Stirring up the waste in the system and making yourself miserable is not the best approach. **The trick is to get the "stuff" down the toilet.**

As toxic waste exits the fat person's body, a roller coaster effect is often encountered because all of the body systems that have been on hold or barely functioning begin to wake up and respond. The products in the Tissue and Liver Protocol™ package **ease** the roller coaster effects associated with cleansing and protects the body from very powerful wastes circulating in the system while boosting liver function.

### Eat Less • Live Longer

Little food is required to maintain good health **if** high vitality food is consumed in place of the usual and customary "stuff." That is the purpose of the basic four Young Again™ SUPER FOODS and the advanced Taoist™ SUPER FOODS. These provide wonderful nourishment with little digestive stress on the liver and other organs. Please remember, it is "food" that ultimately heals the body and restores health. Unfortunately, good food is NOT enough to do it once health issues and aging are fully in progress. The Young Again™ protocols are used to get the person "out of jail" and restore organ function so the body can respond to good food.

These foods, along with fresh vegetable juice (beet and carrot) comprise my breakfast. Evening meal includes beans, potatoes, meat, a fresh salad or vegetables from the garden. There is no longer a need for lunch. For obese people, juicing tow times a day would certainly speed **de**acidification of the tissues. People who follow this regimen rarely hurt for energy and feel good—and the fat disappears, too!

**Avoid over-cooked food. Eat one third of your food RAW! Learn to "chew" your food.**

It has been demonstrated over and over again that animals live longer when their food intake is reduced to approximately 75% of "optimum" intake level. To reduce food intake and not feel hungry, nourishment is **critical**. Nourishment, digestion and a healthy liver cause the body to reduce fat stores and increase metabolic activity. When food intake is reduced, what food is eaten had better be nourishing.

Fat MUST be understood in terms of energy management, as well as in terms of what, when and how much food is eaten. Nutritious food and body friendly water **do** count. Restoration of the "terrain" is the ultimate controlling factor and that is accomplished through the Young Again Protocols™. For women, energy management, metabolic rate and toning of the tissues is solved with B.T. Thyroid Creme™.

### Sabotage & Body Instinct

A bio-junk diet and unfriendly water stand in the way of a healthy lifestyle. They short circuit fat burning enzymes and shut-down fat burning pathways by blocking mitochondrial oxidation (burning) of excess body fat. Once the system slows, it is hard to get going again.

**Body fat contains massive amounts of toxic waste. But before the body will burn its fat, it MUST be assured that the wastes left behind will be flushed from the system.**

The body has *innate intelligence.* It is intuitively smart. It knows what to do to keep itself alive—like placing toxic wastes in the fat AWAY FROM the vital organs. The body can withstand horrendous abuse—and survive—but it can't do it forever. Eventually, we overload our systems and we die.

Turning on the body's fat burning pathways requires MASSIVE amounts of energy and a lot of effort. The body cannot heal or rejuvenate without energy any more than you can get across town in your car without gasoline.

In a fat body even the most nutritious food can be a *liability.* Anaerobic, left-spin environments like those found in a fat body convert positive energy to fat. **Fat bodies are sick bodies, and sick bodies usually REJECT what they need.** Sometimes the body REBELS against nourishing food. The trick is to provide a protocol that allow the body to **de**acidify.

It's not that the fat body has forgotten how to handle nourishing food. It's that it instinctively "knows" that food in the face of accumulated waste only makes matters worse.

Obesity is often accompanied by diverticulitis, colitis, leaky gut and irritable bowel syndromes. Obesity and constipation go hand in hand. Just because a person has regular bowel movements doesn't mean that their colon is fine or that the bile is flowing freely. You want proof? How about colon cancer being the number TWO cancer. Get the message?

### Kindling Wood & Fat

Once the Young Again Protocol™ is begun, the body will accept high quality proteins, **complex** carbohydrates and fresh vegetable juices. Complex carbohydrates are "long-burn" food molecules—as are multi-grain cereals and whole grain breads made with *blackstrap* molasses.

Complex carbohydrates and quality proteins can sustain a person for many hours. Fresh beet and carrot juice and a few SUPER FOODS sustains your author all day. The **pigments** in juice are the plant's "blood!" Comfrey leaves are very delicious when lightly steamed and dressed with a little olive oil and apple cider vinegar. Kale and collard greens are also excellent choices and provide wonderful fiber.

People confuse complex carbohydrates with worthless starches and sugars found in processed foods. Complex carbohydrates do not make people fat. In fact, the body needs them to oxidize fat. **Complex carbohydrates are to fat burning what kindling wood is to a wood fire.**

In other words, the body can't "burn" fat unless you have something to kindle it and keep it going. Body fat is the **LAST** energy source the body will use to fuel its energy needs because fat is synchronized energy. The body draws on muscle tissue protein BEFORE it will draw on body fat reserves. The body is reluctant to release fat bound toxicity unless it knows that the waste can be safely moved OUT of the system. That is the purpose of the Young again Tissue & Liver Protocol.

## Oxidation Of Fat

Aerobic exercise activates fat-burning enzymes. Exercise should demand 60—80% of the maximum heart rate (MHR) for a minimum of twelve minutes causing the **liver** to produce enzymes that oxidize small amounts of fat during exercise and LARGE amounts throughout the day.

The more exercise you do, the more fat you will burn, NOT because exercise burns fat (it only burns a little), but because exercise increases enzyme and metabolic activity and increases circulation of body fluids—both blood and lymph.

Exercise should NEVER be used to offset poor choices in food, water and lifestyle. Obesity ceases to be a problem when people change their "terrain." The fat person MUST cooperate if he/she wants their life back.

## Basal Metabolism

Basal metabolism refers to the *minimum* energy requirements necessary to keep us alive. Basal metabolic rate is usually measured upon waking which is twelve hours after eating, before pulse and temperature rise or the emotions become stirred. Nutritional needs—as reflected in charts and graphs dealing with height, weight and activity—are based on this rate. Unfortunately, "caloric" intake can be misleading.

For example, I am 5' 11," have a 32 " waist, and weigh 178 pounds. According to the nutrition folks, my body needs approximately 2200 Kcalories a day to meet my minimum requirements based on my *activity* level. This is my total daily energy requirement. Food calorie energy units are derived from

ALL food sources (complex carbohydrates, proteins and fats.

Of the 2200 Kcalories I need, over 80% are used to meet my **minimum** physiologic energy needs—heart beat, body heat, breathing, peristalsis, mental processes, etc. If I add 12 minutes of brisk aerobic exercise to my daily routine, I raise my energy needs by **only** 300 Kcalories—which is very little. If I do NOT add those Kcalories to my dietary intake, my body will **withdraw** them from fat reserves **providing** that my diet is nutritionally sound and toxicity problems are not a threat to my system. Acid waste management is **CENTRAL** to weight control and aging reversal. Manage waste and you hold the keys to a long and healthy life. Liver and colon therapy are a **must!**

Another reason fat people stay fat is that their bodies are "programmed" NOT to lose weight. Terrain management requires **patience** because weight reduction and health restoration are one-day-at-a-time projects. The fat person needs the same focus and patience as the cancer patient. This is where mental control and meditation (yoga) come into play. The body *anticipates*. It has a *sixth* sense. It has *innate* intelligence. **De**aciddificaion **precedes** fat reduction. Fat reduction by any other means becomes a vicious cycle. **The fat person MUST pay attention to the basics!**

Exercise NOT to burn fat, but to form fat burning enzymes. Use aerobic exercise to **circulate** blood and lymph. Obese people are discovering the L/CSF™ machine to be a very effective way to increase metabolic rate, move waste, burn fat and slim down **without** harsh exercise. See Source Page 384.

## Thermogenic Supplements

Thermogenic supplements (*thermo*-heat; *gen*-production of, *ic*-pertaining to) help the body to burn fat. Certain herbs like MaHuang (Ephedra), however, are dangerous because they WHIP the body. Guarana is fine when "complexed" with a full array of other ingredients. Poorly complexed or isolated thermogenics **hype** the system and are just as damaging as synthesized drugs.

ETCV™ has some thermogenic efffects. It works best when taken **with** food. Enhanced PAC's™ assist thermogenic supplementation. So does 14 day old Kombucha tea and Yucca Herbal Blend™. The flushing of stones from the liver and gall bladder causes a dramatic increase in metabolic activity. Water intake is crucial. Men should try to drink 1 gal/day; women, 3/4 gal/day. Include a short squirt of racemized™ sea minerals per glass of water—regardless of what kind of water you are drinking—to keep blood electrolytes at peak levels.

## Oxygen • Exercise • Salt

Fat will NOT burn unless oxygen is present. No oxygen means no oxidation. High ORP water and aerobic exercise supply lots of oxygen to the mitochondria in the cells so the body can burn fat.

If you are obese, exercise may be difficult for you. Obese people find it difficult to get their bodies *moving*—especially aerobically. Use exercise equipment that does not jar the joints. Start slow. Each day increase your time. Exercise to **circulate** waste, **NOT** to burn fat. Follow the Young Again™ Colon Protocol™. Use B.T. Thyroid Creme™ (females) and "sip and chew" fresh vegetable juice each and every day of your life.

Next, get OFF "salt" and **all** prepared foods. **Avoid** restaurant food. Avoid MSG (monosodium glutamate) also known as hydrolized vegetable protein. Use **racemized**™ liquid sea minerals and VitaLight™ tablets. Sea salt is a farce. The only granular salt that is acceptable is Celtic™ salt, available from Grain & Salt Society (800)-867-7258.

Common table salt and sea salt contain 98% sodium chloride. Celtic™ salt contains only 35% sodium. Celtic™ salt contains 65% trace minerals. Sea salt contains none. Racemized™ sea minerals are 99.5% trace minerals with 1/2% sodium. **RACEMIZED™ sea minerals clear Rouleau from the blood and boost energy.** See page 136.

Obesity and sodium toxicity go together. When waste proteins overload and stagnate in the extracellular fluids, water accumulates. Obese people are **endematous** (water retensive). Exercise and tissue **de**acidification move massive amounts of waste into the blood for transport to the liver where bile carries it to the small intestine and down the toilet. PAC^s™ and Yucca Herbal Blend™ act as emulsifiers and buffers.

Cleansing the fluids and cells of sodium occurs naturally PROVIDING plenty of *organic potassium* is available. Fresh vegetables juice is a superb source. Pills are useless.

As the cells **give up** sodium for potassium, cellular mitochondria multiply and produce more energy. Simultaneously, the hepatocytes in the liver convert body fat into usable energy that is used to make ATP. **The body needs ATP to POWER the transformation to a slim, healthy body.**

Obesity ceases to be a problem when the liver is healthy and acid wastes can **EXIT** the body.

## Fats • Proteins • Allergies

Fats and fatty acids are extremely important to normal body metabolism. They should make up 20% of the diet. Do not be afraid of naturally saturated fats like coconut oil and animal fats. They will not hurt you. Butter, olive oil, flax, sesame, sunflower and nut oils are also good choices. The very best form of fatty acids is **R/EFA's**™ (racemized™ essential fatty acids).

NEVER use margarine, soy, or canola oils. Ignore claims by the experts that they are good for us. They are not. Always do the *opposite* of whatever the "experts" tell you.

NEVER eliminate all oils and fats from the diet—the body needs them! In John Noble's wonderful classic *I was A Slave In Russia*, Noble told how, when he was in the Soviet gulag prison system (1945-1954), the human slaves were given a thimble full of sunflower oil each day. Without it, the prisoners would die!

**Up to 40% of the body's energy needs come from essential dietary fatty acids, and without sufficient fats in the system, energy pathways shut-down.**

Without sufficient fatty acid availability **and** a healthy liver, good health is impossible. Cholesterol is the basis of **all** hormone production, and without enough fatty acids hormonal activity collapses. **Fat free diets are killing people!**

Proteins should be carefully scrutinized as to quality, quantity and source. Go easy on meat and avoid cheeses if possible. NEVER eat artificial junk proteins like TVP (textured vegetable protein). When you get to the hereafter and you look in God's recipe book for healthy living, you are NOT going to find any recipes calling for TVP, soy or canola. Manipulated proteins CANNOT sustain life. All proteins, except soy are fine. The smart vegetarians and vegans will use racemized™ algae, predigested liver capsules, harmonic pollen and Taoist SUPER FOODS. If you are a meat eater, be sure your meat is free range organic beef, lamb, free range chicken or deep water fish.

Food allergies are a "red flag" that the body is **TOXIC** and that serious liver clean-up is needed. The answer for allergies, asthma sinus problems, tinitis or lung conditions of all types is the same: Colon therapy and fresh veggi juices in conjunction with the Young Again Tissue & Liver Protocol.™

When someone calls your author and asks for help, I have to be able to get at the **heart** of the issues involved and "teach" the caller what he/she needs to know to get control over their life and health. Dowsing provides me with a quick "gut instinct" method of accomplishing the job—and I am good at it!

I dowse people over the phone to guide me in the direction the conversation should take in order to get at the root of people's health problems. I can dowse in my mind **without** the need of a physical pendulum or vibration chain. I need to be able to differentiate between simple healing crises, poor lifestyle choices and a serious problem. Dowsing is my **"gift"** and I share it freely with everyone who calls for guidance **without a fee.** No one is charged—ever!

Dowsing is a tool, and like most tools it must be used by someone who has a **VALID** medical model. The Young Again™ model provides a **realistic** model of how body physiology actually works—not the way it is **supposed** to work.

Conventional medicine just doesn't have its act together, and all the sick and dying people is proof. Much of alternative medicine's model isn't much better, just less damaging—a better band aid! Now let's get back to the subject of food energy and weight control.

### *Racemized™ Algae & Harmonic™ Pollen*

Racemized™ Klammath™ algae is a superb FOOD product that enhances fat reduction and boosts energy. It is a very powerful, naturally occurring, right-spin food substance. Harmonic™ pollen is another. I include both in my diet each morning with my fresh veggi juice.

Klamath algae is indigenous to Upper Klamath Lake, Oregon. Harmonic™ pollen comes from the wilds of northern British Columbia. Both are pure, raw, and wild. They are "low stress" foods with huge energy footprints. Both products require very little digestion.

The B-vitamins in Racemized™ algae are the "real thing." The vitamin B-12 is especially easy to assimilate—**providing** your body produces sufficient "intrinsic factor." Intrinsic factor is a mucoprotein produced by the cells of the stomach wall. Unfortunately, after age 30 (and particularly in women) production of this mucoprotein slows dramatically. By age 45-50, women and vegetarians/vegans find themselves in trouble. The men get by a little longer.

Cobo-12™ metabolite creme provides a source of vitamin B-12 absorbed directly through the skin and into the blood. Sublingual B-12 is **useless** as it cannot get into the system without interfacing intrinsic factor. The effects of using Cobo-12™ can be dramatic as B-12 affects **all** body organs and systems and is at the **CORE** of health issues.

The minerals and enzymes in Harmonic™ pollen are nothing short of impressive. A couple of racemized™ algae tablets, a spoonful of pollen and an apple makes a very good **low** stress, **high** energy, **no** let-down lunch. Both foods are very complete proteins!

The electrical *signature* of Racemized™ algae corresponds energetically with—and has an affinity for—the lymph more than for the blood which explains its role in **de**acidification. When used together, Klammath™ algae and Harmonic™

pollen enhance the immune system and play KEY roles in fat metabolism, both incoming dietary fats and excess stored fat. Klammath™ algae serves as janitor and free radical scavenger while fine tuning and regulating the entire metabolism. Taoist™ products work in a similar fashion, providing a new dimension in health.

### Raw Milk • Real Food • Obesity

Raw, unpasteurized milk is a wonderful food and a good source of nutrients and enzymes. Few people raise milk cows or milk goats, but they can buy raw milk from someone who has these animals. Older people, especially, benefit from drinking raw milk. It is a very good food. *(Raw milk is neither pasteurized nor homogenized. Both processes destroy this wonderful food.)*

Don't be frightened by the **scare tactics** of the bureaucrats who are doing their best to end public access to raw milk. It is notable that outbreaks of E. coli, cryptosporidium, etc. occur just when they are needed to scare the public into submission on any medical issue.

Bureaucrats like to ***regurgitate!*** They quote *chapter and verse* to justify enforcement of their rules and regulations. They may not be privy to the manipulations of America's food supply or medical agendas, but they ARE are acting in a "official" capacity under the yellow fringe flag in direct violation of their oath and affirmation in violation of Title 42, USC 1986 for "knowledge" and "neglect" of the law. In the end, the public suffers and the people lose control of their lives and health.

**Obesity and good health don't go together. Behind obesity is hunger and behind hunger is dis-ease.**

### Water & Obesity

Water is important to the obesity story because water is CENTRAL to all metabolic function. The three variables of water consumption are: quantity consumed, frequency of consumption and the nature of the water consumed.

For the obese person, these variables are critical because their body is under so much load and stress that the rules of the game for normal body types don't apply.

Metabolically speaking, all systems in the obese body are operating at maximum stress levels, while the actual metabolic rate is slowing. Energy is lacking. The joints are strained. The heart is overworked. Movement of lymphatic fluids is poor. Intercellular waste is beyond description. Waste accumulation in the fatty tissues is a serious problem.

The path to youth and vitality can be difficult even for

normal body types. For the obese, it is better to take an alternate route for reasons of safety as well as compassion. The Young Again Protocol™ provides safe passage for the obese person by dealing with the fundamentals, two of which are "water" and "minerals."

Minerals affect body metabolic rate. VitaLight™ is used primarily for its heavy load of racemized™ minerals that fuel metabolic reactions in unhealthy and healthy people alike. VitaLight™ replaces dozens of supplements that get in the way and overload the liver. Most drinking water is questionable.

BEV™ and Medical Grade Ionized Water™ are made in home from incoming tap water. BEV™ units come in counter top and under counter models. Special self contained (6, 12, 24, 110, 220 volt and solar) models for emergency situations and for 3rd world country use are also available.

All BEV™ models make 2 gallons per hour at standard household pressure of 60 psi. In home models do NOT require electricity. There are no boiler elements to clean . Filters last for years. A BEV™ "conductivity meter" is used to monitor the unit and water quality. Units are made in the USA and the technology behind them is **"proprietary."** They are shipped to the end user ONLY after each unit is **individually** bench tested to ensure it exceeds BEV™ standards. Strict quality control insures customer satisfaction.

**BEV water is strange stuff!** It's ORP potential is near "conception point" and therefore must be kept in its own tank or in glass or special BEV™ bottles—away from atmospheric contaminants so the water will NOT draw pollutants and lower its "ORP." Bottles come in pint, quart, 1/2, 1 and 3 gallon sizes, the latter three bottles come with built in spigots.

## Magnetic Sponge

BEV™ and high ORP waters act like a magnetic sponge in liquid form. When they come into contact with body toxins, they bond to them and carry them OUT of the system. In the process they create positive energy vortexes that EXCITE cell chemistry and stimulate metabolism through the increased production of ATP at the cellular level. Atherosclerotic plaques in the arteries dissolve. Capillaries in the posterior eye, ears and scalp respond. **Excess body fat diminishes.**

BEV™ is a ***proprietary*** water processing system that can stand on its own or provide the foundation water for the creation of Medical Grade Ionized Water(MGIW). While purity is very important, it's the biological activity of BEV™ water that makes it ***unique.*** From an energy perspective, other waters don't come close. Avoid distilled water! It is biologically unfriendly water. Toxic volatiles *concentrate* in distilled water, it tastes flat, it is a breeding ground for viruses and is expensive to make. Your author drinks both BEV™ and MGIW™.

**Fat & Chain Reactions**

Metabolism occurs through a continuous series of biochemical reactions. These reactions stall out if the body is missing the raw materials it needs OR if it labors under **systemic excess.**

When metabolism slows, aging accelerates. The body has but three choices in processing toxic food and water. It can try to dismantle (oxidize) the toxic molecules, expel them from the system, or store the them in NEW body fat made for this purpose.

"Bio-junk" diets and most water contain **radiomimetic** chemicals that "mimic" hormones. These chemicals are so potent that the body often has to isolate and store them in FAT to protect itself. A WEAK liver cannot process these freak molecules for lack of needed catalysts, enzymes and energy.

Besides, most livers and gallbladders are so loaded with **stones** that bile flow is limited. Parasites live on toxic energy, reproduce and spread throughout the body. These acid toxins are too "hot" for the kidneys and must exit the system via the bowels. The Young Again Protocol™ and products are designed to neutralize and safely move acid wastes out of the body as it is released from the body fat.

***Think About It!*** *As body fat and weight increases, blood and lymph circulation slow. Insurance companies use height and weight as the basis for their rates. They know the slim person is healthier and stands a better chance of not dying early.* ***The way to beat the insurance companies—and the medical system—at "their" game is to be slim, healthy and never file a claim!***

**Feel Worse First!**

**During the early stages of deacidification, expect to feel worse BEFORE you will feel better.** It's called two steps forward, one step backwards. Action of any type indicates things are happening! Colon therapy speeds the flow of waste down the toilet. The Tissue & Liver Protocol™ is simple to do. Two weeks of preparation is needed, during which time you lead a **normal** life and eat a **normal** diet. Purges are done at night and are generally done one week apart. Green stones come first, followed by brown, black and finally red. The process is unique, safe and pain free—and it works!

Over one hundred health "issues" are simultaneously dealt when following the Young Again Protocol™, and many benefits occur during the two week **preparation** period.

### Diuretics & Weight Control

**NEVER use diuretics (water pills) to reduce weight!** Diuretics upset electrolyte balance—especially potassium. Potassium pills do NOT replenish lost potassium. Potassium loss promotes sodium invasion of the cells and shut down mitochondria production of ATP. **Potassium drives OUT sodium if the potassium is from live foods as in fresh veggi juices.** Edema is confirmation of EXCESS intercellular plasma protein waste—in the obese and in older people.

When the obese person becomes thin, no one needs to tell him or her that they **ARE** *Young Again!*

**PREVIEW:** *Our next chapter deals with the relationship between lightning, energy, vitality and BROWN FAT!*

### Breast Implants: Silicone or Soy?

Thousands of women suffer from the toxic side effects of silicone breast implants because they trusted the "experts" who told them they were "safe."

ALL of them leak—no exceptions! Silicone is **thixotrophic** (the silicone migrates via intercellular plasma proteins in the lymphatic system) and severely stresses the immune system. Restoration of the system is a big job and "terrain" management is **the** foundation step.

The latest **scam** in "safe" breast implants is "soy oil." Soy oil is an industrial oil. Avoid it in your food, and don't be foolish enough to implant it into your breasts.

The silicone dilemma can be safely handled, but action is mandatory! SOC™ capsules **scavenge** stray silicone as well as heavy metals and removes them from the tissues while dissolving scar tissue and creating a healthy environment. (Order Source Page 384.)

### People Getting Fatter—Kids With Acne

60% of the population is obese. Hormones **control** metabolism, but so does acid waste overload which is **THE** issue behind the acne—in teens or adults. "Think" bowels, colon, hormones, waste overload and you get the idea.

## Get That "Youthful" Appearance!

We are "supposed" to regenerate a **NEW** body every 7 years. But, as we age the process slows; and in sub-clinically sick people it can take 12 years to get a "new body" which is usually poorer than the one traded in.

If you would like speed the aging reversal process and have a *younger*, *stronger* and *better* body than the one you trade-in, implement the ideas in this book—along with some $GH_3$+ and Kombucha tea while you are at it.

**$GH_3$+ is a "terrain" product used in conjunction with 14 day old Kombucha tea for general health and specifically for hair regrowth and color restoration.**

$GH_3$+™ rejuvenates the tissues. The jaw line becomes firmer. Liver spots disappear from the skin—especially when Racemized™ Skin Creme™ is used regularly with SOC™ Lotion. Skin takes on a youthful appearance and white and gray hair returns to its natural color. At 58 years of age, John Thomas' hair is jet black!

Product response is dependent on "terrain" issues and the particulars of the individual. Women respond well, but it take more effort for the ladies because females age more harshly than do males.

**A youthful appearance is PRICELESS! It translates into a good job, respect and high self esteem.**

## R/EFA's—The Rest Of The Story!

Essential fatty acids are fundamental to good health. Formulation, freshness, light and rancidity are important issues here. Freshness, light proof carob encapsulation, a "black" bottle and racemization™ are also part of the story. The brain is 75% fatty acids. Children with learning problems respond nicely. So do adults of all ages.

## Nerve Synapses & Schwann's Cells

▬ ▬ ▬ ▬ ▬ ▬ ▬ ▬ ▬ ▬ ▬ ▬ ▬ ▬ ▬ ▬ ▬ ▬ ▬

A dashed line resembles a nerve fiber axon. Schwann cells control the synapse (gap) signal transmissionin, passing the signal along the axon. Aging and disease cause Schwann cell acitivty to falter and the neurolemma to deteriorate. Nerve related conditions like MS, Lupus, fibromyalgia, peripheral neuropathy, and shingles are conditions that call for the Young Again Protocol™—things like COBO-12™ & racemized™ precursors, colon therapy and fresh juice.

**"The difference between an old man and an old *gentleman* is the way he dresses and looks."**

## The Vaccination Dilemma

Vaccinations are part of life in the Western World. In fact, they are so ***pervasive*** that health-minded people had best "tune in" to the Jeckyl and Hyde nature of vaccines if they hope to enjoy a long and healthy life.

Vaccines are "suppose to" encourage the body to build antibodies against future exposure to contagious diseases. The process involves the introduction of **pathogenic** life forms into the body in a serum of **foreign** proteins.

Immunity and antibodies are desirable, but the long term effects of vaccinations are not. Immune system response to vaccinations is an act of *self-preservation* that does NOT lend itself to tampering by medical madmen.

Natural, cell mediated immunity is *different* from vaccination *induced* attempts to ***force*** antibody formation and immunity. Vaccinations set up "resident" enemy troops throughout the body. Later, when we are weak or old, these foreign troops bring about insurrection from ***within!***

Vaccines create electrical *static* because their ***signature*** is *foreign* to the body. Their vibrational frequency interferes with health and longevity by creating "disharmony" at the *subtle-energy* level of our being.

If you have been vaccinated, it's VERY important that you REVERSE the process and eliminate the foreign protein energy fields from your system. If these substances are not **neutralized** and **driven** from the body, they will **eventually** manifest as chronic degenerative dis-ease.

The best way to deal with vaccination-induced foreign proteins in your body is to **"erase"** their ***signatures*** using full spectrum, homeo**vitic** remedies in mixed, multiple potencies that go beyond homeopathics.

The goals of immunization is admirable, but the side effects can be **heart breaking**—especially in young children whose immune systems are undeveloped. Always **buffer** vaccinations to avoid DEATH, autism, hearing loss or the development of Type 1 diabetes in your child. There are ways to beat the game AND be legal, too!

Request the Young Again™ homeo**vitic** info packet to learn more. For **documentation** on the dangers of immunizations contact the National Vaccine Information center, 512 Maple Ave. West #206, Vienna, VA 22180, and New Atlantean Press, Box 9638, Santa Fe NM 87504. **Knowledge dispels ignorance and fear, so learn what you need to know before you need to know it.** See next page for discussion of homeovitics.

## Homeopathy & Homeovitics

*"Homeopathy is wholly capable of satisfying the therapeutic demands of this age better than any other system or school of medicine."*

Charles F. Menninger, M.D.

**Homeovitic detoxification is a *crucial* step in the treatment of dis-ease and chronic health conditions.**

Homeopathy teaches that *symptoms* of disease are a *natural* part of the healing process and that their expression should be ***encouraged*** rather than suppressed.

**Homeovitic remedies restore the body's vibratory frequency.** They are NOT drugs. Some remedies are very specific; others are very general. Some treat substance problems, while others treat emotional problems. Homeo**vitic** remedies are NOT available in health stores, and they are SUPERIOR to conventional homeopathic products.

**Homeovitic** remedies have an energy *footprint* that is the similar to that of the offending substance. If the body is sick, *systemic* frequency must be reestablished. Homeovitic remedies provide complementary *biogenic* and *nutritional* support and are *vitalized* to 9x, 20x, 30x, 100x, and 200x mixed frequencies to adjust for transitional energy shifts as healing progresses.

***Potentiation*** energizes a substance and makes it more powerful than it originally was. ***Succussion*** (pounding of a substance so it will vibrate at a specific frequency) and ***dilution*** (watering down of the remedy) are employed to bring about *resonance* and *transference*—processes that involve the manipulation of Hertz rate, making homeovitics SUPERIOR to common remedies.

***Vitalization*** enhances the energy *footprint* of a substance by a stepwise series of dilutions + succussions designed to increase ***resonance*** (vibrational frequency) so energy can be transferred from the "vitalized" substance to a less active substance or system—as in a sick body!

**Transfer of resonance** to toxins occurs when the vitalized substance (vitic) is similar (homeo) to the less active one. Thus, all vitalized substances obey the law of similars (homeovitic) which says *"like is cured by like."*

***The cause is the cure*** is even more specific. For instance, the use of the mercury "energy footprint" in its *vitalized* form removes mercury energies from the body through *resonance* and *transference.*

**Transference** of energy from the *vitalized* substance to offending toxin(s) speeds healing and eases stress on the body's vital energy reserves.

**Homeovitic remedies** are "single solution" MIXED *multiple* potencies (9x, 20x, 30x, 100x, 200x) providing *biogenic* support and cellular rejuvenation by dealing with **underlying** health problems at the **subtle energy level.**

Homeovitic remedies are very effective, but are used LATE in the Young Again Protocol™ where they will render the maximum benefit to the user. Ask for the homeovitic information brochure available through the Source Packet (page 384).

***Homeovitics Work!***

# 24

## Brown Fat

*"Where I am, death is not. Where death is, I am not."*
Epicurus

In 1976, Peking, China (now Beijing), suffered a massive man-made earthquake that killed 650,000 people. The events prior to its occurrence were exactly in line with the predictions of the electrical wizard, Nicola Tesla (1865-1942). Tesla said earthquakes could be *created* by manipulating massive amounts of electrical ENERGY!

Tesla predicted a highly charged ionic atmosphere would be exhibited. Buildings and objects may have an iridescent blue green glow about them. Multi-colored lightning—red, blue, and gold—may be seen in the early morning sky around the epicenter for hours prior to the event. The earthquake would be the EFFECT of a massive electrical energy shift, NOT the cause.

The lightning we see in the sky and the electrical phenomenon of the *bio-electric* body have much in common. BOTH are *expressions* of electrical energy. Both are electrical phenomena.

The *physical* body is ***condensed*** energy (i.e., frozen light) that we can see and touch. It belongs to our Third Dimension world. The *electric* body, however, belongs to the world of the Fourth Dimension—an electrical world that is *invisible*, but is there nonetheless.

Our aura also belongs to the Fourth Dimension world. It is a "generated" energy field that radiates from the physical body. Energy that is *generated* must have a source—something that is producing it. We are interested in the body's source of its generated energy because **energy** DEFINES the aging process in terms of *rate* and *ability* or *inability* to control aging. *Bio-electric energy* is the body's version of *lightning!*

### *Bio-electric Lightning!*

Animals produce electrical discharges similar to lightning. For example, electric eels and electric rays— creatures of the ocean—release enough electricity to light the dark at night or even kill a man.

The Portuguese Man o' War—a jelly fish—is but a mass of transparent protoplasm, yet it can kill any living thing that comes within the grasp of its umbrella of tentacles. It kills with a MASSIVE discharge of bio-electric *lightning.*

Consider the electrical spectacular that occurs when the human sperm enters the ovum at fertilization. At that instant, over 480,000 volts of electricity (Yes! 480,000 volts) are released!

The discharge of electricity coagulates the outer surface of the ovum and prevents penetration by other sperm. The event is the beginning of a new organism. It is an *electrical* event of massive proportions that *generates* a new life! Death is a similar—but opposite—electrical event where "spirit" energy returns from whence it came and metabolism synchronizes.

While we are on this earth, it would behoove us to understand the SOURCE of *lightning* that keeps us alive. Understanding it is the key to becoming *Young Again!*

### The Body *"Electric"*

The body is a flesh and blood electrical storage battery and power generation system in one. Peak health depends on the bio-electric body's ability to generate and store electrical ENERGY! We are dependent on a source of *fuel*, a storage system, a *transmission system* to distribute our energy and a method to *control* the ebb and flow of that energy. Energy is a **two way bridge** between youth and old age.

We draw on our electrical energy reserves as needed and we replenish them through rest, **de**acidification and nourishment. When we fail to restore electrical balance, we lapse into partial or total energy synchronization. A *decomposed* corpse is an example of total energy synchronization. Aging is the abbreviated version—the *crock-pot* version! Aging confirms the LOSS of electrical vitality. Aging is *slow* death. **Lose control of the "terrain" and vital organ function and ATP energy production slows and eventually ceases.**

## The Mitochondria

The mitochondria are bacteria that inhabit the cells of all animals. They were first observed through the microscope around the year 1800. However, they were not officially identified as "living" organisms—capable of independent existence and given a name until approximately 1935.

The *mitochondria* derive their name from the Greek *mitos*—a thread, and *chondros*—a grain. These root words describe their shape, NOT their function. Originally, the mitochondria were thought to be artifacts (waste) or organelles (tiny bodies) found within the cells. Eventually it was discovered that they are our SOURCE of *bio-electric lightning!*

Life is **impossible** without the mitochondria. They process our glucose sugars and produce the energy molecule **adenosine triphosphate (ATP).** ATP energy *is* our *life force.* Glucose is our sugar fuel. It is stored in the liver and muscles as glycogen. When energy is needed, the cells convert glycogen to glucose and the mitochondria oxidize glucose sugars through **glycolysis and the Krebs Cycle** into ATP.

Conversion of body fat to energy takes place in the liver. Aerobic exercise helps the liver's functional cells (the hepatocytes) to produce enzymes that CONVERT body fat into usable **glucose fuel** that the mitochondria can burn. The mitochondria CONTROL aerobic "cellular" respiration which is also called *internal* respiration because it occurs inside the cells as opposed to *external* respiration, which occurs in the lungs.

## Mitochondria Control Aging

The mitochondria are BOTH power generators and storage batteries. They convert food energy into metabolic electricity. They are referred to as the **power house** of the cell.

The mitochondria replicate (reproduce) on their own. This is important! They are **NOT** dependent on the host even though they reside in our cells and are influenced by the body environment. They have their own DNA code. (Think of DNA as cellular programming *software,* genetic instructions, *ability to make their own hormones* and a road map all in one.)

**Mitochondrial activity is what *drives* anabolism—the process of build-up and repair of body tissue. Anabolism is a youthful condition and the opposite of catabolism.**

As we age, anabolism gives way to catabolism. When we reach our ***anabolic peak,*** growth and repair of body tissue slows. Energy production slows. Hormone production slows. Health and vitality diminishes and aging becomes reality.

Mitochondrial ATP is right-spin, positive energy. It keeps us **alive.** When mitochondrial activity diminishes, the effects are seen in the mirror. When energy production falls short of our minimum requirements, life ceases.

## Growth Plates

Medical science's *dividing line* between youth and old age is based on long bone extension. When the growth plates between the diaphysis (shank of the long bones) and the epiphysis (end of the long bones) "close," science says we cross the threshold into that *twilight zone* between youth and old age. Whatever growth or lack thereof that has occurred is a done deal. We have officially *stopped* growing. This event usually occurs between ages 18 and 22. Science's definition of aging focuses on the extension of long bones. It is incomplete.

Our definition of aging focuses on the body's *shift* from anabolism to catabolism, which can be accelerated or reversed at will. Our focus is on ***perpetual growth and repair*** of body tissues, instead of long bone extension. We are NOT concerned with closure of the epiphyseal plates.

When the mitochondria cannot produce enough ATP to meet the body's needs for growth and repair, we age. Aging and the passing of *bio-electric* TIME are one and the same. Our friends, the mitochondria, control TIME.

**We must learn HOW to assist the mitochondria if we want to reverse aging and stop the passing of TIME.**

## The Sweat Zones

The sweat zones of the body are areas of heat production and waste energy release. Concentrations of mitochondria in the sweat zones confirm the relationship between mitochondrial function and waste ENERGY release. These zones experience heavy lymphatic fluid movement (lymph is our non-blood body fluid). Good lymph flow is crucial to good health.

**The lymphatic system is cancer's electrical highway. The lymph nodes are the power stations. The lymph nodes are most plentiful in the sweat zones of the body.**

The lymphatic system's job is multiple in nature. It includes toxic waste management and recirculation of extracellular fluids. Most importantly, the lymphatic system is the body's primary **"protein communication system."** The lymph nodes ***hold*** toxic energy fields and release them only when the body can handle them. Swollen tonsils are a good example.

Body hair is found in areas of high toxicity and high lymphatic activity—like the groin, arm pits, scalp, face and legs. The purpose of body hair is to siphon-off and releases toxic energy stored in the fat layer below the skin.

**Hair Analysis**

Hair analysis measures EXCESSES **leaving** the body. It is NOT a measure of *deficiencies* within the body because we do NOT suffer from deficiencies, only **excesses**. Hair analysis is a window into the body—a PAST TENSE window.

Let's say hair is analyzed and found to contain mercury. The metal may be coming from the amalgam fillings in the teeth or from the diet. Whatever the source, the person IS excreting mercury —via the hair. That's good! We know that the body is releasing the mercury.

But let's say hair analysis shows NO mercury even though there are amalgams in the teeth? What does this mean? It means the person's skin (and hair, hair being an extension of the skin) isn't working efficiently and dangerous levels of mercury are building-up in the tissues. Remember, there is NO such thing as deficiencies! The only thing deficient in this example is the limited and backward thinking by practitioners using hair analysis and live blood cell microscopy to "prescribe." **Hair analysis and live blood cell analysis are tools of observation ONLY and are useless for diagnosing.**

Unfortunately, live blood cell microscopy is commonly used to prescribe **in direct conflict** with Dr. Guenther Enderlein's ground breaking microscopic work a century ago. The misuse is based on the FALSE premise that we suffer from deficiencies when there is **no** such thing. Such thinking is just a **backward** as the germ theory and vaccinations.

Healthy fast growing hair, and natural colored hair over the entire body are desirable. Basic lifestyle changes and the Young Again™ protocols cause it to happen.

**Healthy hair is related to your level of BROWN fat and the activity level of the mitochondria in your scalp.**

**Insects • Birds • Sperm**

Insects and birds have heavy concentrations of mitochondria in the muscles that are responsible for flight because that is where the ATP energy is needed, stored and used.

The sperm makes the long trip into the woman's fallopian tubes to fertilize the ovum with *power* generated by the mitochondria. The base of the sperm's tail is heavily laden with mitochondria. When the sperm fertilizes the egg (ovum, ova plural) the electrical discharge of 480,000 volts of electricity comes from both the sperm and the ovum. Both are energy bodies—one is **HUGE** the other is **miniscule**.

The electrical discharge of the ovum generates only .19 volts. The discharge by the sperm is 25,263,157 times GREATER than that of the ovum—a huge difference!

Moreover, there is a massive difference in physical size between the sperm and ovum. The volume of the ovum is 1,760,000$^3$ microns. The volume of the sperm is only 21$^3$ microns. When we divide the size of the ovum by the size of the sperm, we find that the egg is 83,809 times greater! These differences in **physical size** and **electrical potential** fuels the release of the 480,000 volts we call *bio-electric lightning!*

## At Birth

Mitochondrial count and their activity level at birth are very high. So is the level of BROWN FAT which we will discuss shortly. This is why children and "young" people are warm blooded and people whose metabolism is slowing suffer from coldness. Behind "coldness" is a sluggish to poorly functioning thryroid gland. B.T. Creme™ remedies coldness.

The mitochondria produce the huge amounts of energy a child requires to grow to adulthood in a few short years and be able to stay warm even when subjected to cold conditions.

As we grow, we experience the ebb and flow of energy called health and sickness. By the time we reach adulthood, the growth plates in the long bones have closed and we reach our maximum height. When we cross the threshold of our anabolic peak, we experience an energy shift and we begin our descent into old age—UNLESS we are willing to **take control of our life** and **responsibility for our condition and REOPEN the puberty window and reverse the aging process.**

As the *bio-electric* body becomes toxic and hormonally unbalanced, mitochondrial production of ATP falls. Next, mitochondiral replication (multiplication) falls. Then, ATP reserves diminish as BROWN fat disappears from the system causing dis-ease to manifest and the doctor an opportunity to provide a diagnosis.

So aging is really just loss of function in the vital organs, hormonal imbalances and toxicity of the tissues. **It does NOT have to be this way!**

## Rest • Detoxification • Illness

Rest is a part of the rejuvenation process. Rest allows the *bio-electric* body to heal. It *frees* and *redirects* ATP energy so critical metabolic processes can rebound.

Illnesses ARE healing crises. When someone suffers

with the flu, hepatitis, cancer, etc.—there is NOT enough available energy to both heal the body and carry on normal activities—so we must seek rest!

**Infants and sick people need lots of rest because their bodies are growing and are stressed.**

When we force the body to work under conditions of high stress—be it a *diagnosed* illness or mental stress—we "squander" mitochondrial ATP that should be used for detoxification and healing. To restore energy and vitality, the mitochondria NEED our assistance. They automatically increase their numbers and activity if we do our job by flushing the system of EXCESS metabolic wastes, balancing the hormones and eating good food.

Mitochondrial replication involves the doubling of DNA and genetic material —so two bacteria are created out of one. This process is called *mitosis*. As the mitochondria increase their numbers, ATP production increases also.

When the mitochondria are unable to return to former activity levels, we break through a TIME "barrier" and experience aging. All of us have seen our parents and friends jerk and slip their way *down* the catabolic side of the pyramid. Metabolic slowdown results in a *plateau* effect. **Aging accelerates in direct relationship to slowing of cellular respiration, loss of mitochondrial activity, build-up of acid wastes in the tissues, hormonal shortfalls and slowing of bile flow. Aging in the bowel is a "given."**

### Sodium & Waste

Aging, toxicity and catabolism are peas in a pod; and where you find one, you will find the others. Toxic substances come in many forms. Sodium chloride is one of them.

Sodium chloride (table salt) is of particular importance to our discussion of the mitochondria. Sodium in excess is a *poison*. Sodium is also a *preservative*. Sodium ions are electrolytes. Sodium conducts electricity in solution—like the ***inter***cellular fluids in the spaces between the cells, as well as in the blood. Extracellular (interstitial) fluid is composed of blood plasma proteins and is found between the cells while blood SOLIDS circulate in the blood vessels. These fluids are NOT sterile as commonly taught in medical schools. They are dynamic, live ***organism-bearing*** fluids whose energy profiles are *easily* altered by diet and stress. The elimination of the Rouleau effect (see page 136) from the blood is accomplished with racemized™ sea minerals which work by changing the electrical charge on the red blood corpuscles.

**Soft drinks dramatically alter blood and lymphatic**

**fluid pH and should be considered as toxic as alcohol.**

*Deterioration of brain neurons and nerve fibers throughout the body is linked to consumption of soft drinks, heavy metal (mercury) accumulation and build-up of acid wastes in the system. Hormone issues grossly affect the Schwann cell count and activity at the nerve synapses as well as repair and maintenance of the myelin sheath protecting the nerve fibers. The Young Again Hormone Protocol™ helps restore nerve deterioration when done in conjunction with other Young Again Protocols™. For women over age 40, nerve and connective tissue deterioration are as predictable as prostate issues are for men. Alzheimers is certainly most affects nerve tissue. Unfortunately, once deterioration has been diagnosed, it is too late, Prevention is the* ***KEY!*** *Read Beating Alzheimers and Our Stolen Future which are available from Source Page 384.*

It is almost impossible to get too little sodium. Yet, a huge percentage of people suffer from symptoms associated with low blood electrolytes. Conventional medical *protocol* calls for increased sodium intake in hot weather. This approach fails to address the issues of insufficient hydration, EXCESS toxicity and a broad based electrolyte intake. Sodium can save your life from heat stroke and heat exhaustion, but racemized™ sea minerals work a thousand times better.

Under **normal** conditions, all but a fraction of sodium remains OUTSIDE the cell membranes—out in the **extra**cellular fluid—**between** the cells. Potassium is sodium's twin. Potassium remains inside the cell membrane, (i.e. in the cytoplasm (*cyt*-cell, *plasm*-fluid). A healthy body maintains a balanced ratio of sodium to potassium. When we eat devitalized and processed foods, we ingest EXCESS sodium and insufficient potassium and we upset the balance between them. The more sodium we consume and the more acid waste we accumulate, the greater is the loss of potassium from the cells. Excess sodium brings on death. *The word d**eat**h is mostly **"eat."***

### STOP The Salt

Under normal conditions, few sodium ions ($Na^+$) are allowed inside the cells. Excess sodium ions gain entrance to the cells as potassium ions ($K^+$) are given-up by the cells for use elsewhere in the body. This ***one for one*** trade occurs in the face of sodium **excess.** As each $K^+$ ion leaves the cell, it is replaced by one $Na^+$ ion. A poor diet FORCES the body to *steal* potassium from the cells to sustain itself. Fresh veggi juices provide a wonderful natural source of potassium as well as **de**acidification of the body tissues and fluids.

The body depends on the process we call *biological*

*alchemy* to meet its dietary needs. It can make what it needs **if** all systems are functional, but the alchemy process fails under conditions of **excess.** Sodium also affects hormone balance. **Sodium plays an important part in the menstrual cycle.**

Sodium and potassium ions BOTH carry a (+) charge and are close in size; hence, EXCESS sodium drives out potassium. When $Na^+$ ions invade the cells, mitochondrial activity slows, vitality wanes and dis-ease follows as acidification increases. It is under these conditions that auto digestion (self cannibalism) of muscle proteins occurs.

Older people and people suffering with degenerative dis-eases build-up **MASSIVE** amounts of toxic wastes in their tissues. To repeat, conditions of EXCESS, as in edema, appear as turgor is lost (turgor is resistance of the skin to deformation). This *waterlogged* condition is common in the extremities (hands, legs, ankles, and feet).

Edema is **more** than water retention. It is a SIGN of excess waste plasma proteins in the tissues, diminished heart function and kidney slowdown. NEVER use diuretics for edema! Instead, **de**acidify the tissues, use racemized™ sea minerals, PAC[s], and racemized™ asparagus (Aspar-Max™).

Allopathic medicine relies on diuretics (water pills) to force EXCESS fluids from the tissues. In the process, potassium is lost and the body is forced to cannibalize its muscle proteins and fats as alternate fuel sources. When it runs out of reserves, the person's weight **collapses overnight**—leaving skin and bones—an extremely serious condition.

As waste and toxicity increase, body hair decreases. Body hair loss is very common among older folks who become "bald" all over their body, especially the legs. Fungus under the toe nails and feet irregularities are also SIGNS.

**When body hair is lost, the system is on its way down. Hair is crucial to detoxification of the skin and body and will regrow over the entire body if the procedures outlined are followed.**

**STOP** the use of table salt at the dinner table. Never use the salt a recipe calls for. Instead, dissolve a "pinch" in a little water and add to recipe for desired effect. Better still, use home grown food. It doesn't need salt. It is loaded with mineral ions.

Salt's effects are insidious, and cancer loves high sodium environments. Cancer tumors and masses surround themselves in a field of sodium saturated tissue. Sodium doesn't singularly cause cancer, but it is a serious factor.

**Cancers are strong, sodium saturated energy fields. Cancer TUMORS "import" and "condense" toxic energy. Cancer MASSES export negative energy (see page 307).**

The invasion of sodium into the cells is the equivalent

of shutting off the power in Jurassic Park. When the power goes off, nature's dinosaurs—the cancer viruses—ACTIVATE and take control of the DNA and RNA software and multiply in our cells. Their proliferation rate is exponential (2, 4, 8,16, 32, 64,128, 256, etc.). Their job is to eliminate weak organisms.

**Viruses ONLY gain entrance and proliferate in our cells when our electrical defenses have been sabotaged. We are our own saboteur when we include table salt in our diet!**

BEV™, Medical Grade Ionized Water™ and racemized™ sea minerals are VERY helpful in sodium **de**acidification because they are PERFECT *carrier* solvents due to their high ORP potentials. They transport excess sodium OUT of the cells and OUT of the body. **Sodium must be DRIVEN OUT of the cells. The body voluntarily withdraws potassium to meet its daily needs if DAILY dietary intake is insufficient.**

As the sodium in the cells is replaced with potassium, the mitochondria come alive, multiply, and produce ATP! Cellular **repolarization** always precedes increased ATP production by the mitochondria.

Pricking the finger is one way to gauge overall health. If you prick your finger and the blood fails to stand-up with a very distinct "pearl," and instead produces a low profile ball or flows or oozes onto the skin, you are in trouble! **De**acidification is mandatory. So is fresh veggi juicing daily. Blood should be BRILLIANT red, never dark red. Blood with a low *crown* and dark color is in a ***pre-cancer*** state and Rouleau will be present.

## Brown Fat & Mitochondria

Brown fat has a great deal to do with vitality and rejuvenation, for it sheds light on WHY some people are fat, skinny, sick, energetic, long lived, etc.

Officially, brown fat is called *brown adipose tissue* or BAT. BAT was only recently discovered. BAT is brown because of the extremely heavy *concentrations* of mitochondria. It is very active, biologically speaking. Except for the word **fat**, BAT has NO resemblance in appearance or function to its shirt-tale relative, *white adipose tissue* or WAT (normal body fat).

Officially, BAT is responsible for **"non-shivering thermogenesis"**—the generation of heat in the absence of shivering. Shivering is a normal body function that is part of heat production under cold OR high stress conditions (people shiver during and after a serious accident). BAT is heavily vascularized (lots of blood vessels) compared to WAT.

Babies have much higher concentrations of BAT than do adults. People who live and work in cold climates have more BAT than people in warm climates. Japanese women skin divers have very high concentrations of BAT and are able to bear frigid ocean waters for hours at a time. They can do this because of the high concentrations of BAT in their tissues and because of a right-spin energy diet. BAT generates much ATP.

**Healthy people have more BAT than do sick people. Thin people have more BAT than fat people. The more BAT you have, the leaner you will be and the more energy you will have!** To understand BAT, let's review the physiological process called ***thermogenic hyperphagia.*** Dissected it looks like this: *thermo*-heat; *genic*-pertaining to the production of. *hyper*-above normal; *phagia*-that which eats.

**People who are subclinically sick or who suffer with degenerative dis-ease have low concentrations of BAT!**

Obese people do not have enough BAT. Instead, they have too much WAT (white adipose tissue). As WAT increases in a person's body, BAT decreases. Obesity is the most obvious SIGN of metabolic slow down, accumulation of EXCESSES, and hormonal imbalance.

When we reach our **anabolic** peak, loss of BAT accelerates, obesity becomes a problem, vitality diminishes, and aging accelerates. **This downward spiral begins in the middle twenties to early thirties.**

In industrial societies like the USA, BAT loss among women is *epidemic!* Premenopausal symptoms are now appearing 20 years AHEAD of official onset of menopause. Symptoms that used to manifest in the late forties and early fifties are now RAMPANT among women in their late twenties and early thirties. **Signs and symptoms of aging develop in direct relationship to loss of BAT, development of hormonal excesses and acidification of body tissues.**

The use of **racemized**™ hormone precursors encourages BAT formation and reverses menopausal and andropausal symptoms in BOTH sexes by **reopening** the puberty window. All of the Young again™ protocols assist in BAT formation and increased metabolism as does moderate aerobic exercise and use of the L/CSF™ machine. Use of the Young Again™ Lymphatic Roller helps break-down cellulite. Subjecting the body to cold is VERY beneficial. Swim regularly in a cold pool, ocean, or lake. Never plunge in as it can cause temporarily paralysis and death due to the "gasp reflex." Do yard and garden work and take walks during the cold months dressed in only a light, short sleeved shirt to encourage BAT formation and strengthen the immune system. Finish bathing with an ICE COLD shower!

**My favorite cold therapy is to work out on my Nordic Trac™ aerobic exerciser OUTSIDE in nothing but boxer shorts—year around! "COLD" workouts stimulate brown fat formation and trains the mind to focus.**

ETVC™ increases BAT activity. B.T. Thyroid™ creme warms cold bodies through increased metabolism and regeneration of connective tissue. Muscle has more mitochondria than fat.

Increase BAT and you will back your way UP the aging pyramid (see page 21) to your **former** anabolic peak. When you reach that peak, you will be *Young Again!*

**PREVIEW:** *Our next chapter is going to SHOCK you! You are going to learn WHY men and women are going bald—and what can be done about it! You are also going to discover the relationship between certain cooking oils and the HIV/AIDS virus.*

**Look at all the sick and dying people!**

**Medical Studies & "Your" Life**

People rely on the advice of their practitioner. Practitioners, in turn, foolishly rely on the *credibility* of medical studies to guide them.

Unfortunately, most medical studies are flawed. For the patient, *bogus* medical studies mean the difference between life and death at worst or pain and suffering at best. For the doctor, flawed studies are disheartening.

In front of me is a news article captioned, *"Fraud Mars Breast Cancer Research."* Investigators uncovered more than a *decade* of fraudulent breast cancer research. And another report condemns mammograms for damaging women's breast tissue.

These reports are frightening, but the **message** is clear. Your MUST learn to think for yourself because you cannot afford to rely on scientific "studies" and "experts" to save you. Hopefully that is why you are reading this book. **And please, do NOT fall into the trap** of conjuring reasons why tried and proven techniques outlined in this book will not work for you. **If you want your life back, be willing to do what needs to be done.** Excuses do not wash. Health and longevity are gifts we experience in the **wake** of *personal* responsibility and informed action. So go to work and experience the miracle in YOUR life as I did in mine. It feels wonderful to be age "19" at age 58.

**P.S.** Your author asks that you "consult" **before** ordering Young Again™ products. There is "no" fee of any kind, and what you will learn will astound you—and set your free of the medical system!

# 25

# Bald Heads & Oils

*"Hair on my legs, hair on my chest, but no hair on my head?"*
Uncle Ross

Balding is a SIGN of premature aging. So is thinning hair. Balding is *loathed* by men, yet it is accepted as inevitable if it "runs" in the family. The *experts* tell us balding is a genetic trait. They are **wrong!** Balding is neither inevitable nor genetic, nor does it have to be permanent. Balding is steeped in poor liver function, acid **excesses**, dietary and digestive short falls, hormonal issues, electrolyte problems in the blood and poor diet. **Hair follicles die or go dormant in a toxic scalp!**

Scalp toxicity and congestion are linked to the consumption of certain dietary oils. If you eat the oils the *experts* tell you to eat, you will likely go bald or develop thin hair as well as succumb to degenerative conditions like arthritis, gout, heart problems, stroke and cancer.

Almost ***everything*** the public has been taught about dietary oils and fats just isn't so. We have been manipulated and lied to. It's time to wake up.

## A Short History Of Oils

Beginning in the 1930's, cotton seed oil became the primary "liquid" dietary oil substitute for fats like butter and lard. During WW ll, cotton seed oil was **hydrogenated** to create a butter substitute that was SOLID at room temperature. They called it **oleo**margarine, margarine or *oleo* for short. War mentality caused the public to accept oleo and by the 50's—when I was growing up—margarine was considered an *acceptable* butter substitute. By the early 1960's, Americans experienced ANOTHER fundamental shift in the TYPE of dietary oils and fats they were eating. This time, the move was even further away from solid fats like butter, lard and oleo to "healthy" oils and tastier margarines.

While the media and the *experts* vilified butter and lard, the Cholesterol THEORY of Cardiovascular Dis-ease became the new scientific "buzz" within the halls of academia which spilled over engulfing the populace with fear and almost total rejection of butter, lard and eggs.

Later, more cliches and buzz words were added to the American vocabulary, such as "unsaturated" and "poly-unsaturated." Corn and safflower oils then appeared replacing cotton seed oil for those with finer tastes and fatter wallets. Oleo was history and margarine was in its hey-day. Fewer people were eating butter. Lard was only for the poor.

By the late 1960's, SOY BEAN oil began to appear on supermarket shelves and in thousands of *processed* foods. Cotton seed, corn and safflower oils were still in wide use, but there was a new focus—health! Soy bean oil became synonymous with ***health** and the **health food movement.***

The shift away from natural fats—like butter, lard and and coconut oils—to liquid and semisoft *hydrogenated* margarines coupled with chlorination and fluoridation of public water supplies caused Americans to experience a dramatic increase in degenerative heart dis-ease.

The ***experts*** blamed naturally occurring *saturated* fats and *cholesterol* for the rise in cardiovascular problems and the increase in degenerative dis-ease while they **ignored** the dietary alterations inherent in **"processed"** foods. They see "balding" to be a "genetic" problem, NOT a dietary one. In the process, God was indicted for his stupidity and error in failing to construct a functionally healthy human model.

*The experts like to razzle dazzle us with scientific hocu pocus. They control the flow of information in schools and the media so the "folks" never make the connection between cause and effect on hundreds of health issues. Balding is just one of them. LOOK at all the folks with balding heads and thinning hair. Ignore the experts!*

With the advent of the new "healthy" oils and soft margarines, balding and *thinning* hair increased in both sexes, young and old. The only person who noticed that something was WRONG was Dr. Carey Reams, who worked in the agricultural arena. He was a voice crying in the wilderness.

**Please acquaint yourself with the following terms so we may continue our story with better understanding.**

**Arteriosclerosis**—hardening of the walls of the arterioles (small arteries) due mainly to fibrous thickening of the connective tissues in their walls, hyalinization, and infiltration of lipids (fats) into the intima (innermost wall) of the arteriole.

**Atherosclerosis**—a form of simple intimal arteriosclerosis with atheromatous deposits within and beneath the intima of the arteries.

**Atheromatous deposits**—the fatty *degeneration* of the artery walls with infiltration of those walls by lipids (fats)—as in arteriosclerosis. Cellular debris, toxic waste and calcium deposits are usually involved.

**Intima**—the innermost layer of the three layers that compose the artery wall.

**Hyalin**—a clear substance that has undergone amyloid degeneration; material deposited in the glomeruli filters of the kidneys.

**Amyloid**—abnormal hyaline deposits in the tissues during pathological state (dis-ease).

**Hyalinization**—infusion of hyaline seen normally in the matrix of cartilage and abnormally elsewhere; any alteration within the cells or extracellular spaces which involves the deposition of hyalin.

**Plaque**—a cholesterol containing mass in the intima or tunica of the arteries; means *patch.*

## The Soy Connection

Dr. Carey Reams often commented on the rise in balding, but it was my friend, Tom Mahoney, who provided the clue that solved the puzzle. It was an *agricultural* clue.

Tom talked of a strange family of plants known as the **Fabales**. He observed that if cows or sheep were allowed to graze on soy for any length of time, their health would suffer and their hair would **thin,** and/or **fall out.**

Tom's observations were the trigger I needed to solve Dr. Carey Reams' thirty year old observation. Reams was sure there was a link between the dietary soy, balding and aging.

## Soy Oil & PHG

Soy bean oil and soy bean curd (tofu) contain a toxic biochemical called **phyto-hema-glutinin** or PHG for short. Dissected, the word looks like this: *phyt(e)*-that which comes from plants), *hem(e)*-blood, *glutinin*-a vegetable protein "glue."

**PHG is a large protein molecule that has proven to be specific in its ability to *agglutinate* human blood.**

Agglutination means to "glue," to cause to "adhere," to form a "mass!" The Rouleau effect we have been referring to is a good example of agglutination. Soy oil—and soy products—are rich in PHG and promote Rouleau (see page 136).

PHG causes blood circulation to slow and to clot. It combines with impurities in the blood and forms plaques on the walls of the arteries and arterioles and clogs the fine capillaries in the posterior eye, ears and SCALP. It magnifies the Rouleau "sticky blood" problem affecting 95% of Americans. PHG numbs the immune system's T cells, and it negatively influences the central and peripheral nervous systems. It alters hormonal activity and it influences endocrine and exocrine activity while it slows vital organ function.

PHG kills rats DEAD! It is poisonous to *all* living things. As with any systemic poison, the *quantity* consumed, *length* of exposure and *individual* predisposition are factors that hint at why the body tolerates soy oil and proteins even though they are "bad news!" **The effects of soy PHG are "cumulative."**

## Soy & Digestion

Soy interferes with *normal* digestion. Soy beans produce gas and upset body chemistry. Peanuts are another *famous* member of the Fabale family of plants, and many people cannot digest peanut products. Peanuts contain very little PHG in comparison to soy. More examples of the Fabale family of foods are garbanzo beans (chic peas), fava beans, lentils, and mung beans. These contain *almost* no PHG.

Two Fabale legumes that cause serious long term problems for *grazing* animals are clover and alfalfa. In the field, they can be deadly toxic and cause bloating in ruminants. Cows, horses and sheep thrive on grasses which contain **growth energy** proteins and sugars. Grasses have a different "spin" on their nutrient molecules than do legumes like alfalfa, clover and soy.

Soy PHG reacts with circulating minerals and dissolved blood gases like chlorine, chloramine and fluorine forming substances that resemble bath tub scum—like that which comes from using Grandma's lye soap in hard water.

*Municipalities use chemicals like sodium hypo-chlorite (sodium hydroxide + chlorine) to treat public water supplies. Sodium hydroxide* **(lye)** *is what Grandma used to make her lye soap. It is extremely alkaline (pH 12). Chlorine is extremely acidic (-2 and +2 pH) and is used to kill bacteria. The hydroxide is used to drive up the pH so that the acidic water will not kill you. Halogenated (chlorinated and fluoridated) tap water reacts with dietary oils and other circulating wastes and produces plaques that are combination of these ingredients. (Note: plaques are NOT difficult to clear from the body using the Young Again™ protocol outlined in this book and in the Source Packet.)*

Lipids (oils and fats) are absorbed by lymphatic capillaries called **lacteals**. Unlike carbohydrates and proteins, lipids are NOT absorbed directly into the blood capillaries. Lacteals feed into larger ducts that join the blood at the left subclavian vein which empties into the superior vena cava, returning the blood to the right side of the heart. Incoming blood rich in bad fats and **inorganic** minerals and other waste (soy) form arterial plaque that leads to heart dis-ease.

The heart then pumps the blood to the lungs for oxygenation AND energy *transference* before it is returned to the left side of the heart for distribution to the body. The liver receives a **double** blood supply. Oxygenated blood via the hepatic artery and deoxygenated blood via the portal vein. Only AFTER the blood has run its course is it returned to the liver for cleaning. Forty percent (40%) of the blood leaving the heart feeds the head via the carotid arteries. Precipitates, called **plaque** collect on arterial walls are electrically "charged" substances that slow blood flow, interfere with oxygen delivery, harden blood vessel walls, thus raising blood pressure. Plaque causes the lining (intima) of the arteries to harden and deteriorate and form clots. When plaque breaks lose, it can migrate up the neck and into the brain and cause a stroke. If, on the other hand, the oxygen supply to the heart becomes severely limited due to plaque formation, a heart attack will result. Fresh beet and carrot juice and the Young Again Colon Therapy Protocol™ reverses these problems.

As blood enters the neck, waste sticks to the artery walls, narrowing the carotid arteries that feed the head and brain. Waste finds its way into the VERY FINE capillaries that feed the cells of the posterior eyes, ears and scalp, closing them off. Plasma proteins that escape into the extracellular spaces further clog the lymph capillaries compounding problems for the scalp, ears, eyes, hair follicles and nerve fibers.

Balding and graying are SIGNS of deterioriation. Removal of **acid** wastes from the body causes hair to grow. Kombucha tea and $GH_3$™ speed the reversal process.

## Alfalfa Sprouts

Alfalfa sprouts are a popular vegetarian delight, but there is a caveat that comes with them. Alfalfa **sprouts** contain powerful ***phytotoxins*** and are detrimental to people with weak immune systems. In dry leaf form, as used in food supplements, alfalfa does not pose a problem. But "fresh" alfalfa sprouts should be avoided like the plague! Cancer patients should NEVER, EVER eat **alfalfa** sprouts because the phytotoxins in them depress immune function and create EXCESSES that fuel cancer. Clover and mustard sprouts should also be avoided. Other type seed sprouts are fine.

***Occasional sickness is good. It means that your immune system is functioning and that your body KNOWS when things are out of balance.***

## Eyes • Ears

The forces **driving** glaucoma, retinitis, and macular degeneration are the **same** forces driving hearing loss, hair loss and graying. Translated, this means *insufficient* oxygen and and **acid** waste overloaded and hormonal issues. Why hormones? Because tissue **regeneration** is hormone driven in both males and females respectively. In women, sluggish thyroid function is a **HUGE** factor. B.T.™ creme remedies hypo thyroid issues. Kelp tablets help, too, but they do not solve the problem by their self. SOC™ capsules open blood capillary flow into scarred, congested areas. Colon therapy and fresh veggi juice are standard operating procedure.

Hair follicles are heavy energy feeders. They require good blood and lymph circulation. Slow growing hair and nails are a SIGN of low metabolic activity. Thinning hair is but another version of balding. Gray hair speaks for itself.

Loss of body hair—especially leg hair—is a SERIOUS condition and a red flag. Waste accumulation brings on problems in the feet, like "restless legs syndrome," corns, bunions, deformed toes and nerve and connective tissue disorders that cause pain and the feet to "burn." Behind these problems are conditions of **EXCESS** acid waste plasma proteins and hormone irregularities. These problems are reversible.

## Supplementary Information On Soybeans

Soy beans are *unlike* other beans. Soy is a *toxic* plant! It is one of two **toxic** seed oil plants grown for their "industrial" oils. Insects seldom touch soy. Soy bean plants—and canola too—thrive on toxic soil and air. Soy proteins have a powerful left-spin and should never be consumed. Soy converts and stores toxic energies in its "oil." **Humans do likewise by entombing toxic waste energy fields in fat layer under the skin. Energy is never lost, it merely changes form.**

Few people know that soy beans were genetically altered in the middle 1950's with that "harmless" process called *irradiation.* This was done to INCREASE the soy bean's oil content and to create a plant that would prosper on toxic soils.

Powerful interests made sure "corporate" government funded soy research. The same people who promote vaccinations and touted the Cholesterol and Germ Theories. They needed an oil crop that would grow on negative energy soils treated with synthetic salt fertilizers and poisonous sprays. The soy cartel is not concerned about the long term effects of soy on people. **Soy oil is an "industrial" oil that is being peddled as a food oil. Soy protein is a waste spin-off.**

### Sticky Oils • Sick People

The toxic nature of soy has been known for a long time, yet, soy oil is added to THOUSANDS of **processed** and **prepared** foods. Soy is often substituted for dairy products. Soy baby formulas are deadly. *(See page 382 for baby formula.)*

Heat olive oil, butter, or lard in a skillet and you will observe that they become "thinner." Soy and canola oils thicken and become gummy—especially after they cool. Put soy and canola oils into a 98.6°F human body and you have a recipe for dis-ease. Soy oxidizes in the body and produces free radicals. **Industrial oils do not belong in the human body.**

Peanut oil is an interesting oil. Edgar Cayce said it was a nice massage oil for the skin. But put it in the body and all hell breaks loose. It is toxic inside the body, but not outside.

The best dietary oil to use is OLIVE OIL, followed by sunflower oil. Olive oil is the product of a **fruit**—the olive! If olive oil was good enough for Jesus, it ought to be good enough for you and me! Nut oils and sesame oil are fine, too. Flax oil is **highly** unstable and is best **AVOIDED** due to issues of rancidity. Avoid corn, safflower, and cotton seed oils, too.

Tofu is a **very** popular food among vegetarians. Tofu is the curd of the soy bean. It is rich in PHG and is therefore, toxic. If you make Tofu a regular part of your diet, long term health will suffer and you will grow OLD and see your connective tissues break down. Tofu should NEVER be eaten by recovering cancer patients! NOTE: 99% of vitamin E capsules use soy oil as the carrier. Wheat germ oil is a better choice. PAC®are even better than vitamin E in regard to antioxidant activity.

Many people ask, *"What about soy protein?"* My answer

is "avoid it!" Soy protein has a left spin. It's the wrong "kind" of protein. Scientists tell us that protein is protein, but then they tell us sugar is sugar i.e. maltose, sucrose, lactose, etc. and the body doesn't know the difference. All substances have an energy "signature"—including proteins. Soy protein is extremely difficult to digest because it contains large quantities of trypsin, a harmful substance that inhibits digestion and enlarges the pancreas. Foods high in trypsin fuel cancer too!

Soy is also high in phytates, which are salts of phytic acid. Phytates cause widespread mineral imbalances because soy has the highest phytate content of any food plant **EVER** studied. Vegetarians who consume soy and tofu eventually experience degeneration of the connective tissues and the build-up of **excesses** in the system. Phytates deprive the body of zinc which the body uses to ward off diabetes (pancreas) and strengthen the immune system. Soy produces connective tissue disorders in laboratory mice and in children affecting bones, cartilage, muscles, tendons, ligaments, and skin, and the myelin sheath protecting the nerve fibers. Soy is trouble!

Soy baby formulas are ***synthesized*** junk that creates serious problems for infants. **Toxic chemical SOLVENTS are used to extract the oil from the soy bean leaving residue.** High heat processing denatures soy proteins and makes them unhealthy. Heavy metal contamination makes soy formula a real threat. Mothers wrongly turn to soy formulas due to infant cow lactose intolerance. Breast milk is the **BEST** choice, then goat milk, followed by the recipe on page 382. Regardless of the formula vehicle, Young Again R/C™ and Microbe-ize™ used in tandem does wonders for sickly, colic troubled babies.

Food intolerance (so called "allergies") in adults and children is tied to acid waste overload, poor liver function, "leaky gut syndrome," antibiotics and the effects of non steroidal anti inflammatory drugs (aspirin, etc.) and medicines. Adults with food allergies, sinus problems, and asthma **MUST** follow the Young Again™ colon therapy protocol, and the Tissue & Liver cleanse protocol if they expect to become whole.

## Debating The Issues!

I am fully aware that the contents of these pages are totally contrary to what the **experts** are saying about the benefits of soy ingestion. A week doesn't pass that some new "study" or ***soy miracle*** marketing scheme doesn't land on my desk with a note asking me to debate the issues regarding soy. **Sorry! There is nothing to debate.** Believe whomever you like. The choice is yours. Go ahead. Believe the experts. In the end, I can assure you that the scoffers will be "dead" right!

## Rotenone • Fish • Insects • Soy

Rotenone is used by organic gardeners as a "natural" organic pesticide. It is also used for poisoning unwanted fish species in lakes throughout North America. Rotenone comes from the *soy bean. Roten* is Japanese for *derris.* It means to destroy, to tear apart. "Derris" is the specie name for the soy bean within the family Fabale. Home gardeners have been told by the *experts* that rotenone is great stuff. However, if you read the label you will be warned against breathing the dust.

When inhaled, rotenone is absorbed through the mucous membranes. These membranes are a direct conduit into the blood and lymph and provide easy access to the body's IMMUNE system. A breath of rotenone dust is a direct shot at the central and peripheral nervous systems. It is the **glycosides** in the rotenone that brings on paralysis of the muscles.

*We can LEARN from watching an insect that has been dusted with rotenone. Insects react to rotenone in a matter of seconds with TOTAL paralysis! This* ***harmless*** *(?) stuff from SOY BEANS shuts down the insect's nervous system and muscles. Soy foods do the same thing to people, but it does it a day at a time over a period of years!*

In lakes, rotenone causes a complex *series* of changes in metabolism that prevent fish from extracting ENERGY from nutrients! **Rotenone can kill ALL the fish in a lake with an application as small as 1 part per million (ppm).**

One-half pound of rotenone is equivalent to 60,000 ppm. One-half pound equals 8 ounces or 7,500 ppm per ounce. The *experts* tell us that it would take **1 ounce** of rotenone to kill a 150 pound man. If 1 ppm can kill all the fish in a lake, do you think it would require a concentration that is 7,499 times greater to kill a human being? It appears that the *expert's* calculations as to what is a "safe" amount of this ***poison*** that the human body can handle is off a bit. The truth of the matter is that the *experts* don't know or care what is a safe amount. These are the same "experts" Rachel Carson struggled against in her effort to warn mankind of the inherent danger of pesticides. I suggest you read *Silent Spring* and *Our Stolen Future* (see the Source Page 384). When you ingest soy , you are ingesting PHG—which gums up your blood and puts your IMMUNE and NERVOUS systems under severe stress. Avoid it!

## Sweet Proteins

Glycine is an amino acid. It is one of approximately twenty-three amino acids that form larger molecules called proteins. Sow peas (soy beans) are very rich in glycine containing proteins because they have been *irradiated* and *genetically engineered* to produce proteins that are high in glycine. Industry, in turn, concentrates glycine through a process called hydrolysis. The result is a glycine-max (glycocide) concentrate. Liquid glycer**ol** is extremely sweet and syrupy. These molecules have an *alcohol* molecule attached. Glycolysis is part of the Krebs Cycle and occurs within the cells in the **absence** of oxygen and **within** the mitochondrial electron transport chain and results in the energy molecule ATP. (*glyc*-sweet, *lysis*-to cleave, divide or split the sugar molecule glucose.)

*Saponification* (the same process Grandma used to make her lye soap) produces glycerol (an alcohol) and alkali fatty acid (soap). An **-ol** on the end of a chemical name means the molecule is an alcohol. Alcohols are excellent *non-polar* solvents, that is, they dissolve fatty substances like those that comprise our cellular membranes. Alcohols destroy our cells and attack the myelin sheath that protects our nerve fibers.

The chemical industry likes *glycine-max* glycer**ol**. It is widely used as a *solvent* and as a **plasticizer** in the manufacture of hundreds of plastics.

*BEV™ water should NOT be stored or transported in common plastics because it reacts with the plasticizers, causing them to leach into the water. Bottled water—**especially distilled water**—is loaded with chemical isolates leached from the plastic bottle. That is one of the reasons distilled water tastes so bad. Concentration of volatile chemicals is another shortcoming of distillation. Volatiles gas-off during distillation. Common "drink and toss" bottle water is bad news due to the isopropyl alcohol residues left in the bottles prior to filling. AVOID them!*

**When the soy molecule is subjected to heat in the presence of organic compounds like those in our blood, "thermoplastic" resins are formed.** The result is **sticky blood** that gums-up the capillaries. Keep in mind, this is a "subtle" process that occurs SLOWLY over a period of years! The body cannot tolerate these resins, so it stores them in the the soft tissues and **fat layer** under the skin. Blood vessel degeneration and plaque formation are part of this scenario.

### Glycosides • Opium • Morphine • Atropine

Glycosides (rotenone) from soybeans cause physiologic reactions in humans and animals. *Morphine* and *atropine* are examples of drugs that contain high concentrations of glycosides. Morphine comes from opium and skews the **central nervous system**. It affects muscle control, pupil dilation, and is extremely reactive in the body. *Atropine* comes from the belladonna family of plants. It alters response to electrical signals and causes paralysis of the **parasympathetic nervous system,** the part of our nervous system over which we have NO direct control—like the heart muscle, breathing muscles, and intestinal muscles. *Digitalis* is a glycoside that comes from Foxglove. **Morphine, atropine,** and **digitalis** are "legally" controlled substances that have been *isolated* and *concentrated.* **Synthetic** glycosides are openly substituted for the real thing with serious side effects for patients. The experts tell us there is no difference between *real* and *synthesized.* Really?

## Soy & Dog Food

In front of me is a label from a can of a well known brand of dog food. From 1993 -1998 you could find it on your supermarket shelves. It says **"Soy FREE • Highly Digestible."**

The implications of the words on the label and those on TV ads (January 6, 1994) indicate that there is a serious problem with soy protein in dog food. Some dog food manufactures tout ***digestibility*** because they have **REMOVED s**oy. MANUFACTURERS are closed mouth about the **long term** *degenerative* effects of soy on dogs. They are afraid of retaliation by the soy cartel and the feds.

The dog food and grazing animal connection confirms the problem of soy oil and soy protein in HUMAN metabolism. Soy causes serious degenerative problems in humans, but it is NOT being taken out of our food. Instead, it is being **promoted** by **expert after expert** as a "perfect" food. The barrage of soy wonder "stories" backgrounds the introduction of soy "miracle" products—along with the usual hype and an army of experts!

If food that contains soy is toxic to dogs **(carnivores),** and grazing animals **(herbivores),** what do you think it will do to human beings **(omnivores)** who are a little of both? Maybe people should decide what pedigree they would like to be so they can qualify for *soy free, highly digestible food—arf, arf!* Avoid foods that contain soy! Period!

Note: Private soy interests—via government—recently strong armed the largest hamburger chain in the world (guess who) from going back to using animal fats for their french fries. It appears that soy cartel interests "control" government.

## Conclusion

We know the cumulative effects of soy bean oil, canola oil, tofu, and alfalfa sprouts on humans and animals. We know their effects on the blood, the central and peripheral nervous systems, the immune system, and how they "block" hormonal receptor sites and foul the environment. **The evidence is**

**obvious for those with eyes to see!**

Please **do not** call the publisher making demands for "documentation." There is more than enough information contained in this book for those who can think without the blessings of higher authority. **Ignore the experts and you stand a much better chance of becoming *Young Again!***

**PREVIEW:** *In our next chapter, you will learn about the connection between blindness, glaucoma, and canola oil!*

---

**30 Years Old & 7 Months Pregnant**

It doesn't get any better than that, and lucky is the woman who can "freeze" this magical moment, **regardless** of age. Learn how by referring to pages 72 164, 212 and 274.

---

**"Bone density tests don't offer any solutions!"**

---

**The Gulf War Connection & Your Life Today**

Gulf War veterans were "ordered" to take a drug called Pyridostigmine Bromide (PB) every day. This drug interferes with *acetylcholinesterase*—an enzyme that is critical to nerve synapse function (nerve signal transmission). **The side effects were known & predictable!**

PB produces the symptoms being experienced by Gulf War veterans. The question is WHO ordered its use and WHY? The answer is "the experts!" The same experts who tell us to eat soy and canola, promote birth control pills, vaccinations, estrogen replacements and "harmless" organophosphate poisons like malathion.

Anyone who has taken medications of any variety should "clear" those molecules from their body's neuro and hormonal receptor sites by using racemized™ hormone precursor products and following the Young Again Protocols™.

Improvement in nerve signal function, renewal of the myelin sheath, and Schwann cell activity at the nerve synapses must precedes the formation of healthy tissue and restoration of health.

The Young Again Protocol™ works equally well for veterans, osteoporotic women, hyper active and attention deficit children, men with "male" problems, etc—all of which have receptor site "lock up." Women with SIGNS of premature aging or menstrual difficulties experience a rebirth, while men with prostate problems get to stop worrying. The process is called "aging reversal." The experience is quite a lofty feeling. At age 58/19, your author can **attest** to what is in store for people who are willing to take responsibility for their lives.

## War In The Marketplace

It takes twenty years to create a market for a new product. Early on, consumers resist change IF the enemy can be "created" in the consumer's mind. In time, fight gives way to resistance. After twenty years, fatigue sets in, memory fades, and the metamorphosis is complete.

The rules for *creating* a bogus market are the same as for waging war. I refer the reader to Sun Tzu's 6th century B.C. book *The Art Of War*, summarized as follows: *Outline an agenda, disseminate disinformation and misinformation, create confusion and dissension, raise an army of experts, use subversion, quote statistics, and finally create fear. Fear leads to panic, and panic to victory.*

Perhaps now you can see how the soy and canola oil cartel(s) developed antipathy towards butter, coconut oil, and lard while creating a high demand, consumer-friendly market for **industrial** oils like soy and canola.

Sun Tzu was correct! The game is called **divide and conquer!** It's simple. It works. His book was the official training manual in the rise of the Soviet empire. ***Hear*** what the experts preach. ***See*** which way the masses are moving. ***Tune-in*** to what the media is pushing. **Now! Go the other way as you spread the word!**

## The "250" Club

The "250" Club is for anyone who would like to live to the age of 250 vibrant, healthy years *young!* Please do not dismiss such a goal as impossible or ridiculous. It's within the reach of anyone who desires to see it become a reality.

Society needs goals and role models. Think of the good things that would spin-off from a core of people who have healthfully lived five generations? Instead of each generation starting over every fifty years losing wisdom and experience, the "250" Club would act as a *transition* team to help other humans to learn to live in harmony as God intended.

Think of the suffering and strife that could be eliminated through the transfer of correct living to our great grand children. Life on Earth would become a joy. So clean up your body and follow the Young Again Protocol as best you can and "250" might just happen for you. **The "250" Club is a testimony to the world.**

## Inflame-Away™

Finally, a safe and fast acting answer for inflammation and joint pain anywhere in the body. Over 300 times the activity of traditional herbal products (see Source Page 384).

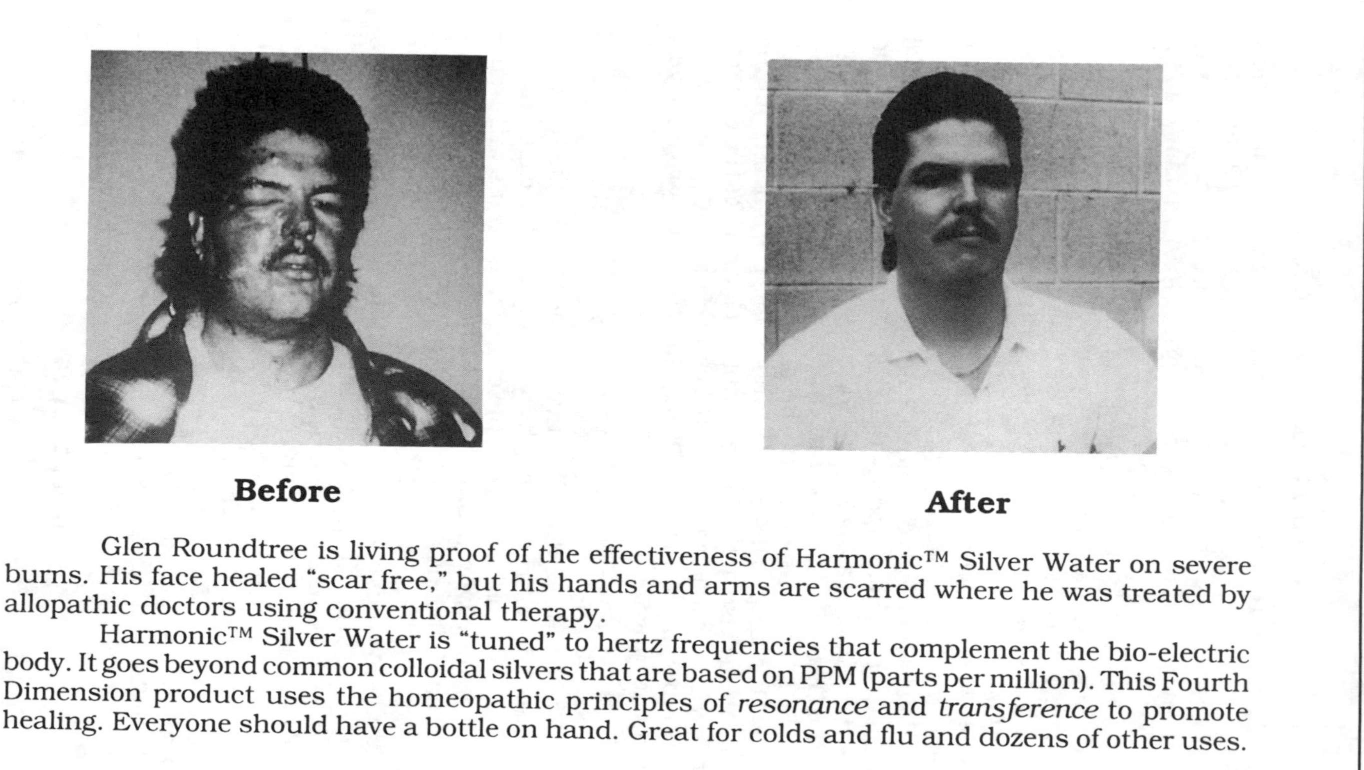

**Before** **After**

Glen Roundtree is living proof of the effectiveness of Harmonic™ Silver Water on severe burns. His face healed "scar free," but his hands and arms are scarred where he was treated by allopathic doctors using conventional therapy.

Harmonic™ Silver Water is "tuned" to hertz frequencies that complement the bio-electric body. It goes beyond common colloidal silvers that are based on PPM (parts per million). This Fourth Dimension product uses the homeopathic principles of *resonance* and *transference* to promote healing. Everyone should have a bottle on hand. Great for colds and flu and dozens of other uses.

# 26

# Blindness & Oils

*"Since the days of revelation, the same four corrupting errors have been made over and over again: submission to faulty and unworthy authority; submission to what was customary to believe; submission to prejudices of the mob; and worst of all, concealment of ignorance by a false show of unheld knowledge, for no other reason than pride."*
Roger Bacon

Millions of people have suffered the loss of their vision from glaucoma, a dis-ease involving *atrophy* (deterioration) of the optic nerve. For years, the *experts* have been telling people that glaucoma results from fluid pressure buildup in the eye which causes the optic nerve to deteriorate. This THEORY was based on an incorrect medical model. **They were wrong!**

The *experts* now admit that these things are NOT true and have given birth to a new theory that says glaucoma is caused by a deficiency of oxygen and blood flow. Finally, they are on the right track. In the end, they will discover that glaucoma is the result of insufficient blood flow and agglutination (clumping) of red blood cells, metabolic waste build-up in **inter**cellular fluids and spaces, and hormone irregularities.

Agglutinated blood CANNOT squeeze through the extremely fine capillaries of the posterior eye (over 80 miles per eye) and, therefore, cannot deliver oxygen and nutrients to the cells and the mitochondria, nor can it remove cellular waste.

Death of the mitochondria in the cells of the *posterior* eye is due to oxygen starvation, sodium toxicity, and waste accumulation. When the cells die, the tissues of the posterior eye *atrophy* and the dead cells create acid waste. Acid waste build-up, nutrient starvation and hormone short falls are also behind hair loss, Alzheimers, multiple sclerosis, cerebral palsy, fibromyalgia and hearing disorders. For sure, hormonal issues must be addressed if the body's receptor sites are to be cleared of hormone analogs. (A hormonal "analog" is a molecule that fits neuro receptors and blocks normal function.) Yeast is also a major contributor to eye, ear and sinus problems. "Floaters" in the eye is YEAST. Bt age 47 your author was plagued with floaters. Today, I have none!

**Rape or Canola?**

The name **canola** is a "coined" word. It is not listed in anything but the most recent reference sources. It is a word that appeared out of ***nowhere!***

The flip side of the canola coin reads: RAPE! You must admit that canola sounds better than *rape*. The name *"canola"* masked the introduction of **rape oil** to America.

Canola oil comes from the rape seed, which is part of the Mustard family of plants. Rape is the **MOST** toxic of all food oils. Rape is a toxic plant and insects will not eat rape. It is deadly poisonous. **The oil from the rape seed is a hundred times more toxic than soy oil!**

Canola oil is a *semi-drying* oil that is used as a lubricant, fuel, soap and synthetic rubber base and as an illuminant for the slick color pages you see in magazines. Canola is an **industrial** oil. It does NOT belong in the body!

Canola oil—like soy oil and soy protein—has some interesting characteristics *and* affects on living systems. For example, it forms latex-like substances that cause ***agglutination*** of the red blood corpuscles just like soy, only MUCH more pronounced. Loss of vision is a **known** characteristic side effect of rape oil. Rape oil ***antagonizes*** the central and peripheral nervous systems. Deterioration takes years to manifest.

**Rape (canola) oil stresses the body's terrain in general, and contributes to multiple symptomatic conditions in the bodies of ANIMALS—and humans.**

Rape oil was in widespread use in animal feeds in England and Europe between 1986 and 1991 when it was thrown out. Do you remember reading about the cows, pigs and sheep that went **blind,** lost their minds, and attacked people? They had to be shot!

*Not long after the first edition of this book appeared, a woman called me from Chicago to tell me that she was in England at the time the Mad Cow Disease was at its peak. She told me that she witnessed a news report on television that told people not to panic if they had been using rape oil in their diet and were over 65 years of age. The "experts" added that the effects of rape oil ingestion take* ***at least*** *ten years to manifest, and in all likelihood, most of these people would be dead by then anyway. Interesting!*

"Experts" *blamed* the erratic behavior on a viral disease called *scrapie.* However, when rape oil was removed from animal feed, scrapie disappeared. A thoughtful reader sent your author a serious, in depth study of the affects of Canola on dairy cattle in Canada. The results was disastrous to the animals. Now Americans are growing rape seed and using rape (canola) oil in the USA. Canola oil is now *our* problem. It is widely used in thousands of processed foods—with the blessings of government watchdog agencies, of course.

Officially, canola oil is known as "LEAR" oil. The acronym stands for *low erucic acid* ***rape.*** The *experts* in the industry love to tell the story of how canola was developed in Canada and that it is safe to use. They admit it was developed from the rape seed, but that through *genetic engineering* (irradiation) it is no longer rape seed, but instead "canola!"

The experts love to talk about canola's "qualities"—like its unsaturated structure, omega 3's, 6's, and 12's, its wonderful digestibility and its fatty acid makeup. They malign **naturally** saturated oils and fats and come to the rescue with canola oil. They even tell us how Asia has warmly embraced canola due to its distinctive flavor. *Isn't it wonderful how multinational oil cartels "help" third world people? Doesn't their story remind you of the introduction of microwave ovens?*

In the old west, there was an **earthy** expression that sums up the industry flim-flam that accompanied the smoke and mirror introduction of rape oil into the diets of unsuspecting people world wide. It was, ***"Horse Shit & Gun Smoke!"***

The term *canola* gave the perfect cover for cartel interests who wanted to make billions. The name "canola" is a warm fuzzy, but powerful interests have nothing to worry about. The public has already bought the farm!

## Chemical Warfare

The chemical warfare agent, MUSTARD GAS is derived from rape oil. This is the chemical agent that was responsible for blistering the lungs and skin of hundreds of thousands of solders and civilians during WW I. Recent reports from the French indicate mustard gas was used during the Gulf War.

Between 1950 and 1953, white mustard seed (rape seed) was ***irradiated*** in Sweden to increase seed production and oil content. *Irradiation* is the same process the *experts* want to use to make our food *safe* to eat. Genetically engineered fruits and vegetables—which will soon have innocent things like hepatitis-B spliced into their DNA—are another example of man's misuse of technology and abuse of public trust by powerful interests and "head in the sand" watchdog agencies.

Canola oil contains large amounts of **iso-thio-cyanates** which are **cyanide** containing compounds. Cyanide INHIBITS mitochondrial production of ATP. ATP is the chemical acronym for adenosine triphosphate, which is the energy molecule that fuels the body and keeps us healthy and *YOUNG!*

**Canola Oil & Body Metabolism**

Many substances *bind* metabolic enzymes and *block* their activity in the body. In biochemistry, these substances are called *inhibitors.* Throughout this book we have used terms like "bio-junk food," "toxic/acid waste," "negative energy," "drugs," "left-spin energy," etc. to describe inhibitory energy fields.

Toxic substances in canola and soy oils encourage the formation of covalent bonds. Normally, covalent bonds are *irreversible* and CANNOT be broken down by the body once they have formed. This is particularly true of hormone analogs contained in birth control pills, estrogen replacements and anabolic steroids. Environmental zeno estrogens are so ubiquitous that they are unavoidable. **The Young Again Hormone Protocol™ is used to reverse system damage.**

Consider the pesticide **malathion.** It binds to the active site of the enzyme ***acetylcholinesterase*** and stops this enzyme from doing what it is supposed to do, which is to divide acetylcholine into choline and acetate. Malathion is the "harmless" pesticide spray used to kill the Med Fly and blanket every living thing in California in the early 90's, again in 1994, and in Texas in 1995. Malathion is an **organophosphate**.

**Nerve Function & Organophosphates**

**Acetycholine is critical to NERVE impulse transmission. When inhibited, nerve synapses do not function normally and the muscles do not respond.**

For example, think of your garage door opener. If no signal is sent, the door does not open. In the case of the body, your hand or leg does not respond. Perhaps you have noticed the tremendous increase in disorders like systemic lupus, multiple sclerosis, cerebral palsy, restless legs syndrome, pulmonary hypertension and peripheral neuropathy in recent years. Soy and canola oils are players in the development of these dis-ease conditions. So are the **organophosphate** insecticides used in food production in the name of efficiency.

**Acetylcholinesterase inhibitors cause paralysis of the striated (skeletal) muscles and spasms of the respiratory system.**

That is why malathion is the pesticide of choice by the

*experts*. It kills insects by causing **muscle paralysis**—just like *rotenone* from soy beans! It inhibits the insect's *enzymes* and it inhibits human enzymes, too!

Agents *orange* and *blue* were used in Vietnam to defoliate jungle cover are organophosphorous compounds. The Vietnam Vets and the Vietnamese people know first-hand about them. Government *experts* who okayed their use and chemical companies that manufactured them have finally owned up to their toxic effects on PEOPLE and the environment. Nevertheless, present day *experts* in academia and government continue to **"abba dabba"** the public with stories of "safe" science and cheap food through the use of poisons.

**Canola oil is rich in glycosides. Glycosides cause serious problems in the human body by blocking enzyme function and locking up nerve and hormone receptors.**

Glycosides interfere with the biochemistry of humans and animals. Consider the effect of a rattlesnake bite. Glycosides in the venom **inhibit** muscle enzymes and cause instant immobilization and tissue necrosis.

### Canola Oil • HIV & AIDS

Soy and canola oil glycosides depress the immune system. They cause the **white blood cell defense system**—the T-cells—to go into a stupor and fall asleep on the job. These oils alter the body "terrain" and promote dis-ease.

The alcohols and glycosides in canola and soy oils shut down our protective grid—the immune system. Fluoride, immunizations, antibiotics and bio-junk food play complementary roles in immune system collapse.

An *alcohol* is a chemistry term for the "reactive" chemical group on an organic molecule. The "-R" group is what makes organic compounds work—for good and bad! Canola alcohols and glycosides are very reactive. They are just as toxic as alcoholic beverages, but their effects manifest differently. **The damage takes years to show up.**

When the medical experts check your blood for the presence of the HIV virus, they are looking at your white blood cell count. If the numbers are normal, they will tell you that you do NOT have HIV. What they don't see is that the T-cells are in a toxic *stupor*. This *opportunistic* condition allows life forms in the blood and lymph to metamorphose and manifest as hepatitis, pneumonia, herpes, **HIV** and to *bypass* the body's immune system defenses (the T-cells) and get a foothold. As Claude Barnard said, *"The terrain is everything!"*

**Once inside the cells, HIV takes over the RNA and DNA. It uses the mitochondria to produce energy for its**

**own use. Quietly, the virus multiplies (replicates) and one day—BANG!—you wake up and you are dying of AIDS.**

### AIDS & Green Monkeys

In his earth shaking book, *AIDS The End of Civilization*, Dr. William Campball Douglass asked, *"Do you really think some Green Monkey all of a sudden bit some guy in the ass and presto, AIDS all over the world?"*

Dr. Douglass was examining the hype that the Centers for Disease Control in Atlanta was *peddling* to the public about the AIDS virus—HIV. Douglass' book tells the "whole" story of the development of HIV at the Ft. Detrick, Maryland military installation. His story is well documented and confirms the theme of the futuristic movies *Outbreak* and *The Twelve Monkeys* which I highly recommend you see.

### Lorenzo's Oil

Another movie, *Lorenzo's Oil*, offers another good example of how far off course medical science has strayed and how muddled is the scientific mind. Early on in the movie, the *experts* said the problem with the dying child was not in the math (i.e., pH). They were wrong.

Had the experts determined the pH of the saliva, urine and blood they would have *instantly* known what they were up against. That dying boy had a chronically low total body pH! So low that his body fluids were *dissolving* the myelin sheath that protects the nerve fibers. This was causing his nervous system to disintegrate. *Does this description smack of the dozens of degenerative nerve related disorders plaguing people today?*

The boy was given Lorenzo's oil to boost energy output and act as a detoxifier of metabolic poisons. The oil *shocked* his body into a LESS acid condition. Lorenzo's oil is OLIVE oil! When given in large quantities, olive oil SHOCKS the body and causes it to adjust pH by dumping acid wastes and bile.

Shortly after Lorenzo's Oil was released, my brother witnessed a TV talk show where an expert claimed Lorenzo's oil was rape oil. This was a lie. Give rape oil to a sick person and you will seal their doom. Here is another good example of "disinformation" in the public domain. These falsehoods should cause every thinking person to question the molding of public opinion by **"shadow"** interests behind the scenes.

### Blood & Oils

By now it should be obvious to the reader that congested blood and lymph flow negatively affects every part of the body. It should be equally obvious that there is a direct link between dis-ease, diet and the water we drink. Moreover, the astronomical increase in the use of processed foods that contain canola oil, soy products and chemical additives CONFUSE the body and weaken the immune system.

It should also come as no surprise that anyone wanting to enjoy peak health and longevity MUST take control of their life and personal responsibility for their health. Fortunately, most health conditions can be eased and even reversed.

**The "health care" industry is an oxymoron. It protects its own health and economic interests. Learn to protect YOUR health and economic interests by learning HOW to take care of yourself and acting upon that knowledge immediately.**

**Note:** *ABC news just aired the results of a damning medical study that confirmed that soy and canola oils are definitely linked to prostate cancer in men. The report aired on February 15, 1994.* Now the *experts* are promoting soy oil breast implants for **unsuspecting** women. Amazing!

**PREVIEW:** *Our next chapter looks at the connection between onions, your liver and aging.*

---

**It's important to hang and s-t-r-e-t-c-h every day. Yoga and Pilates are very good for superb health!**

---

***"Everything In Excess Is Opposed By Nature."***
Hippocrates

**Comfrey Greens**

In the good old days, before the FDA decided to save us from the evils of comfrey, it could be found in health stores. Today, if you want comfrey, you have to grow it yourself or have someone grow it for you. And, if you are smart, that is exactly what you will do.

Obtain a few crowns with a few shoots and plant each one flush with the soil surface. In a few weeks, you will see luxurious plants spring out of the ground and grow up to 5 feet high and 4 feet wide. Allow plenty of space. Pick greens and blossoms from spring to frost. Nothing bothers comfrey. The roots grow to forty feet. I often cut the plants down to force new, tender growth.

The leaves may be mixed in salads or put on sandwiches. Eaten like spinach, the leaves and blossoms are at their very best! Steam until wilted, yet bright green in color. Add a little olive oil and apple cider vinegar, and you've got a highly nutritious meal.

The FDA says comfrey is dangerous. If that's true, my family and I should all be dead! We've eaten comfrey several times a week for years and love it.

Plant comfrey once, and you will have "free" food forever—food that is outside the reach of the bureaucrats! It can also be grown in pots on the patio or inside and is easy to divide and repot over and over. Pulverized comfrey root and aloe heals peptic and intestinal ulcers! Maybe that is why the pharmaceutical companies had the fed's ban it?

**What Is A Precursor?**

A precursor is a molecular substance that precedes the formation of something else. A racemized™ precursor is the accelerated version of the same. All racemized™ precursor products produce excellent results that dwarf common supplements. Racemized™ products are a wonderful way to get MORE bang for your dollar. Ten times the "effect" for the same dollar is a pretty good trade. Call and ask for guidance in choice of protocol and products that will help your "get a better life."

**Pesticide Free?**

I recently saw a *huge* canola oil display in a store. The sign said, "Pesticide Free." What they didn't mention was that canola oil is a long term "systemic" **poison!** The bugs won't eat it anyway. "Pesticide Free!" Right!

# 27

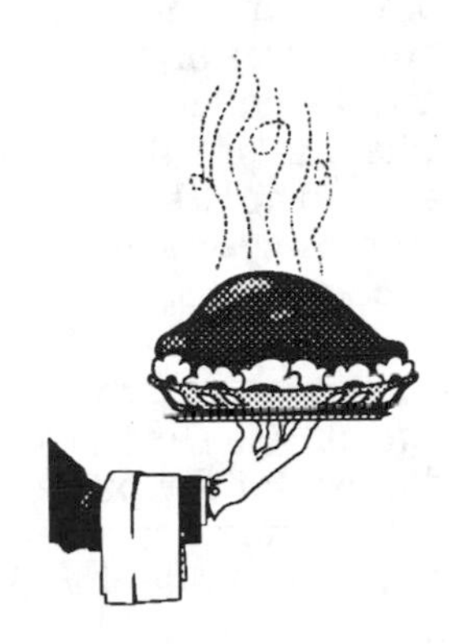

## Liver & Onions

*"As goes the liver, so goes the body!"*
Anon.

The liver is **THE** most abused organ of the body. It is the body's *primary* waste removal organ. A healthy liver is essential to good health and central to the aging reversal process.

The liver is a phenomenal chemical factory that is responsible for *thousands* of biochemical reactions. It is the second largest organ in the body and the ONLY organ that will *regenerate* itself on its own volition—even when only 25% remains in tact. The liver's regenerative ability is an indication of its importance. The liver's functional cells are called **hepatocytes,** (*hepat*-liver, *cyte*-cell) and are classified as *parenchyma* cells.

The liver metabolizes food, drugs, pesticides, wastes and alcohol that arrive via its **dual** blood supply. These substances impose heavy physiologic stress on the liver and, in turn, on all the other organs and glands of the body.

When the liver becomes overly toxic, the hepatocytes die. The spaces left behind are filled by "scar" tissue comprised of *stroma* cells that normally cover the "outside" of the liver, plus solidified bile that takes the shape of the biliary ducts and form "nails." This occurs in cirrhosis of the liver, a condition of EXCESS that often manifests as a nutritional deficiency disease, when in fact it is not. Cirrhosis causes the liver to "yellow" and "harden."

The liver is **heavily** vascularized with blood vessels. It receives a DOUBLE supply of blood. *Oxygenated* blood from the heart is supplied via the hepatic artery and nutrient laden *deoxygenated* blood comes from the intestines via the hepatic portal vein. If waste accumulates on the walls of the portal vein, blood pressure rises and it's called *portal hypertension.*

The Kupffer's cells that line the blood vessels of the liver are of *immense* importance to health and vitality. Kupffer's cells are both **hepatocytes** and **phagocytes** (*phag*-to eat, *cyte*-cell.) Phagocytes remove microbes, foreign matter, and worn out red and white blood cells from circulation.

The liver filters toxic waste from the blood and normally disposes of it through the bile via the intestines and bowel. Bile also acts to emulsify dietary fat for proper assimilation. Fats provide NEEDED cholesterol necessary for the forming of all of the corticosteroid hormones made by the adrenal glands (cortisone is a steroid).

In a sick or aged body, liver function becomes so compromised that the body instead builds fat and cellulite, both of which represent acid waste build-up.

The liver consumes large amounts of energy in the performance of its job. If the body is under stress—mental stress (negative thinking; worrying, anger, fear, etc.) or physical stress from drugs and toxic food and water—fatigue and dis-ease eventually follow.

**Acidification of the blood, lymph, joints and soft tissues of the body ALWAYS involves a compromised liver!**

Hepatitis (*hepat*-liver; *itis*-inflamation of) is a liver condition. So is mononucleosis, Epstein-Barr, lyme disease, malaria, Nile fever and Chronic Fatigue Syndrome. EXCESS waste overload in the system and hormonal issues go hand in hand. Practitioners blame nature's garbage crew—the viruses—for the damage inflicted on the liver, but they are wrong.

Thanks to Dr. Guenther Enderlein, we know the exact sequence of microbial metamorphosis that occurs along the trail of degenerative dis-ease. We also know what to do about it as described in *Hidden Killers* (out of print).

Officially, hepatitis manifests as type A, B, C, D, or E. All are currently prevalent in the USA and are **not** difficult to reverse if the person is willing to cooperate.

Rene's tea is being used intravenously in mainland China for viral blood conditions with great success and for distemper in dogs and cats by a few US veterinarians. PAC's and Yucca Herbal Blend™ are very helpful as is Kombucha tea. Deacidification, hormone precursors, exercise, good water and rest all play an important part in healing.

## Choleric Personalities

As people age, their personalities change. One personality type—the choleric—reflects the condition of a person's liver. The *choleric* has a *bitter* personality that is vile and difficult. The word *choleric* comes from *chole* which means bile in Greek. *Chole* refers to the liver's digestive juice and waste product, bile. A "bilious" person has a foul personality. Alcoholics and some older folks are notorious for being *bilious*. (The Greeks believed there were four basic personality types: choleric, melancholy, sanguine and phlegmatic.)

Much of Western medicine's disastrous history was the result of the theories of the Greek physician and medical writer Claudius Galen (circa A.D. 130-200). He was the personal physician to the Roman Emperor, Marcus Aurelius.

Galen believed in the four basic personality types. He called them "humors." A humor is a body fluid that was believed to influence personality. Galen's theories were, for the most part, in total error. His personality types, however, are still in vogue, but under new "personality" names like type-A, type-B, etc. ***Humoral*** *immunity refers to circulating antibodies and antigens in the blood and lymphatic fluids.*

## Hydrogen Chloride • Bile & Aging

Aging of the vital organs and leaky gut syndrome limit our ability to process food, FLOODING the body with a never ending flow of toxic/acid waste. Insufficient production of hydrogen chloride by the stomach cells LIMITS protein digestion and allows parasites and their eggs to PASS into the gut for absorption into the blood stream. Indigestion and acid reflux is often blamed on too much stomach acid, but exactly the **opposite** is the case. Indigestion are terrain issues linked to leaky gut syndrome, poor liver function and sluggish bowels. Colon therapy relieves "hiatal" hernia pain by relieving abdominal "pressure" on the diaphragm—a **very common** complaint closely linked to **"acid reflux."** Sadly, the public buys into the relentless diatribe, ignorant of better options available.

Stomach acid has a pH as low as .8. It is so acidic that a drop of it on the skin will eat a hole in it. Healthy mucous membranes protect the stomach's walls from this powerful acid. **When the issues discussed thus far are addressed, the membranes return to health.**

Peptic ulcers occur on the stomach's walls. Duodenal ulcers occur on the walls of the small intestine. Aging, stress, and H. pylori (a bacteria) all underwrite peptic ulcers. Vitamin B-12 assimilation is also a "stomach" issue, but here the issue is insufficient secretion of intrinsic factor from the stomach wall. Sublingual B-12 tablets don't work, either, and women run out of this vital substance 20-30 years ahead of men. B-12 is not specific for anything, yet it affects virtually everything. Cobo-12™ creme easily enters skin blood capillaries and is wonderfully useful for dealing with anemia issues in women.

The liver strongly affects digestion. A sick liver does NOT discharge enough bile for digestion of a heavy or greasy meal. A healthy liver produces about **1 quart** of bile a day. Bile is a yellowish-brown or sometimes olive-green juice with very alkaline pH. Bile contains mineral ions, **chole**ster**ol** and bilirubin from worn-out red blood corpuscles. Bilirubin gives bile its yellow, brown, and green color. If we dissect the word **"chole**ster**ol,"** we get *chole*-bile. *ster*-a fat and *ol*-alcohol.

Gall stones indicate digestive problems. They are very common and can be serious and are 10 TIMES more prevalent in **women** than in men! Gallstones are LIVER stones that have migrated out of the liver, hardened and settled in the gallbladder and range in size from lentils to golf balls. A little Yucca Blend™ with meals eases gallbladder complaints. The Young Again™ Tissue and Liver Protocol™ **solves** the problem.

Partially digested food (called chyme) exits the stomach and enters the first of three sections of the small intestine which is called the *duodenum* where it is mixed with secretions from the pancreas and bile from the liver. These secretions are VERY **alkaline** and are designed to raise the pH of the chyme so carbohydrate bonds can be broken and the sugars digested.

**Note: drinking fluids with meals dilutes stomach acids and digestive enzymes creating the perfect environment for parasites and accelerated aging.**

## Micelles

Bile (and Yucca Blend™) work like dish soap. They break-up and emulsify large fat globules into pin head droplets called *micelles.* Micelles have more surface area, making it easier for the body to process and absorb fats.

The gallbladder stores bile secreted from the liver and digestion triggers the release of bile into the small intestines. **Bile is to digestion as detergent is to greasy dishwater.**

Without enough bile, dietary fats cannot be digested. Partial digestion robs the body of energy because up to 40% of our energy comes from the oxidation of fat. The formation of micelles is central to the absorption of the fat soluble vitamins A,D,E and K. Poor fat metabolism results in serious health problems and low energy as evidenced by "fat free" diets.

Bile contains "heme" iron which has the cobalt atom at

its core, hence, the use of Cobo-12™ creme for anemia problems. Loss of heme iron means low hemoglobin, low metabolic rate and loss of energy and vitality particularly in women. anemia and low energy issues are remedied with racemized™ algae and liver, and Cobo-12 creme.

**Heme** iron should be reabsorbed in the gut. Heme is not the same as dietary iron. If there is a shortage of heme iron in the body, there will be a corresponding shortfall in mitochondrial oxidation of glucose (conversion of glucose into ATP, our energy molecule) and diminished oxygen blood levels that fuel the mitochondria as well as the hepatocytes. Elevated blood sugar levels (diabetes) is closely akin to low heme iron levels, hormone imbalances and leaky gut syndrome.

Iron supplements are disastrous to the body. Iron is an oxidizer and participates in the formation of free radicals. Pregnant women should NOT take them!

If the liver is toxic and cannot remove bilirubin from the blood, waste backs-up into the entire body. Jaundice is the result of excess bile and bilirubin in the blood and produces a yellow coloration in the whites of the eyes. People with hepatitis, cirrhosis, and mononucleosis often reflect a jaundiced appearance. Jaundice is a SIGN of serious liver malfunction.

**Children often suffer from liver malfunctions. Acne, boils, jaundice, constipation, appendicitis, psoriasis and learning difficulties are symptomatic of liver problems and systemic toxicity, poor diet and leaky gut syndrome.**

Lecithin is the fat emulsifier in bile that keeps cholesterol in solution. As the body ages and pH shifts, cholesterol, salts, drugs and minerals in the bile settle-out and cause gallstones to grow in size. Gallstones **originate** in the liver and **grow** to giant proportions in the gallbladder.

If gallstones BLOCK the bile duct connecting the gallbladder and the small intestine, gangrene will set in a matter of hours. Gangrenous tissue is dead tissue; necrotic tissue. A gangrenous gallbladder must be removed or the person will die from toxic shock poisoning (toxemia). **Loss of the gallbladder usually results in diabetes within 20 years unless action is take to prevent it.**

Modern medicine has made quick work of gallbladder removal. However, people need to understand the CAUSES behind gallstone formation and NOT rely on "magic bullet" technology and invasive surgery to save them from death's pall. Gallstones account for some **8,000** deaths and over one BILLION dollars in medical costs in the USA every year.

**Gallstones are a confirmation that the aging process is accelerating—no matter what your calendar age!**

Loss of the gallbladder equates to accelerated aging and

life at the subsistence level UNLESS proper action is taken to assist the body. We can live without a gallbladder, appendix, spleen, tonsils, testicles, ovaries, etc., but health and vitality are sacrificed. Remedial action to offset their loss is critical and can restore a person's quality of life and add many good years.

Try to avoid losing your gallbladder. Once removed, the liver drips bile directly into the intestine instead of in mass at meal time, creating multiple health issues. Insufficient and untimely bile secretion means poor absorption of essential fatty acids, incomplete digestion and marginal health. Chewing one's food is of crucial importance in proper digestion.

## Liver Hygiene

People with cancer should temporarily abstain from eating meat, cheese and fish. These are **heavy, high stress** proteins that drain the system unless heavy digestive supplementation is used. It is far better to rely on easy to process, highly nutritious SUPER FOODS. Since there is only so much energy to go around, the more energy directed to healing rather than processing of food the better and quicker healing occurs.

Dr. Max Gerson used fresh, organic calf liver "juice" to treat cancer patients. It is LOADED with biologically active nutrients and enzymes, but horrible to ingest. In the USA, fresh liver is NOT an option due to the sick condition of the animals. The same goes for dessicated liver. A safer alternative is **predigested** racemized™ organic liver capsules. They allow everyone—and especially vegetarians and vegans—to add some balance to their lives (see page 344).

Fresh, organic vegetable juices (beet and carrot) are VERY therapeutic to the liver. "Raw" milk products like yogurt, buttermilk, and kefir are healing. Kombucha tea and fresh lemon juice are very helpful dietary additions.

## Anatomical Location Of The Liver

The liver is located directly under the anterior right rib cage (page 46). It is above the ascending colon, below the right lung, next to the stomach and opposite the spleen which is under the left anterior rib cage.

Intestinal parasites often reach the liver via the portal vein and by migration up the primary bile duct. It is COMMON to find colon bacilli (E. coli bacteria) in an inflamed liver—a condition that goes with cirrhosis. parasites, constipation and bowel problems. Similar infections occur in women's vaginal canal, but here HORMONAL issues are involved.

### Distended Belly

A distended abdomen is a classic SIGN of a person with a compromised liver and a body under siege. An enlarged belly is partly body fat and **mostly** an engorged and distended colon—a tell-tale SIGN of trouble in the making. This condition goes hand in hand with colitis, irritable bowel and leaky gut syndromes, diverticulitis, prostate, gout, arthritis and heart problems. A congested bowel is a breeding ground for dis-ease and a fast ticket to the grave, and ALWAYS indicates liver trouble. Cellulite on women's hips and thighs is another indication of "abnormal" acidification of the body and liver stress. Bowel problems, heart problems, kidney problems, skin problems etc. are all spelled "liver!" **Hopefully, the reader now understands why chewing your food, proper water intake throughout the day, exercise and good food are so crucial to the aging reversal process.**

### Liver Breath

Certain foods—like raw onion—cause some people to get *liver breath*. Raw onion is a potent detoxifier that produces a "metallic" odor in the breath of some people.

I once overheard my biochemistry teacher's assistant discussing her health problems with another. When she came over to help me, I got a whiff of her breath and I recognized the odor instantly. The lady had a stressed liver.

People with stressed livers get hepatitis, mononucleosis and chronic fatigue syndrome. They are the ones who suffer with psoriasis, heavy dandruff, ringworm, impetigo, athlete's foot, dry skin, weak nails, cancer, periodontal gum dis-ease, constipation, diverticulitis, colitis, Crohn's and celiac dis-ease, irritable bowel and leaky gut syndromes, parasite infestations, Alzheimers, and more.

**Fully 90% of the population have stressed livers. This is why your author has stressed the need to restore liver function following Young Again™ protocols.**

*There are different paths a person can take to achieve super health, and I support all of them. But, if your health has slipped or you are aging or dealing with dis-ease and you have been on the "health food" path—then you need to face the fact that the rules change after age 40.* ***I woke up at 45 and found myself in trouble. But instead of continuing on the same dead-end path so popular in the health movement, I cut a NEW path and at 58 years young I got ALL of my life back.***

**Mineral Baths & The Liver**

Throughout history, mineral springs, hot pools, and mud holes have attracted health-minded people. As a child, I remember going with my family out to Desert Hot Springs, California where we would see people soaking in mineral water pools and taking mud baths to improve their health.

*I can attest to the detoxifying effects of mud and mineral waters. Most people are invigorated by them, but they exhaust me! People with weak livers must be careful when using hot pools because they cause the body to release too much acid waste into circulation. And , if you are not prepared for it, you will become exhausted. Loss of mineral electrolytes also occurs here and we will discuss them in the next chapter. Drink large quantities of water with plenty of racemized™ sea minerals when detoxing the tissues through the skin.*

A FIR™ sauna is a wonderful way to experience the benefits of a mineral hot spring right in your own home. This marvelous device dissolves and flushes acid wastes from the soft tissues and restores the liver. The device does NOT work on the basis of hot lights, steam or heat (see Source Page 384).

A healthy liver leads the way to becoming *Young Again!*

**PREVIEW:** *Our next chapter deals with energy flow, limitless vitality, and the body's toll road system.*

**Racemized™ SUPER FOODS**

Here is the list of racemized™ SUPERFOODS used in the Young Again Protocol™. Use them to nourish your body and restore your "terrain." Always purchase good, clean food from health stores; avoid super markets. Organic eggs, free range beef and chicken are good examples.

H/E™ Powder
Taoist Rice Polish™
Taoist 5 Elements™ &
Taoist High Performance
Racemized™ Algae
Racemized™ Liver
VitaLight™ Tablets
Harmonic™ Pollen
Biogenic™ Skin & Body Toner
Biogenic™ hGH
Racemized™ Ginger

Most racemized™ super foods are taken as a meal, ideally with fresh vegetable juice (beet and carrot). DiSorb Aid™, Yucca Blend™, and R/HCI™ should accompany juices for maximum effect (see page 294).

## Aluminum Poisoning

Aluminum is a **heavy** metal that is extremely toxic to the body. It—along with mercury, cadmium and lead—accumulate in brain tissues, short circuiting neuron function and eventually becoming a major contributor, if not the actual cause, of conditions like "Alzheimers."

Aluminum contains fluoride as does tooth paste and much of the municipal water supplies in the USA. Aluminum ions in the body are bad enough, but in the presence of the halogen gas "fluorine," (the gas disassociates from sodium once in the body; sodium fluoride is the name of the molecule) and becomes even more toxic and biologically active.

Aluminum cookware is another source of aluminum ions as evidenced by the "pitting" seen on the cooking surface of such cookware. Non-stick resins coatings are applied over aluminum and present a whole different set of problems for people using this cookware. When the coating deteriorates, aluminum becomes another toxic issue.

One of the **least** suspected and **MAJOR** sources of aluminum ions is common baking powder and dill pickles. Look at any can of baking powder and you will see alum on the ingredient list. AVOID all commercially prepared baked goods that use baking powder as the leavening agent. Non aluminum baking powder is available from health food stores.

Alum is an "approved" food additive and is on the FDA's "gras" list (generally recognized as safe). Obviously, government watch dog agencies don't have the public's best interest in mind or they would not approve alum and tens of thousands of other additives and colorings for dietary consumption.

In the body, aluminum reacts with acid wastes and attacks the *nervous system* and accelerates the onset of degenerative conditions like MS, neuropathy, cerebral palsy, fibromyalgia, lupus and, of course, Alzheimers.

Colloidal mineral products are loaded with heavy metals and are best avoided. It is the molecular "form" that the elemental metals are in that is the issue.

The human body needs ALL of the elements in the periodic table for good health. The **deciding factors** are **FORM** and **SOURCE**. Elemental metal ions should derive from home grown, organic food or from racemized™ sea minerals, both of which have gone through the **carbon cycle** as discussed in Chapter 28.

SOC™ capsules and racemized™ algae act as chelating agents to carry heavy metals across the blood brain barrier, out of the body's tissues and down the toilet. Fresh beet and carrot juices are heavy in the "pigments" and are also very good.

## Why "Racemization™"

*"Racemized™ formulas are combinations of circular, overlapping energy fields unified to achieve maximum viability and biological activity."*

**Racemixed™ products work** because they are *extremely* biologically active, and quickly produce maximum benefits for the body's "terrain."

The word *viability* best describes the effect ***racemization***™ has on FOOD nutrient molecules. *Viability* refers to biological *usefulness* and *activity* rather than potency. Racemization™ greatly **enhances** nutrient energy profiles by increasing the energy "footprint."

Racemized™ products carry a dual rating: "biological activity" and "energy footprint." These indicate ***potential*** available energy and ***expected*** biological response. They are NOT a measure of carbohydrates, fats, proteins or calories, but they are a measure of **life force** activity in living systems.

The racemization™ scale is 0-10. All right-spin substances receive a ***static*** reference score of "0" keyed to their energy profiles. The racemization™ process then raises the reference score by a factor of ten times (10x). This 4 step *proprietary* process ***unifies, boosts, stabilizes*** and ***locks*** energy frequency(s) so individual and composite fields cannot revert to a lesser energy state or deteriorate during shelf life.

*Racemization*™ does **not** involve the use of magnetics, homeopathy, or other known processes heretofore used in the health arena and, therefore, has no historical analog. ***Unification*** of overlapping nutrient energy fields into a unified composite field increases the ***rate*** of spin and ***depth*** of the ***composite*** energy field—thus, enhancing biological activity in the body.

All Young again™ products carry a 10/10 reference score and are far more ***viable*** in the body than the same formulation in a non racemized™ state. They offer **incredible** value and results to anyone using them.

Racemized™ products have NO equal in the marketplace and are ONLY available to the end user.

# 28

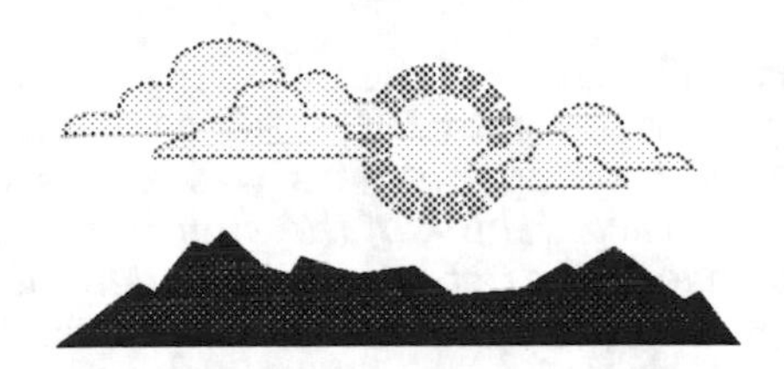

## Soil To Sea

*"Man does not die; he kills himself."*
Seneca

People love the seaside! The "ionized" air makes them feel good. It buzzes with electricity. The "ionized" water invigorates their bodies. Barefoot, the sand siphons away the toxic energy from the reflex points in the feet. *Charged* ionic minerals give the sea's air, water and sand its healing qualities.

The sea is nature's storage battery of right-spin ENERGY! It is a phenomenon of tremendous importance. Understanding the source of the sea's energy is central to the aging reversal process and health.

Mineral ions in solution are called ***electrolytes***. Ions are atoms that have gained or lost electrons. Ionic compounds are two or more ions that have bonded together. Ionic compounds are crystals—like table salt (sodium+chloride). Salts are STABLE and maintain their crystal form UNTIL they are *hydrolyzed* (dissolved) in water.

When salts dissolve in water or body fluids, the molecules disassociate (split) into and become *unstable* mineral ions, chemically speaking. If the ions come from a non living source—like table salt or calcium carbonate—they **de**stabilize the system and create conditions of **excess** in the body. In contrast, racemized™ sea mineral ions balance the system.

SOME ions are capable of conducting electricity in solution; others cannot—an important point that can save a life if heat stroke, heat exhaustion and heart attack are involved.

The blood and lymph contain electrolytes. Our nerve

fibers and cells are lined with them. Electrolytes relay electrical energy and are responsible for transferring electrical signals from one end of the body to the other via the nerve fibers and mineral ions. No mineral ions, no nerve response.

### Toll Road

It is helpful to think of the nervous system as a toll road where a price must be paid BEFORE each energy signal is allowed to cross a synapse on its way to its destination—perhaps a finger or leg. *(Think of the synapses as "toll booths" along the nerve axon. The Schawnn cells keep the gate open by producing hormones that polish the receptor sites at the synapses, while mineral ions supply the energy to BOOST the signal, "jump" the gap and continue. See diagram page 248).* The body conducts its daily affairs using electrical currency. A unit of electrical *currency* is called a mineral *ion*. As nerve impulses cross the synapses, mineral ions give up their electrons which supply the energy for the process.

The body needs a **constant** supply of ions. Minerals that are **not** in ionic form do not suffice—INCLUDING colloidal minerals. A body with enough ions enjoys health and vitality, otherwise, sickness and lethargy rule.

Disrupted electrical signals produce spastic motions that make it difficult for a person to move and function. Cerebral palsy and multiple sclerosis (MS) are classic examples of sporadic, *uncontrolled* electrical impulses. Shingles and peripheral neuropathy are closely related, as is loss of Schwann cells at the synapses and deterioration of the myelin sheath. SOC™ capsules and Biogenic™ Skin & Body Toner are helpful in restoration of the nerve sheath. Racemized™ hormone precursors provide the hormonal activity needed to reestablish the Schwann cells.

### Athletes

Electrolytes are VERY important to athletes who associate performance, strength and vitality with electrolytes. They know their bodies will NOT perform without them and will excel when they are in full supply. Sport drinks are poor substitutes.

Athletes need large quantities of electrolytes because their bodies are under heavy *physical* stress. Regular people also use electrolytes, but unlike athletes—who burn-out in a few short years—people take years to bankrupt their ionic mineral account. They do it in *slow motion*—a day at a time!

All mineral ions are NOT equal. Those that have gone through the carbon cycle and are in **racemized**™ form are FAR more active in the body. When racemized,™ their activity level is unequaled. These mineral ions plus BEV™ water are the basis for the creation of Medical Grade Ionized Water™.

*Synchronized*, ancient sea bed deposits dug out of the ground and hydrolyzed into a "toddy" containing mineral ions in *colloidal* form are **not** a good idea. Their signature and electrical footprint is **inferior** to racemized™ sea mineral ions AND they are LOADED with **heavy** metals like lead, cadmium and mercury. Racemized™ sea water ions keep blood electrolyte levels at optimum level and unequaled in reducing "Rouleau" in the blood.

Table salt is composed of sodium and chlorine. Sodium ions are *electrolytes*, and assist the body in the flow of electrical impulses. We **need** sodium in VERY **small** amounts. Too much sodium upsets the sodium to potassium ratio in the body and sets the stage for cancer.

**When the body is given NO other option, it will use sodium ions in lieu of more desirable trace mineral ions.**

### Sports Drinks • BEV™ • Energy

Many athletes use commercial sports drinks to meet their ionic mineral needs. Sports drinks are bad news! Their energy footprint is unfriendly to the body and their signature is incomplete. Athletes who depend on them experience rapid aging of the vital organs and connective tissues. Smart athletes make their own sports drink for pennies using concentrated **racemized**™ sea water ions.

My children **voluntarily** lugged their ionized BEV™ water to school each day in their special BEV™ bottles. They loved it and did better in the classroom and in sports. They called it *"power water!"* All their buddies bummed water from them because wanted to benefit from it, too!

BEV™ water has a "conception point" ORP. Its high energy ***footprint*** comes from the **restructuring** of the water molecules and erasing of the memory of the toxic contaminants that are in native water. The BEV™ process enhances hydrogen and molecular bond angles and changes the *vibratory* frequency of the water—making it biologically friendly. BEV™ water resonates (vibrates) at a "healthy" frequency. Add racemized™ sea minerals for unequaled drinking water.

Transference of energy can be demonstrated in other ways. For instance, walking barefoot in sand or grass, or hugging a tree bare-footed. These protocols alter abnormal body frequencies and cause the body to ***vibrate*** with Mother Earth. Five minutes a day spent walking in this manner releases MASSIVE amounts of toxic energy and stress from the body. I have seen people with severe back pain, unable to stand up straight, walk in beach sand for 15 minutes, straighten up and return to normal! A vibration chain can be used in a similar fashion. Chiropractic acknowledges that vertebral orientation is directly related to stress in the vital organs—and walking in sand draws-out toxic energy from the body causing pain and health problems to vanish.

**Electrical "current" is the movement of energy *along a metal wire.* In body fluids like blood and lymph the current is carried by activated mineral ions.**

### $10,000 For A Bag Of Salt

Ions in solution allow electricity to flow. No electrical flow means no ions are present. Electricity flowing through a liquid creates electrolysis (*electro*-electricity, *lysis-dissolution of*). Blood electrolyte levels are **CRITICAL** to good health.

Dr. Carry Reams was once paid $10,000 for solving a electroplating problem in a chroming shop that involved ions and electrolysis. No one—including the manufacturer of the equipment—could make the electricity flow in the processing tank. Reams came along and poured a few pounds of common table salt into the solution; and, bingo, the electricity flowed through the solution of water and salt and the plating process proceeded. Sodium chloride solved the electrolysis problem because sodium is an *electrolyte*.

The human body requires a **constant** supply of balanced, electrolytic mineral ions for optimum health. Substitution of table salt as s source of sodium ions "masks" the immediate problem leaving the cause untouched. Sodium creates conditions of EXCESS and accelerates the aging process. Sodium in excess is poison!

### Sugar

Sucrose (table sugar) is a crystal, but sucrose will NOT conduct electrical current when dissolved in water. It is a non-electrolyte because it contains no mineral ions. Sugar is a "concentrated" left-spin energy substance that lowers the body's vibratory frequency and dims the aura.

Sucrose *sabotages* the flow of energy in the body. It does this by **bonding** with our mineral ions. When ions bond with sugar, their energy is **neutralized.** When the supply of ions in the body is low, a health crisis occurs and aging accelerates.

Most people live out their lives on the edge of starvation—their diet supplying them with just enough mineral ions to exist between subsistence and dis-ease.

**If you choose to eat food laced with table sugar, you will lose your vitality and grow old.**

*Earlier, we discussed Kombucha tea. It is important that the reader understand that the Kombucha organism has the ability to convert a left-spin substance—white sugar—into a right-spin energy field that is loaded with enzymes, hormones and healthful organic acids. It does this by way of biological alchemy. Kombucha is a live food product whose energy field has been reversed. The sugar is gone, but the energy remains.*

The experts tell us sugar is sugar. *They* tell us there is NO difference between sucrose, maltose, dextrose and lactose except in their molecular structures. *They* tell us that mannitol and sorbitol are harmless—and **aspartame**, too! *They* tell us that the body does not care because it all becomes glucose. *They* tell us the sugar *blues* that haunt millions of people are "imagined." The experts are wrong. They should know better.

**The body differentiates between sugars as it does with oils. It differentiates based on the energy SPIN.**

Some sugars accelerate aging by neutralizing the body's supply of mineral ions. White and artificial sugars destroy food energy through "ionization" or scrambling of food molecules. Translated, the food molecules are altered through the gain or loss of electrons and mineral ions. Purified sugars (table sugar, fructose, corn syrup) and artificial sugars—like **aspartame** (better known by the red, white, and blue "swirl") and food additives and coloring agents have ***radiomimetic*** qualities that mimic the effects of nuclear radiation on cellular DNA. These poisons "zap" body energy and are no different than eating microwaved food. They bring on graying of the hair, wrinkles and diminished glandular activity and hormone imbalances by "locking up" body receptor sites. The effect produced is characteristic of "zeno" molecules. The Young Again Protocol™ reverses this "aging" process.

Foods processed with large amounts of sugar and salt do not spoil because their enzymes have been scrambled. Bugs seldom eat sugar and salt laden food. They are not stupid.

**If you MUST make a choice between table sugar and artificial sweetners, choose white sugar! VitaLight™ tablets help buffer the effects of sugar by loading your system with mineral ions—but try not to make a habit of it!**

## Major & Minor Minerals

The body needs the **major** minerals and the minor (trace) minerals to function. Science has known about the major minerals like calcium, iron, sulphur, and phosphorous for a very long time. The TRACE minerals like manganese, boron, iodine, molybdenum, and sixty or so others have only recently been recognized to be of any importance in human nutrition. *(Science is reluctant to acknowledge man's mineral dependence, yet it* ***rubber stamps*** *the use of soy and canola, aspartame and genetically altered foods.)*

We KNOW minerals are crucial to good nutrition and aging. What is NOT widely known is that the "form" the mineral is in is as important as the mineral itself. Form determines the mineral's effect on health.

Elemental mineral compounds are of little use to the body. Calcium carbonate is an elemental compound used to supplement ***misdiagnosed*** so called calcium deficiencies (as in osteoporosis) It is composed of calcium and carbon. The *-**ate*** tells us that it is in a *salt* form—a *crystal*.

**Elemental mineral compounds do NOT belong in the body. They foul our nest and create secondary health problems.**

Taking calcium carbonate to get more calcium is an absurdity. It is the equivalent of a postpartum woman drinking milk so she can produce more breast milk for her baby.

**Chelated minerals** cause problems in the body. They are elemental mineral compounds bonded to a "carrier" amino acid that transports the minerals through the GI tract and into the blood. **This is NOT desirable!** Tricking or forcing the body to accept that which it otherwise would not is ludicrous. Elemental mineral compounds have NOT gone through the carbon chain. They stress the system and create **excesses** by"trading" one problem for several new ones. Do NOT use them.

The chelation process *tricks* the body into admitting substances into the blood that otherwise could NOT gain admittance under normal body protocol. These elemental substances are the equivalent of a *bogus* $20⁰⁰ bill!

**Biologically active mineral ions come from healthy plant juices, good "unprocessed" food, healthy animal tissues, racemized™ sea minerals and SUPER foods like racemized™ algae, Biogenic predigested organic liver and Harmonic™ pollen.**

**Enzymes • Minerals • Nitrogen**

*Enzymes are mineral-dependent.* They are protein molecules that function as **on-the-job** engineers within the body. Enzymes create *hot spots* within the body that throw the switch so blood and lymph can deliver nutrients to the areas in need.

Nitrogen plays a KEY role in the life process. All proteins and amino acids contain nitrogen. Nitrogen is NOT a mineral ion in the classical sense (it's a gas), but it can function like one.

Nitrogen (atomic symbol "N") is very important to electrical conductivity and energy *transference* in the body. Nitrogen has many molecular forms. In it's *pseudometallic* form, nitrogen conducts electricity like an *electrolyte.*

Life CANNOT exist without nitrogen. The atmosphere is composed of 78% nitrogen. Plants and animals require nitrogen to grow. Unfortunately, the *experts* use nitrogen to FORCE plants to grow on the premise that food is food. They *think* they can bribe Nature into building high vitality food with nitrogen based **salt** fertilizers. Nature responds with left-spin energy food that is high in "funny" proteins.

### Funny Proteins

**"Funny proteins"** are "unavailable" proteins—that is, proteins that confuse the body—soy is a "classic" example. Food protein is measured by its nitrogen content. When you hear a nutritionist or farmer talk about a crop or a food's protein percentage (%), they are actually referring to the nitrogen content. Nitrogen is a gas. Unbuffered, it is an **acid** gas (pH 1-2). When proteins are digested and broken down into their constituent parts, nitrogen is released (think of a compost heap, a pile of fresh grass clippings, or a rotting carcass).

Nitrogen has many different forms. Funny proteins contain nitrogen in the **wrong** form. When funny proteins are turned loose in the body, they create EXCESSES. Massive amounts of calcium are required to buffer the effects of funny protein nitrogens that are released into circulation during the digestion process.

Environmental deterioration, high-powered synthetic salt fertilizers, and poisonous sprays are part of the reason that more and more **funny proteins** are entering the food chain. As **FREAK** protein levels rise, so does degenerative dis-ease.

Look at a bag of dog or cat food. It will list total protein and crude (unavailable) protein. If you subtract one from the other, you can calculate the amount of available protein. There was a time not so many years ago when the amount of unavailable or "bastard" protein was under 1/2%. Today we are seeing unavailable protein levels as high as 2%—and more!

**Each time the level of *funny* protein doubles—say from 1/2% to 1%—the amount of calcium needed to stabilize blood pH increases by 200 times! Think about it!**

I have repeatedly stated that there is no such thing as a deficiency condition or a deficiency dis-ease. Problems and deficiencies are the result of conditions of EXCESS within the system. In the case of osteoporosis, the problem results from an "excess" of funny protein nitrogen in the blood, hormonal imbalances (unopposed estrogen dominance and blocked receptor sites), and build-up of "excess" metabolic acids.

Body tissue is comprised of nitrogen based proteins. Billions of cells die each day; and if they are not promptly removed from the system, they release **nitrogen** into the blood, making it ever more acidic. When you see someone aging at an accelerated rate, understand that their body is **acidifying**. The fastest way to **REVERSE** acidification accomplished with the Young Again Tissue and Liver Protocol™. Fresh beet and carrot juice taken as breakfast each morning, combined with the Young Again Colon Therapy Protocol™ should be practiced by everyone—young or old. Drinking Medical Grade Ionized Water™ is another way to fast-track the process.

As the level of *funny* protein nitrogen rises in the blood, the body goes into survival mode and begins withdrawing minerals from the bones in an effort to **BUFFER** the **acidic** condition of the blood. Medical science labels the resulting process "osteoporosis" and shouts **"deficiency"** of calcium. Not so! The body has innate intelligence and it knows what to do to keep itself alive when it encounters conditions of **excess**.

***HOWEVER,*** *when the neuro and hormonal receptor sites are "locked up" from hormonal and chemical zeno estrogen analogs in food and water, the body becomes confused because it cannot get a "hand shake" from receptors on the receiving end of the signal. Grid lock best describes this condition.*

## Nitrogen & Plants

Nitrogen is the unit of **electrical currency** that opens the plant's toll gates so energy and mineral ions can pass on their way to enzyme created *hot spots* in the plant's tissues.

Chemical agriculture has learned how to manipulate the life process in plants and trick them into taking unwanted minerals and poisons into their tissues. The process is similar to that of chelation of elemental minerals to trick the body into ignoring its own normal protocol.

The need to **chelate** elemental mineral compounds and force crops to grow on them is based on the **assumption** that God and Nature are stupid, plants are stupid, the body is stupid, but the *experts* are smart. Chelation of minerials smacks of the same mentality that says, "*genetically engineered and hydroponically raised food is just as good as naturally grown food.*" These **mutant** processes **moot** the need for *real* soil. The same goes for microwaved food vs. conventionally cooked food, and chemically fertilized crops being just as nutritious as crops raised using biodynamic techniques.

**Nature designed things so that the elements would have to pass through the carbon cycle before gaining legitimate status and a ticket into the human body.**

## The Carbon Cycle

The carbon cycle explains how earth minerals are ionized and assimilated into food molecules and sea water. **CARBON CYCLE = rain + soil + sun + microbe + plant + animal = biologically *enlivened* mineral ions.**

The carbon cycle transforms biologically inactive earth minerals into active, right-spin *energy* fields that people can use to stay or become strong and healthy.

Bacteria in the soil are the bankers for earth minerals. Ions are "made available" when minerals react with weak acids like carbonic acid, which is atmospheric carbon + hydrogen that is **secreted** from plant roots. The bacteria hold and modify mineral ions and live off their electrical energy until the plant withdraws them from its mineral ion account. Enzymes act as the cashiers and oversee the exchange. The mineral ions are the currency (electric money). Plants combine ionic and solar energy to produce proteins, fats, carbohydrates, vitamins and enzymes—all of which contain biologically active mineral ions.

Animals eat plants and deposit their waste on the soil. Plants grow, die and leave their residues on the soil for the bacteria, yeast, and fungi to consume. In time, nutrient ions make their way to the sea where they become a ***solution*** of biologically active *ionic minerals.* Mineral ions give sea water its characteristic salty flavor, just as racemized™ trace mineral ions provide the body with ENERGY—the same energy that provides peak health, youth, vitality, etc. All of Mother Earth's mineral ions are present and in a dynamic, high energy state when sea water is racemized™. Their affect on the body is **confirmation** of their valence condition and energy footprint.

## Vitamins

Vitamins **cannot** function unless mineral ions are present in balanced form. Vitamins are NOT well understood, but we do know that they are mineral dependent. Science has had to *shadow box* with vitamins, learning of their importance through **so called** *deficiency* conditions.

Pellagra is one of these conditions. Pellagra is a ***marker*** "condition" that *supposedly* indicates a deficiency of the B vitamin niacin (B-3). The "condition" responds well to B vitamin therapy, but good food and things like racemized™ algae and liver are better.

The word ***vitamin*** derives from "vital" meaning *necessary* and "amine" which is the chemical name for a nitrogen bearing "—R group" molecule. The word *amino*—as in *amino* acid—is also related to *amine*. Aminos join and form proteins that contain nitrogen. SOC™ supplies racemized™ carbon and sulfur for building the sulfhydryl bonds that link the proteins.

When SOC™ capsules and lotion are used regularly, the body AUTOMATICALLY goes to work dissolving internal and external scar tissue by replacing it with live, functional tissue. The body is 90% connective tissue and the older you become the more SCAR tissue you have which is what is behind that old **STIFF** body. Yoga and Pilates also help.

Amino acids, fats and carbohydrates are organic molecules produced by anabolic activity in living things. Organic molecules contain oxygen, nitrogen, sulfur and carbon. **Carbon** grants the title, "organic!" **Carbon**aceous matter (leaves, grass, wood, etc.) contains carbon. **Carbo**hydrates contain carbon. Life is impossible without carbon. So, a vitamin is a nitrogen containing substance that also contains **carbon** in an amine —R group.

*Earlier, we talked about a family of chemicals called "chlor**amines**." Chemicals used by cities throughout the USA to treat public water supplies produce chloramines. When amines bond to organic substances like bacteria, toxic substances are formed. Here, chlorine has been combined with an organic amine group to kill bacteria in drinking water. Toxic chemicals of all types **penetrate** the skin when bathing, stress the liver and **DEVASTATE** the lining of the gut, hence, the development of leaky gut syndrome in people of ALL ages.*

Your author rejects the use of all but a very few **food based** vitamin supplements because most are synthesized, even if they are labeled "natural." Man-made vitamins STRESS the liver and are toxic to the body and cannot build healthy tissues. Real, live food is as good as it gets!

In biochemistry and nutrition, vitamins are referred to as *cofactors* or *coenzymes*. Vitamins and mineral ions need each other to work. Please engrave the following statement into your consciousness and *never* forget it. **We DO NOT live on vitamins, minerals, and enzymes—but from the *energy* released by the chemical reactions they fuel.**

## The Carbon Connection

In his timeless book, *The Carbon Connection*, my friend, Leonard Ridzon defined carbon as *"The governing element that determines the vitality of food crops [and life on Earth]."*

Carbon is extremely important in the aging process. It

is THE common denominator between high vitality food and healthy soils. Carbon is the barometer of the soil's aura and magnetic field. It is the basis of all life.

Carbon can combine in **millions** of combinations because of its unique molecular form. *Bogus* science uses carbon to create organic poisons like pesticides and herbicides.

Soil that is highly magnetic is usually described as **para**magnetic (i.e., *para*-beyond). Soil that is paramagnetic grows right-spin energy food with a complete energy signature.

Devitalized soil has NO paramagnetism; and the food grown on it will NOT produce healthy human beings, barnyard animals, or plants. Sick soil is LOW in carbon and microbial activity. Crops "force-grown" on sick soil means sick people.

The fastest and best way to convert sick dirt to vibrant soil is through the use of biodynamic principles as described in the book *Biodynamic Farm.* Another approach about this marvelous field of *esoteric* agriculture is *Biodynamics I & II by Alex Podolinsky* (see Source Page).

**Another way to avail yourself of a biodynamic principles and turn polluted soil into a nice garden the first year WITHOUT the use of synthetic chemicals is the product "BioGrow" (see Source Page 384).**

The best we can hope for is to eat home grown food that's packed with life giving nutrients with a right-spin energy footprint. If our food doesn't contain all the minerals we need, we must get them from the next best source available—**racemized**™ liquid sea minerals and VitaLight™ tablets.

Your author obtains his vitamins from fresh veggi juice, and my minerals from good food and SUPER FOOD supplements as outlined in the pages of this book.

Your author wishes to stay YOUNG for a very long time, and mineral ions help make it happen. They are my electrical *currency.* They trigger my biochemical processes, prevent Rouleau in the blood, and make me feel good!

If you tend to the basics, you won't become OLD and you won't die prematurely. Each of us must take responsibility for our lives. Hopefully, this book is your **catalyst to action** so you, also, can become *Young Again!*

**PREVIEW:** *Our next chapter is about the immune system and cancer and how to avoid things like AIDS.*

> The reflex points in the feet are wired to the vital organs; and so are the nerves feeding from the wall of the colon. The Young Again Colon Therapy Protocol™ boosts organ activity.

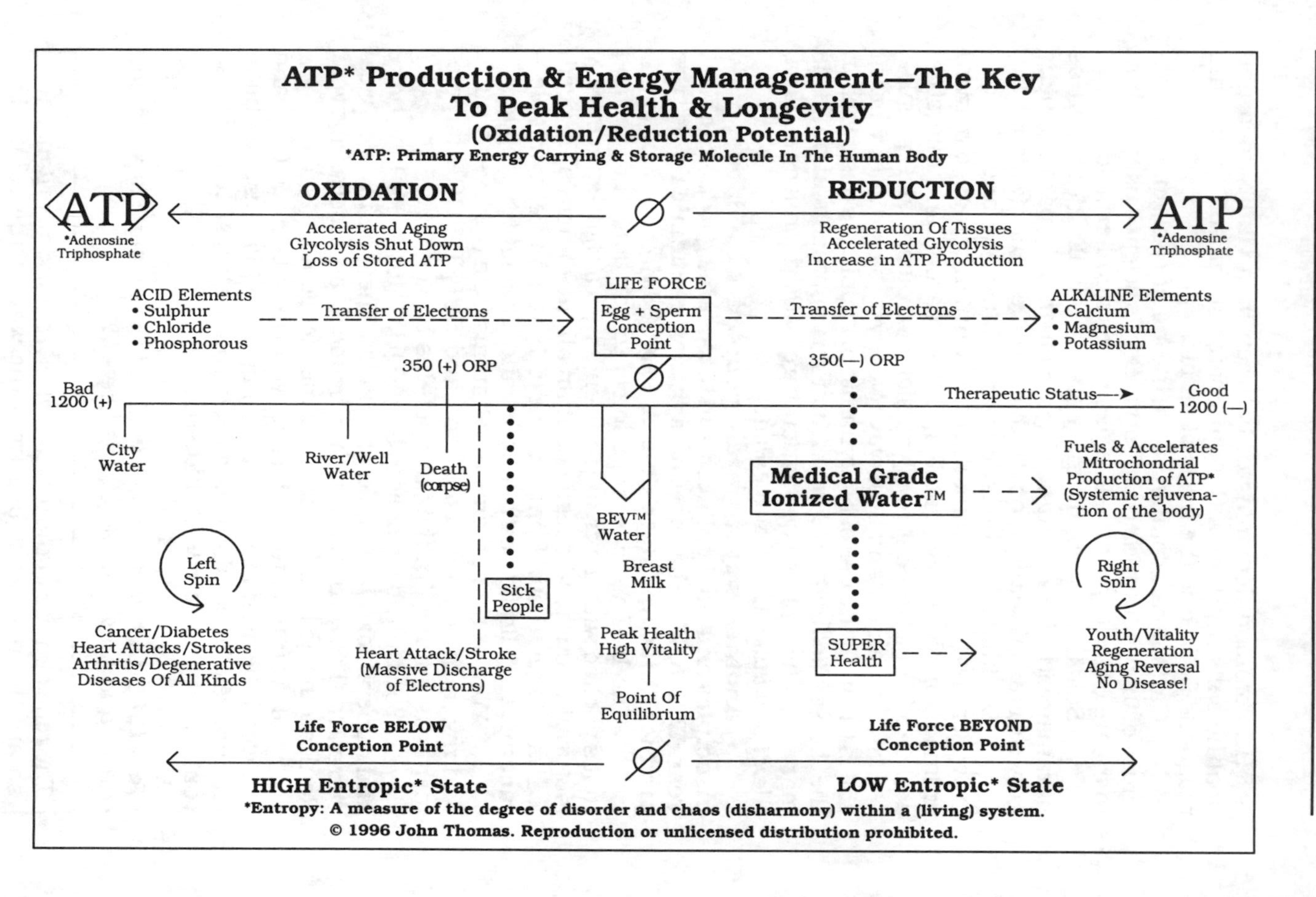

ATP* Production & Energy Management—The Key
To Peak Health & Longevity
(Oxidation/Reduction Potential)
*ATP: Primary Energy Carrying & Storage Molecule In The Human Body
ATP
*Adenosine Triphosphate
OXIDATION
Accelerated Aging
Glycolysis Shut Down
Loss of Stored ATP
REDUCTION
Regeneration Of Tissues
Accelerated Glycolysis
Increase in ATP Production
ATP
*Adenosine Triphosphate
ACID Elements
• Sulphur
• Chloride
• Phosphorous
Transfer of Electrons
LIFE FORCE
Egg + Sperm Conception Point
Transfer of Electrons
ALKALINE Elements
• Calcium
• Magnesium
• Potassium
350 (+) ORP
350(—) ORP
Bad 1200 (+)
Therapeutic Status—
Good 1200 (—)
City Water
River/Well Water
Death (corpse)
BEV™ Water
Medical Grade Ionized Water™
Fuels & Accelerates Mitrochondrial Production of ATP* (Systemic rejuvenation of the body)
Left Spin
Sick People
Breast Milk
Right Spin
Cancer/Diabetes
Heart Attacks/Strokes
Arthritis/Degenerative
Diseases Of All Kinds
Heart Attack/Stroke (Massive Discharge of Electrons)
Peak Health
High Vitality
SUPER Health
Youth/Vitality
Regeneration
Aging Reversal
No Disease!
Point Of Equilibrium
Life Force BELOW Conception Point
Life Force BEYOND Conception Point
HIGH Entropic* State
LOW Entropic* State
*Entropy: A measure of the degree of disorder and chaos (disharmony) within a (living) system.
© 1996 John Thomas. Reproduction or unlicensed distribution prohibited.

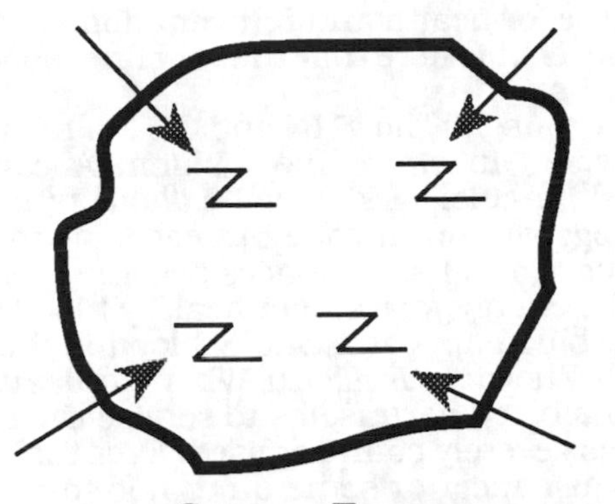

**Cancer Tumors**
**Import & Condense Energy**
Tumors calcify; appear on
X-rays, CAT Scans, & MRI's
can be felt with hand; do not
have an occult phase.

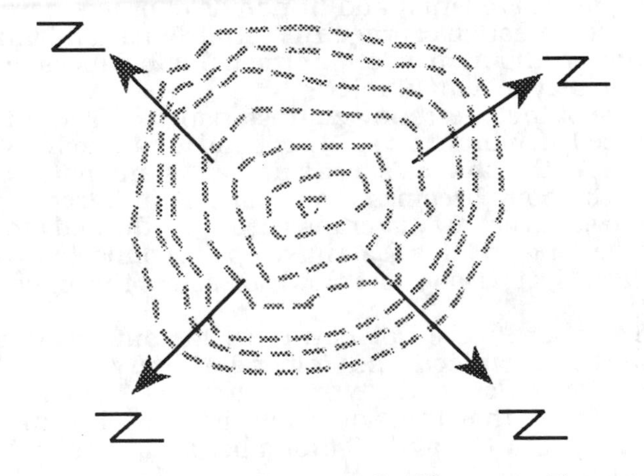

**Cancer Masses Export & Disperse Energy**
Masses don't calcify or appear
on X-rays; CAT Scans, MRI's;
soft to touch; invisible
during occult period.

## Cancer Tumors vs. Cancer Masses
## They are NOT the same!

## The Rouleau Effect

The battle for health and rejuvenation is WON or LOST at the cellular level. It is here that the very fine blood capillaries interface the cells.

Blood corpuscles "flow" IN and OUT of the fine capillaries (arteriola/vena) in single file fashion. A corpuscle is a *denucleated* cell, that is, a blood cell *without* a nucleus. Think of a chicken's egg without a yoke. An egg is a single cell.

As the cells and tissue spaces become overloaded with **acid** wastes, the energy *footprint* of healthy blood shifts to the left and ***sticky*** blood appears. Sticky blood is the EFFECT of what is officially known as *Rouleau.* When Rouleau sets in, free movement of the blood corpuscles to service the cells and the tissues becomes severely compromised. Eventually the condition manifests as cancer or some other not-so-nice dis-ease.

**SLOWDOWN** in the *bilateral movement* of oxygen, nutrients, carbon dioxide and waste **across** the cell membranes is called **aging.** Aging is just another word for self inflicted fouling of our own nest—and the fouler we become, the faster we age.

Stagnation of the **intra**cellular fluids inside the cells causes them to die. Conditions like cancer, arthritis, fibromyalgia, scleroderma and hundreds of others have their roots in a combination of **stagnant** extracellular and intracellular fluids. Without question, hormonal imbalances and excesses also play a MAJOR role.

One of the interesting characteristics of SOC™ is that it softens cell membranes so nutrient and waste exchange can accelerate. As the process speeds up, aches and pains disappear and the body becomes more "limber" and free moving. SOC™ provides the raw materials needed by the body to build **sulfonyl** bearing proteins that make up the connective tissues that replace "scar" tissue as it slowly dissolves throughout the body.

To break up the Rouleau effect in your blood, add a short squirt of **racemized**™ sea minerals to every glass of water you drink—regardless of the type of water it is! The effect is an energy response that translates into good health and high vitality. See pages 136 and 294 for a better understanding of these issues.

If you want to regain your health or hold onto what you have, it's VERY important that you provide your body with a **constant** flow of racemized™ sea mineral ions that effectively provide the same effect as blood thinners, but in a natural, safe way, along with needed mineral ions for good health. Fresh veggi juices and the Young Again Colon Therapy Protocol™ are **extremely** important to terrain management and aging reversal. Rouleau is a **TERRAIN** issue! Don't forget it.

# 29

# Body Fluid Dynamics

*"When science falters, it is because no one is asking the right questions."*
Charles Walters

Blood is central to all body metabolism. It carries oxygen and nutrients to the cells and carbon dioxide and acidic wastes OUT of the cells and OUT of the system by way of the kidneys, bowel, lungs, and skin.

Blood is systemic. It ***interfaces*** ALL body systems and is, therefore, an excellent medium for testing. It is a good barometer of present or pending dis-ease and is one of **two** sources of information derived from body fluids.

The blood has a fraternal twin that performs many similar functions. This "other" system has NO heart to act as a pump. Its fluid color is straw to clear—not red. Unlike blood, no one will buy it from you. If there is a medical emergency, no one will ask you to donate any of this other fluid. This fluid is called LYMPH and it is part of the *lymphatic* system.

Healthy lymph is central to health and vitality. It is impossible to reverse aging without good lymph circulation. We promote lymph circulation by vigorous walking, running, aerobic exercise, swimming, calisthenics, deep breathing and load-bearing work. We do more of these activities when we are young, and we tend to **avoid** them as we grow older.

The lymphatic system is a network of capillaries and vessels similar to the arteries and veins with some notable differences. Lymph capillaries begin as blind alleys, while blood capillaries are continuous. The lymphatic system has nodes where the blood circulatory system has none.

The lymphatic system is primarily a "plasma protein" communication system that is responsible for the movement of 75% of the body's liquid proteins. Its capillaries remove wastes and service the **extra**cellular fluid in the spaces between the cells. Lymph capillary walls are *more* permeable than blood capillaries and they ONLY work in one direction. Once extracellular fluid enters a lymph capillary, it cannot escape until it joins the blood at the subclavian vein near the anterior base of the neck. Blood is filtered by the kidneys and liver.

***It is VERY important to recognize that the lymph "nodes" are really energy storage sites. TOXIC energy fields are stored and held there for safekeeping until the body can manage them. When you feel swollen lymph nodes under the jaw, in the armpits, under and outside the breasts, or in the groin (above and to the outside of the hairy area), you are feeling "condensed" energy. That is why they are swollen and hard. They should be soft and pliable—not swollen! The tonsils are lymph nodes. They swell and become inflamed during illness. Rebounding and use of the lymph rolling helps circulate lymph fluids. So does colon therapy. The very best method calls for the L/CSF™ machine. Nothing equals it!*** *(See Source Page 384.)*

Blood is pumped; lymph fluid is not. Blood corpuscles (red blood cells without a nucleus) are *pumped* into the arteries under pressure from the heart. 10% of the blood that leaves the heart *escapes* as **plasma** through the capillary walls into the **extracellular** spaces BETWEEN the cells. This **extra**cellular fluid is what actually services the cells and tissues.

The lymphatic system performs critical functions that the cardiovascular system cannot. The veins return 90% of blood fluid volume to the heart. The lymph ducts return the other 10% to the blood as lymphatic fluid.

**Insufficient exercise and water intake lead to congested tissues, acidification and dis-ease.**

## Lymphatics & Aging

The lymphatic system is one of the most important systems in the body. BOTH health and dis-ease have their roots in the watery fluid called lymph. If lymphatic circulation is active and body fluid pH is balanced, toxins and wastes will NOT accumulate in the tissues. Otherwise, acid wastes mix with metabolic poisons, tap water minerals, salts and fats FOULING our tissues and shutting down vital organ function.

When the tissues are congested and the body is unable to cleanse itself, oxygen and nutrient flow slows. As wastes accumulate in the **extra**cellular fluids between the cells, body pH shifts and the sodium/potassium ratio is upset.

The body requires a constant supply of organic potassium. If it does not get it, it **STEALS** it from **inside** the cells. As potassium exits the cells, sodium invades and replaces the potassium. This ultimately shuts down mitochondrial production of our ATP energy molecule in the cells.

**Cancer BEGINS in the lymphatic system and metastasizes (spreads) by way of the body's plasma protein highway—the lymphatic system.**

The lymphatic organs of the body are the lymph nodes, thymus gland (between the heart and base of the neck), tonsils (we have three kinds), spleen and red bone marrow. Lymphocytes and macrophages are part of the lymphatic system.

### Fats & The Immune System

The lymphatic system transports dietary fats out of the intestines and INTO the blood. The **lymph**ocytes and **macro**phages in the blood and lymph fluids protect the body from invading microbes and foreign material.

**Lymph**ocytes include the T-cells and B-cells, both of which the HIV virus infects or circumvents. B-cells originate in the bone marrow. Some of them become **plasma** cells which secrete **anti**bodies. Antibodies concentrate and conduct their warfare in the blood and lymph.

A sluggish lymphatic system is an OLD system! Fluid retention in the legs, ankles and feet is due to the accumulation of EXCESS wastes. Where proteins are, water accumulates.

Fungus under the nails is related to poor lymph circulation and acidity. Loss of body hair is also an acidity issue. These SIGNS are **red flags** of dis-ease in the making. They are also related hormonal complications.

### Exercise & Lymphatics

Exercise has tremendous influence on lymph flow because lymph movement depends on body movement and muscle contraction. The mini-trampoline, called a *rebounder*, greatly enhances lymph circulation. Women try to improve lymph drainage in the breast and chest region when they hold their arms high and move them excessively while walking. They would be **better off**, however, allowing their arms to swing as God made them to do. A swinging arm is an ***exaggerated*** lever. **Swinging arms exert more force** on lymph movement than the ridiculous antics prescribed by the *experts.*

Here is an interesting exercise that demonstrates the dynamics of lymph movement and ion energy. First, have the person stand erect and extend their arm straight out to the side of the body level with the shoulder. Next, attempt to gently but forcefully pull down on the arm and note the amount of "resistance" the person generates. Then, have the person run in place while actively moving the arms and lifting the knees high for about 10 seconds. Now, repeat the arm deflection exercise and note the loss of resistance and strength. The loss of strength is related to lymph displacement and use of charged mineral ions (please recall that ions give up their energy in exchange for the passage of electrical signals).

### Lymph • Red Bone Marrow • Fluoride

Red bone marrow is the part of the lymphatic system responsible for red blood cell production. Red bone marrow is located in the flat bones of the body AND in the epiphyses (ends) of the *long* bones. Between the *epiphyses* and diaphysis, which is the shank of the long bones, is where the growth plates are located. The growth plates give us our physical height.

**Fluoride** interferes with the production of red blood cells. It blocks enzyme activity and weakens bone integrity. Toothpaste and drinking water that contain fluoride suppress red blood cell production and promote *pernicious* anemia.

Anemic people have poor vitality and tire easily. Fluoride's affect on health and energy is similar to taking chemotherapy for cancer except that it occurs in SLOW MOTION! Table salt negatively affects body metabolism. When you combine sodium with fluoride, the effects spell trouble.

***The Romans knew the power of table salt. When they defeated Hannibal's Carthage, they made sure that Carthage would NEVER rise again by salting her soil.***

***Excess sodium stresses body metabolism, while fluorides limit oxygen-carrying capacity of the blood (fewer blood cells produced by the red bone marrow means less oxygen). Together, they reduce ATP production.***

The lymphatic system services the colon, which **begins** at the cecum (see page 46). The cecum is the juncture of the lower small intestine (ileum) and the beginning of the large intestine (colon). The *appendix* dangles from the cecum. This area is the **MOST toxic site** in the body. It is loaded with lymph nodes (called Peyer's patch). Lymph nodes isolate and manage toxic waste overload and prevent death. **Appendicitis is confirmation of toxic waste overload to the point of death!**

A sluggish colon and lymphatic system are **symptomatic** conditions related to a toxic liver which, in turn, leads to bowel problems. People who experience appendicitis, diverticulitis, colitis, or irritable bowel syndrome are under **indictment** for MORE serious health problems to come unless remedial action is taken.

### Acne & Scars

As lymph fluid circulation slows and acid wastes accumlate in the basement membranes of the outer facia, the skin becomes clogged, the connective tissues break-down, and acne becomes a problem (adults get a little extra: wrinkles!).

Acne is nothing but an acute case of a sluggish lymphatic system in the sub-cutaneous layers of the skin and toxic waste overload. A TOXIC liver is central to this problem.

Scar formation and a congested lymphatic system go hand in hand. Scars result from damage to the *parenchyma* cells which are the ACTIVE, functional cells of an organ—like the skin. Scars are like the battlefield where armies of competing energy fields wage war. Scars are **proof** that the negative energy forces won. Acne scars and blemishes are easily cleared with regular use of SOC™ lotion and capsules and racemized™ Skin Creme™ . The former soften scar tissue; the latter encourage the formation of new "clear" skin.

Injuries that do trauma to the *parenchyma* cells result in scars when acid waste is stressing the system. The parenchyma cells will **erase** acne scars if the tissues are cleared of its waste. Formation of new tissue requires the presence of sulfhydryl carbon and sulphur. SOC™ provides these.

***An astute surgeon can tell the physical age of his patient by the amount of scarring in the tissues.*** *Due to an accident, I had a hernia repaired when I was 48 years old. My doctor was astounded because my* ***vital organs*** *were those of a 15 year old! We captured it on video. But, I must tell you that my* ***connective tissues*** *were in poor condition, partly due to a "vegetarian" diet for eight years and partly due to the effects of male menopause. I have since totally reversed the aging.*

*One of the negative side effects of the vegetarian, fruitarian and macrobiotic diet is systemic* ***breakdown*** *of the connective tissues. I have since renewed my entire body by doing the things outlined in this book and returning to a more balanced dietary approach. SOC™ has done wonders at rebuilding the joints and connective tissue, and I can attest that I look and feel better at 58 years "young" than at any point in my life. I did it!* ***And so can you!***

## Burns • Scars • New Limbs

In 1983 I suffered a *severe* burn in a welding accident. The skin and underlying tissues of the inside of my right elbow were burned and destroyed by a hunk of red hot 5,000° F steel that fell and landed in the crook of my arm.

At that time, I was age forty. By medical standards, I was old and should have scarred horribly. Instead, healing progressed without ANY scar formation. I did not see a doctor. Why was there no scar formation? The answer is related to vital organ function, blood/lymph circulation, and lifestyle.

The body can regenerate itself—limbs, nerve tissue and bones. I am talking about TOTAL limb regeneration as well as total restoration of function with no evidence of scar formation. These things have been amply demonstrated by Dr. Robert Becker and Dr. Melvin Saunders and recently by the Japanese who helped a diabetic grow a missing foot using Medical Grade Ionized Water™! The Japanese video is available and is best understood with the help of the Water Book, both of which are available (see Source Page 384).

*The miracle of "regeneration" was personally experienced by Mitchell May who made medical history by growing new skin, bone, and nerve tissue after suffering over forty breaks to his femur (thigh bone).*

Medical **miracles** are closely aligned with the principles of vibrational medicine and the manipulation of subtle energy forces in the bio-electric body. True health is healing without scars and the formation of new tissues in spite of the defined laws of science and medicine.

## Clogged Arteries & Lymph

**Athero**sclerosis (clogging of the arteries) is a major problem in the USA. Yet, **nothing** is said of the relationship of the lymphatic system or hormones to cardiovascular problems.

The two main trunks of the lymphatic system join the blood system at the origin of the subclavian veins at the base and front of the neck just below the collar bones. The subclavian veins feed into the superior vena cava vein which feeds into the right side of the heart to complete the circulatory loop.

**The heart pumps blood to the lungs where TWO things occur: the blood is reoxygenated AND toxic energy is RELEASED into the atmosphere.** The blood is then returned to the left side of the heart for distribution to the body. As the blood leaves the heart by way of the aortic artery, the left and right coronary arteries branch off and feed the heart muscle. These are the arteries that become blocked and require coronary bypass surgery.

Toxic fats like soy, canola, and hydrogenated margarines COMBINE with *chlorine, fluorine, and chlor**amines*** (all from tap water), and metabolic acid waste in the blood. Atherosclerotic plaque formation is the **"predictable"** result.

Some people age so rapidly in their vital organs that they simply drop dead! *Angina pectoris* is a good example of chest pain that results from oxygen deficiency AND low ATP production. A reduced oxygen supply to the heart is called ischemia (*ischein*-to hold back. *hemia*-pertaining to the blood). When a heart attack occurs, some of the heart muscle tissue dies for LACK of oxygen due to blocked arteries that feed it. This is called *myocardial infarction.* If a blood clot is involved, it is called a *coronary thrombosis.* A clot is a *thrombus.*

### People & Plants

Human beings and plants have MUCH in common. They also have ONE major difference. That difference has to do with MOBILITY and fluid movement.

Humans rely on physical activity to assist the movement of lymph fluid, and we have the heart to pump our blood. By comparison, plants have no heart and must depend on capillary action, osmosis, enzymes and mineral ion energy to overcome gravity and move water and nutrients up into their tissues and back to their roots.

Humans depend on the mitochondria to produce the ATP energy that fuels body processes. Plants rely on mineral ions, photosynthesis and solar energy to fuel their metabolic processes. Humans rely on red blood corpuscles and hemoglobin for their supply of oxygen. Plants rely on chlorophyll and the chloroplasts. Circulating human body fluids are called "blood" and "lymph". Plant fluids are called chlorophyll and sap. Human beings need movement, exercise, and load bearing work for repair and maintenance of body tissues. Plants enjoy little mobility, and are dependent on their circumstances.

**Lack of exercise and load-bearing-work SLOW blood and lymph flow, leading to the CURSE called, dis-ease.**

Blood and lymph are flip-sides of the same coin. A disease condition in the lymph mirrors trouble in the blood. The lymphatic system directly influences blood chemistry.

When we learn HOW to control body terrain, we control the aging process. Aging reversal requires that we assist the body in cleaning-up and maintaining the lymphatic system through increased ***body fluid dynamics.*** Examples are load-bearing-work, rebounding, exercise, use of the lymph roller and, of course, the L/CSF™ machine.

**Dis-ease "develops" in the lymph. Later, it appears in the blood. Maintain the lymphatic system and dis-ease will not be found in the body.**

We ***limp*** our way into old age. We must ***lymph*** our way UP the aging pyramid—back to our anabolic peak, for it is there at our former PEAK, that we become *Young Again!*

**PREVIEW:** *Our next chapter is the "cancer" chapter! Learn HOW to avoid becoming a cancer statistic.*

---

**Ring, Ring Goes The Bell!**

And so it does, 150+ times a day. The question is, "Does the caller really wish help or is he/she just spinning their wheels? People who are ready, run with the ball. How about you?

---

**Stroke & Heart Attack**

Damage following a "stroke" can be minimized by giving LARGE quantities of SOC™ capsules, TCM™ and racemized™ sea minerals with lots of WARM water. Better yet, place the victim in a tub of tepid water, lower to 86°F for 24 hours before slowly raising the victim's body temperature to 98.6°. Presto, little—if any— brain damage. For heart attacks, the doctor needs to intravenously administer magnesium IMMEDIATELY!

---

**Life! A Dual Perspective!**

We grow old and die in the *invisible* realm of the Fourth Dimension **BEFORE** we see and experience aging in the Third Dimension where we live out our lives.

Acidification of the body requires a **dual** perspective to be truly effective. For example, colon therapy accelerates the release of toxic metabolic wastes on the physical level, while Enhanced Homeopathic™ bring about tissue memory "clear-ing" on a higher "invisible" level. When we ***erase*** toxic energy conditions in the Fourth Dimension, we deal with **underlying** health issues and promote true healing in the Third Dimen-sion. Life is the manifestation of what we in the West refer to as *spirit, soul, grace,* and what Eastern thought calls *life force, chi, qi* and *prana.* Good health and rejuvenation demands a dual perspective. So does spiritual enlightenment.

---

**Howdy Doody Facial Lines**

*Lines* from *the corners of the mouth to the sides of the chin* indicate colon/liver problems, hormonal imbalance and a body that is in **trouble—and full of parasites!** Follow the Young Again Protocol™ to rid those Howdie Doody lines from your face. You didn't have them when you were younger, so why do you have them now? It's your "terrain!"

**A Typical Day**

**1.** Wake up early the same time each day & immediately drink a QUART of water with a fresh whole lemon and a short squirt of racemized™ sea minerals.
**2.** Get on the rebounder and "rock'n roll" for 5 minutes.
**3.** Stretch and do calisthenics followed by a lymph roller "rolldown." Drink a glass of Kombucha tea.
**4.** Do pull ups (both over and under hand); get on a good aerobic exerciser and raise heart beat to 80% of your maximum heart rate and HOLD it there for 12 minutes. Do this in cold, fresh air with a minimum of clothing using *mind over body* to stay warm. I use the Nordic Trac™.
**5.** Drink another glass of water on the way to the shower.
**6.** Take a hot shower followed by a long ice cold shower. Shave, make-up and dress.
**7.** Make a big glass of beet and carrot juice. Sip and chew the juice. NO GULPING! Super Foods™ are generally taken at the same time as the juice. If you are still hungry, eat something that is good for you. No junk!
**8.** Each time you urinate throughout the day, drink more water with the racemized sea minerals in it.
**9.** Lunch. Generally, you won't want lunch if you do the above. But if you insist, repeat the SUPER FOODS list on page 292 and detailed in the Young Again Source Packet, and you will ZOOM the rest of the day. An apple or fresh veggies are always acceptable. A short walk in fresh air, some relaxing music, meditation, good conversation, breathing exercises, prayer, whatever—as long as it's uplifting and relaxing makes for a nice lunch break. **P.S.** Don't buy into other's problems and don't worry about your own.
**10.** Hold your bladder to promote bowel movements. Use Biogenic™ Colon Prep Formula to increase bile flow and bowel activity.
**11.** Do some load-bearing work every day. Move boxes. Lift things. Do gardening work by hand (no rototiller). DO yoga or Pilates. Walk to the store. *Carry* your groceries home. Pump some iron. Do some calisthenics. Hang and stretch twice daily, preferably by your feet; by your hands is fine if your shoulders will take it. The body was made to work. If it hurts, take some SOC™. If you are weak, be patient and you will become strong.
**12.** Eat a healthy dinner and enjoy your family/friends.
**13.** Retire the same time each evening. Sleep outside if possible or in a well ventilated cold room. Pray. Give thanks for being alive. Look forward to better tomorrows.
**14.** Get a life and people will seek the same path you are on because it is the path of TRUTH.
**15.** Remember, poor health is a matter of **CHOICE!**

### Microbiology Of Drinking Water

The principal bacterial agents known to be involved in intestinal dis-eases associated with drinking water are: *Salmonella typhi: typhoid fever; Salmonella paratyphi: aparathyphoid fever; Salmonella species: enteric fever, salmonellosis; Shigella bacteria: bacillary dysentery; Amebas: amebic dysentery; Vibrio cholerae: cholera; Leptospira species: leptospirosis; Yersinia enterocolitica: gastroenteritis; Francisella tularensis: tulararemia; Escherichia coli (E. coli): gastroenteritis; Pseudomonas aeruginosa: various infections; Cryptosporidium: cryptosporidiosis.*

Enteric (pertaining to the small intestine/gut) bacteria like E. coli, Salmonella, and Shigella are classified as *facultatively anaerobic*, that is, they can function and live with or without oxygen. They **ferment** sugars and produce toxic organic **acids** (acetic, formic, lactic, etc.) and gases (mixed-acid fermentation).

Unlike bacteria, viruses are **intra**cellular parasites and cannot replicate outside the host's cells. Hepatitis-A (infectious hepatitis) is the product of a notable water born virus. So is poliomyelitis (polio).

Viruses and bacteria are prevalent in raw untreated water. Therefore, conventional treatment of public water supplies involves steps like coagulation, sedimentation, filtration, and disinfection (chlorine, **chloramines,** mercuric acid, etc.) to produce *potable* water. These steps reduce organism count. However, during the warm season, the organisms can multiply in the lines with disastrous results.

The BEV™ process removes parasites, pathogenic bacteria and viruses from drinking water, and they are **flushed** from the BEV™ system so as not to develop a breeding ground for the spread of dis-ease. No other water system offers biologically friendly water with an elevated ORP and the potential to make Medical grade Ionized Water™.

**The United States is headed for a cataclysmic crisis in public drinking water. Protect yourself!**

---

### Laxatives vs. Bile

People use laxatives to "force" bowel activity, but the there is a HUGE difference between naturally moving the bowels and "forcing" a bowel movement with laxitaives—regardless if they be chemical or herbal in nature. It is the free flow of "bile" that carries the acids from the system and moves the bowels—and without bile flow, you will grow old. That is what the Young Again Protocol™ is about. Think "bile!"

# 30

# Cancer & Salt

*"Well organized ignorance, unfortunately, often passes for wisdom."*
anon.

Salt (sodium chloride) is a paradox. It is part of life, yet it is involved in death. A little salt will hurt you a little bit. More than a little will *eventually* kill you.

History can be written according to salt. In ancient China, two big tablespoons of salt was a socially acceptable mode of suicide. Salt has served as money, an item of barter and a cathartic (laxative). For over 100 years, medicine's focus has centered on salt's relationship to *high blood pressure*. We will instead focus on salt's systemic AFFECTS on the "terrain."

Mankind has chosen to upset Nature's balance. We use salt to *hype* our food, and in so doing we hasten old age. Nutritious food does NOT need salt because it has plenty of mineral ions in it to give it flavor. Marginal food requires salt to create the *mirage* of taste—and to keep it from **spoiling**. Look at any can or package of processed food and you will find that it is loaded with salt—as a preservative agent.

Canned foods came about in 1859 when the H. J. Heinz company produced the first of its Heinz 57 varieties. Salt was used to create a brine environment that was hostile to Clostridium botulinum. Clostridium is a *facultative* anaerobe. It can survive with or without oxygen. Its wastes are the most toxic systemic poisons known. We call the condition produced by these toxins *botulism!*

Sailors of old suffered miserably from *salt*-preserved beef and pork. So did civilian populations. When meat is preserved with salt, it loses its energy force and nutritive qualities. Sodium chloride (table salt) is a preservative that upsets the potassium:sodium balance in the body. Salt puts money in the mortician's pocket.

Organic foods are naturally high in potassium and low in sodium, while bio-junk and processed foods are exactly the opposite. Sodium upsets the ion balance in the body and destroys energy balance in the soil. Salt fertilizers create conditions of EXCESS in the soil, as does table salt in the body. Salt is a concentrated, left-spin energy field that does not belong in the body.

**NOTE: A little flour, salt, and water mixed together makes a wonderful play dough for children. However, when it dries, it turns as hard as concrete!**

### Natural Preservatives

Dr. Carey Reams taught that quality produce will dehydrate before it will rot. He proved his point by entering a watermelon he had grown in the local county fair for three years in a row! Quality, fresh food is high in natural sugars and earth minerals. Quality produce has a right-spin energy signature.

*Acres USA* once carried a story about a salesman who carted around three cabbages in his car for nine months without spoilage. On the weekends, he would roll them under a shade tree until Monday morning when he would peel away a leaf and hit the road again. When the salesman was challenged, the nine month old cabbages were cut and eaten raw. The point here is that high mineral and high sucrose levels go together in high quality fruits and vegetables.

*Homemade ice cream containing too much sugar will NOT set up regardless of the amount of salt applied to the ice to lower the freezing point. Oranges that are high in natural sugars will wither and shrink, but they will NOT rot. Home grown lettuce and greens can be kept in the refrigerator for over a month and will still be crisp and tasty with no spoilage! High sugar levels in the juices of food crops indicates high mineral content, excellent flavor, and good keeping qualities.*

*Trace minerals and humic acids applied to plant foliage as a foliar spray raise the sugar/mineral levels in the juices of plants and protect them from frost damage. A high sucrose level in a crop is an excellent marker of nutritious food. Proper glucose (sugar) levels in the blood and glycogen levels in the muscles are closely related to peak health in humans. Dis-ease cannot survive in a high energy, right-spin environment where mineral ion levels and sugars are balanced and excesses do not exist.*

In the old days, a bushel of fresh green beans weighed 32 lbs. Today, a bushel of beans weighs only 24 lbs. The difference is the lack of earth minerals AND lower concentration of sugar energy. The more concentrated the positive energy fields, the heavier the crop vs. crops raised with salt fertilizers and poisons that produce sick, weak populations of human beings.

## SALT: Paul Bragg vs. The Athletes

Here is a true story about how salt affects health and vitality. In the early 1960's, Dr. Paul C. Bragg, a famous health crusader and one of my mentors, challenged a group of college athletes to a 30 mile hike across Death Valley. The temperature in August was 130° Fahrenheit.

The *experts* advised the athletes to take "salt tablets!" The athletes were given all the "cold" water and food they wanted. Bragg drank *only* warm distilled water (in those days BEV water was not available), took NO salt, and fasted—taking no food. Bragg was the only one to finish the hike. The athletes—every last one of them—were carried off for medical care. They suffered from heat exhaustion and heat stroke. Bragg finished the hike in 10 1/2 hours, camped overnight, and repeated the return hike the following day. He was in his mid *sixties!* He was YOUNG and active. **He avoided all salt!**

Rommel's German-Afrikan Corps used no salt in their diets, yet they fought tremendous desert battles. When they were finally captured, they were in peak condition and unaffected by the intense desert heat. The Americans used salt tablets, they salted their food and the heat got to them.

Native peoples consume little salt. When *civilized* man comes along and introduces salt into their diet, their health deteriorates. Salt isn't the only issue in dis-ease, but it is ***always*** a player in the development of subclinical illness that eventually gives way to SIGNS and the diagnosis of dis-ease.

## Cells • Sodium • Mitochondria

When sodium levels are high, the body is in a negative energy condition. A high sodium diet upsets the body's sodium:potassium ratio and speeds the LOSS of potassium from the cells. Potassium is the predominant ion *inside* cell membranes, while sodium is the predominant ion *outside* of cell membranes in the **extra**cellular fluid.

When sodium levels are high, the body steals potassium from the cells and replaces it with sodium. Both ions have a positive (+) charge and both are electrolytes. However, sodium spins left while potassium spins right. **Edema (fluid retention in the tissues) is a SIGN of excess sodium and excess plasma protein wastes in the intercellular spaces.**

Once inside the cell, sodium short-circuits cellular machinery, sedates the mitochondria, and eventually kills the cell. Dead cells create acids that must be removed. Marginal cells that are between life and death produce little ATP and become a drag on the system. The presence of dead and sick tissue needlessly ***consumes*** vital ENERGY. ATP energy that could be used for growth and repair is squandered in the presence of sodium-imposed stress.

The mitochondria **cannot** function in a high sodium environment. They **cannot** replicate (reproduce) when sodium has invaded their territory.

### Energy • Free Radicals

We have spent a lot of time discussing and describing energy using terms like *left-spin, right-spin, negative, positive, aerobic*, and *anaerobic* in an effort to help the reader understand the nature of energy and its relationship to aging.

The term "free radical" is a term that comes to mind in regard to energy and cancer. A free radical is a molecule that contains an *odd* number of electrons. This makes it highly reactive and EXTREMELY unstable.

Free radicals are very much a part of **every** person's life. Poor choices of lifestyle, diet, and water are greatly compounded by environmental poisons that bombard the bioelectric body from every direction.

In a healthy body, free radical reactions take place continuously and look like this: $O^2 + O^2 + H^2 <\!\!\longrightarrow H_2O_2^{=} + O_2$ (the double arrow means that the reaction can **reverse**). In a stressed body, **reverse** chain reactions cause electron theft to go out of control. The end result is accelerated aging.

Free radical production tremendously influences aging and the formation of cancer in the body. For our discussion here, I want the reader to understand that these *wild* reactions drive the production of ***non differentiated*** tissue (cancer tissue) and systemic EXCESSES.

*Nondifferentiated* tissue is the tissue from which we evolve PRIOR to hormonal influences that cause the formation of skin instead of muscle, bones instead of brains, etc. We are talking about OUTLAW tissue with no identity. Tissue *insurrection* best describes the process. Uncontrolled oxidation of the tissues builds EXCESS toxic waste in the system, drives hormone disturbances and acid waste overload that eventually manifest as *so-called* deficiency dis-eases.

Free radical reactions within a stressed body leads to loss of control over the "terrain." Cancer absorbs and uses cellular ATP to proliferate. In compliance with the second law of thermodynamics, energy is NEVER lost, it merely changes form. Once excess toxic energy **EXCEEDS** the body's ability to cope, the formation of a tumor or a mass will begin. We will discuss their individual characteristics shortly.

Uncontrolled free radical oxidation can be prevented through deacidification and the use of various racemized™ products and protocols outlined thus far. Consumption of Medical Grade Ionized Water™ is perhaps the ultimate tool for terrain control. Do understand this: health is a "cumulative" state of being as is dis-ease. **Health and dis-ease are also a reflection of the choices we make.**

### Energy • Cancer

Cancer is a manifestation of a negative energy condition. Cancer **tumors** surround themselves in a zone of SODIUM. They **concentrate** energy by acting as *anaerobic* black holes, siphoning away and isolating the host's life force.

The tumor is NOT the "enemy." Rather, it is a statement by the body that all is not well. Moreover, a tumor is a self-defensive measure taken by the body to preserve itself through the **condensation** of deadly toxic energy. We are talking about toxic energy that the body is unable to neutralize or dispose of through normal exit portals like the lungs, kidneys, bowel and skin. Tumors—even benign tumors—are a warning SIGN.

In the early stages, a cancer tumor goes unnoticed. As it concentrates more energy, it becomes more "dense." It can now be seen by X-ray, CAT scan and MRI. It can even be *felt* with the fingers if it is not too deep in the body.

Cancer tumors are NOT the same as cancer masses. Tumors are energy-**importing** clusters of tissue that the body forms to ISOLATE toxic energy fields and get them OUT of circulation.

Tumors are *nationalistic.* They stay within their own territory and import their energy needs. They do NOT spread as commonly believed. When *antagonized by surgical intervention,* the body is weakened sufficiently to precipitate the formation of new tumors rather than son and daughter tumors. Generaly, cancerous tumors should NOT be removed.

Sometimes the body chooses to **dissolve** a tumor. In most cases, however, it chooses to **calcify** (deposit minerals, petrify) the tumor and tie up the toxic energy on a permanent basis. The tumor is an effort by the body to preserve itself rather than the enemy. The enemy is usually the person who inhabits the body. Healing requires focused effort and reprogramming of the way people think. Even in the face of doing everything right, negative thinking will get you because "negative" is what you **believe. The mind is 90% of the battle.**

Conversely, the positive thinking, happy, loving person can outlast the worst of cancers. However, correct mental choices need to be duplicated on the physical level if success is expected. God performs miracles for people who make correct "choices!" GET IT?

When a **malignant** tumor (or mass) is discovered, immediate action is needed. Radiation and chemotherapy are NEVER wise choices. Torture and financial strain make little sense. Alternative treatment is safer and more humane if the patient has discipline and is willing to face down death.

Alternative therapy requires that a person have a laid-back, happy-go-lucky attitude and outlook. There is absolutely NO room for doubt, fear, worry, hate, blame or anger—only love! **The desire to live must be intense and beyond the fear of death.** I highly recommend the book, *Your Body Believes Every Word You Say* and *Holographic Universe* (see Source Page 384).

**The ONLY things cancer tumors and masses have in common are that both are *virus* havens and both like left-spin, anaerobic, high sodium environments.**

### Cancer Masses

A mass is **not** a tumor, and the terms should **NOT** be used interchangeably. A mass is not dense like a tumor. It cannot be felt because it has no definitive boundaries. A mass is soft, spongy, porous and difficult to feel—never hard.

A mass takes form, grows and establishes outposts quietly. Masses exist in the twilight zone *between* life and death. They rarely appear on X-rays, CAT scans, ultra sound or MRI's and it is almost impossible to differentiate where sick and healthy tissue begin and end. Masses are *invisible* because they have low density and hide behind other tissues.

Masses are ***offensive*** in nature. Think of them in terms of outposts for colonial expansionism in a third world country (your body). Masses colonize during a 7 year period, referred to in medical circles as the "occult" period (*occult* means hidden). Long before a cancer *mass* announces itself to the host, it is there, growing and spreading. Masses follow the lymphatic highway and sabotage the host's Immune system while the host notices nothing and even feels good! By the time a mass announces itself, the host is in **deep** trouble

### Cloaking Period & Sodium

During the occult period, a cancer mass is concealed, invisible and non-detectable by the host and conventional testing. In other words, a mass employs a cloaking technique so as to go undetected. The years preceding the end of the occult period are often some of the very best years in terms of OUTWARD appearance of good health. On the inside, however, confirmation of the person's lifestyle, thought patterns and choices have come home to roost. Aging is in full swing.

Masses cause the body to gain weight with little or no increase in body measurements because water is heavier than fat on a volume basis. Therefore, weight gain without inches is reason to question what is occurring in your terrain.

A person who is sodium-toxic always suffers from edema (water logging of the tissues), partly from the sodium and partly from the accumulation of plasma proteins in the **extra**cellular spaces between the cells.

Edema is a SIGN. Edema is abnormal. *Chronic* edema is the equivalent to a quiet proclamation of WAR and must not be ignored. Edema signals the *invasion* of sodium at the cellular level and GROSS accumulation of plasma proteins in the interstitial spaces between the cells. Look for puffy, water filled skin that "dents" easily when pressed and does not spring back quickly. Be alert to swelling in the legs, ankles, feet and hands. This SIGN also goes with congestive heart failure and is **very** hormone related.

People in the *early stages* of a cancer "mass" formation often experience substantial weight gain for no particular reason—usually WITHOUT any noticeable change in dietary habits. Near the end of the occult period, they get the *"I just don't feel up to par!"* syndrome. Finally, out of the blue, the person becomes **skin** and **bones**. Their body **evaporates!** When this occurs, the *mass* type cancer has removed its cloak, the occult period is over, and the final struggle begins.

***Edema is cancer's cloaking device.*** **People do NOT recognize edema for what it is! They don't understand. They think everything is okay—*"Just a little old age!"*** During the cloaking period, the cancerous body is **cannibalizing** itself. It is experiencing severe free radical oxidation and is digesting its own tissues—a process called **auto digestion.** The body is living on *stored* energy. The body is now in a catabolic high acid state. Once the body has used up its energy reserves—BANG!—the game is over. Because of the *invisible* nature of cancer masses, exploratory surgery is pushed onto the unsuspecting patient by *blind men and women in white robes.* Exploratory invasive surgery sabotages whatever energy reserves remain and weakens the person beyond hope.

A positive "confirmation" of **CANCER** is not a blessing because it does a "number" on the sick person. By this time, their weight has plunged downward and their energy is nil. The victim becomes skin and bones overnight. Terror sets it.

**When sodium levels in the cells and the plasma proteins in the tissues reach the critical point, cancer *turns off* its cloaking device and announces itself.**

### It's Your Life

There are no tests to determine sodium toxicity at the cellular level, but there are SIGNS. There are no tests for plasma protein toxicity at the **extra**cellular level either, but there are SIGNS. Learn to pay attention to them.

Pay attention when you see people (and children) gaining weight. Be alert to gyrating blood sugar levels that manifest as mood swings/depression. PMS and menstrual problems are serious business. Acne, boils, balding, ongoing "subclinical" illness and low energy all tell a story. Bladder infections, prostate problems, bowel conditions and graying hair have long-term consequences.

If you are in trouble, seek help. But be forewarned that you will be bullied into conventional therapy. People feel **"relieved"** when the enemy has been identified, i.e., cancer. They want to **"believe"** their physician. **FORGET IT!** Identifying the enemy means you are focusing on what you **don't** want. Medical fairy tales are a fraud, and fraud always results in bogus decisions. Instead, decide to take personally responsibility for yourself and **GET A LIFE!** Forget about dying. You could have died any day in your life, but you did not. If you want the **MIRACLE**, you have to do your part. Forget the games! You must do your part. Remember, the **body** does the healing. As steward of that body, it is YOUR job to provide the environment where healing can occur. **Control your "terrain!"**

**Colon therapy is crucial and tissue deacidification is a MUST.** Limit food intake by using Taoist™ products. Juicing is mandatory. Restoration of liver function—yes! Hormone issues MUST be addressed. Biologically friendly water is crucial. Electrolyte intake is a must. Lymphatic circulation cannot be ignored.

Walking is beneficial. Positive thinking and visualization are crucial. Use of the L/CSF™ machine has no substitute. Laughter and fun are basic prerequisites. Worry and fear are **not** allowed. GUARD your thoughts or you will become a self-fulfilling prophesy. Remember the power of prayer, both for yourself and others. Meditation and deep breathing are powerful tools. Time spent in a garden (bare foot), growing food and enjoying Nature is as close to heaven as you can get. Take time to focus on and **help others**. The more you give, the more you receive. Get plenty of rest. Sleep on a Biogenic™ Medical Grade Mattress Pad to turn your rest periods into "healing" periods.

### Self Diagnosis & Treatment

The simplest tools for diagnosis are a pendulum and vibration chain. Used properly, they are fantastic devices. Use them to establish the depth of your aura today, so you will have a reference for the future. Combined with your "bio-electric age," you now have TWO reference tools.

It is NOT easy to drive sodium from the body—especially a body diagnosed with cancer. Copious amounts of organic potassium are needed and fresh veggi juice is a great source. Eat whole fresh foods like carrots, cabbage, onion, lemon and beet. ***Sip*** and ***chew*** your juices. **Do NOT gorge!** Remember, it takes 5-10 minutes to properly eat an apple, but only 2 seconds to drink the juice. Juices are like jet fuel. Use moderation and be certain to add a little Yucca Herbal Blend™, DiSorb Aid™, and R/BHCl™ for maximum degestability and benefit.

Fresh juices are VERY powerful detoxifiers and can flood the body with wastes to the point that the liver and adrenals become *exhausted* and the kidneys *overloaded*. Colon therapy lifts the overload burden very effectively.

In the face of cancer, the Young Again Colon Therapy Protocol™ is done 3-5 days a week. The results are incredible! Best of all, you can stay home and heal. Colon therapy represents 50% of the prerequisite to healing.

Liver is a wonderful food—if you can stand it! I use racemized™ ***predigested,*** organic beef liver capsules. Cancer therapy should **always** include liver. Domestic liver products are contaminated; avoid them. Do not use *dessicated* liver! If you are a vegetarian or vegan, you must change your ways or you will not get well. Same for heavy meat eaters.

Coffee colonics are NOT called for in the Young Again™ protocol. Kombucha tea is wonderful. Lymphatic work with an L/CSF™ machine and body roller is most helpful (see page 366). RHYTHM and regular hours are most critical.

Detoxification of plasma protein acid wastes does NOT happen by itself. You must assist your body. Once released into circulation, wastes MUST exit the body and be sent down the toilet! Avoid tap water and distilled water. Distillled water in plastic bottle is loaded with plasticizers. Those who advocate it have their feet in cement. Better choices are available.

### Expect To Feel Crummy

EXPECT to feel crummy as you detoxify! You are paying for your sins. Do NOT forget the power of prayer and positive thinking. Try to find strength within YOURSELF. It's nice to have a "strong" person to help you through the transition back to the world of the healthy, but they are few.

Once the potassium begins exchanging places with the sodium inside the cells, the mitochondria will come alive and replicate themselves. The more of them that come alive and multiply—the more *ENERGY* there will be available for your body to rebuild itself. At first, you will feel worse. In time, you will feel better. **It's two steps forward, one step backwards.**

Deacidification can be tough on people. It's a kind of **mind game.** The body shouts, *"I feel crummy!"* but you must ignore and reassure the body that all is **under control.** Talk out loud and tell your body *what you expect* and *what you desire.* Never go hyper at the first sign of a metabolic rebound—guard your energy at all costs! Good days are followed by bad days. In time, you will enjoy more good and fewer bad days. **If you panic or cut and run, you will NEVER be healed!**

### Chemotherapy

Chemotherapy is defined as the prevention or treatment of infectious disease by *chemicals* which act to promote "antisepsis" in the body while avoiding serious side effects in the patient. If we dissect the word *antisepsis,* we get *anti-* against' *sepsis*-a general fever producing condition caused by bacteria or their toxic by-products. In light of this dictionary definition, do you think that *chemotherapy* as used on cancer patients meets this description? Did you know that you must sign a form *before* you get your *magic bullet* cancer therapy?

### NOT Approved

Drugs used in cancer chemotherapy are *magic bullets.* They are NOT APPROVED as safe for the treatment of cancer. They are administered to unsuspecting people. Medicine and the pharmaceutical companies side step the "liability" problem by having people sign away their rights *beforehand,* so they cannot bring suit for the horrible side effects that follow.

When people sign the ***"standard"*** form, they are giving the legal AND medical systems *jurisdiction* over them. The name of the game in our legal system is *jurisdiction!* Either medicine and the courts have jurisdiction over a person's body or the person does, but NOT both at the same time.

*"Standard" forms are no different from entering a courtroom where the judge has committed constructive treason by placing the yellow fringe on a Title 4, U.S.C. 1 flag of "peace" of the united (note small "u") States of America or displaying it inferior to a ball, eagle or spear on the pole, or placing it on the right as you face the flag, or placing it inferior to any other flag. The judges do this to "create" a foreign "state" in order to deny citizens their constitutional rights. JURISDICTION is everything!*

When the medical system has jurisdiction, the person does not. When a person grants jurisdiction over their body, medical "science" is free to maneuver with impunity.

For the cancer patient, the options "within" the medical system are nil. Sign the form or be refused treatment because jurisdiction was not granted—a limited liability contract where ONE side shares the benefits and the patient assumes ALL the risk! The medical system needs ***jurisdiction*** because they are using EXPERIMENTAL drugs in the treatment of cancer and the destruction of YOUR body—with the blessings of so called watch-dog government agencies, of course!

Everyone MUST come to understand something known in legal AND medical circles as the "Rule of Probable Cause." It states: *"...experimental drugs may be used IF the side effect of the drug is NO worse than the end effect of the untreated disease."*

**"For Experimental Use Only"**

Regardless of the specie of cancer drug, it will be stamped with the tell-tale sign of a **"magic bullet"** medicine—"For Experimental Use Only."

How do you like that? How does it make you feel to know that the MAXIMUM risk to the poor patient is no worse than if treatment were not rendered at all. What an alternative—sign on the dotted line, and let us milk you of your life and savings or go home and die!

**"For Experimental Use Only"** is a fact that should be sufficient SHOCK therapy to motivate every thinking person to immediately begin the aging reversal process. No matter how you figure it, you are on your own. So go home and live! "Magic bullets" don't work! Self treatment is less risky and the odds of recovery far greater—at a fraction of the cost.

Believe me when I tell you that your health and life are worth more than all the money you can throw at the medical system in the futile effort to buy back your life. **Good health isn't for sale!** Instead, it requires commitment, discipline, responsibility, and choice. AVOID the horror of cancer and degenerative dis-eases by implementing what you have learned throughout this book.

### Cancer & Root Canals

**According to Dr. Issels, a German doctor, only 20% of the population has root canals, yet, 90% of cancer victims have root canals in their mouth!**

Cancer and root canals in the teeth are related. The implications are scary, but options like dentures, bridges, implants also have shortcomings. Your "terrain" dictates the outcome and viability of all of these procedures.

I have a problem with root canals if the body's **TERRAIN** is weak. For some people, "dead" teeth in the mouth produce an auto immune response that compromises good health. But if you are in PEAK health or are willing to get yourself in PEAK health, root canals need not become a health issue. It's the "terrain" that dictates whether you can enjoy good health and a long life with root canals in your mouth. From fillings to root canals, ALL dental procedures are less than desirable, so take care of your teeth. Got it?

If you have an **infected** root canaled tooth, get it **OUT** of your mouth. And if you are facing serious dental work, PLEASE call and learn how to prepare your body for mercury amalgam removal to avoid ***dental shock*** associated with a sick **"terrain."** What you do BEFORE major dental or amalgam removal dictates the outcome. Control the TERRAIN, and you will become *Young Again!*

**PREVIEW:** *Our next chapter deals with the world of Time and Space and its relationship to the Fourth Dimension, ageless living and the vast UNKNOWN!*

***Our Stolen Future* explains the "hormone" story.**

**It's Your Life!**

**Some things are worse than death.** Becoming a victim of *conventional* cancer treatment is one of them. **Never** rejoice because insurance is paying the bills. **Do** be concerned about what "they" are doing to you. **Do** be independent. **Do** keep your dignity. **Do** maintain control of your life. **Do** stay away from doctors. **Do** these things and you will leave your loved ones with more than the ugly memory of the **"torture"** that preceded your death!

**CHOOSE to live and die on your own terms!**

# 31

# Time & Space

*"Time and Space are the shadows by which man defines his existence."*
Sepio

Time is duration—Space is extension. We do not think of Time and Space as entities, but we do consider the bodies and events that occupy them as entities. If we acknowledge the existence of material bodies because they occupy space, then what is an event? An event is a group of circumstances that occupy Time. Therefore, material objects are also events, and both are entities.

Mankind attempts to define those intangibles we call "Time and Space," using words and concepts. We have no physical sense organs for Time and Space. We anticipate them through our "intuition." Intuition, then, must be a sixth sense—a projection of the physical body—something we invoke to comprehend Time and Space.

Philosophy tells us that Time and Space consist of relations between entities—that there is co-existence and succession of entities or events. Metaphysics (*meta*: beyond) tells us that Time and Space are indistinguishable as long as neither is excluded. Yet, we are aware of the *passage* of Time.

Plato stated, "Time and space is the "substance" which contains the identity and the diversity in one." If we think of Space as something that is created, then something must create it. What? *Meta*physics answers, *"Time."* Okay. If there is creation, then motion must also exist. If there is motion, then there must be a mover or source of motion. Metaphysics tells us that Time is the source of motion and, if this is so, then Time is *ENERGY*.

Is Time *energy* or is energy created in the passing of time? If energy is created, the results are perpetual motion which is not a straight line, but a curved line that returns to itself—like a circle. Therefore, Space becomes Time's trail. But a trail does not move, so Space cannot move either, since it was Time that generated ENERGY in its expansion—creating Space. Time and Space can also be demonstrated to be static, indistinguishable or non-existent. Let us illustrate.

Suppose we are in an airplane that is traveling at the same speed as the Earth's rotation or approximately 1080 miles per hour and we are heading West following the sun at its own speed. We begin our three hour trip in New York City at exactly twelve o'clock noon, and, when we arrive at Los Angeles, it is still exactly twelve o'clock noon.

What has taken place here? Time became a motion of Space and Space the relaxation of Time. We moved from one point to another point on the surface of the earth, but Time did not change. We are in a quandary—caught between Time and Space—a kind of cosmic cul-de-sac. The mathematician working on our dilemma would have difficulty making his calculations respond to our problem—so he would give the *unknown* condition a name: "fourth variable," and reestablish his equilibrium by imposing the ingredient Time so his calculations could continue as if Time were a fixed point.

When we ponder the situation, we must conclude that Time is NOT a fixed point to which we can anchor our lives, but a mirage on a phantom's shroud. Once we admit that Time is not a fixed point, we lose our center and our reference point—yet, our *intuition* tells us there should be such a center.

To compensate, man divides Time into three parts: *present, past,* and *future*. However, this does not solve the problem because present is but the transition from past into future—a transition that lacks both dimensionality, and duration. The present is the future before we think of it, and the moment we think of it, it is the past. Under these circumstances, self examination of our thought processes and sensory experiences becomes impossible. Is Present but the "living fringe" of our memory tinted by expectation? And if it is, what of our dilemma between the poles of eternity—past and future?

These extremes—past and future—have delivered us into the *enigma* we call the Fourth Dimension—the "unknowable." Because man *seems* capable of comprehending only three dimensions related to his physical world—that of length, width, and height—the idea of the existence of another dimension that is totally invisible only compounds his dilemma. **Yet, the existence of the Fourth Dimension cannot be denied. Intuition is real. It is more than an intangible tool by which we interpret Time and Space. It is an extension of our mind.**

Perhaps the Fourth Dimension is not unknowable at all, but simply misunderstood? If so, there is no reason for man to have to die and emerge from his terrestrial envelope before he can come to *know* this *Unknowable* dimension.

Knowledge of the existence of this *other* dimension is quite different from understanding it. Consider Jesus, who passed through the wall in the Temple. He was a Third Dimensional being with a physical body, yet He passed through that wall! Since both He and the wall were solid matter, shall we chalk up this event to Deity? Did He violate some Natural Law? Or did He invoke knowledge of the Fourth Dimension?

When we enter the arena of the Fourth Dimension, necessity demands that we visualize a *hyper-space* that is measured with *meta*geometry (*meta*-beyond). Our three dimensional world of length, width, and height becomes but a section of *hyper-Space*. Let us examine this in more detail.

The *length* of a procession of events is not contained in three dimensional space. Extension in Time is a projection into unknown space—or the Fourth Dimension. Because Space and Time are interchangeable at specific points, Time becomes a dimension of Space. That is, Time is Space in motion becoming the future or the past. Therefore, Space is time projected—horizontal Time—Time that persists, Time that moves. And since Space can only be measured by Time, and Time is defined by the speed of light, we must conclude that there is no difference between Space and Time ***EXCEPT* that our consciousness is defined in Time.**

We are, therefore, *forced* to acknowledge that the present is eternal—that Time per se does not exist, but is relative to the person with the *notion* of time. **Events do not ebb and flow. It is we who pass them by!** The more we wrestle and try to understand, the deeper we get into the vast unknown.

**The creature we call man exists in two worlds: the visible and the invisible.** The invisible world is the realm of negative and positive "energy" forces that ultimately determine our perception of reality in the visible world in which we find our existence. The visible world and the physical body, in turn, act as our compass and bridge into the sphere of the unknown — where the *electric* body exists and functions.

People who have become *OLD* tell us, "Time seems to *fly;* and the older you get, the *faster* it flies!" Their day disappears before it has begun. Is this a figment of their imagination or is it reality? And if it is reality, by what measure do we scale this phenomenon?

We cannot measure the Time phenomenon in Third Dimension terms, for neither Time nor Space exist here, leaving us, once again, wrestling in the shadows of the *unknown*—a Fourth Dimension world where we are totally dependent on our intuition—our sixth sense.

We must invoke our *intuition* to measure the passing of Time because it passes at the **subatomic** level of our existence—the level of the invisible "electric" body. Therefore, it stands to reason that Time DOES pass more quickly for the person who is catabolic, who has passed their anabolic peak, and whose cells are aging at an *accelerated* rate.

Time passes slowly when we are YOUNG—when we are climbing up the anabolic side of the pyramid. When we are young, we experience *slow* Time. After we reach our anabolic peak, we experience *fast* Time as we *slide* down the catabolic side of the pyramid (see page 198).

We have arrived at the answer we have been seeking. It is the *thesis* of this book, summarized as follows: **Slowing the aging process slows the passing of Time and transcends the physical and material world. And though the physical body is confined in Time and Space, the *electric* body is FREE. It is an extension of the *self* and a fixture of the unknown Fourth Dimension where our mind and emotions are but windows to our soul. The electric body is our spirit and our soul.**

**Buying Time!** By stopping our bio-electric clock, we buy Time. Time provides us the opportunity to exchange an old body for a young one and is the equivalent of *recycling* the sand in an hour glass. This recycling process does NOT mean that we relive our earlier experiences. Rather, it means that we recycle Time itself. This is what is meant when we talk about becoming *YOUNG AGAIN!*

**PREVIEW:** *Our next chapter deals with rejuvenation of the bio-electric body through rest, fasting, and avoidance of self-imposed physiologic stress.*

**Bran Muffin Recipe:** 1/4 C honey, 1/3 C blackstrap molasses, 1 tbsp. non aluminum baking powder, 1 egg, 2 C unbleached white flour, 1/2—1 C water, 1 C bran, 2 tbsp. olive oil, 1/4 C sesame seed, 1 C raisins, 1/4 C wheat germ, 1/2 C chopped walnuts, perhaps a little pumpkin pie spice. Recipe makes six muffins. Bake @ 400° until medium brown. Mix/stir ingredients lightly. Do not knead.

**Taoism & Taoist™ Super Food**

Ancient Chinese Taoists (pronounced *Dowists*) viewed man as a small reflection of the universe. They perceived that ***cyclic*** change governs all living things. They laid down principles and correlations that described the effect of Nature on man and the response of man to Nature. They described these principles in terms of ***Yin*** and ***Yang***.

Taoist Masters believed that Five Elements describe the natural cycle of life and that man follows Nature's *cyclical* patterns through the "universe within."

Herbals were formulated to help man adapt to nature. Taoist Masters strove for *total* balance and harmony, promoted *self-cultivation*, thought enhancement, *shen* clearing, and *jing* building through manipulation of the Five Elements. Their discoveries are now confirmed by modern advanced physics.

The **Wood** Element represents the liver and gallbladder which control emotional harmony and the smooth flow of Chi (energy) necessary for a strong nervous system and the clearing of toxins from the body. The **Fire** Element is represented by the heart and small intestine and addresses the blood, lymph, and cerebral systems, plus physical and mental health and growth. The **Earth** Element represents the stomach and spleen and *extracts* and *separates* pure from the turbid within the body. The **Metal** Element represents the lung and colon and is said to dominate respiration and maintain defensive Chi (the immune system). The **Water** Element represents the kidney and bladder systems. Taoists believed that *Jing* (the very *essence* of life) is within body water and is expressed as hormonal and reproductive systems responsible for maintaining youthfulness and glandular function.

Taoist philosophy teaches that the body has the power to ***regenerate*** itself when stress (physical or mental) occurs. Taoists believe that the body is designed to run on whole food. They teach that *accountability* underwrites superior health and is reflected by the "universe within."

Through Taoism, people achieve ***enlightenment*** through balance, awareness and expression of the *person* within. Enlightenment and truth bring *understanding*. Taoist™ SUPER foods, colon therapy and juicing restore health and speed rejuvenation (see Source Page 384).

**Taoist™ SUPER food are 3500 year old formulations in racemized™ form.**

**Especially For You!**

*Young Again!* was written to help people understand the forces in their lives that **CHEAT** them of health and happiness—forces that **CONTROL** them and **LURE** them to an early grave.

The author has endeavored to use examples that are meaningful. Every effort has been made to help the reader develop a practical foundation in the *recognized* sciences and in the *para*sciences.

The reader is reminded that knowledge must be **applied** and that the return of health and rejuvenation requires much **time, focus and patience.**

Sometimes rejuvenation isn't fun. But if you are willing to devote your energies to this worthy goal, you will be rewarded beyond your greatest expectations.

Each day brings new opportunities to make "healthy" choices. Each step in the right direction brings improved health and slows physical degeneration. Each day is the first day of the **rest of your life.**

***Young Again!*** is a statement, an offer and a model all in one. It is the product of the author's personal life experiences, observations, philosophy and lifestyle. It was NOT written to satisfy pretentious *experts.*

The author is not an "expert." *Experts* claim to have answers, but they can't demonstrate proof in their own lives. They suffer from dis-ease despite their knowledge. Their *magic bullets* do not save them. They talk the talk, but they don't know how to walk the walk.

Medical science will not be fond of this book. They will quote chapter and verse in *defense* of themselves. They may scorn and belittle—even accuse the author of oversimplification. They will demand "scientific proof," and their demands will be ***ignored.***

This book was written for those who seek results rather than *endless* debate. It's contents can benefit anyone who is seeking TRUTH.

Remember, old age is not fun. It is not a joyous process. People age through **ignorance**. Ignorance is a lousy excuse. **You can do better.**

**Health & sickness is a matter of choice.**

**A person's mind changed against their will is of the same opinion still!**

# 32

# Rest & Fasting

*"Dine with little, sup with less; do better still: sleep supperless."*
Benjamin Franklin

We dig our grave with our teeth! Powerful words—and true! Is the problem what we eat? Do we eat too much? Do we eat too often?...or all of the above?

The deleterious effects derived from eating the wrong things have already been discussed. Now let us look at the *degenerative* problems that spring from *other* dietary habits—habits that accelerate the aging process.

### Food a'Plenty

Americans live in a country where food is plentiful and inexpensive. We have become accustomed to treating our dietary habits with total indifference. As children, we are encouraged to eat as much as we want, to gorge ourselves where less would do, to snack between meals and particularly at bed time. We are taught that food is food. We believe that hunger is a signal that it's time to eat. We think a full belly is better than a lean one. We carry our beliefs and habits into adulthood—and eventually to the grave.

It is unfortunate that bio-junk food has become the dietary norm. But it is our failure to develop *dietary discipline* regarding *what, when* and *how much* to eat that clouds the issue and **compounds** the problem.

## Food-Induced Stress

When we are physically tired, mentally fatigued or spiritually depressed, we think nothing of getting additional sleep. After all, sleep is considered *normal;* and everyone accepts this at face value.

Yet, few people realize that the vital organs also need rest. When we eat too much, the organs are *forced* to process that extra food. Overeating stresses the glands. Digestion is NOT a voluntary activity. We eat, and the vital organs react. If we eat too much or too often, they become *hyper* stimulated, leading to exhaustion, overload, and crisis.

Digestive tables shown earlier indicate that the body requires a certain amount of time to digest food. **Digestion is influenced by stress, physical activity, food quantity, liquid intake, time of day, how often food is eaten, enzyme and saliva production and the condition of the TERRAIN.**

Vigorous exercise should be avoided for one hour after eating a meal. The body needs time to begin digestion before it can transfer the blood *away from* the abdominal area. This explains the energy drain experienced after a meal. The heavier the meal, the more we experience a drain on energy. If the meal is loaded with toxic substances like food additives, soy or canola, salt and processed sugars, energy drain and free radical formation can be substantial. Snacking creates the same effect as overeating and denies the vital organs rest.

## Pot Belly

A distended stomach is seen when the gut hangs over a man's belt line or fills a woman's pelvic area. People refer to abdominal excess as "fat," but distension (stretching) of the connective tissues that anchor the visceral organs AND a congested, constipated colon are the real problems. In the case of older people, spinal compression and forward extension of the visceral organs [those organs of the abdominal (visceral) cavity which include the liver, kidneys, adrenals, intestines, spleen, pancreas, ovaries, prostate and bladder] occurs due to settling of the spinal column (see the skeletal depiction of the dowager's hump on page 100).

The gut (small intestine) and colon (large intestine) are held in place by connective tissue called the *mesentery* (apron). Over time, due to the accumulation of mucoid matter and gravity, the bowel becomes heavy, overly bulky and *stretches* the mesentery beyond normal—producing the pot belly effect.

Colon therapy combined with lymph activity restores tone to the viscera and connective tissues (see Source Page 384 and diagrams on page 366).

If you are older and if you are SHORTER than you once were, hanging and stretching are **mandatory** procedures. I recommend hanging from a bar, rafter, beam or tree branch several times a day. Start slowly if you are older. Hang for five seconds, then ten and so on until you can hang for several minutes.

The idea of hanging is to s-t-r-e-t-c-h the joints, the connective tissues (ligaments, tendons, muscles), and open the spinal column to blood and lymph flow so it can be rebuilt. In other words, get oxygen and nutrients in, fluids and waste out. Use SOC™ capsules to rid your joints of pain, restore limberness to your joints and dissolve scar tissue, and use racemized™ hormone precursors to encourage new tissue growth.

Do lymph activity every day. Do stretching exercises. Lift weights. Get into colon therapy. Learn about yoga and Pilates. Drink BEV™ or some kind of filtered water. Plant a garden. **Train your mind.** Detox, detox, detox! Do these things and you will get your life back and get to live it over again in THIS lifetime. Your author plans to make it to 250 years.

*Think of the good things people could accomplish with hindsight! Think of all the exciting things the future holds! Life should be a celebration!* ***Life will be easier the second time around.***

## Gluttony

"Gluttony" is an old word. As a child, I was taught that gluttony was a sin against the sixth commandment. Whether gluttony is a sin is not the issue here. What is a concern is the *premature* old age and death that result from gluttony. When we eat beyond *minimum* satiety (please review chapter nine), we overload the system with waste, free radicals, and more. Avoid liquids with meals. Proper chewing eases food-induced stress and the tendency towards obesity. Racemized™ products like DiSororb Aid™, R/HCI, and Yucca Blend™ complete the job.

"Gluttony" is the act; obesity is the effect. Gluttony is one of the primary reasons industrial man is dying of degenerative dis-ease. Gluttony may be driven by genuine hunger, but it's usually the product of "true" dietary starvation. The quickest way to rid yourself of the need to eat is by getting some real nourishment from real food. Certainly the Young Again™ SUPER foods shine in the nourishment arena.

## Space Your Meals

The body was not meant to be under constant dietary load twenty-four hours a day. The organs require rest and an occasional day off for rejuvenation. The glands **must** be allowed to rest between meals. Late night meals and snacking deprive the body of the vital energy it needs for deacidification, tissue repair and growth—all of which occur primarily during the sleep cycle. **Mineral absorption occurs at night.**

*Plants have a cycle too. They manufacture food during the day, but they grow and repair their tissues at night. Visit your garden in the wee hours of the morning and "hear" the corn growing. It crackles and pops. During the day the Earth exhales. At night it inhales. The "dew point" has special meaning. When the dew forms on the ground, plant and microbial activity are at their PEAK!* **Rhythm is vitally important to good health.**

## Sleep • Oxygen • Detoxification • Glycolysis

The body feels refreshed after a "good" sleep because it has processed acid wastes and neutralized abnormal energy fields. Sleep should be a time of energy transformation.

Neutralization of lact**ate** occurs during the sleep cycle. Anyone who has experienced muscle soreness and fatigue from over exertion has experienced the effects of lactate formation in the muscles. *(SOC™ capsules can be taken before or after hard physical work to avoid and ease muscle soreness. SOC™ also speeds healing and reduces scar tissue formation when used prior to any type of surgery.)*

Lactate formation occurs in the early stages of the sugar burning process we call glycolysis. Lactate formation is the result of **insufficient** oxygen in the cells and **incomplete** burning of the sugars. Lactate is a transitional waste product. Rest and sleep provide the vital energy needed to *recycle* lactate. In other words, lactate formation is the product of a system that has gone *anaerobic* at the cellular level.

The ***ate*** in lactate tells us that lact**ate** is the salt of lactic acid. Salts are *bound* energy. To prevent lactate formation and fatigue, drink plenty of water with racemized™ sea minerals every 30 minutes during work or exercise along with some SOC™. Lactate is a byproduct of *fermentation*—just the same as in alcohol production.

**Alcohol is made by "anaerobic" fermentation. Kombucha uses "aerobic" fermentation to produce high amounts of glucoronic acid for healing sick bodies.**

Oxygen deficiency in the cells stops the conversion of glucose into the energy molecule ATP by the mitochondria.

Oxygen deficiency sabotages energy production in the *Krebs and Citric acid cycles and in the Electron Transport Systems* (where the mitochondria produce ATP). Aerobic exercise, BEV™ and Medical Grade Water™, use of the L/CSF™ machine, rebounding and lymph rolling heal sick bodies through waste movement in the lymphatic system and by increasing tissue oxygen levels.

### Sleep • Digestion • Metabolic Hype

During the sleep cycle, the body uses large amounts of VITAL energy to heal and grow. Sleeping on a full stomach sabotages the deacidification process and blocks healing. *Normal* digestion slows or comes to a halt. We wake up with that *full* feeling—sluggish, not well rested!

Even good food can create a toxic condition if taken before retiring. Sleeping on a full stomach brings on *anaerobic* fermentation and foul gas. **An**aerobic conditions produce **putrefaction** of undigested food in the intestines and releases toxic waste molecules. Avoid late night meals and bedtime snacks if you can. But if you can't, you had best use some DiSorb Aid™, Yucca blend™, and R/BHCI™ with your snack.

**Poor digestion and absorption produces excesses in the system and acid wastes. Illness and dis-ease result.**

Adequate sleep and dietary rest are important ingredients for good health. Failing to get enough rest is no different from using a battery powered golf cart during the day and forgetting to recharge it at night, with one notable difference. **We are not golf carts!** Without adequate rest and deacidification, the body is forced to draw upon its energy reserves. This kind of lifestyle produces stress and metabolic "**hype.**"

Just because we have the ability to "drive" our body is not justification for doing so. The ability to psyche the body with the power of the brain (Fourth Dimension energy over Third Dimension reality) is a "dangerous" *skill* that comes with a very high price tag.

### Discipline • Spacing Of Meals • Snacking

Learning not to overeat requires *discipline*. Spacing meals requires *discipline*. Putting *rhythm* in our lives requires discipline. Health and rejuvenation require DISCIPLINE, good food, proper digestion and adequate hydration.

Allow four hours between meals—including snacks. Snacks are *mini* meals. They interrupt the body's rest break. When we snack, we become a *slave labor boss;* and we force the glands to overwork and become exhausted. How would you like it if every time you tried to get some needed sleep, some inconsiderate person woke you up? So it is with frequent eating. The smart solution to *snacking* is to incorporate the SUPER foods into your diet. In their presence, hunger vanishes. Your author can attest to this fact by going from 3-4 meals a day to someone who juices in the am and only eats a regular meal once a day. I'm simply NOT hungry, yet I look and feel better than I ever have in my 58 years.

Children are *growing* and *repairing* tissue so they must eat more. But children today are malnourished because the food is so poor. Children MUST have nutritious food, good water and racemized™ sea minerals. Well nourished children don't snack incessantly. All soft drinks MUST be stopped. Their long term effects are WORSE than alcohol, but in a different way. **Do NOT encourage children to develop habits that will *lure* them to an early grave. Bad habits become an unhealthy lifestyle. Be a good example.**

Spacing of meals provides *rhythm* and *control* of dietary habits. Nourishment *tempers* hunger. Home-grown food and the alternative SUPER foods mentioned are examples of foods that build strong bodies and minds.

Nourishment and deacidification strengthen will power. Will power is the product of healthy body and mind. A sick body has little will power. Smoking, drinking, gambling, drugs, gluttony, obesity, etc., have their roots in malnourishment and acidification of the tissues.

Nutritionally deprived people constantly cry for *nourishment.* They snack and eat their way into old age and hasten their appointed destiny with the grave—*decades* ahead of schedule. They are *early birds* in the truest sense.

## Rhythmicity

One of the secrets of health and longevity is the establishment of regularity in our lives. Rhythm is so terribly important that reversing the aging process will *stall out* if we ignore this simple secret.

*Rhythmicity* is rhythm in the sense of the ebb and flow of energy in our daily life. Up each morning at the same time, meals taken within 1/2 hour of the appointed times, plenty of water, exercise, going to bed at the same time, sleeping for 7-8 hours—EVEN if you can operate on less. Practice rhythmicity, and the balance of the lessons in this book will become patterned habit and easy to maintain. **Health and vitality flow on the wires of rhythmicity. The lifestyle of Dr. Paul Bragg and his daughter, Patricia speaks for itself!**

## The Miracle of Fasting

*This is a true story, told exactly as it happened. I hope you will enjoy it.*

It was May 1, 1993, Santa Barbara, California. I was attending a dinner party following a publishing seminar when a cute lady approached me and said, "Did you get one of my apple cider books?"

I answered in the negative, and as she proceeded to hand a book to me, I got a square look at her face and said, "Who are you?"

"I'm Patricia Bragg!" she answered.

At that moment, I knew that the path upon which Bob McLeod—who you met in chapter one—had set me adrift twenty-two years before had reached its destination. I was standing before the daughter of the Great Wizard, Paul Bragg!

"Please come sit down," I said. "We must talk!"

I began, "Your father saved my life. I cannot tell how thrilled I am to meet you! You look exactly like your picture in your father's book on fasting."

So we talked and laughed. The following day I was able to sneak away long enough to visit the Bragg Worldwide Headquarters in Santa Barbara, where I stood in awe of a twenty foot high painting of the wonderful Wizard, Paul Bragg.

"How did your father die?" I asked. "I have heard several rumors and I am anxious to know the truth."

"He died in a surfboard accident in Hawaii. He drowned. They could not revive him!"

"Please tell me, what was his age?"

"My father was 97 years *YOUNG!*—and if he had not died when he did, I have no doubt he would have lived to be 125 years young!" she snapped.

"What is your age, Patricia?" I asked with a lump in my throat.

"I am like my father. I AM AGELESS!"

And so she was. Sweet! Cute! And very much a senior citizen by the calendar, but you would never, ever guess! Patricia looked to be in her late forties, but had the energy of a teenager.

Paul and Patricia are PROOF positive that each of us can experience agelessness. I am forever thankful for getting to meet this wonderful human being—the daughter of the Great Wizard himself. Like her father, she has helped millions of people. I am proud to continue in their footsteps.

Patricia's father, Paul Bragg, was a Wizard of a man. A recent U.S. Surgeon General (the "highest" *official* medical doctor in the USA, politically speaking) made the comment,

"Paul Bragg did as much to help the health and vitality of Americans as any medical doctor." Considering the source, that is one very big compliment.

Many readers will be too young to remember Paul Bragg. When you read his wonderful book, *The Miracle of Fasting*, be sure you are *wide awake!* Bragg speaks simple TRUTHS and in simple terms. He was a "low tech" Wizard, but a Wizard just the same.

Thanks Dr. Paul C. Bragg and Patricia Bragg to whom I dedicated this book. Because of them, I am *Young Again!*

**PREVIEW:** *Our next chapter deals with the world's MOST toxic element, and it's in YOUR body and drinking water. You will also learn what you can do about it.*

**Meat Eating vs. Vegetarianism**

Please turn to page 367 for a common sense discussion of a volatile health issue. As for your author, *"I've been there! I've done both!"*

**Acres USA**

This monthly publication has had **profound** influence on my life. If I could only receive one publication, this is the one. Order a trial subscription, and see what I mean. Call (800) 355-5313. I accept your thanks in advance.

**Ear Problems!**

From ancient times to the present, people have had trouble with their ears. Ear wax, infections, water in the ear, pain, poor hearing, ringing and so on.

If the problem is in the outer ear (wax, etc.), the Bio-Magnetic Dental Irrigator can double as a ear cleaning tool. To use, put one drop of Taoist™ Ear Oil in each ear in the evening before bed. Upon rising, fill the irrigator with warm water, turn down the pressure knob to low, and go to work while leaning over the sink. When you dislodge the wax, you are done. Repeat if necessary.

If the problem is INSIDE the ear (severe pain, ringing, fever and pressure), take OX™ & R/C™ and do colonics daily until problem stops. If a child is sick, give the child an "enema" several times a day.

Over 600,000 adenoidectomies and tonsilectomies (ear/tonsil surgeries) are performed each year as a result of ear infections. 50% of all children's surgeries and 25% of hospital admissions are due to ear related complications.

# 33

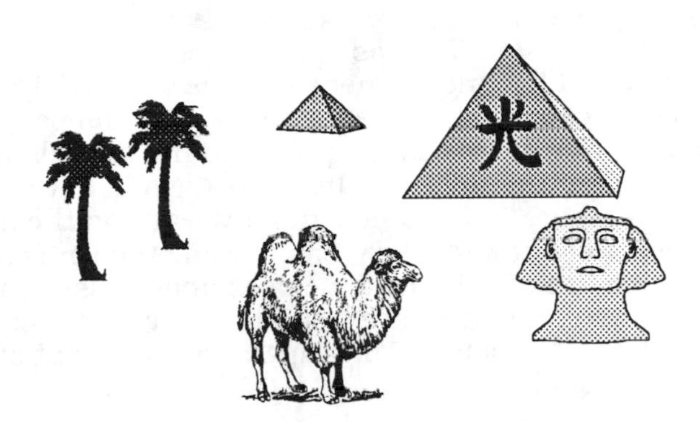


## The Camel Or The Palm Tree?

*"Truth will come to light; murder cannot be hid."*
Shakespeare

"Kibyo" is Japanese for *strange disease.* Kibyo described the series of strange conditions that appeared during the 1950's in the small fishing village of Minamata on the southwest coast of Kyushu, Japan.

The conditions came to be known as "Minamata Disease." In 1957 mercury was discovered to be the toxic agent behind the strange symptomatic conditions and SIGNS.

Cats went crazy. Crows fell from the sky. People experienced dizziness and tunnel vision; their nervous systems failed; numbness was experienced in their extremities; and their legs burned. ALL life forms in the area suffered from the high mercury levels in the air, water and soil. The mercury came from an industrial plant up the coast from Minamata.

### Mercury & Aging

Mercury is the **MOST** toxic substance known to man! It is the only elemental metal that occurs naturally in the "liquid" state. Sometimes it is referred to as *quicksilver* due to its elusive nature. A broken thermometer allows mercury to splatter and run. It **evaporates** like water!

Mercury is of importance to the "aging" story because of its toxic nature and ubiquitous (everywhere) presence in the environment. It has been used in industry for several hundred years. The fur industry used mercury to process animal furs as far back as the time of the Industrial Revolution. Mercury poisoning was diagnosed as long ago as 1865, but it continued to be used by the fur industry into the 1950's!

The expression "mad as a hatter" refers to the tremors and insanity that hat and garment workers suffered. Industrialists did NOT care what happened to the common people. If a doctor dared to create a fuss, he quickly found himself without a license to practice medicine. In those days, a hat worker's widow was given a "gold watch" and a wreath on the casket. Today, we get neither. Mercury has become the equivalent of industrial bio-junk food. Medicine goes about assigning new names to mysterious dis-ease conditions—usually with the word "syndrome" attached. The Japanese equivalent of syndrome is "kibyo!"

**About Mercury**

Mercury has the ability to cross the placental barrier and deform the unborn fetus. It lodges in our vital organs and short circuits their activity. Mercury poisoning leads to disintegration of the nervous system and damage to the kidney's nephrons (blood filters). **Mercury poisoning usually occurs slowly over many years. It is involved in thousands of diseases plaguing millions of people.**

Acute mercury poisoning leads to vomiting, bloody diarrhea, nervous tremors in the extremities, eyelids and tongue. People with moderate poisoning seldom are aware of what ails them. Fatigue, insomnia, headaches, nervous anxiety, and loss of appetite are common side effects. Erythism (redness as in blushing of the face) is a characteristic symptom of mercury poisoning. So is night time leg pain in older people.

Sources of mercury poisoning include tuna fish, shell fish, water based house paint, insecticides, fungicides (bathroom fungus cleaners), wall sizing and tens of thousands of products that people come into contact with everyday.

Mercury is so *ubiquitous* that it is in ALL commercially produced food. The only way around it is to grow your own food. The microbes in a healthy soil *denature* mercury, lead and toxic organic metals and chemicals. The use of Bio-Grow™ soil rejuvenator (a biodynamic right-spin soil catalyst) is the fastest way to develop a healthy right-spin soil environment.

The GREATEST source of mercury in the United States comes from tap water. Mercury—in the form of mercuric acid salt—is widely used to treat public water supplies. Recent events bear out the severity of the problems we face. For instance, during the fall of 1993, hundreds of innocent people became sick and some DIED from drinking tap water that was contaminated with pathogenic (dis-ease related) bacteria.

The cities were Milwaukee, Washington, D.C. and Chicago. We do not know if more cities were involved because these things are hushed up quickly to prevent panic. In Milwaukee people died! The authorities blamed the bacteria, but the problem was related to mercury.

Here is the problem. Cities throughout the country are treating water with **mercuric acid** to kill the bacteria. This is done "without" public knowledge and is vehemently denied by authorities. Mercuric acid is used during the "warm months" when demand outruns water processing capability. Population growth creates additional pressure. Cities do NOT have time to treat the water before pumping it into the distribution lines, so they use **mercuric acid** (remember "mercurochrome" used on cuts and scratches?).

Cities use the same dirty sand filters over and over. They seldom change them! Instead, they use mercuric acid to kill the bacteria and viruses that breed in them and send the water to the gullible public to drink! Municipal water filters deserve more attention than a cat litter box—which we change regularly. We know better, and so do our water officials.

In the Fall when the hot season is over, cities stop using mercuric acid. If they miscalculate, the results are sick and dead people from an explosion of pathogenic bacteria in the filters and lines—like what happened in Milwaukee, Washington, D.C., and Chicago.

Without mercury, public water supplies are a potential source of an epidemic of pathogenic dis-ease. With mercury, the people are drinking their way to dis-ease, old age and an ugly death. Mercury creates lots of sick people to fill the hospital stalls—all of them demanding a *magic bullet!* Sick people are good business.

The best solution to the water dilemma is to equip your home or apartment with either BEV™ water unit so you can avoid the chemicals and avoid developing leaky gut syndrome which these chemicals ultimately produce.

**SOC™ has a VERY strong affinity for heavy metals and can be used by anyone to rid the tissues of mercury—even when amalgam fillings are still present.**

Water pollution in public water supplies is a "time bomb" waiting to manifest as dis-ease in the bodies of people who are ignorant enough to drink it. AVOID WATER FROM PUBLIC WATER SUPPLIES!

**Deregulated Death • Bombs & Munitions**

The U.S. Department of Agriculture has established a **"zero"** tolerance for mercury. I repeat, a ZERO tolerance! At the same time, the FDA has established a "safe" level for mercury. Safe levels imply safety and a watch dog function. People feel protected. Nothing could be further from the truth.

Federal and state regulatory agencies are *supposed to* enforce food and water purity laws. Powerful interests see to it that mercury's use in industry goes unrestricted. **Mercury is a $6,000,000,000 (billion) dollar industry!** "Corporate" yellow fringe flag government refuses to regulate it. So much for that government "safety net" you thought was there!

Mercury is divided into three classes. Elemental vapor (mercury evaporates like water), mercurous/mercuric salt solutions like mercurochrome (for minor cuts, now outlawed)! and mercuric acid and **a third form that is found bonded to food "proteins."** Every reaction in the body requires **protein** enzymes to occur. Mercury shuts them down and blocks vital biochemical reactions.

"Corporate" U.S. Government, via the Atomic Energy Commission (AEC), is the biggest supplier of mercury to industry. After WWII, they held huge stockpiles of mercury. Government policy shifts allowed this "silver death" element into the market. They know about mercury toxicity, but they dumped it on the market anyway.

**The bombing of the Oklahoma City Federal building in April of 1995 may have involved the use of large amounts of mercury to accelerate the explosion. Pictures of the bombed building show that the explosion GAINED velocity as the force went up the face of the building—instead of dissipating as in non-mercury related explosions.**

Agriculture uses massive amounts of mercury in the production of FOOD! In 1914, chemists discovered that mercury was an effective fungicide. Over six million pounds of mercury have been used in FOOD production in the past forty years, and over two-hundred million pounds since 1900.

Mercury is used to treat crop seeds, and in the paper industry as a slimicide. **AEROBIC** bacteria convert industrial mercury into highly toxic forms like ***methyl* mercury.** Methyl mercury is difficult to remove from body tissues. Your author uses SOC™ capsules, racemized™ algae, PAC™, colon therapy, and fresh vegetable juices. Homeovitic remedies are used "later" to "erase" the **vibratory memory** of mercury from the tissues. SOC™ has a strong affinity for heavy metals. It takes about **10 years** to rid the body of mercury!

**Mercury Fillings In Teeth**

Dentistry has been promoting the use of mercury amalgam (so called "silver" fillings) for over one hundred years. In the mouth, bacteria convert elemental mercury into *methyl* mercury which "bleeds" into the tissues and goes about its dirty work quietly, producing ever new health *syndromes*.

Amalgam fillings are BIG business! Dentists are taught in dental school that amalgam fillings are non-toxic. **Dentistry likes mercury amalgams because they are a quick "drill and putty" operation.** The *ignorant* patient is told the only difference between gold and amalgam is the cost and appearance. Dentistry avoids using the word **"mercury"** and instead calls these mixed metal fillings *amalgams* or "silver." It is a sin to fill innocent people's teeth with the most toxic element on Earth. Its use renders *predictable* results—just as in the hat industry. Mercury amalgam fillings bring on S-L-O-W death. Professionals who install them claim ignorance and lack of "scientific proof," while their patients lose their health and lives.

Gold also creates problems, but of a different sort. Gold fillings and crowns are composites of dozens of different metals. Elemental metals are toxic to the body. These "anti-life" energy fields are measured in milli-volts (thousandths of a volt). They interfere with body metabolism.

If you have mercury in your mouth, do NOT remove it until you have prepared your system as outlined throughout this book. Removal is FAR more dangerous than placement due to a weaker immune system and an older patient. **I have seen many people sicken and suffer from mercury removal because they did NOT prepare. Allow 6 months minimum!**

NEVER, EVER go to a regular dentist for amalgam removal. They are antagonistic to the idea and they are careless in their technique. They will try to convince you that you have been hoodwinked. They will use the old, professional glass hand approach. AVOID THEM!

Be very careful to avoid johnny-come-lately dentists who are NOT certified holistic, biological dentists! If the dentist also offers amalgam fillings on the pretense that some patients want them, you have the wrong dentist!

Racemized™ algae bonds-to and removes heavy metals—like mercury—from the tissues. So does fresh vegetable juices and SOC™. PAC®s act as a **buffer** to protect the thyroid and liver from mercury damage during removal.

**The Camel Or The Palm Tree?**

Today, more than ever, people are faced with the

dilemma of choosing between conventional medicine and holistic therapies. Making the right choice is easy. Let me emphasize "false" alternatives with a childhood story.

When we were children, one of our favorite jokes involved finding an empty Camel cigarette package and showing it to whomever we could get to listen.

"Assume you are in this picture, and it is raining cats and dogs and you must run for cover. Would you get under the palm trees or would you get under the camel?" (On the face of the package is pictured a camel, some palm trees, and several pyramids.)

Some people answered they would take cover under the palm trees, while others said they would take their chances under the camel.

Regardless of the answer, the person was wrong. You see, we did what conventional medicine does to *desperate* people. We only offered two alternatives, and **BOTH of them were bad choices!** The smart answer was to go around the corner of the package and take lodging in the hotel!

In the world of conventional medicine and expert opinions, you are constantly faced with "camel or palm tree" decisions. Do not allow yourself to fall for false alternatives in matters of health, or you will grow old and suffer miserably along the way. Heavy metal poisoning—be it from tap water, food, colloidal minerals or dental fillings—is serious business.

***Would you rather drink water that is contaminated with pathogenic microbes, mercury, sodium, chloramines and fluoride or water that is "safe" according to industry standards?"***

The answer to this camel or palm tree question is, **None of the above!** Do whatever you need to do to protect yourself from heavy metal poisoning and you will become *Young Again!*

**News:** The world's second biggest manufacturer of mercury amalgam has agreed to post ALL dental offices in California with signs WARNING patients about the carcinogenic, mutagenic and teratogenic effects of mercury—especially in children and unborn fetuses.

Scandinavian countries—along with Germany and other European countries—have BANNED mercury amalgam fillings. The American Dental Association and its lackeys are too damned proud and greedy to admit their mistakes!

### Dental Alternatives

Mercury removal requires that special protocols be followed for your safety. Composite plastic is the replacement material of choice. These fillings require more skill and time than "drill and putty" mercury fillings. If composites are done correctly, they have a long life.

Do not accept porcelain fillings. A dentist that tells you that composites don't hold up isn't doing them correctly. Price is not the issue here. Your health is! To find a holistic dentist, look in the yellow pages, call health food stores, ask around. Conventional dentists don't like these guys. Holistic biological dentists are hard to find. Call your author for guidance and help **before** amalgam removal. Do NOT remove your amalgams if you are female, older or in poor health. **Call for guidance.**

**PREVIEW:** *In our next chapter, you will learn about tobacco and how it relates to health and vitality. The American Indians knew the answer!*

### Red Flags

**Show me a lady with** a cold body, memory complaints, excess fat, thinning/graying hair, yeast/bladder infections, PMS, fibroid tumors, aching joints, receding gums and low energy **and I'll show you someone whose "terrain" is our of control. Show me a man who** is fat, impotent, lost his sex drive, has prostate troubles, low energy and gray or missing hair, **and I'll show you a man who is NOT in control of his body's terrain.**

### Take Time For 12 Things

Take time to **Work.** It is the price of success.
Take time to **Think.** It is the source of power.
Take time to **Play.** It is the secret of youth.
Take time to **Read.** It is the foundation of knowledge.
Take time to **Worship.** It is the highway of reverence and washes the dust of earth from our eyes.
Take time to **Help and Enjoy Friends.** It is the source of happiness.
Take time to **Love.** It is the one sacrament of life.
Take time to **Dream.** It hitches the soul to the stars.
Take time to **Laugh.** It is laughing that lightens life's loads.
Take time for **Beauty.** It is everywhere in nature.
Take time for **Health.** It is the true wealth and treasure of life.
Take time to **Plan.** It is the secret of being able to have time to take for the first eleven things.

## HELLO, THERE!

Few people comprehend the **"true"** state of their health. And only 1 out of 10 are willing to take responsibility for their lives and STOP the whining.

Some folks **rationalize** circumstances; others **utter** excuses and **blame** everything and anyone for their condition. Many simply give up and live out their lives.

I **can** help anyone who wants to experience aging reversal and perpetual good health, but only if that person is willing to do their part. Interestingly, what is done to **AVOID** serious medical problems and loss of good health is **EXACTLY** what is done to remedy the problem. *Truth cuts **both** ways!*

In **"my"** life, health food, vitamins, herbs, juice, yoga and exercise were not enough to keep the reaper away from my door—and these things **alone** will NOT keep the reaper away from **your** door, either.

Most alternative modalities stop short of the fundamental issues controling the body's terrain. High profile big-shot practitioner's make lots of noise, but they, too, grow old like their followers. The reaper **waits** at their door, too!

Results count, and the *Young Again Protocol*™ definitely produces results for anyone who is **short** on excuses and **long** on responsibility.

If you would like to experience RESULTS in your life, feel free to call and ask me for guidance. **But, please be willing to do YOUR part.**

It takes years to lose control of our lives. It takes **PATIENCE** to reverse the process called "aging."

Patience, friend! Patience!

**John Thomas**

# The "Sacred" Three Sisters

*"First, the Creator gave us tobacco."*
*"Kanonsionni-Kayeneren-Kowa"*
The Iroquois

*If you control the dietary health of a nation, you control the people. If, in addition, you control the creation of that nation's money supply, you have the perfect monopoly.*

When the white man came to the Americas, he discovered that the main staples of the Indian diet were corn, beans and squash. The Indians called these foods the "sacred three sisters."

The Indians understood the importance of these foods in their diet. They also understood the importance of another FOOD—a food which they held in the *utmost* esteem. That food was TOBACCO!

The Indians told the white man, *"The Creator gave us the sacred three sisters. But before the Creator gave us corn, beans and squash, He gave us TOBACCO!"*

The Indians considered tobacco *sacred.* It was considered sacred because the Indians had discovered tobacco's NUTRITIONAL characteristics. Their discovery was incorporated into their religious beliefs.

**The status of tobacco in the Indian psyche was based on DIETARY need, but it was respected on a religious level. Smoking was the extension of the dietary status tobacco held in Indian culture.**

When native peoples elevate certain foods and events to religious status, there is a reason. Unfortunately for millions of people, the white man failed to take his cues from Indian dietary habits and religious beliefs. The white man did NOT make the connection between diet and health until four-hundred and ninety-eight years later (1990). The connection was made by a lone individual named Tom Mahoney.

### Tobacco

Despite its negative image, tobacco has significance to the aging process AND to general health and vitality. Tobacco is **terribly** misunderstood by the American public. They know NOTHING of its therapeutic or dietary value because their eyes can't see through the smoke, not to mention the TRUTH that they have been denied. They have ONLY heard of the negative aspects of tobacco. They have been told nothing of the real tobacco story. **Their ignorance is NOT an accident!**

Prior to the discovery of America, Europeans did NOT grow or eat corn, beans, or squash. These important foods were absent from European diets. Dietary imbalances created the EXCESSES that plagued the white man and his "civilization."

The *Three Sisters* were taken back to Europe, and for a while people's nutritional status improved. Corn was easy to grow and became the "dominant" food staple of the poor. By the seventeen hundreds, corn's dietary dominance manifested as excesses and dis-ease throughout Europe, and particularly in the Mediterranean countries of Italy, Spain, Greece and Portugal. The condition of *excess* had no name—yet!

### Casal's Necklace

In 1735 the Spanish physician Casal described a disease condition by one of its key SIGNS. He called it *mal de la rosa.* This means "red sickness." People on farms who ate a lot of corn suffered the most. They typically had a red ring around their neck which came to be called *"Casal's necklace."* In the American South, corn's dominance among farmers and the poor caused the phrase "red neck" to come into usage.

In 1771 an Italian doctor described the SIGNS of an unknown dietary EXCESS condition when he wrote of "rough, painful skin." *Pellagra* is the English corruption of Italian and summed up the condition nicely. Until the 1900's, however, no connection was made between corn intake and the condition of EXCESS that had come to be called *pellagra.*

*Like most conditions, pellagra operates behind a cloak in the early stages. It includes loss of energy, weight loss and poor appetite. The four 'D's' dizziness, depression, dementia and delusion best describe pellagra's SIGNS. There are tens of thousands of people suffering from these SIGNS today.*

In the United States, similar dis-ease conditions occurred beginning in the 1850's. After 1859 when H. J. Heinz produced the first "canned" food, the problem grew worse. Canned food contains salt to keep down botulism. In addition, heat processing destroys and denatures food enzymes. This was the beginning of bio-junk food.

The Civil War wrought massive upheaval in people's dietary habits—especially farm people in the South. Excesses became very prevalent. Economic conditions were blamed, but *pellagra* had its roots in the shift from a *balanced* agricultural society to an unbalanced *industrial* one. The poor did not eat a balanced diet. They ate too much corn and not enough greens and proteins. An unbalanced diet produces EXCESSES in people, plants and animals—no matter what the food. *Excess* corn creates an acid pH condition with many side effects.

By the turn of the century, the dis-eases of pellagra and beriberi became widespread. Poor people were eating too much corn—hominy, corn meal, grits, and corn meal mush—especially in the South. (The South continues this practice to this day.) Worse, the corn being consumed was "bolted." Bolted corn has had the germ removed. The germ is what causes a seed to sprout and grow. It is the seed's LIFE force!

The food processing companies discovered that bolted, *de-vitalized* corn meal keeps better. It was one of the first "natural" bio-junk foods. Bolted corn meal is like white bread. Both were and are perceived by an ignorant public as *status* foods. Processed food became "value added" food and commanded higher prices and higher profits. People didn't realize they had been taken. They are **STILL** being taken.

Pellagra became *endemic* (related to certain geographic areas and diets). Tens of thousands of people suffered from *pellagra* and *beriberi*. In dogs, pellagra is called black tongue. These dis-eases could have easily been prevented IF the white man had payed attention to the Indian diet—which included tobacco. Tobacco contains the "entire" vitamin B-12 complex. Tobacco is very valuable FOOD!

**Non-hybrid, non-bolted corn is good food.** Too much corn, like anything, brings on excesses and acid driven dis-ease conditions in the body. Excesses are easily offset with a diet that includes fresh green leafy vegetables (alkaloids), high quality proteins and VARIETY. Digestive short falls and hormonal imbalances affect how the body responds to even the best of food—which brings us back to the "terrain."

*The Mexican custom of soaking corn in lime water offsets corn's acidity and prevents the incidence of pellagra in Mexican populations.* The custom was adopted from the Indians, along with the combining of corn and beans for dietary balance.

### The B-vitamin Story

The B-vitamins (B's) offset dietary excesses and do away with pellagra and beriberi by rebalancing the system. Specifically, "niacin" has been credited as the active pellagra cureative agent. **(This is NOT true, but for the time being, let us *assume* it is true.)**

Niacin is referred to as vitamin B-3. Niacin is involved in ALL of the body's metabolic pathways. These pathways are a very complex series of reactions that keep us alive, healthy and happy. The healthy *bio-electric* body is a reflection of strong activity in the reactions of these critical pathways.

Niacin contains two molecules, NAD (*nicotine* dinucleotide) and NADP (*nicotine* adenine dinucleotide phosphate). These substances are used in the Krebs and Citric Acid Cycles and the Electron Transport System where the energy molecule ATP is created, burned and converted into cellular lightning!

All of the B's, including niacin, are involved in the FUSION reactions of the gut and liver. The mitochondria need B's to produce energy to fuel the body, build, and repair the tissues, and to keep our immune system strong.

### B Vitamins • pH • Soft Drinks

The Indians knew about tobacco's life giving properties. Tobacco is the richest natural source of the B's in the world—nothing compares to it—**nothing**! Concentrations of the B vitamins run as high as 30%! When **"small"** amounts of green or dried tobacco are put into stews, beans, and salads, we get the B's. Care must be taken in the choice of variety. Most importantly, fresh lemon juice or apple cider vinegar MUST be used to bring green tobacco within digestion range.

The pH of edible tobacco is Ph 10-11. Lemon juice and vinegar have a pH of 2. Stomach acid (HCL) is between pH -1 and +1. For each # up or down the scale (pH 7 is neutral, above is alkaline, below is acid), pH changes by 10 times. So, a pH of 10 is 1,000 times more alkaline than pH 7.

The side effects of soft drinks **loaded** with phosphoric acid are incomprehensible and go beyond just pH. When ingested, the body is **forced** to draw on bone calcium to "buffer" the acid introduced into the blood stream which skews the calcium:phosphorous ratio and *grossly* alters body physiology. When the side effects of *aspartame* sweetener (think red, white and blue swirl) are added, it's a wonder we don't just die!

### Synthetic vs. Natural B's

Real B vitamins are potent right-spin substances, even in small amounts. ALL commercial B-vitamins—unless derived from a natural FOOD source—are "synthetic" and left-spin, and require high doses to *mimic* the real thing.

REGARDLESS of claims on the label promoting "natural," unless B vitamins are food derived, they are **synthetic.** Synthetic niacin, B's, vitamins A, D, and E, are not the same as naturally occurring vitamins. The body is UNABLE to build healthy tissue with synthetic vitamins. When the body's supply of natural B's diminish, energy fusion reactions slow, and pernicious anemia (chronic shortage of oxygen carrying hemoglobin and red blood corpuscles) announces itself—and if ignored, will eventually bring down the immune system.

When we are sick, white blood cell count should go UP. If this fails to occur in response to a threatening condition, health is lost and dis-ease manifests. Without sufficient B's, the body CANNOT defend itself. Other excellent sources of "real" B vitamins are racemized™ Biogenic™ liver tablets, racemized™ algae, fresh green leafy vegetables and organic RED meat (if available). COBO-12™ is racemized creme form of vitamin B-12. It was specifically developed for women.

Green tobacco is loaded with B's. Green tobacco juice contains nicotine as an alkaloid. Dried tobacco contains nicotinic acid. Nicotinic acid, niacin, and nicotinamide are the acid forms of nicotine.

*Niacin* is promoted as the 'heart' vitamin, which is true IF it is from a natural food source. Natural niacin improves blood circulation and has anti-agglutination (anti-clumping) qualities. The *experts* tell us the FLUSH that accompanies niacin ingestion is due to its vitamin activity, but, this is NOT true. The *flush* effect is a mild "shock" type allergic reaction to *synthetic* niacin molecules and binders. Food sources are the only safe sources of B-vitamins.

Fresh organic greens are one of the best sources of the B's. Meat has limited amounts of the amino acid trytophan which the liver converts to niacin (60 mg of trytophan=1 mg of niacin). It is **most** suspicious that government authorities (FDA) outlawed this amino acid. Your author supplements his diet with Biogenic™ predigested, organic liver capsules from healthy range free animals and racemized™ algae.

Food alkaloids can be **poisonous** if you overdo. Alkaloids are nitrogen-containing compounds with "marker" physiologic properties. In other words, alkaloids make things happen in the body! Alkaloids are alkaline on the pH scale. Other alkaloid foods that we commonly eat are SPINACH and SWISS

CHARD which explains why many people have difficulty digesting them. These nutritious vegetables must be eaten or prepared with lemon or vinegar to be of benefit to the body. Other well known plant derived alkaloid drugs are digitalis (foxglove), belladonna (nightshade), lobelia, and marijuana. There are many kinds of Indian tobacco (Rustica, Lobelia, Aztec, etc.), but they are NOT for consumption. Do not confuse garden and commercial tobacco varieties with edible tobacco. (For seed, see the Source Page 384).

## The Niacin Story

Nicotine was named for Jean Nicot—the French ambassador to Portugal who sent tobacco seeds to Paris in 1550. By 1571, crude nicotine had been isolated. In 1828, purified nicotine was isolated. In 1867, *nicotine* was demonstrated to cure black tongue and pellagra, but it was **ignored**.

Natural nicotine is a FOOD nutrient source. Nicotine is EXTREMELY poisonous in **purified** or **synthesized** forms. When ingested in tobacco leaf form in small amounts, natural nicotine is not a problem. The Indians used it judiciously.

Nicotine in dried tobacco is not as toxic as we have been led to believe. If it were, people who smoke and chew would react and die on the spot. I would remind the reader that the mucous membranes of the respiratory tract are the avenue of choice where fast absorption is desired. Cigarettes are BAD news because of what is in them —and I am not talking about "tobacco!" Cigars do not share the dangers of cigarettes—and you can tell the difference by the smell.

## History Of Vitamin P-P

From the turn of the century, nicotinic acid was known by the disguised name of—"P-P factor," short for **P**ellagra **P**reventive. (This name was used until the generation then alive had died. Later, in the 1930's when the word "vitamin" was coined, P-P factor became known as "vitamin P-P.")

In 1899, Dr. Joseph Goldberger of the United States Public Health Service, launched a study into the effects of P-P factor and its relationship to pellagra. He dragged his feet for 16 years before he penned his study regarding the relationship between P-P factor and pellagra—something that had been known since 1867! This was NO accident. There was a reason for the delay.

In the meantime, pharmaceutical and oil industry interests went to work developing "synthetic" P-P factor. They did NOT want people to know they could treat pellagra and beriberi—and the spin-off dis-ease conditions that resulted from them—by **"growing"** their own cure in the form of tobacco. They did NOT want people to make the association between P-P factor, nicotine and tobacco.

Pharmaceutical interests figured out a way to manufacture SYNTHETIC "P-P" cheaply and easily using pyridine carbon rings from inexpensive charcoal and petroleum. Synthetic P-P factor is not the same. Real vitamin P-P spins right and supports good health. The other spins left.

**The pharmaceutical companies could NOT "patent" tobacco, but they could patent "synthesized" molecules. This is exactly what they did to women with their damnable hormone analogs contained in female replacement hormone drugs aand birth control pills.**

### Keep The People Confused!

"Niacin" is a *bogus* term. It is a coined name—like "canola!" It was invented by the medical establishment and pharmaceutical interests in the 1950's. It was coined to hide the fact that "nicotinic acid" (the acid form of nicotine in dried tobacco) is the *active* ingredient that balances the **excesses** that bring on pellagra and beriberi. **Certain "corporate" interests wanted control over America's health. There was a massive effort to VILIFY tobacco. That effort continues to this very moment.**

To create confusion and cover their tracks, the *experts* divided the B-12 vitamin complex into separate vitamin *factors*, called B-1 through B-12, and offerred a "fix" for people health problems using synthetic formulations.

After age 30, B-12 absorption drops dramatically as intrinsic factor secretion from the stomach wall collapses. Women run out of B-12 about 20 years before men due to loss of blood from the menstrual cycle. The cobalt atom is central to the hemoglobin molecule. Anemia issues reflect loss of cobalt, hence, the introduction of Cobo-12™ skin creme. Sublingual tablets and oral sprays do NOT solve the problem. B-12 is a **HUGE** issue for women because it affects virtually everything about their body physiology, yet it is not specific for any condition. B-12 shots are, at best, a synthetic "band aid!" *Intrinsic factor* is critical to "cold" FUSION reactions in man's gut and liver. Without B-12, pernicious anemia appears and the immune system takes a nose dive—especially in females!

### Cobalt & Health

Cobalt 60 is a *naturally occurring radioactive substance*

that must be present in order for life to exist. It is a crucial element in the fusion reactions in the *bio-electric* body of man and animal. It is involved in the production of the massive amounts of energy needed to keep us alive. Tobacco is loaded with cobalt blue. It is full of the B-vitamin complex. When we eat whole natural foods like fresh green leafy vegetables and tobacco—we provide the body with natural NAD and NADP, cobalt 60, and all of the B-vitamins needed to assist the mitochondria in the production of the ATP energy molecule.

Everyone should grow tobacco. It is legal to grow, so far. It can be eaten fresh or steamed and can be frozen or dried. The tobacco cultivar of which I am speaking is a beautiful plant. It stands 6-10 feet tall and 3 feet wide. The bugs will not eat tobacco. It is simply too potent.

### The Dilemma

On one hand, the public is told that tobacco and nicotine are bad for them. On the other hand, they are told that niacin and the B's are good for them. We are NOT being told the whole truth!

A long-term campaign began early in this century to get people to stop using tobacco in all forms. Today the effort is **massive!** The public is being DRIVEN into a frenzy over the smoking and chewing of tobacco. Every dis-ease condition from lung problems to cancer is being blamed on tobacco. **Tobacco is a scapegoat, and the experts are LIARS!**

The TRUTH of the matter is that less expensive, cheaper substances—synthetic substances—have been *substituted* in many tobacco products. People have been smoking and chewing TOXIC substitutes instead of the real thing! If you want to smoke, get a good cigar and go outside.

### Lies & More Lies

Personally, I do NOT like smoking or chewing. However, the issue here is not personal preference, but the fact that we have been lied to about something that can powerfully boost our immune system at a time when our food supply is deteriorating at a fantastic rate!

At the same time that tobacco is being vilified, the U S Government is "the" biggest grower of **hybridized** tobacco in the world! The implications are scary, but tobacco isn't the issue. What is the issue is the parallel "corporate" government called the "U"nited States Government, which is NOT the same as the "u"nited States of America. The former operates under the yellow fringe flag—a war flag; the latter under the Title 4

USC, Section 1 American Flag of Peace.

One reason tobacco is being socially vilified is to cover the deleterious side effects of billions of tons of toxic waste chemicals being burned in waste incinerators across the USA. Tobacco is the perfect cover. The pharmaceutical companies and "corporate" government are the problem. Improve your health by growing and eating tobacco in SMALL amounts, and by growing a home vegetable garden.

**The more something is believed to be true, and the greater the number of people who believe it to be so, the greater are the odds that it is NOT true!**

Old time farmers from Tennessee and thereabouts knew that if you wanted to have the finest horses in the world, you had to feed them TOBACCO! It seems to me that people count as much as horses. You can also use tobacco in **small** quantities in stews and salads. Freeze it green or dry it for later use during the year.

Tobacco was the American Indian's gift to the white man. We accepted the Sacred Three Sisters, BUT we ignored the greatest gift of all. Home grown tobacco strengthens the immune system, improves mitochondrial oxidation (energy production), and boosts metabolic reactions in the liver.

Pellagra's disappearance in 1935 had nothing to do with "enrichment" of the food supply with *synthetic* vitamins. Pellagra ceased to be a problem when **dietary variety** and **quality proteins** found their way onto people's dinner plates.

Today, people suffer with *subclinical* pellagra, living *marginal* lives and suffering from dietary excesses. When health breaks down, medical science says, ***"syndrome."*** The Japanese say, *"Kibyo."* Your author says, *"Old age!"*

**PREVIEW:** The title of our closing chapter comes from a poem by the same name. Please read it and think about its meaning.

## The Appendix

The appendix extends downward from the cecum in the most toxic area of the body (see page 46). It was put there to siphon away "**excess**" toxic energies from the cecum. The appendix is surrounded by clusters of lymph nodes called "Peyer's patch." The cecum is the end of the small intestine (gut) **and** the beginning of the large intestine (colon). It's where parasites hang out. It is 6 feet up from the anus and the **end of the road** when doing colon therapy. The medical folks consider the appendix a vestigial leftover, when, in fact, God put it there quite "on purpose!" People who have their appendix enjoy better health than those who don't.

## Making It Happen In Your Life!

Good health is a one step at a time process in reverse. Here are some basic steps to health and vitality.

1. Drink biologically-friendly water, and enough of it.
2. Complete the Young Again™ Tissue & Liver protocol.
3. Eat "good" food; avoid junk. Juice carrots & beets daily.
4. Avoid extremes. Seek balance in ALL areas of your life.
5. Get into the Young Again™ Colon Therapy Protocol.
6. Add some racemized™ super foods to your diet.
7. Restore/balance your hormones; open receptor sites.
8. Avoid all bio-junk food.
9. Get some aerobic exercise. Learn yoga and Pilates.
10. Use racemized™ hormone precursors EVERYDAY!
11. Stay away from doctors.
12. Get control of your mind.
13. Laugh! Love! Help others!
14. Don't buy into hate, anger, greed, envy, blame, etc.
15. Avoid medications, recreational drugs and alcohol.
16. Follow your instincts.
17. Visualize good health and the life you desire.
18. Refuse to buy into negative thinking, but be realistic.
19. *Erase* "vaccine" energy fields from your body.
20. Remove mercury and heavy metals from your tissues.
21. Develop a healthy, regular prayer and meditation life.
22. Use a rebounder or L/CSF machine daily.
23. Use a Biogenic™ lymph roller on your body 2x a day.
24. Use ETVC™ for energy; leveling blood sugars; burn fat.
25. Live today. Forget yesterday. Leave tomorrow alone.
26. Drink Kombucha tea & use $GH_3$+ to grow & darken hair.
27. Do load-bearing work everyday.
28. Simplify your life in every way possible.
29. Remove those mercury dental fillings from your mouth.
30. Use racemized™ sea minerals in your water.
31. Grow a garden! Grow a garden! Grow a garden!
32. Learn to use a pendulum and vibration chain.
33. Use Taoist™ SUPER foods for superb health.
34. Eat only organic food; don't buy food in grocery stores.
35. Don't consume soy or canola oils or soy products.
36. Give thanks each day to be alive.
37. Be patient with yourself; good health takes time.
38. Experience the *miracle* of rejuvenation.
39. Live life 90% correct; don't worry about the 10%.
40. Do **whatever it takes** to have & enjoy a healthy life.

**Young Again™ protocols produce results, while racemized™ products restore the "terrain."**

# 35

## Unforgiven

*"Most wonderful; with its own hands it ties*
*And gags itself-gives itself death and war*
*For pence doled out by kings from its own store.*
*Its own are all things between earth and heaven;*
*But this it knows not; and if one arise*
*To tell this truth, it kills him unforgiven."*

Tomasso Campanella, *The People*

Reversing the aging process is a one-step-at-a-time process that occurs one-day-at-a-time, in reverse.

Ask yourself these questions. *"Am I willing to take responsibility for my future and create the miracle of agelessness in my life? Am I willing to do whatever it takes to keep my youth or gain back the years I have lost? Am I willing to act in my own best interest today? Right now?*

Everything in life comes at a price. Pain! Suffering! Money! I hope you will join me and pick up your yoke no matter how difficult it may be. Never scream *"Uncle!"* Health and vitality belong to whoever is willing to take personal responsibility for their life.

May you become *Young Again!*

Sincerely,

John Thomas

## Hormones & De-acidification

**What's can I do to speed the aging reversal process?" is the question asked most.**

I respond, *"Water, fresh juice and colon therapy are the fundamentals. Next, is restoration of liver function and clearing acid wastes from the fat layer under the skin and clearing of stones and nails from the liver."*

It stands to reason that the body can't return to a more youthful condition when **wastes** have accumulated in the soft tissues and vital organ function is compromised!

The information and supplies needed to complete the Young Again Tissue and Liver Protocol™ come as a package. The process takes 8 weeks to complete. During this period, your lead a normal life.

The **only** time special provision is made is the night of the purge and the following morning. Most people do their purges on a Friday or Saturday night, so they can rest up the following day. It takes 2 weeks to prepare the body for the first of six purges, thereafter, they are performed weekly. There is **nothing** dangerous or **difficult** about the process. Think of Young Again Protocols™ as a means of "breaking out of **prison**"—your own prison!

**OF EQUAL IMPORTANCE** is balancing of the body's hormonal systems and "deblocking" of the hormonal receptor sites. Ideally, the 90 day hormone program is completed at the **same time** as the tissue and liver program. The function of each organ is dependent on the other organs.

Purging of waste **lightens** the load on the system. Women learn how to measure, map and restore their "hormone cycle" so they experience the equivalent of **30 years old and 7 months pregnant.** Meeting the body's thyroid needs is another HUGE female issue, as is vitamin B-12 shortfalls. Both problems are easy to remedy.

Tissue/Liver purging gets you out of **prison**, while the hormone program **"flips"** your breaker switches on your electrical panel so the *energy* can flow—literally!

The Young Again Protocol™ helps the body restore itself. Common "health" approaches are NOT ENOUGH to "recapture" the years that may have slipped away. **Damage control** is the first order of the day. Then comes the miracle of rejuvenation—complete with a slim, energetic, warm body with a full head of natural colored hair. Sex drive returns, problems diminish and go bye bye. See you there!

## FIR™ Saunas & FIR™ Energy

**The Earth is bombarded** with energy rays in the far infra red (FIR™) band of the light spectrum. Humans can't see "fir" energy, but it's there, nevertheless. Soldiers use special equipment and infra red light to see at night. The Japanese have DISCOVERED how to use "fir" energy to promote **health** and **longevity.**

"FIR™"*energy* is **right-spin** energy and is both safe and good for the body and the organs. The most practicable "fir" technology available is the **FIR™ Sauna** that for a few cents converts regular electricity into "fir" energy.

**FIR™ Saunas have captured your author's attention** because they fit into most any home or apartment, are easy and safe to use, and beam "fir" energy into the tissues **without** the need for steam or heat or lights.

"FIR™" energy is sometimes referred to as "soft heat." It breaks down toxic acids in the skin and sub cutaneous tissues. Translated, that means an end to aching joints, arthritis, deteriorating skin, winter time blues, old age complaints and body odor.

People THINK **"infra red"** is the same as a far infra red sauna, but it is **NOT** the same! Almost all saunas use infra-red technology. Infra-red energy has a 750-920 nanometer wave length, while the far infra-red spectrum is 920-1020 nanometers. FIR™ technology uses a specific proprietary wave length to provide health benefits. Use the **wrong frequency** and you don't get the benefits. Medical "cold" lasers with the wrong frequency produce no mitochondrial activity and no healing.

**Acid** waste produces inflammation, swelling and pain if allowed to build up in the tissues. **Excess** waste brings on degenerative dis-eases like cancer, arthritis, and diabetes, just to name a few. Older people move more freely and their temperament "sweetens" when they incorporate the use a FIR™ sauna into their daily regimen.

"FIR™" energy **stimulates** basal metabolic rate for people with degenerative disorders like arthritis, fibromyalgia, lupus. The therapeutic effects of "fir" energy is real. Heart and stroke patients can safely enjoy a FIR™ sauna, too! FIR™ saunas are well engineered, modular in design, easy to set up and move around, carry a 5 year warranty and have a beautiful cedar interior and beautiful, furniture grade oak exterior (see page 60).

FIR™ saunas come fully equipped with stereo speakers, and reading lamp and offer excellent value and improved health.

**"Unplug" from the medical system by "plugging-In" to a FIR™ sauna from *Young Again!***

**Dr. Bronner's castile soap (almond/pepermint) is a superb, and healthy, body soap that is available in health stores nationwide. Just don't use it on your hair, ladies, as it takes out perms and color.**

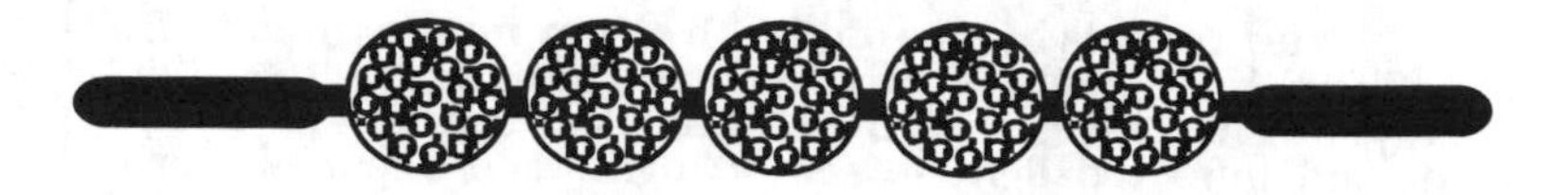

**Biogenic™ Lymph Roller**
**A Powerful Health Building Tool!**

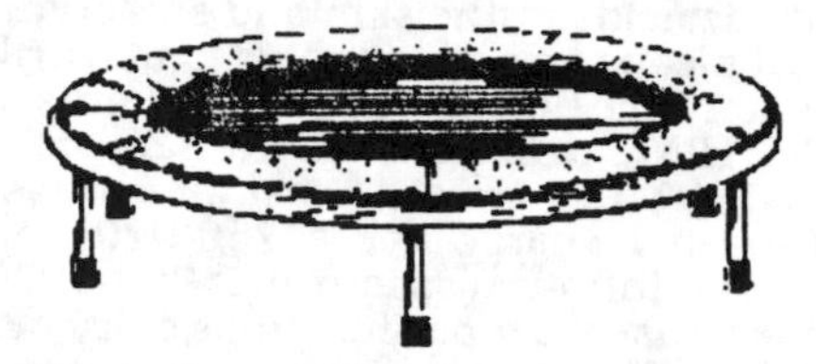

**Rebounder or Mini Trampoline**
**Available from many department stores.**

**The L/CSF™ machine**
**(See details in the Source Packet)**

## The Way It Is!

### Meat Eater or Vegetarian/Vegan

*"The savvy person is neither a heavy meat eater nor radical vegetarian. Balance is the key!"*

Deep within the heart of the health movement is the **dogma** that "vegetarians" are *smarter* and *healthier* than meat eaters, and "vegans" are smarter than BOTH. When sick, aging, meat eaters go "vegetarian," their health improves and they soon look and feel better.

**The question is** "why?" do heavy meat eaters enjoy improved health when they include fresh vegetables in their diet? Because meat eaters need **"balance;"** and fresh juice and live food provide balance.

Having been on **both** sides of the fence, first a heavy meat eater and then a radical vegetarian, your author **returned to his senses** many years later, mellower and smarter. Here is what I learned first hand.

1. All foods impose stress on the body.
2. How we digest food dictates the results.
3. Dietary balance is the key.

Like it or not, plants have eyes and ears and blood and parasites just like animals and people. They are every bit as much alive as "flesh and blood" creatures. Pulling a plant from the ground or cutting its branches and leaves is **NO** different than slaughtering an animal.

It is our inability to fully process "food" that dictates long term health and longevity—NOT whether we are meat eaters or *vegetarians*. **In fact, the less we eat, the longer we will live.** Fresh beet and carrot juice tremendously enhances people's health if used according to the Young Again Protocol™. And for those of you with "spiritual" hang-ups about eating meat, remember every living thing eats other living things. It's the way it is!

*Racemized*™ liver is a ZERO stress food because it is **predigested.** It is my **"meat"** of choice. Take 1-2 capsules 2x daily with racemized™ hydrogen chloride and DiSorb Aid™ to insure complete assimilation.

Vegetarians **enjoy** better health and maintain their appearance longer than people who eat too much meat. However, vegetarians DO experience secondary health problems due to lack of *variety* and the ***inability*** to PROCESS proteins (same problem for meat eaters) causing both to experience connective tissue problems. The "vegan" suffers far worse and ages much faster! **Here are a few tips.** Red meat is better for you than chicken. Fish is in between. Butter is good for you. Margarine is bad news. Soy and canola are deadly.

# The U.C.C. Connection

Throughout this book your author has alluded to and pointed out that our legal system is in serious trouble. The problem is that we have two **parallel** systems operating side by side—one constitutional, the other unconstitutional—the latter being the source of most of the troubles we labor under every day of our lives—as well as the social injustice emanating from the attorney controlled courts of "corporate" America.

Perhaps you are wondering why your author would raise this subject in a book about health and aging reversal? Because when TRUTH is cast aside, FRAUD takes its place; and the people and their children suffer unnecessarily and in vain.

Citizens labor under layers of mistruths and half truths relating to law, medicine and politics—**and the fastest way to expose a lie is to tell the truth.**

Want to learn about our so called "justice" and "money" systems and learn how they relate to the Uniform Commercial Code? Order the UCC Connection from Source Page 384. The Yellow Fringe Flag 12 hour cassette tape course is an eye opener, too!

**P.S.** Why do Americans salute the "flag" when they recite the pledge of allegiance? Want to better understand the events of September 11, 2001? Read *Barbarians Inside The Gates,* available from the Source Packet on page 384.

## Colon "MYTHS"

People have lots of misconceptions and hang-ups about colon therapy. Even your author labored under half-truths and mis-truths for over 25 years, until further examination caused John Thomas to "question" popularly held dogma on this health modality.

Here is what I discovered. An enema is NOT a colonic and neither is 5 gallons of water Colonics do NOT cause dependency, they do NOT steal your friendly flora or electrolytes, they do NOT cause constipation and lastly, the purpose of doing colon therapy is NOT to clean the colon.

The reader will find the rest of the pieces of the "riddle" throughout this book. If you would like to know **why** YOUR future includes colon therapy, call John Thomas and ask for an explanation about the Young Again Colon Protocol™.

**Sandra says, *"Its time to stop hanging onto your crap!"***

## *"Eat your vaccine, dear!"*

Did you know that government, the medical establishment, the pharmaceutical companies and the multinational food giants have hatched a devilish plan that will have disastrous effects on the health of people worldwide and especially in the USA?

The scheme involves using genetically altered fruits and vegetables to transport the likes of hepatitis B, polio, measles, mumps, tetanus, swine flue and rubella into YOUR body via the food you eat.

**Gene splicing of the food supply will produce millions of sick people. It will render "forced" immunization moot while it keeps the hospital rooms full.**

If you want to live a healthy, happy life, you MUST plant a garden, grow some fresh food in containers on your patio, share a community plot or hire someone to grow "safe" vaccine and chemical-free food for you.

Home grown food—even in small quantities—produces astounding effects on health. The best way to get into gardening is to start today! Normally it takes several years to build up soil and neutralize negative energy fields in the soil. Now, with the use of a product called Bio-Grow™, it is possible to convert dirt into live soil in one season. Bio-Grow™ creates a positive energy soil environment where microbes and plants prosper. This is a Fourth Dimension ENERGY product that parallels the effects of biodynamic agricultural techniques, but with less work. *Biodynamics I, II* and *Biodynamic Farm* help understand agricultural energy phenomenon (see Source Page 384).

---

### Hyper Active, Attention Deficit Children

These children all suffer from messed up livers, neuro receptor site "locked up," sluggish bowels, poor diet and insufficient water and electrolyte intake. To solve the dilemma, call and ask for some guidance. You already know drugs are NOT the answer, so ask for some help!

---

### End Your Cravings!

If you "crave" food, cigarettes, alcohol or drugs, "purge" tissues and liver, do the Young Again™ Colon Protocol, eat SUPER foods, and your cravings will simply..........go away.

---

**Anal itching often accompanies deACIDification.**

---

# Glossary

**Acetylcholine**-a nerve impulse transmission chemical.
**Acetylcholinease**-an enzyme that splits acetylcholine.
**Acid**-any substance that liberates hydrogen ions; ion donor.
**Acid reflux**-entry of stomach acids into esophagus; a bowel, liver & diet disorder; treatable.
**Acid stomach**-describes upset stomach/poor digestion; related to HCl, poor bowel & liver activity.
**Acne**-confirmation of poorly functioning liver and highly acid condition of body terrain.
**Acupuncture**-alternative manipulation of body energy fields with pins or their electrical equivalent.
**Adenovirus**-a virus associated with upper respiratory infections, associated with AIDS/HIV.
**Adhesion**-water's tenedency to coat the surface of things.
**Adrenals**-a pair of ductless glands; located on top of each kidney.
**Aerobes**-bacteria that require an oxygen rich environment.
**Aerobic**-with air.
**Aerobic exercise**-exercise that produces a high oxygen state.
**Aging process**-begins at anabolic peak and ends with death; cumulative
**A/G ratio**-ratio between albumin & globulins in blood, range 100-240; the higher the number the better; at 232, a person is in peak health; below 160, serious trouble lies ahead.
**Agglutination**-clumping of the red blood corpuscles; see soy.
**AIDS**-Acquired Immune Deficiency Syndrome.
**Albumin**-a blood protein; abnormally found in the urine.
**Alcohol**-end product of fermentation; anaerobic process
**Algae**-lowest of plants; some edible (klamath, spirulina, chlorella)
**Alkaline**-above pH 7.0.
**Alkaloid**-alkaline plant juices; physiologically active.
**Allopathic medicine**-conventional cut, burn, and drug medicine.
**Alum**-double sulfate of aluminum; toxic; food additive; pickles.
**Aluminum**-a metal that releases toxic ions into food and water.
**Alzheimer's** -atrophy of brain; produces dementia, violence, anger in elderly.
**Amalgam**-toxic metals used to fill the teeth; up to 60% mercury; erroneously referred to as "silver" fillings.
**Amenorrhea**-absence or suppression of menstruation.
**American Dental Association**-"official" dentistry.
**Amyloid**-a complex protein substance without structure.
**Anabolic, anabolism**-build up of tissues; repair of tissues.
**Anabolic Peak**-high point of anabolism; end or youth, beginning of old age.
**Anaerobes**-bacteria that can live in the absence of oxygen.
**Anaerobic**-without air; oxygen deficient.
**Analog**-a synthetic molecule; "—R" group moved; a patented drug.
**Andropause**-male version of menopause in women.
**Angina pectoris**-chest pain due to lack of oxygen in muscles.
**Anemia**-low number of circulating red blood corpuscles; low blood hemoglobin levels.
**Anions**-the smallest form of energy released during a reaction.
**Antegenic Protein**-Protein for formation of body at conception; used with hGH precursor.
**Antibiotic**-anti: against; bio: life; ic: pertaining to; drug.
**Arthritis**-deterioration/inflammation of the connective tissues and joints.
**Arteriosclerosis**-hardening of arteries; see atherosclerosis
**Antenna**-device that receives a radio (energy) signal.
**Antibody**-immunity related blood immunoglobulin; product of a previous infection.
**Applied kenesiology**-hocus-pocus version of muscle testing; see muscle testing.
**Aspartate**-salt form of aspartic acid; aspartame (Nutrisweet™); toxic.
**Atherosclerosis**-plaque formation/deterioration of arteries.
**ATP**-(adenosine triphosphate)-energy carrying molecule of body; product of mitochondrial oxidation of blood glucose; produced with and without oxygen; glocolysis (lactic acid conversion to ATP).
**Atrophy**-deterioration and death of body tissue/gland/organ.
**Avogadro's Number**-number of atoms in 12 grams of carbon-12.
**Autonomic Nerve Complex**-nerve fiber complex stimulated by colon hydrotherapy.
**Aura**-the electric body; invisible body; see Fourth Dimension.
**Bacteria**-microorganisms; microbe.
**Bactericidal**-a non-selective killer of bacteria, antiseptic.
**Balding**-loss of hair; related to $O_2$ deficiency and toxicity.
**Basal metabolism**-minimum resting energy expenditure.
**Basement membrane(s)**-primary support/connective tissues.
**B-12**- (vitamin B-12) part of vitamin B complex; cyanocobalamin; required for making hemoglobin; related to anemia; intrinsic factor secretion in stomach necessary for absorption; Cobo-12™ creme.
**BAT**-brown adipose tissue; not related to WAT (see).
**Bent molecule**-the water molecule. Also known as a polar molecule.
**BEV**-biologically friendly, conception point drinking water.
**Bile**-liver and body waste product; fat emulsifier; digestive enzymes.
**Biogenic**-stimulation of body to produce new, healthy tissue and heal self.
**Bio-dynamic**-agricultural manipulation of energy for production of biologically live food.
**Bio-electric age**-true age based on health of the vital organs.
**Bio-electric body**-the physical and energy body's combined.
**Bio-junk food**-adulterated food; toxic; negative spin effect.
**Biological alchemy**-transformation of the elements in liver, gut via bacteria; fusion reactions.
**Biological Theory of Ionization**-life is the product of the energy released by the breaking of ionic bonds that hold minerals together.
**Bio-magnetics**-the use of therapeutic magnets in healing.
**Bio-magnetic Irrigator**-dental hygiene device; prevents/ dissolves/removes plaque from the teeth; manipulates hydrogen ions and the water molecule; plaque (-) minus charge; treated water (+); joining of these is called oxidation.
**Bladder**-the urine storage organ in animals.
**Blood**-one of two key body fluids; lymph is the other.
**Body odor (BO)**-odoriferous product of microbial oxidizing of skin waste.
**Bonds**-the energy link between elemental atoms and between and within molecules.
**Bone spur**-abnormal mineral deposit in/on joints and bones.
**Bowel**-the colon or large intestine.

**B-vitamins**-the B-1-17 vitamin complex.
**Brix**-a unit of measure of the sugars in plant juices.
**Brown fat**-see BAT.
**Calcify, calcification**-soft tissue invasion by mineral salts (calcium/magnesium/sodium/potassium).
**Calcium**-mineral element; a metal in elemental form, a salt crystal when combined with other elements; anion; 229 known forms of.
**Calculus**-dental plaque; tartar.
**Cancer**-systemic deterioration/collapse of the body "terrain."
**Canola oil**-same as rape oil; toxic; mustard family; see soy oil.
**Capillaries**-smallest blood vessels; can be venous or arterial.
**Carbohydrate**-sugars, starches, dextrins, and cellulose; contains carbon, oxygen, and hydrogen; classes of nutrient; other classes are protein/fats.
**Carbon**-essential element to all living things; atomic element #12.
**Carbon cycle**-the path of carbon from atmosphere through bacteria, soil, plant, animal, ocean, and back to the atmosphere; requirement for life/creation of positive energy food.
**Carbon dioxide**- atmospheric gas; animal waste gas, $CO_2$.
**Carcinogenic**-poisonous.
**Cardiovascular disease**-dis-eases of the circulatory system.
**Carpal Tunnel Syndrome**-occlusion/deterioration of nerve & nerve paths in bones of wrist; loss of motion and/or function.
**Carrion**-spoiled animal flesh.
**Casts**-albumin/amyloid, proteins, salts; wastes deposits of the kidney's tubules; indicates deterioration of nephrons.
**Catalyst**-a substance that causes a chemical reaction that would not occur without its presence; used over and over.
**Cataract**-the clouding of the lens of the eye or its capsule.
**Cation**-smallest form of (-) energy released during a reaction.
**Catabolic, catabolism**-break-down or self-digestion of body's tissues; failure/inability to rebuild or repair tissues; old age; opposite of anabolism.
**Cavities**-rotting away of the teeth; decay.
**Cecum**-junction of small/large intestine; gut/colon (bowel).
**Cellulose**-a carbohydrate; fiber.
**Chemotherapy**-treatment of dis-ease w/negative energy drugs.
**Chloroform**-toxic substance; source: chlorinated water/drugs.
**Chlorine**-a halogen; a gas; "a wildcat," used to treat water.
**Chloride**-a salt form of chlorine (sodium/pot./alum chloride).
**Chiropractic**-modality for correction of alignment of spine.
**Chiropractic (Network)**-advanced holistic form of chiropractic
**Chloramine**-highly toxic form of chlorine combined with carbon organic molicules; a byproduct of chlorine reaction with organic substances; absorbed while bathing; drinking; avoid.
**Chlorinated water**-water treated with some form of chlorine.
**Cholesterol**-a body fat; an alcohol; part of bile; a phospholipid.
**Cilia**-hair like projections in small intestine/respiratory tract.
**Cirrhosis**-hardening of glandular tissues; inflammation of.
**Clinical Disease**-a diagnosed medical condition with measurable signs.
**Cloak(ed)**-under cover; hidden; can't be detected; subclinical; occult stage.
**Cobalt**-mineral element; related to anemia/B-12/absorption; intrinsic factor production; fusion reactions in gut; critical to hemoglobin production (blood iron) and high metabolic rate; female issue.
**Co-enzyme**-necessary for the function of an enzyme.
**Cohesion**-water's tendency to stick together; hydrogen bond.
**Colloid**-substance that stays in suspension; mineral colloids not as effective in nourishing body as minerals in racemic ionic form.
**Colon**-large intestine; bowel.
**Colonic**-stimulation of nerve activity to vital organs; accelerated bile (acid waste) flow; washing of colon; done at home or professionally; together with fresh beet and carrot juice, modality controls the "terrain."
**Collagen**-connective tissue; 30% of body protein.
**Comfrey**-garden plant grown for spinach like leaves; heals ulcers.
**Coral Calcium**-biogenic coral; used for rejuvenation.
**Crypts of Lieberkuhn**-where food nutrients are absorbed in gut; located between intestinal villi.
**Crystal**-a salt; combination of halogen and a metal ions.
**Currency, electrical**-energy money; mineral ions.
**Cyanide**-contained in rape (canola) oil; toxic.
**Cyanocobalamin**-cobalt atom combined with an amine; B-12; poor absorption via oral route.
**Cytoplasm**-fluid inside the cell.
**DNA**-genetic code of living things; deoxyribonucleic acid.
**Deacidification**-removal of environmental and metabolic wastes from body tissues and fluids.
**Defecate**-a bowel movement.
**Deficiencies**-imaginary causative circumstance behind disease(s); invalid theory; see excesses.
**Degenerative dis-ease**-systemic oxidation and acidfication of the tissues.
**Denature**-alteration in form, function and/or shape of food enzymes/proteins.
**Holistic dentistry**-biologically friendly dentistry.
**De-energize**-neutralization/synchronization; loss of effect.
**Deodorant**-a chemical used to mask BO; most are toxic.
**Dermis**-the true skin; beneath the epidermis (outer skin).
**Detoxify**-removal of waste from the body.
**Devitalized food**-loss of vitality; neutralization of energy.
**Diabetes**-dis-ease of pancreas; related to blood serum levels of insulin; loss of organ function; closely related to liver, adrenal and thyroid function; old age, adult onset called Type-II; Type-1 childhood diabetes; Type-1 onset tied to vaccinations and puberty related stress.
**Digestion**-breakdown/conversion of nutrients into energy.
**Dilution**-homeopathic remedies.
**Dirt**-unproductive, dead, synchronized soil.
**Dis-ease**-the opposite of health; a left-spin condition.
**Diuretic**-agent that forces excretion of body's extracellular fluids.
**Dogma**-established authoritative opinion.
**Dowager's hump**-hunchback condition due to loss of bone mass and connective tissue; degenerative.
**Dowsing**-technique for measuring nature of energy and direction of spin.
**Drugs**-chemical substances that cause a physiologic effect.

**Ductless glands**-glands that do not excrete into a lumen or duct.
**Dynamic Reflex Analysis**-kinesthetics.
**ETVC™**-super food that builds muscle, burns fat, boosts energy and levels blood sugars.
**E. coli**-un/friendly bacteria of the gut.
**Eczema**-inflammation of the cutaneous layers of the skin (dermis); dermatitis; toxicity related.
**Edema**-excess tissue fluids; plasma protein/lymph toxicity; potassium loss;
**Enema**-a swallow, partial cleansing of the lower colon.
**Electrolytes**-mineral ions capable of electrical conductivity; necessary for nerve signal transmission along nerve axon; keep down Rouleau effect in blood; assist in acid waste movement in blood.
**Electron flow**-movement of electrons along metal wires.
**Endocrine system**-body's system for hormonal transmission of energy and messages via the blood.
**Energy**-electrical phenomenon.
**Energy field**-a field of electrical influence; signature may be left/right spin.
**Energy imbalance**-bio-electric stress; dis-ease.
**Energy manipulation**-alteration of signature and frequency of an energy field.
**Energy meridian**-an energy highway or path.
**Energy (scrambled)**-effect of radiation/irradiation/food additives/halogens on food energy molecules and/or enzymes.
**Enzymes**-biological catalysts; all body functions require them.
**Estrogens**-group of female horones (estrone, estradiol, estratriol, etc.); total of 12 known forms.
**Exit portal**-waste removal avenue(s) in bio-electric body.
**Excesses**-causative condition behind manifestation of all diseases; opposite of deficiencies.
**Exocrine glands**-glands which secrete enzymes into lumens or hollow organs like the stomach or gut.
**Extracellular fluid**-fluid between (outside) cells; interstitial.
**Fabale**-a family of plants; parent family of the soy bean.
**Facultative anaerobes**-bacteria that can function with or without the presence of oxygen.
**Fats**-food category that may be healthful/bad; excess adipose body tissue.
**Far Infrared**-healing part of the light spectrum; therapeutic.
**Fever (febrile)**-elevated body temperature due to infection/toxins.
**Fission**-splitting of atoms/molecules; catabolic; nuclear.
**Fluorine**-a halogen gas; toxic; a wildcat.
**Fluoride**-the form of fluorine gas combined with metal ions to form a salt..
**Fluorosis**-fluoride toxicity.
**Food**-nutrient energy; energy footprint may be lert/right.
**Footprint**-descriptive term indicating spin direction, intensity and depth.
**Fourth Dimension**-an invisible/intangible energy dimension.
**Free radical**-negative electron scavenger, reactive; aging related effect on cell life and health.
**Functional cells**-healthy tissue cells; parenchyma cells; vitality producing.
**Fusion**-anabolic transmutation/formation of molecules.
**Gallbladder**-holding sack for liver's bile; dumps into gut.
**Gallstones**-deposits of precipitates from bile.
**Gas**-free moving matter; non-solid; invisible energy; w/o form.
**Gastric**-related to stomach.
**Genetically engineered**-manipulated life forms; synthetic.
**Germ Theory of Disease**-allopathic medical theory; disease diagnosis.
**GI tract**-gastrointestinal tract.
**Glaucoma**-a group of eye dis-eases involving atrophy of retina.
**Glucose**-blood sugar; in storage form called glycogen; energy fuel for body.
**Glycerol**-glycerin with alcohol(s) attached; present in fats.
**Glycine**-a nonessential amino acid; sweet; glycine max.
**Glycolic acid**-a natural substance used to peel skin; rid face of wrinkles.
**Glycosides**-inhibit muscle enzymes; soy/canola contain them.
**Glycolysis**-splitting & oxidation of glucose; Krebs cycle; formation of ATP.
**Glands**-body organs with special functions and tissues.
**Goiter**-swollen thyroid gland; stressed ovaries, pancreas, liver and adrenals.
**Gout**-uric acid toxicity in blood and joints; degenerative.
**Gua Sha**-acupuncture without needles; lymphatic manipulation.
**Greens**-collards, broccoli leaves, spinach, cabbage, chard, etc.; good food.
**Gut**-small intestine (includes duodenum, jejunum, ileum.
**HCL**-(hydrochloric acid); stomach acid; breaks peptide bonds joining amino acids; critical for health.
**Halogen**-an extremely unstable, acid gas; a wildcat; toxic.
**Harmonic**-a healthy frequency; causes body to resonate health/vitality.
**Heart attack**-insufficient oxygen available to heart muscle.
**Herbicides**-man made organic poisons.
**Hemorrhoids**-swollen, congested, displaced veins in the anus.
**Hepatitis**-inflammation of the liver (hepatocytes).
**Hepatocytes**-the functional cells of the liver.
**Herpes**-group of viral conditions; sexual or non sexual in nature; fever blister, genital blisters.
**High blood pressure**-hypertension; abnormal; sign of systemic problems.
**hGh**-should be used in racemized™ form with Skin & Body Toner.
**HIV**-Human immunodeficiency virus; the precursor virus to AIDS.
**Hologram**-a multidimensional energy message.
**Homeopathic medicine**-the medicine of similars; remedies.
**Homeovitic**-qualities of homeopathy plus energy and nutritional support.
**Hormone**-chemical messenger; powerful energy field; product of vital glands.
**Hormone Cycle**-female cycle independent of menstrual cycle; occurs monthly from puberty until death; must be resurrected and maintained; can be measured and mapped; vitally important to all women.
**Howdy Doody Lines**-Facial lines that indicate stress in vital organs/colon.
**Hyaline**-albuminoid tissue substance that reflects amyloid degeneration.
**Hyalinization**-infusion of hyaline into cells or tissue.
**Hybrid food**-food produced from genetically weak seed.
**Hydration**-the water level in the tissues of the body.
**Hydrochloric acid**-see HCL.
**Hydrogen**-an element; high energy; bonds easily; bioactive; acidic.
**Hydrogen peroxide**-$H_2O_2$; therapeutic; antiseptic; oxidizer; ages tissues.
**Hype**-unrealistic thinking; mind over matter; biojunk food induced stress.
**Hyperspace**-Fourth Dimension energy space.

**Hypertrophy**-increased/abnormal change in organ function.
**Hypoglycemia**-low blood sugar.
**Hypotrophy**-decline; abnormal change in organ function; diminished organ size; atrophy.
**Hypovolemia**-low blood fluid volume (also lymph).
**Ileum**-end of small intestine; joins colon at cecum.
**Ileocecal valve**-gatekeeper between small intestine and cecum (lg. intestine)
**Immune system**-our bio-electric defense system.
**Immunization**-bogus introduction of foreign microbial protiens into body.
**Impotence**-inability of male to get an erection; female clitoris non responsive.
**In-camera**-consideration of all body systems as a whole; not isolated.
**Inflammation**-redness; swelling; edema.
**Indols**-toxic whole molecules produced/absorbed in the gut.
**Insulin**-A blood protein; controls glucose flow into the cells.
**Integument**-the skin (subcutaneous, dermis, epidermis).
**Internal environment**-status of the cells/fluids/tissues.
**Intercellular substance**-mix of materials between the cells.
**Interstitial fluid**-fluid between the cells; extracellular fluid.
**Intestine**-small intestine (gut) and large intestines (colon).
**Intima**-innermost layer of the artery blood vessel wall.
**Intoxication**-alcohol saturation of tissues beyond liver's to breakdown and the kidneys to excrete; or, toxic acidic waste condition of the tissues.
**Intracellular fluid**-fluid inside the cells.
**Intrinsic factor**-secreted by stomach; B-12 absorption impossible w/o; after age 30 production drops.
**Intuition**-instinct; extension of the min beyond 3rd dimension.
**Invisible**-not seen; the electric body; Fourth Dimension.
**Iodine**-an element; needed for health; related to thyroid goiter.
**Ion**-an atom that has gained or lost an electron.
**Ionic bond**-bond between two mineral ions.
**Ionic minerals**-minerals that have gained/lost electrons.
**Ionization**-exchange of energy and electrons; anions/cations.
**Irradiation**-destruction/scrambling of food molecules/tissues.
**Iridology**-reading/interpretation of health via iris of eye.
**Ischemia**-reduced oxygen supply to heart muscle.
**Isotope**-an atom with same number of protons, but different number of neutrons; a different molecular form of the same element.
**Jaundice**-toxic liver effect; bilirubin; yellowing of eye sclera.
**Juice capsules/tablets**-concentrated right-spin dried plant juices.
**Kombucha tea**-dynamic home preparaton used for rejuvenation.
**Kidney**-primary excretory organ of the body; exit portal.
**Kidney stones**-mineral/fat/waste precipitates in the kidneys.
**Kinesiology**-study of body movement.
**Kinesthetics**-muscle sense tests; identify toxic food/drugs.
**Krebs Cycle**-cycle for production of energy molecule ATP; glycolysis part of; includes electron transport chain within the mitochondria; includes citric acid cycle.
**Lactate**-the salt form of lactic acid.
**Lactic acid**-product of anaerobic fermentation; incomplete oxidation of glucose; acid waste; produces muscle soreness; liver recycles and oxidizes.
**Laying on of hands**-healing through energy transfer; similar to chi gong.
**L/CSF™**-device for increased circulation of lymphatic and cerebral spinal fluids; very effective.
**Lecithin**-emulsifier and component of oils/fats/bile; soy derived.
**Left-spin**-negative energy; catabolic; anti life;
**Lemon juice**-powerful de-toxifier(if fresh); acidic.
**Lice**-creatures that live on filth and negative energy.
**Life expectancy**-length of time we can expect to live.
**Lightning, cellular**-energy produced by the mitochondria.
**Limb regeneration**-regrowth of bone, nerve and tissues.
**Live blood cell analysis**-dark field microscopy used for diagnostic purposes; not reliable.
**Liver**-primary chemical/fusion/detox organ of the body.
**Liver breath**-bad breath resulting from stress liver; smells like onions and/or metallic.
**Liver stones**-natural waste product of body; slows bile flow; accelerate aging.
**Load-bearing work**-work involving movement and weight.
**Localized condition**-a condition that is not systemic.
**Lungs**-organs of external breathing.
**Lye soap**-saponification of fats/oils with lye (sodium hydroxide).
**Lymph**-fluids in lymph vessels; a body fluid.
**Lymphocyte**-immune system cell; B-cell; part of lymph. systen
**Lymphotrophic**-change in lymph fluid; T-cell.
**Lyse**-to split, cleave or break apart.
**Macrophage**-non circulating immune system 'attack' cell; defensive.
**Macular degeneration**-deterioration of macula of eye and loss of vision; aging issue for women; waste,oxygen and hormone related; related to loss of hearing & osteoporosis.
**Magic bullets**-medical science hype; false hope; drugs.
**Magnetism**-the effect of a magnetic field.
**Magneto hydro dynamics**-dental plaque removal therapy.
**Malathion**-a toxic man-made organic poison.
**Malnutrition**-insufficient right-spin food energy.
**Manganese**- trace mineral; builds serum iron via bioalchemy.
**Mastication, masticate**-chewing of food.
**Mass**-energy exporting tissue; cancer/benign.
**Matter**-condensed energy.
**Matriarchal society**-blood line follows the woman.
**Matrix**-collagen framework for deposition of bone minerals.
**Meat**-dead animal tissue; may be right/left spin energy.
**Menopause**-negative shift in hormonal flow; the "climactic."
**Menstruation**-monthly shedding of endometrial lining of uterus in women from puberty until menopause; not same as female "hormone cycle; periods w/o ovulation occur for 3-8 years before periods stop; see hormone cycle and pages 72 & 212 in 5th edition of Young Again..

**Mental age**-how old a person thinks.
**Mercury**-extremely toxic element; quicksilver; evaporates.
**Mercuric acid**-extremely toxic heavy metal agent for treatment of water during warm months; an acid form of elemental mercury.
**Metabolic rate**-rate of metabolic activity in a living system; thyroid, liver and hemoglobin related..
**Metabolism**-a change in energy via biotransformation of food energy to ATP.
**Metabolite**-byproduct of metabolism.
**Metaphysics**-beyond normal physics of length, width, height.
**Microbes**-microscopic life forms; bacteria.
**Microwave oven**-a negative energy cooking device.
**Medical Grade Ionized Water™**-reduced/oxidized water with very high ORP pH in both acid and alkaline forms; a therapeutic water; made from BEV™ water plus mix of racemized™ liquid minerals; NEVER make from "tap" water; used in Japan to heal people with diabetes, cancer, arthritis and cardiovascular disease; acid form can destroy viruses, bacteria, fungi and yeast; water BEYOND conception point.
**Mitochondria**-bacteria within all cells that produce the ATP energy molecule; Krebs Cycle.
**Modality**-a form of therapy.
**Molds**-lowest life forms.
**Molecular bond**-bond between molecules.
**Mononucleosis**-inflamed lymph nodes/liver; severe immune system stress.
**Monosodium glutamate (MSG)**-a salt of sodium and glutamine.
**Morbid**-dis-ease related; death related.
**Multiple sclerosis**-inflammation of central nervous system; myelin sheath deterioration of nerve fibers.
**Muscle tone**-resistance of muscles to elongation or stretch.
**Mustard gas**-chemical agent of war; made from rape oil.
**Muscle testing**-subjective/unreliable misuse of dowsing; never use for diagnosis or treatment.
**Myocardial infarction**-see heart attack.
**Myelin**-protective nerve fiber sheath; destruction pH related.
**Myelinoma**-deterioration of the nerve sheaths.
**Myxedema**-low thyroid function/metabolic rate; thyroid atrophy; low BMR; hypothyroid.
**Naturopathic**-alternative therapeutic modality; similars.
**Necrotic flesh**-dead, non-gangrenous tissue; not same as carrion.
**Negative energy**-left-spin energy; catabolic.
**Negative inhibition**-feedback system to control metabolism.
**Nephron**-kidney blood filter; critical to detoxification.
**Nerve gas**-toxic agent of war; blocks enzyme function.
**Neti pot**-device used with Clear Head™ to purge sinus cavities of infection and mucous.
**Neurolema**-the outer sheath of nerve fibers (includes the Schwann cells).
**Neuropathy**-syndrome of nerve fiber (myelin) deterioration; pH related.
**Neutralize**-denature; detoxify; energy shift; synchronize.
**Niacin/niacinamide**-names for bogus vitamin B-3; synthetic.
**Nicotine**-if natural, a good source of complete B-vitamins; an alkaloid.
**Nicotinic acid**-acid form of nicotine; natural source: dry tobacco.
**Nitrogen**-elemental gas; critical for formation of nitrogen in food molecules; 3 forms, 1 metallic.
**Nodes**-part of lymphatic system; also known as nodules.
**Nonfunctional cells**-cell that do not grant permission to life.
**Nonshivering thermogenesis**-heat produced w/o shivering.
**Nourishment**-positive food energy that fuels anabolism.
**Obesity**-slowdown in metabolic & vital organ function.
**Old age**-dis-ease; loss of vitality; acidification/breakdown of conective tissues
**Open pollinated seeds**-seeds that produce true to type; non hybrid.
**Opportunistic**-condition where microbes proliferate; low tissue vitality.
**Organic**-a misnomer; a molecule containing carbon; healthy food.
**Organic poisons**-poisons built on a carbon skeleton.
**ORP**-Oxidation/reduction potential; measure of life force (electrons) in Medical Grade Ionized Water™; symbol (+) means water is in oxidized state and missing electrons; and exact opposite (-) for reduced water; high pH plus high ORP is rejuvenatory to body; electrons fuel mitochondrial production of ATP;
**Osteoporosis**-loss of bone mass; acidification of tissues and fluids; aging.
**Ovaries**-glands that produce female reproductive cells (egg).
**Oxidation**-aging factor; related to free radical production; Krebs Cycle and glycolysis; conversion of glucose (sugars) molecule to ATP; chemistry term indicating loss of electrons indicated by symbol (+).
**Oxygen**-gas; atomic element; oxidizer; aerobic; anabolism.
**Ozone**-$O_3$; therapeutic; bactericidal to pathogenic organisms.
**PACs**-racemized™ formulation of proanthrocyanidins; very useful for free radical management and minimization of damage to healthy tissues during Young Again Tissue & Liver Protocol™.
**P-P Factor**-pellagra preventive agent; part of the B-complex; known as B-3, niacin; most commercial sources are synthetic.
**Palliation**-relief of signs/symptoms without cure of cause.
**Pallor**-poor color; abnormal color.
**Pancreas**-vital digestive organ; both duct and ductless; stress linked to liver.
**Paradigm**-a new model along side an older model.
**Paralysis**-loss of muscle function; degenerative.
**Parasite(s)**-foreign life forms in the human body, living on wastes, poisoning/destroying organ function.
**Parasympathetic nervous system**-involuntary nervous; no control; part of autonomic system.
**Parathyroid**-four tiny glands next to the thyroid; (ductless).
**Parenchyma cells**-functional cells of a gland or organ.
**Pathogenic**-pertaining to dis-ease; dis-ease causing; stress terrain.
**Patriarchal society**-blood line follows the male.
**Peer review**-undressing in public; submission to convention; following the protocols of "legitimate" medical science; control of independent thought.
**Pellagra**-dis-ease related to unbalanced dietary intake; B-vitamin related.
**Pendulum**-an antenna; a tuning device; a transmitter; a tool.
**Peristalsis**-intestinal wave-like motions that move food/waste.
**Pesticide**-organic poison; man-made; attached to carbon atom.
**pH scale**-normally from 1-14; 7 is neutral; ea. # increases 10x.
**Phagocyte**-a cell that eats the body's invading enemies/antigens.
**Phenols**-toxic whole molecules produced/absorbed in the gut.
**PHG**-phytohemaglutinin; a vegetable protein glue; soy beans.

**Phytates**-substance that interferes with digestion; heaviest in soy.
**Phytohemaglutinin**-see PHG.
**Plants**-nature's antennas; mediate cosmic energy; build soil; food energy.
**Pituitary**-important ductless gland; linked to all other glands.
**Plicae circularis**-undulating folds in the walls of the gut.
**Plaque**-waste deposits on the artery walls(arteriosclerosis/atherosclerosis) and on teeth (causes decay).
**Plasma Protein**-see lymph.
**Poison**-carcinogenic; deadly; produces negative effects.
**Polar molecule**-the water molecule; a bent molecule.
**Polycystic ovary**-cysts on ovary(s);"incomplete" ovulation (egg stuck in ovary wall);hormone problems.
**Poly/pleomorphic**-microbial ability to change "specie" to suit body "terrain."
**Polluted**-toxic; loaded with poisonous waste; tap water.
**Positive energy**-right-spin; anabolic.
**Positive thinking**-mind over matter; helpful if real; no hype.
**Post mortem**-after death; examination after death.
**Potassium**-atomic element; (+) charge; sodium's twin; alkaline.
**Precipitate**-formation of a solid & settling out of solution.
**Precursor**-a substance that precedes another; beta carotene/vitamin A; used to make hormones.
**Proof**-something medical science demands, but can't deliver.
**Prostate**-male ejaculatory organ; surrounds urinary tube.
**Portal**-an exit point or avenue or system for waste disposal from body
**Portal vein**-venous blood vein from gut to liver; caries food molecules.
**Protein**-one of three food forms; see fat, carbohydrates.
**Proanthocyanidins (PAC)**-plant derived antioxidant/free radical scavengers.
**Puberty**-onset of secondary sex charistics (breasts/body hair).
**Pulmonary system**-blood movement from heart to lungs and return.
**Pulse rate**-beats per minute of heart muscle.
**Pure water**-$H_2O$ only minus all comtaminants; toxic memory erase.
**Purine**-a nitrogenous protein waste from the digestion of animal tissue, or self digestion of body tissue; catabolic; adenine, guanine; nucleic acid end product.
**Pyridine ring**-a synthetic organic molecule used to make artificial B-vitamins; left-spin; will not support life; toxic to body; synthetic Bio-electric age vitamin molecule.
**R-group**-a chemical group that gives an organic molecule its characteristic(s).
**RNA**-Ribonucleic acid; nucleic acid; genetic template material.
**Racemize™**-process that increases spin rate and energy field to boost biological availability and usefulness to body by a factor of 10x.
**Radiation**-energy radiating from a source (nuclear/solar); left/right spin)
**Radionics**-broadcasting of energy frequencies in agriculture.
**Radiomimetic**-ability of a substance alter body frequency to left/toxic state.
**Rape oil**-canola oil; toxic; not a food; radiomimetic.
**Rebounder**-a mini trampoline used to circulate lymphatic fluid.
**Reduced**-opposite of oxidized, oxidation. A high energy state.
**Refractometer**-device for measuring sugars in plant juices as an indicator of mineral load/plant health.
**Rejuvenate**-to rebuild; start anew; anabolism; opposite of aging.
**Remedies**-home/vitic/opathic substances that neutralize negative energy.
**Replication**-multiplication; reproduction.
**Repolarization**-stimulation of cellular matrix and organelles (mitochondria) to normalize cellular function and increase production of ATP.
**Resiliency**-return to previous condition; bounce back.
**Respiration, external**-$O_2/CO_2$ exchange in the lungs.
**Respiration, internal**-$O_2/CO_2$ exchange in the cells.
**Reticular**-fine network of tissues that form the glands/organs.
**Retrovirus**-a virus capable of using a reverse enzyme to access the host; HIV virus is said to be a retrovirus.
**Right-spin energy**-anabolic; positive; aerobic.
**Rouleau effect**-toxins in blood that produce clumping of blood corpuscles.
**Root canal**-removal of tooth's nerve; retention of dead tooth; toxic.
**Rotenone**-a toxic poison from the soy bean.
**Roten**-Japanese for derris: plant family to which soy belongs.
**Rhythm**-scheduled; systematic; regular; habit.
**Rhymicity**-routine; systematic; regular lifestyle and habits.
**Saliva**-secretion of the salivary glands; digestive juice; pH sensitive/indicative.
**Salt**-combination of halogen and metal ions.
**Satiety**-fullness beyond desire; nutritionally full.
**Saponification**-soap making; the hydrolysis or splitting of fat by an alkali; hydrolysis of an ester; (*sapo*-soap;*facere*-to make).
**Scar tissue**-a negative energy memory field; dysfunction in the skin's parenchymal cells during repair due to low energy state; acidification of tissues; confirmation of aging factor in tissues.
**Scientific Method**-medical sciences official system of information gathering.
**Schwann cells**-cells residing at the synapses of nerve axons; necessary for nerve signal transmission.
**Sea water**-naturally balanced mineral ion water; right-spin.
**Sedentary lifestyle**-lack of exercise and load bearing work.
**Senility**-loss of mental faculties.
**Shallow breathing**-insufficient exchange of lung gases.
**Signature (energy)**-energy footprint; related to spin and intensity; 4th dimension factor.
**Signs**-measurable dis-ease conditions; will support diagnosis.
**Silica**-important element; body transmutes to calcium.
**Silicone**-thixotrophic substance used in breast inplants; highly toxic; destroys immune system.
**Similar(s)**-homeopathic principle; cancellation of one energy field by another.
**Single factor analysis**-a form of scientific myopia; "head in the sand."
**Sixth sense**-intuition; Fourth Dimension; extension of mind.
**Skatols**-toxic whole molecules produced/absorbed via the gut.
**Skin**-our outer tube; halographic; an organ; exit portal; very first organ to form and the organ from which all differentiation of other organs and tissues follow.
**Sleep**-detoxification period, rejuvenation of tissues; ATP production..
**Smoking**-oxidation of dried tobacco via flame; bad news.
**Sodium**-an element; a metal; alkaline; always involved in cancer.

**Soft drink**-acid forming; accelerates aging; toxic; heavy metals; avoid.
**Soil**-biologically live dirt; product of microbial and plant activity on earth minerals.
**Solar energy**-anionic energy; right spin; anabolic; life giving.
**Solvent**-a substance that dissolves solids creating a solution; alcohol dissolves fats (non polar); water dissolves polar substances (all other).
**Soy bean**-toxic plant of Derris family.
**Soy bean oil**-degenerative left spinning energy field; toxic.
**Space**-extension of the mind; related to Time.
**Sperm**-male reproductive cells.
**Spin**-direction of energy flow of a substance or thought.
**Spinach**-an alkaloid; Goosefoot family; eat with vinegar/lemon.
**Spirulina**-a complete algae protein; good nutrient energy.
**Sprouts**-sprouted seeds eaten as food.
**Spurs**-mineral/body waste deposits in joints/on bones.
**Standard**-a defined reference point; a known yardstick.
**Stannous**-a tin containing compound.
**Stannous fluoride**-a toxic fluoride/tin containing compound.
**Static**-standing still; not changing; no motion; synchronized.
**Stomach**-food receptacle; digestive organ.
**Stress**-bad energy; negative effect on body, mind and spirit.
**Stroma cells**-nonfunctional structional cells of the glands.
**Sub-atomic**-below atom level; fusion; transmutation; alchemy.
**Sub-clinical**-not diagnosable; symptoms only, health issues prior to signs appearing.
**Sub-cutaneous**-below the dermis or dermal layer of skin; shallow fascia; deep fascia; connective tissues composed of skin, muscle, ligaments, and tendons.
**Sugar**-glucose or other energy molecule; may be right/left-spin; glycolysis.
**Sun**-source of anionic energy; life giver; causes Earth to spin.
**Supplement**-vitamin, mineral, misc. factors added to diet.
**Sweat**-a waste product; extracellular fluid; heat regulator.
**Swiss chard**-an alkaloid; a Goosefoot; eat with vinegar/lemon.
**Symbiotic**-one life form helps the other; buddy system.
**Sympathetic nervous system**-under our conscious control.
**Symptoms**-subclinical; undiagnosable; early stages of dis-ease; Fourth Dimensional; bio-electric; energy related.
**Synapse**-juncture points along nerve fibers where nerve signal is transfered from one side of synapse to the next; where Schwann cells are located; receptor site points along nerve axon.
**Synchronization**-temporary neutralization of energy (electron) transference.
**Synergy**-the coming together of two or more energy forces.
**Systemic**-affecting the entire body; fever for example.
**Synthesis**-energy forces coming together to form a new substance.
**Synthetic**-artifically prepared; man-made analogous molecule.
**T-cells**-defense cells of the immune/lymphatic systems.
**Tartar**-calculus; dental plaque.
**Terrain**-the TOTAL energy state of the bio-electric body.
**Testes, testicles**-glands that produce male reproductive cells, (sperm).
**Therapeutic**-having healing qualities; promotes health.
**Therapeutic touch**-healing through energy transfer; chi gong.
**Thermogenic hyperphagia**-production of heat & the eating of body WAT (fat) through oxidation by mitochondrial brown fat.
**Thixotrophic**-substance that when disturbed turns to liquid state, and then reverts to a gel state when left undisturbed; silicone (breast implants).
**Thymus**-gland of the immune system and lymphatic systems; above heart.
**Thyroid**-controls metabolic rate; serious female issue; goiter/iodine; critical to good health.
**Time**-extension of mind; related to Space; Fourth Dimension.
**Time & aging**-passing of Time defines speed of aging.
**Time made visible**-signs of aging in the mirror.
**Tin**-stannous; see fluoride; toothpaste.
**Tissue**-cells of the body; grouped by type, function, and organ.
**Tobacco**-richest source of natural, complete B-vitamin complex in the world; up to 30%; alkaloid when green; acid when dry; a good food; must be food grade tobacco; must be eaten with lemon or vinegar.
**Tone**-resistance of muscles to elongation or stretch; that state in which body functions/parts are healthy and normal; retention of muscular shape, strength.
**Toxic**-poisonous; acidification; causes tissues to age.
**Toxins**-poisonous; negative energy fields; acidic;
**Trace minerals**-minerals needed in minute amounts; electrolytes.
**Transmutation**-conversion of one mineral or energy field into another in the gut/solar plexus, or liver of animals, or in soil by bacteria.
**Trophy**-change related to nutritional deficiencies or excesses.
**TRUTH**-something that can be ignored, but not denied; something that is.
**Tumors**-abnormal energy importing energy fields in the body; cancer/benign.
**TVP**-textured vegetable protein; avoid; usually soy derived.
**Unopposed estrogen dominance**-female condition where progesterone is lacking or receptor sites are "blocked" by hormone analogs.
**Uric acid**-a waste product of nitrogen tissue breakdown.
**Urine**-waste product of the body; useful therapeutic if drank fresh AM daily.
**Vaccines**-live or attenuated microbes in animal protein serum; toxic.
**Vascularization**-blood vessel invasion into tissue or bone.
**Vibrational medicine**-manipulation of energy for healing.
**Villi**-finger-like projections of the gut wall.
**Vinegar**-acidic; if naturally produced, good for body; aerobic product.
**Virus**-a non-life form; parasitic; steals converts body's energy; proliferate when the terrain is supportive; opportunistic.
**Visible**-tangible; length, width, and height; Third Dimension.
**Vital organs**-ductless glands: ovaries/testes, pancreas, thymus, thyroid, pituitary, parathyroid.
**Vital force**-the effect generated by the vital organs on body, mind, spirit.
**Vitamins**-co-factors; important to health and vitality; use only food derived.
**Waste**-acid byproducts of metabolism.

**Water**-$h_2o$; food; energy source; primary substance in body; polar solvent.
**Water substitutes**-soft drinks, beer, milk, etc.; not acceptable.
**Weeds**-negative energy antenna; detoxify the air/soil; natures garbage crew.
**White blood cells**-part of the immune defense system.
**Wildcats**-name give to the halogen gases (fluorine, chlorine, etc.).
**Wrinkles**-confirmation of the passing of Time; aging of the vital organs; toxicity in the dermal/subcutaneous skin; acidification of the surface fascia.
**Yucca Herbal Blend™**-biological solvent for removing acid wastes from tisues
**Young Again Protocol™**- program designed to restore good health and take control of the body terrain.
**Yellow Fringed Flag**-any flag of government where yellow fringe, ball or spear is used to establish a foreigh "state" or condition repugnant to the constitution and vested rights of the people; bogus; criminal.
**Zeno (estrogen)**-hormone analog; not real; synthetic/similar molecular structure; capable of grid-locking receptor sites in body; confuses body; stresses liver; read *Our Stolen Future*, page 384.

# Parasites

Parasitic infection is at epidemic levels in people throughout North America. And it is a "silent epidemic," too!

Because people can't see the parasites, they don't think they exist. "They" are something that happens to "the other guy." Nevertheless, they are there, and they reek havoc in the body and in the vital organs, in particular. Here are some common symptoms of parasites: gas, bloating, bowel disorders, joint and muscle aches, allergies, skin conditions, nervousness. The list goes into the thousands of symptoms.

While intestinal parasites are what is most often thought of when people think of parasites. Yet, it is the microscopic sized parasites and their eggs that "leak" into the blood through a **leaky gut** and set up shop in the heart, brain, lungs, pancreas, spleen liver, ovaries, testicles and thyroid.

EVERYONE has parasites, some of us have more than others, and some of us have more serious types of parasites than others. The question is: *"What can be done about these unwelcome guests?"*

The **NUMBER ONE** issue of parasite management is "terrain" management. Get your terrain in order and managing the parasites is easy. A toxic terrain is an ACID terrain, and the parasites love an acid terrain because there is plenty of wastes available for them to eat. All life forms on the planet seek the same three essentials: food, warmth and safety. Provide the perfect environment for parasites and they will be there!

99% of disease transmission is via the hand and mouth path. Sanitation is absolutely the best defense against parasites. Second is proper digestion. All life forms are **proteins** and protein digestion occurs in the stomach as the direct result of hydrochloric acid, otherwise known as HCL.

Beyond these two preventative measures, the name of the game is to **de**acidify the body's terrain and kill off existing parasites. That is the purpose of the Young Again Parasite and the Tissue & Liver Protocols™. Kill them off, dismantle them and move out the debris. It is like shedding a 500 pound pack. Lift the burden, and life gets better!

**Germs & Disease & Aging**

While your author totally rejects the Germ Theory of Disease, he is totally in agreement with the medical folks that germs and pathogenic microbes and parasites wage war against us every day of our lives.

When the body "terrain" becomes acid, pathogenic life forms proliferate and cause us to suffer or die. So is it the "germs" or is it the "terrain" that dictates who wins and who loses this silent war going on in our bodies?

The terrain**dictates,**y but the germs, like the parasites know how to READ their environment. The communicate with each other and when the conditions are just right, they "explode" onto the scene with devastating effects.

In small numbers, germs can't accomplish much, and they don't try. But create the right conditions, and their numbers can exponencially multiply and the war is on.

Modern medicine since the time of Pasteur, and especially since Lister and antibiotics, has tried to manage and kill the microbes when the real war should have been focused on the "terrain."

An how do you manage the terrain? Simple, Plenty of water every day (1 gallon). Make and drink fresh beet and carrot juice every day. Do colon therapy 2-3 times a week, every week of your life. Eat healthy food. Avoid the junk.

Next, clear your "terrain" of the acid wastes that have accumulated in your body tissues and fluids by following the Young Again Tissue & Liver Protocol™. Remember, the "stuff" you want to get out of your body is stored in the body fat just under the skin.

When you clear the body of acids and wastes, you change the terrain and deny the germs control of the body.

Never forget: You don't catch a disease, you develop the conditions for the disease to manifest because of conditions of EXCESS in your body.

Excesses stress the system and diminish vital organ function. Excesses provide a perfect environment for sickness and disease to proliferate. Excesses cause us to lose control of our lives and suffer. Excesses cause us to age, grow old and die years ahead of time because we chose the **wrong** path.

Human beings have free will. God gave us the right of choice. When we choose the path of ignorance or bullheadedness we must pay the price. When we make correct choices, we change the outcome of our lives. We have CHOICE!

**Ignorance is temporary. Stupidity is forever!**

### Iron & Disease

Dietary iron is NOT the same as "heme" iron, the latter being the type of iron found in the blood. Heme iron is central to a healthy condition and a high metabolic rate, and is THE oxygen carrying molecule in blood called **heme**oglobin.

Dietary iron is an OXIDIZER. It reeks havoc in the body by fueling the production of "free radicals."

Pathogenic life forms (disease organisms) "feed on" iron metabolites (byproducts) producing even more wastes that weaken the body and stress the immune system.

The best way to build-up and increase "heme" iron in the body is by using racemized™ algae and predigested liver supplements along with Cobo-12™ creme.

The best way to neutralize and throw-off **excess** dietary iron is by using the racemized™ product R/C™, thereby stopping oxidation of otherwise healthy tissue and blood.

Iron provides a breeding ground and fuel for pathogenic microbes and for parasitic activity. The healthy body want neither; the unhealthy body suffers from both.

---

### Chocolat

One of the best movies of the year 2000 was *Chocolat.*

The subject of the movie was the human obsession for the food, chocolate. Women have a particular obsession for chocolate, especially prior to the onset of their menstrual period. Chocolate is also considered to be a "love" food.

What is overlooked in the chocolate story is the fact that good chocolate is very high in fat, and fat is central to hormone production, especially for females. What your author is really saying is that women need lots of dietary fat to make their hormones each and every month of their life from puberty to death. That is why low fat diets are so harmful for women.

Fats are full of essential fatty acids. Fats do NOT make you fat, but they sure make your body physiology function better. Be sure to include lots of olive oil and butter in your diet, especially if your are female.

Better yet, the use of R/EFA™, which is a wonderful formulation of racemized™ fatty acids, insures that people of either sex get enough of these "essential" food molecules to enjoy a healthy life.

Eat chocolate if you like. Make sure it is "good" chocolate, never cheap, additive laden stuff. And while you are at it, include some R/EFA™ and see how much better you feel.

Lastly, ADD and ADHD kids respond well to R/EFA™. That is why they are called "essential" (see Source Page 384).

# Index

**It TV promotes it, and the government loves it, and everyone nags you to do it—IGNOTE IT!**

### Alkalinity vs. Acidity

The pH of the body tissues and fluids is a huge issue for anyone who wishes to enjoy a long and healthy life because pH tells us where you are at, and where you are going.

The sicker the person is, the more acid is their body "terrain," and conversely, the less acid you are the better. After age 25, the body progressively grows more and more acid until we reach the "change" years (the forties) and life get out of control and dis-ease knocks at our door.

"Terrain" management means **less acid,** not more alkaline. **De**acidification is **THE** name of the game!

### Healthy Baby Formula

3 1/2 C. BEV™ water™, 2 ea. racemized™ liver & algae tabs, 1 Disorb Aid™, 1 tbsp. coconut/olive oil, 1 tsp. each TRP™, cod liver oil, & "blackstrap" molasses, contents of 1 SOC™ cap, contents of 1 R/C™ and OX™ cap. Crush/soak/liquify; refrigerate; makes 32 oz. (thin with water; perforate nipple as needed so formula will pass).

### Popcorn • Oil • Brewers Yeast

Popcorn is a good food—as long as it isn't cooked in soy or canola oil and covered with salt. And for a real treat, sprinkle brewers yeast on your 'buttered' popcorn. It adds zest, and you won't need any salt. You'll love it!

### Are You Feeling Overwhelmed?

Making the transition from the "normal" good old American diet to a healthy one can be challenging.

New ways to healthfully prepare food and new types of strange foods is challenging for conventional cooks. The person eating "strange" new foods often doesn't appreciate tampering. Go slow. *Invest in a good vegetarian* cook book like *Foods That Heal* or a healthy "meat" cook book like *Nourishing Traditions* (see Source Page). Visit a health food store or food co-op and buy a supply of basic food staples. Mix them among your regular food dishes on the dinner table. Home made bread is a good dietary addition. AVOID soy products, canola oil, and tofu. Avoid ALL prepared foods. They are a guaranteed ticket to the grave. Convert your family one step at a time!

***"Nothing transforms a person as much as changing from a negative to a positive attitude."*** Paul C. Bragg

***"If we eat wrongly, no doctor can cure us. If we eat rightly, no doctor is needed."*** Victor Rocine

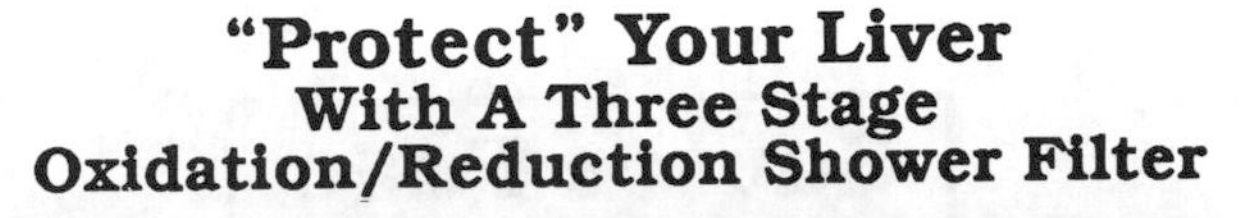

## "Protect" Your Liver
### With A Three Stage Oxidation/Reduction Shower Filter

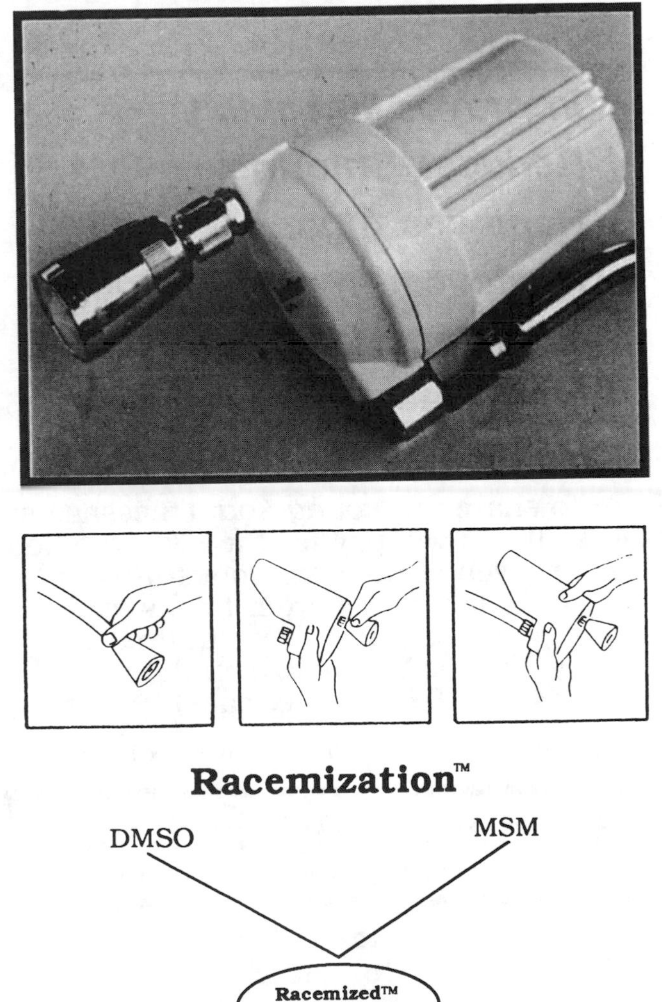


DMSO (dimethylsulfoxide) has been around for over 50 years and except for the fact that it "stinks," it is a helpful product. Then along came MSM. It has a similar molecular structure, but with one less oxygen—which gets rid of the smell. Finally, we have SOC™—a "racemized™" form of MSM that increases biological activity by ten times (10x) without the stink. More results for less money and without any odor. That's progress!

# Source Page

**For Product Information Request The**

**Young Again**

## "Source Packet"

**1-800-659-1882**

Or Write

**Young Again!**

**P.O. Box 1240 Mead WA 99021-1240**

(509) 465-4154 fax (509) 466-8103

## ➥ Free Books

Want to share the *Young Again* message with others? If you will pay for the s&h, the books will be given at no cost. Books must go to one address. To order books, call (509) 465-4154, leave address, Visa or M/C # & exp. date. (36 books per case)

(Publisher reserves the right of limitation or cancellation of offer.)

## Commercial Purchases

**& Resale Discounts Available**

**For Author Interviews Contact:**

**Plexus Press**

**(509) 465-4154**

P. O. Box 1240

Mead, WA 99021

Ph. (509) 465-4154 Fax: (099) 466-8103

**Books Make Great Gifts!**